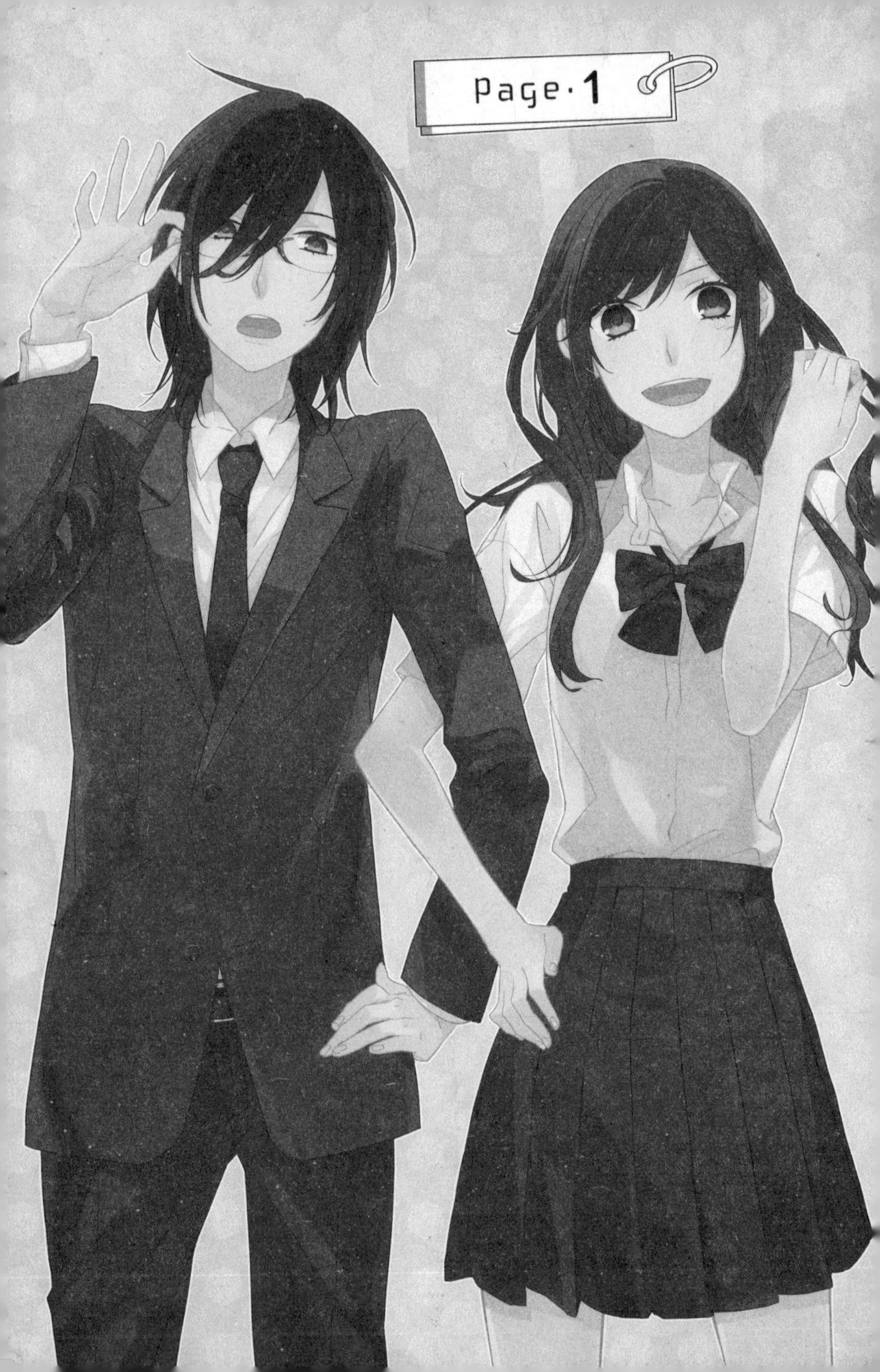
page·1

HORIMIYA

I BET EVERYBODY HAS A SIDE THEY DON'T SHOW ANYONE ELSE.

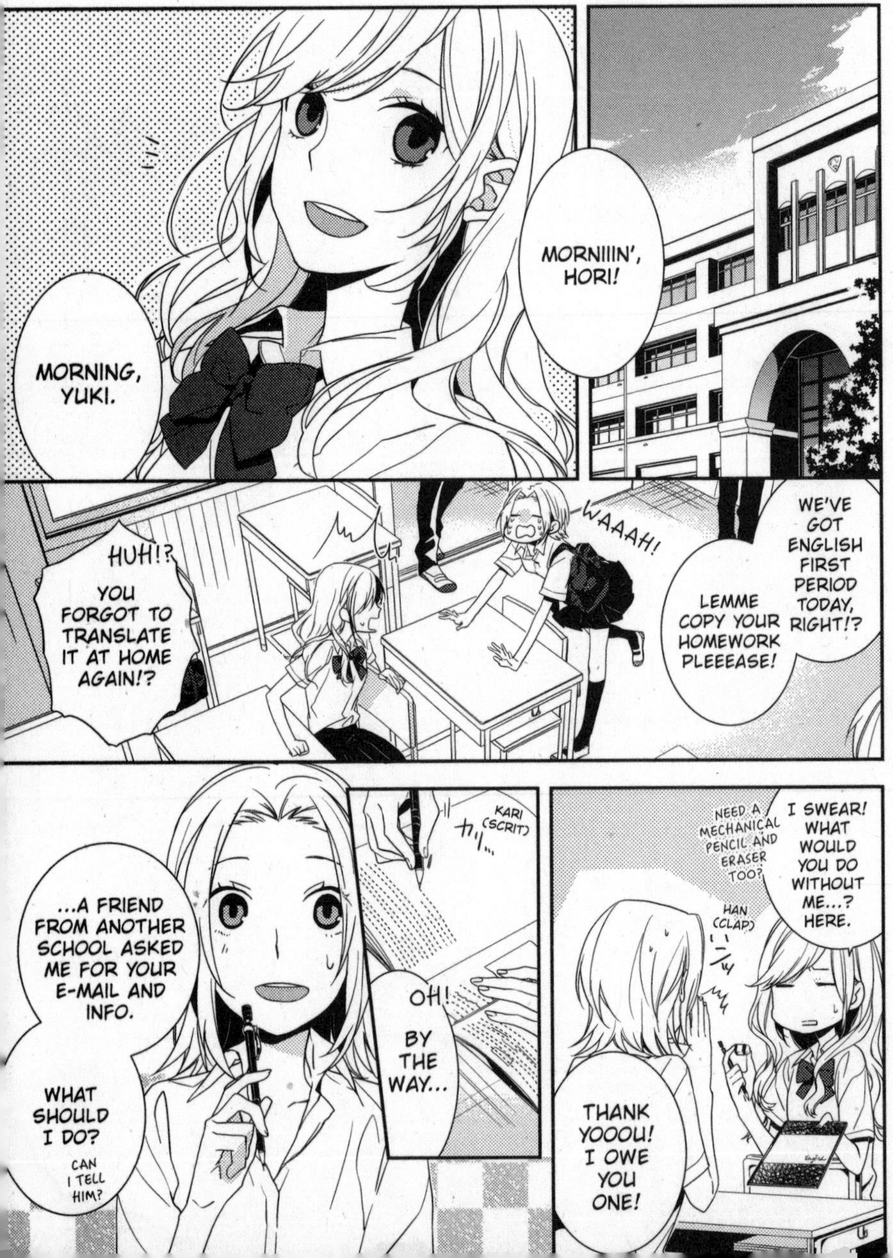
MORNIIIN', HORI!
MORNING, YUKI.
WE'VE GOT ENGLISH FIRST PERIOD TODAY, RIGHT!?
LEMME COPY YOUR HOMEWORK PLEEEASE!
WAAAH!
HUH!? YOU FORGOT TO TRANSLATE IT AT HOME AGAIN!?
I SWEAR! WHAT WOULD YOU DO WITHOUT ME...? HERE.
NEED A MECHANICAL PENCIL AND ERASER TOO?
HAN (CLAP)
THANK YOOOU! I OWE YOU ONE!
KARI (SCRIT)
OH! BY THE WAY...
...A FRIEND FROM ANOTHER SCHOOL ASKED ME FOR YOUR E-MAIL AND INFO.
WHAT SHOULD I DO?
CAN I TELL HIM?

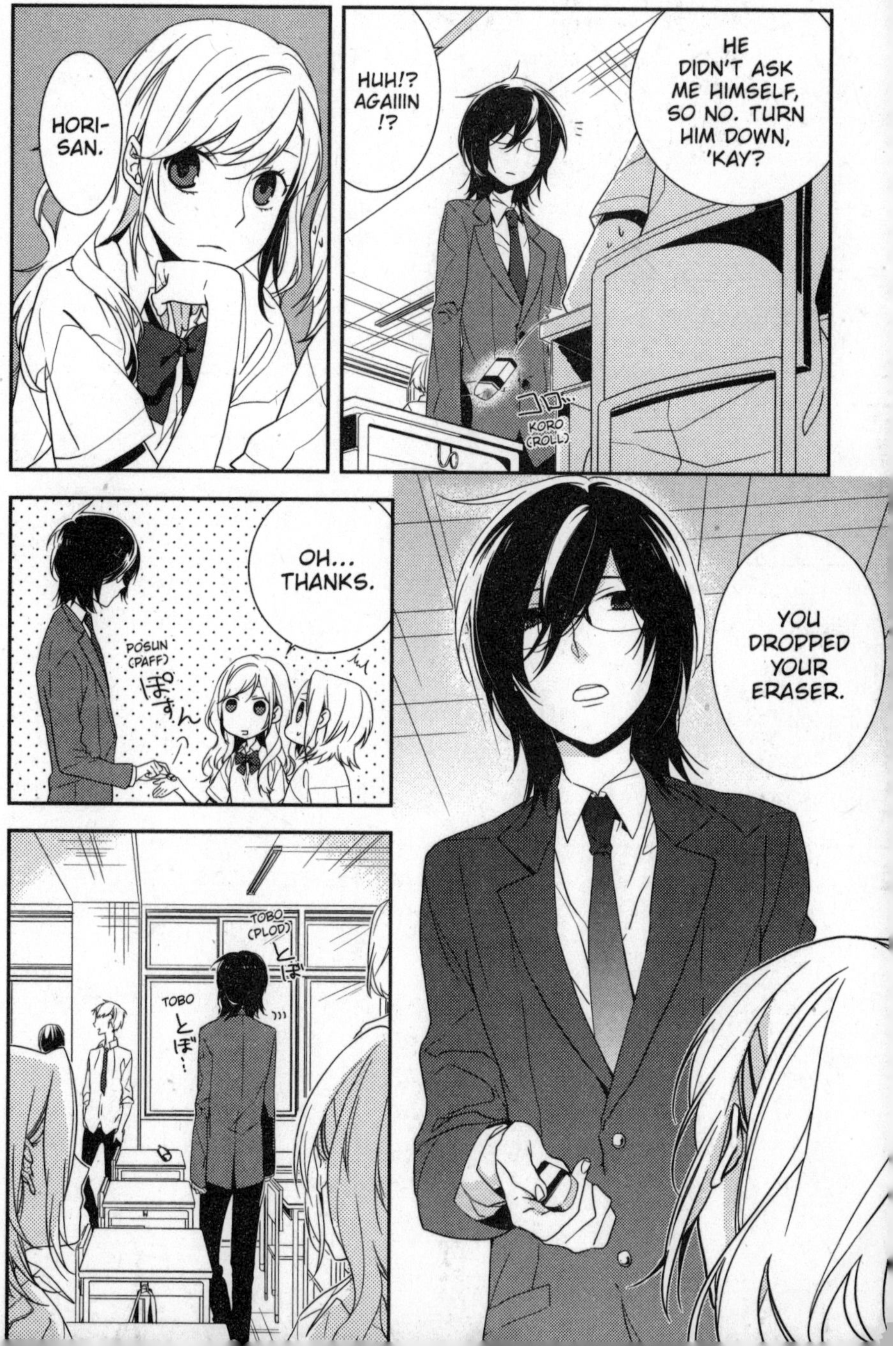
HE DIDN'T ASK ME HIMSELF, SO NO. TURN HIM DOWN, 'KAY?
HUH!? AGAIIIN !?
コロ…
KORO (ROLL)
HORI-SAN.
YOU DROPPED YOUR ERASER.
OH... THANKS.
POSUN (PAFF)
ぽすん
TOBO (PLOD)
とぼ
TOBO
とぼ…

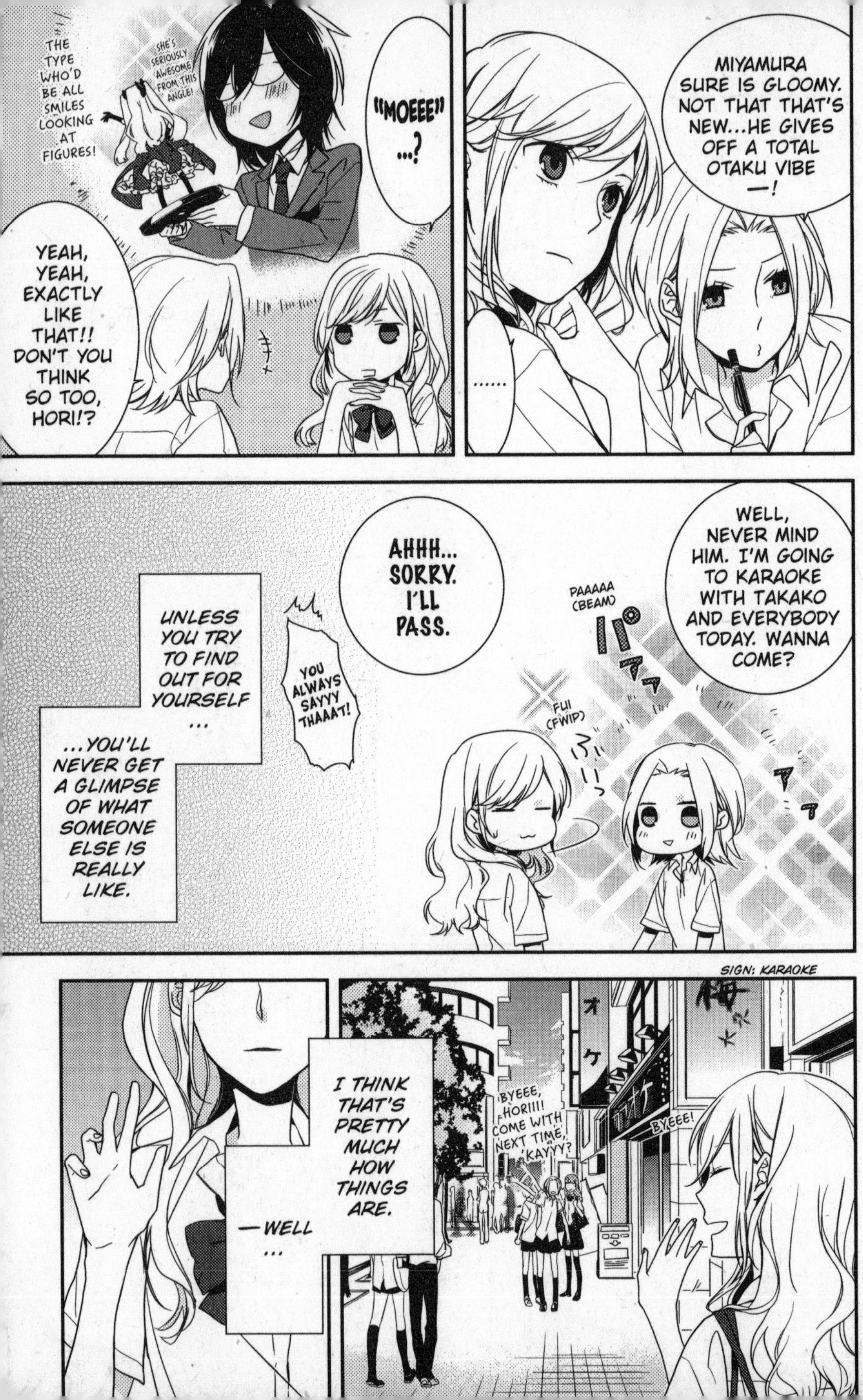
MIYAMURA SURE IS GLOOMY. NOT THAT THAT'S NEW...HE GIVES OFF A TOTAL OTAKU VIBE —!
......
"MOEEE" ...?
SHE'S SERIOUSLY AWESOME FROM THIS ANGLE!
THE TYPE WHO'D BE ALL SMILES LOOKING AT FIGURES!
YEAH, YEAH, EXACTLY LIKE THAT!! DON'T YOU THINK SO TOO, HORI!?
WELL, NEVER MIND HIM. I'M GOING TO KARAOKE WITH TAKAKO AND EVERYBODY TODAY. WANNA COME?
PAAAAA (BEAM)
AHHH... SORRY. I'LL PASS.
FUI (FWIP)
YOU ALWAYS SAYYY THAAAT!
UNLESS YOU TRY TO FIND OUT FOR YOURSELF ...
...YOU'LL NEVER GET A GLIMPSE OF WHAT SOMEONE ELSE IS REALLY LIKE.
SIGN: KARAOKE
BYEEE!
BYEEE, HORIII! COME WITH NEXT TIME, 'KAYYY?
I THINK THAT'S PRETTY MUCH HOW THINGS ARE.
—WELL ...

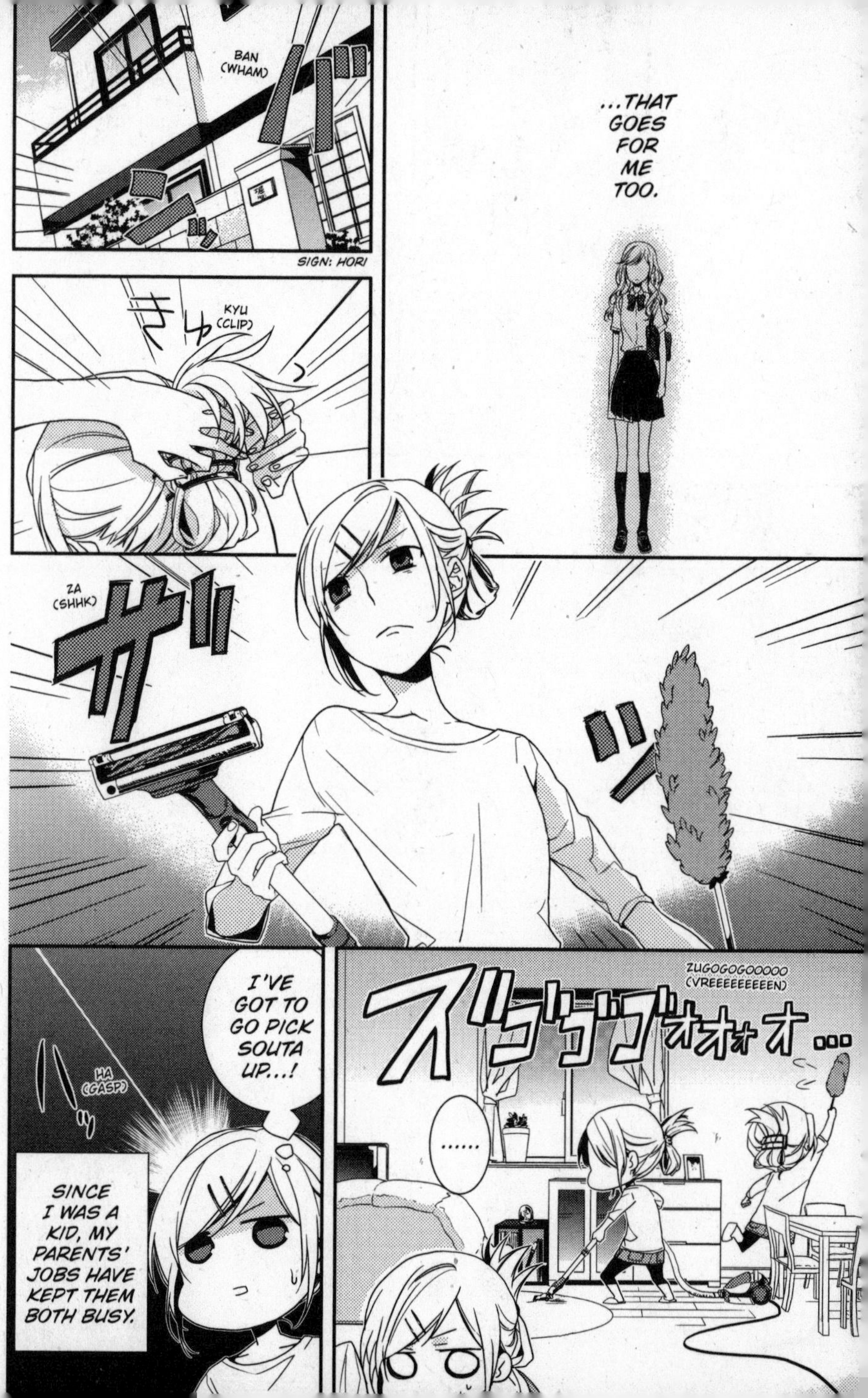
...THAT GOES FOR ME TOO.
BAN (WHAM)
SIGN: HORI
KYU (CLIP)
ZA (SHHK)
ZUGOGOGOOOOO (VREEEEEEEEEEN)
......
I'VE GOT TO GO PICK SOUTA UP...!
HA (GASP)
SINCE I WAS A KID, MY PARENTS' JOBS HAVE KEPT THEM BOTH BUSY.

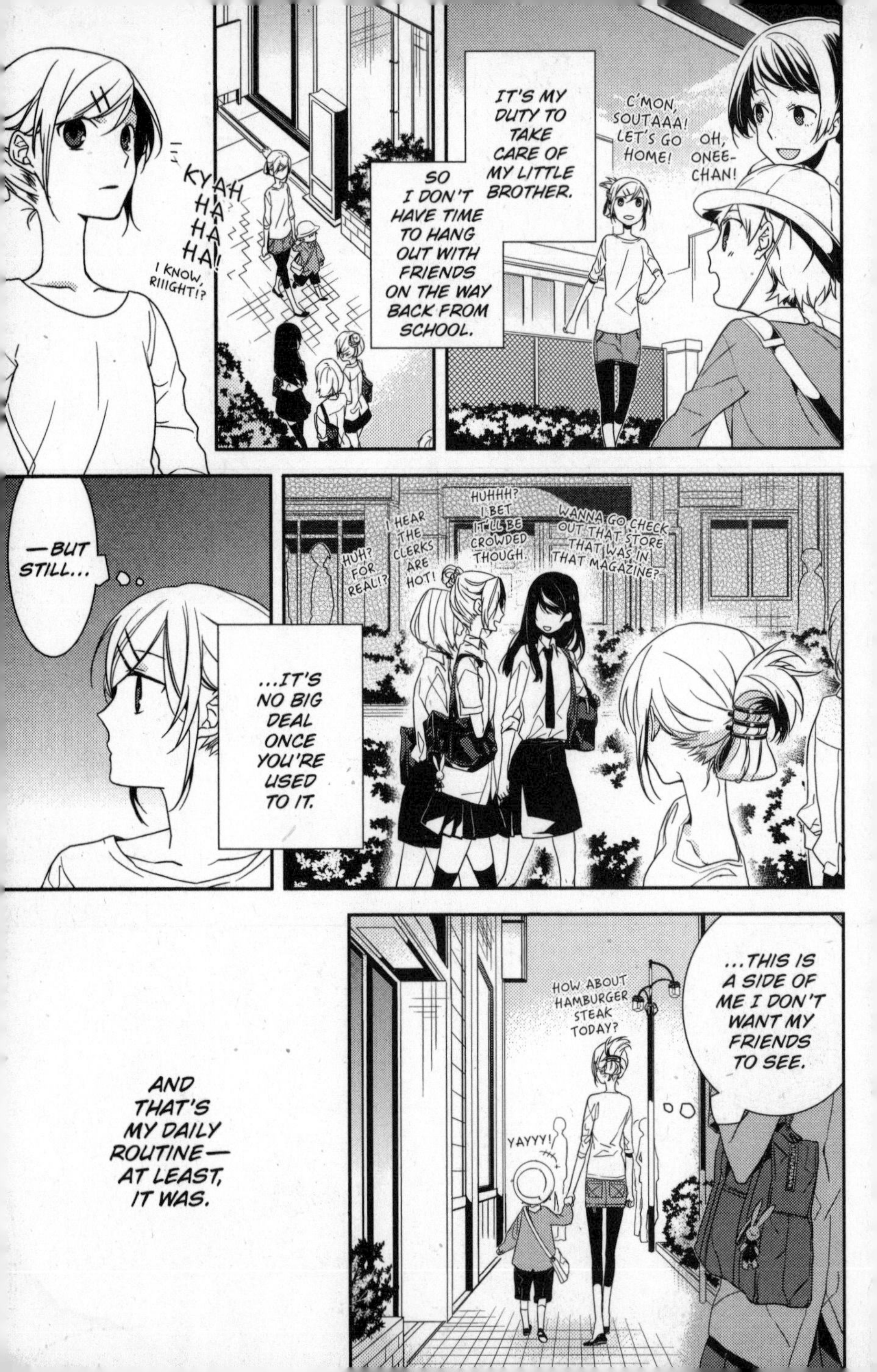
OH, ONEE-CHAN!
C'MON, SOUTAAA! LET'S GO HOME!
IT'S MY DUTY TO TAKE CARE OF MY LITTLE BROTHER.
SO I DON'T HAVE TIME TO HANG OUT WITH FRIENDS ON THE WAY BACK FROM SCHOOL.
KYAH HA HA HA!
I KNOW, RIIIGHT!?
WANNA GO CHECK OUT THAT STORE THAT WAS IN THAT MAGAZINE?
HUHHH? I BET IT'LL BE CROWDED THOUGH.
I HEAR THE CLERKS ARE HOT!
HUH? FOR REAL!?
...IT'S NO BIG DEAL ONCE YOU'RE USED TO IT.
—BUT STILL...
...THIS IS A SIDE OF ME I DON'T WANT MY FRIENDS TO SEE.
HOW ABOUT HAMBURGER STEAK TODAY?
YAYYY!
AND THAT'S MY DAILY ROUTINE—AT LEAST, IT WAS.

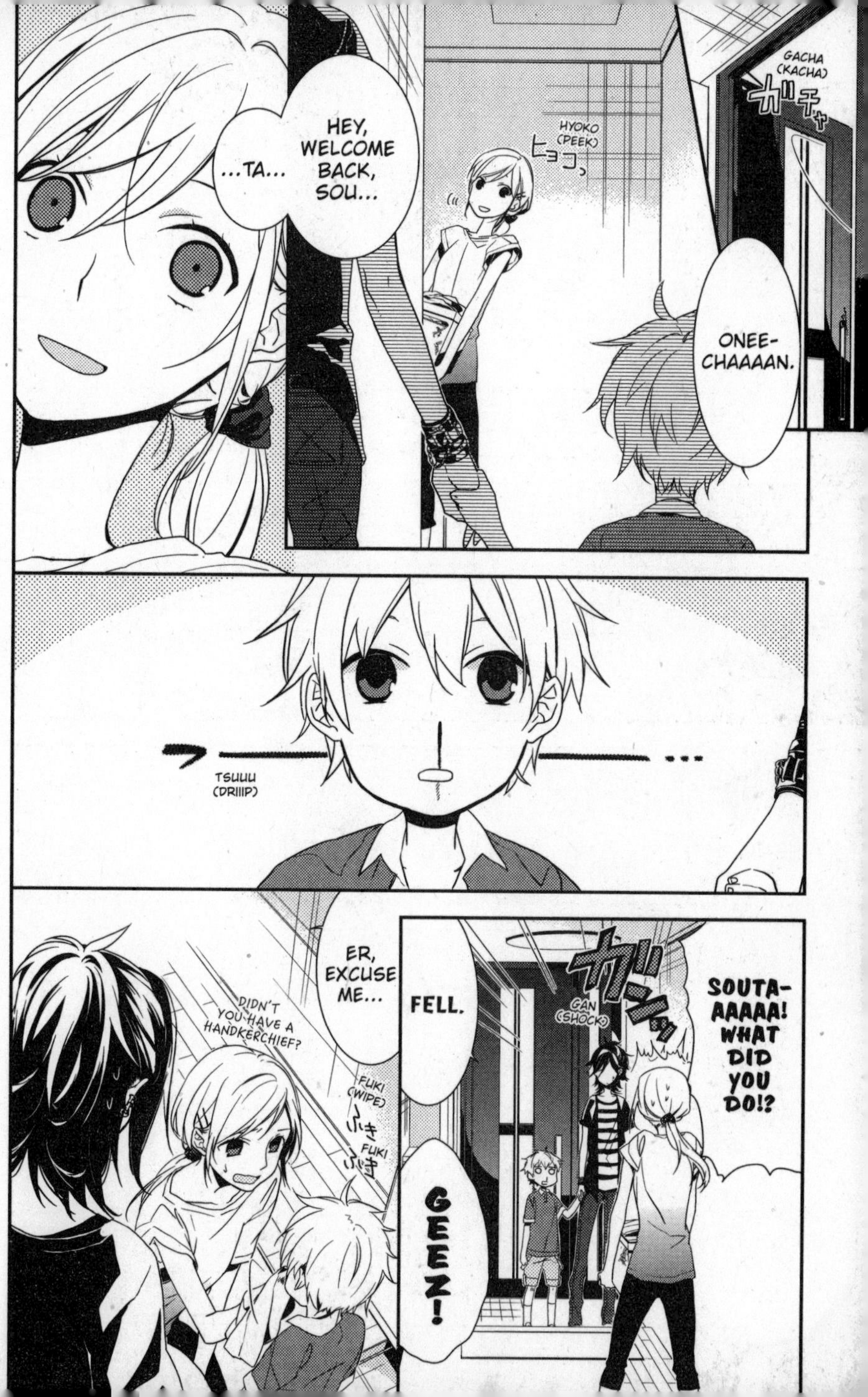
GACHA (KACHA)
ガチャ
ONEE-CHAAAAN.
HYOKO (PEEK)
ヒョコッ
HEY, WELCOME BACK, SOU...
...TA...
TSUUU (DRIIIP)
ッ———————...
SOUTA-AAAAA! WHAT DID YOU DO!?
GAN (SHOCK)
ガーンッ
FELL.
GEEZ!
ER, EXCUSE ME...
DIDN'T YOU HAVE A HANDKERCHIEF?
FUKI (WIPE)
ふき
FUKI
ふき

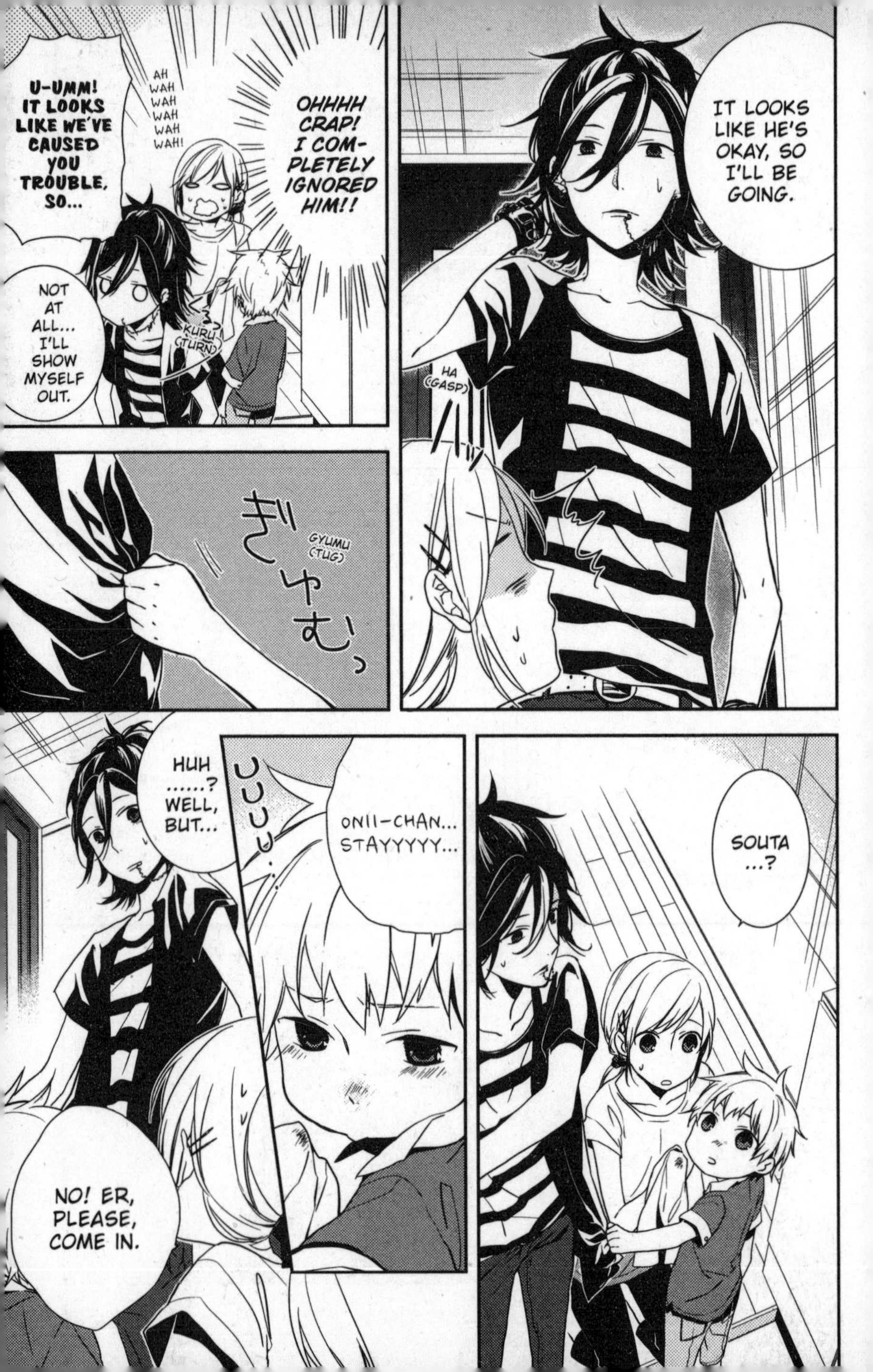
IT LOOKS LIKE HE'S OKAY, SO I'LL BE GOING.
HA (GASP)
U-UMM! IT LOOKS LIKE WE'VE CAUSED YOU TROUBLE, SO...
OHHHH CRAP! I COMPLETELY IGNORED HIM!!
AH WAH WAH WAH WAH WAH!
KURU (TURN)
NOT AT ALL... I'LL SHOW MYSELF OUT.
ぎゅむっ
GYUMU (TUG)
SOUTA ...?
ONII-CHAN... STAYYYYY...
UUUUU...
HUH ......? WELL, BUT...
NO! ER, PLEASE, COME IN.

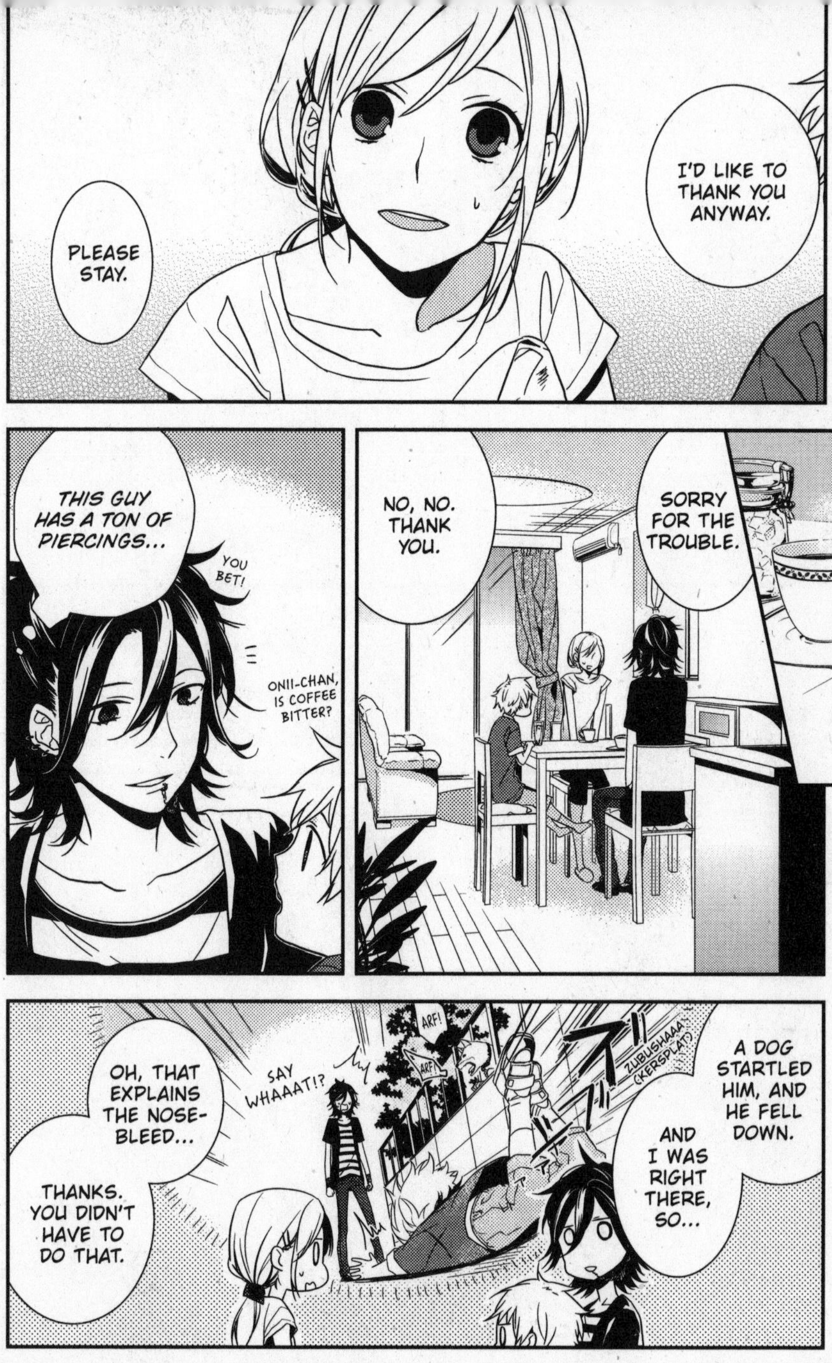
I'D LIKE TO THANK YOU ANYWAY.
PLEASE STAY.
SORRY FOR THE TROUBLE.
NO, NO. THANK YOU.
THIS GUY HAS A TON OF PIERCINGS...
YOU BET!
ONII-CHAN, IS COFFEE BITTER?
A DOG STARTLED HIM, AND HE FELL DOWN.
AND I WAS RIGHT THERE, SO...
ZUBUSHAAA (KERSPLAT)
ARF!
ARF!
SAY WHAAAT!?
OH, THAT EXPLAINS THE NOSE-BLEED...
THANKS. YOU DIDN'T HAVE TO DO THAT.

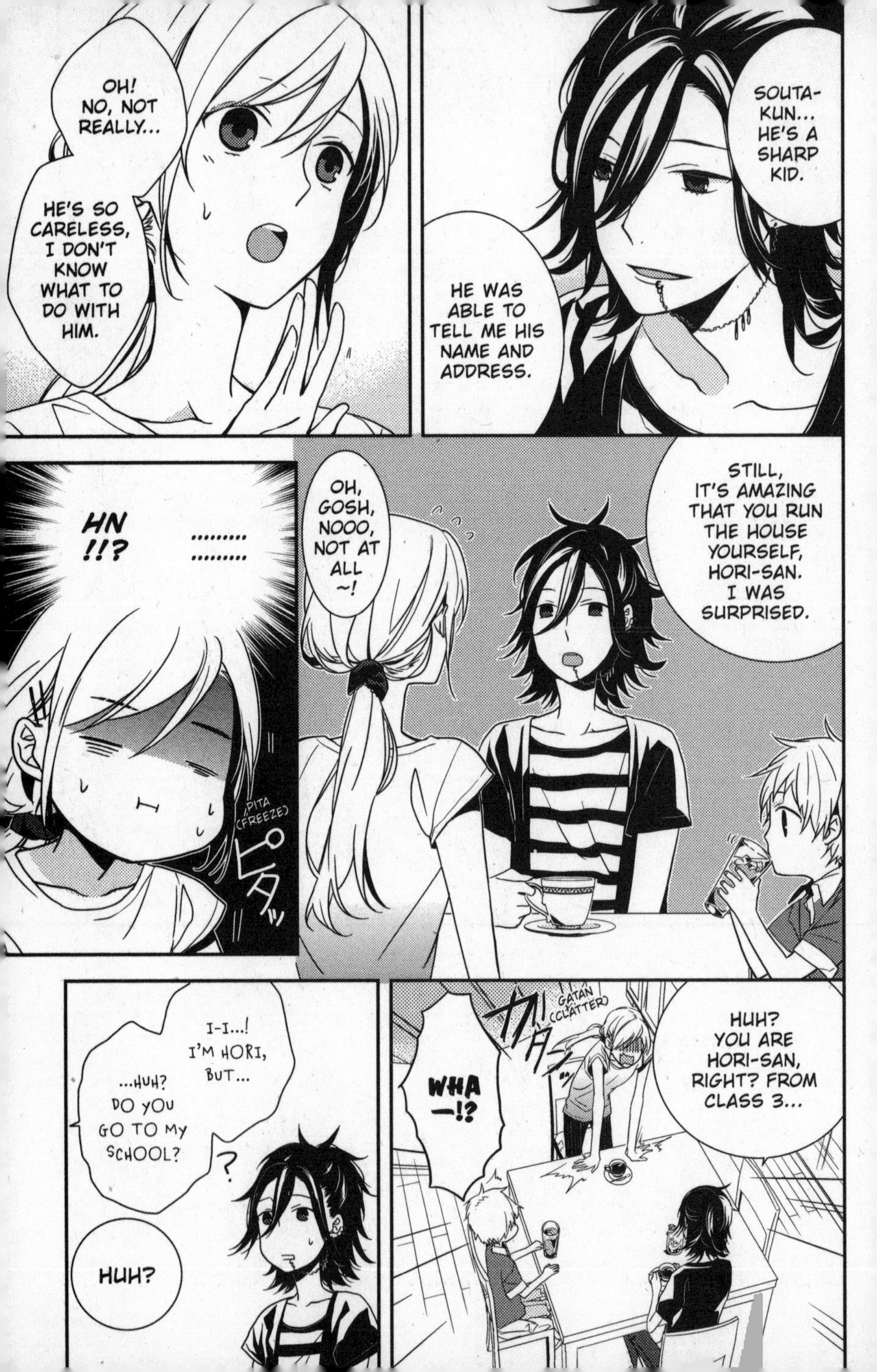
SOUTA-KUN... HE'S A SHARP KID.
HE WAS ABLE TO TELL ME HIS NAME AND ADDRESS.
OH! NO, NOT REALLY...
HE'S SO CARELESS, I DON'T KNOW WHAT TO DO WITH HIM.
STILL, IT'S AMAZING THAT YOU RUN THE HOUSE YOURSELF, HORI-SAN. I WAS SURPRISED.
OH, GOSH, NOOO, NOT AT ALL ~!
HN !!?
....
PITA (FREEZE)
HUH? YOU ARE HORI-SAN, RIGHT? FROM CLASS 3...
GATAN (CLATTER)
WHA—!?
I-I...! I'M HORI, BUT...
...HUH? DO YOU GO TO MY SCHOOL?
?
HUH?

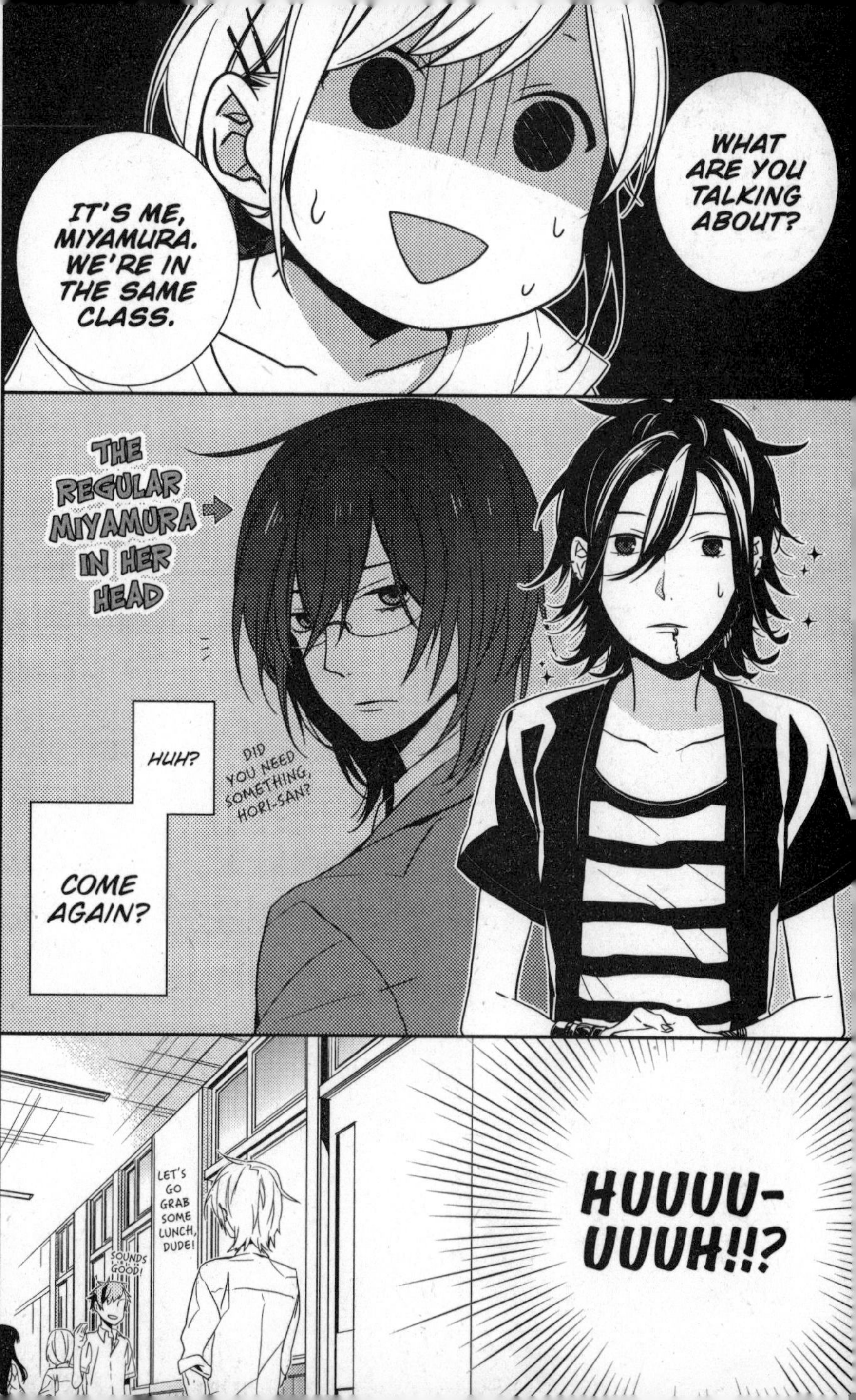
WHAT ARE YOU TALKING ABOUT?
IT'S ME, MIYAMURA. WE'RE IN THE SAME CLASS.
THE REGULAR MIYAMURA IN HER HEAD
DID YOU NEED SOMETHING, HORI-SAN?
HUH?
COME AGAIN?
HUUUU-UUUH!!?
LET'S GO GRAB SOME LUNCH, DUDE!
SOUNDS GOOD!

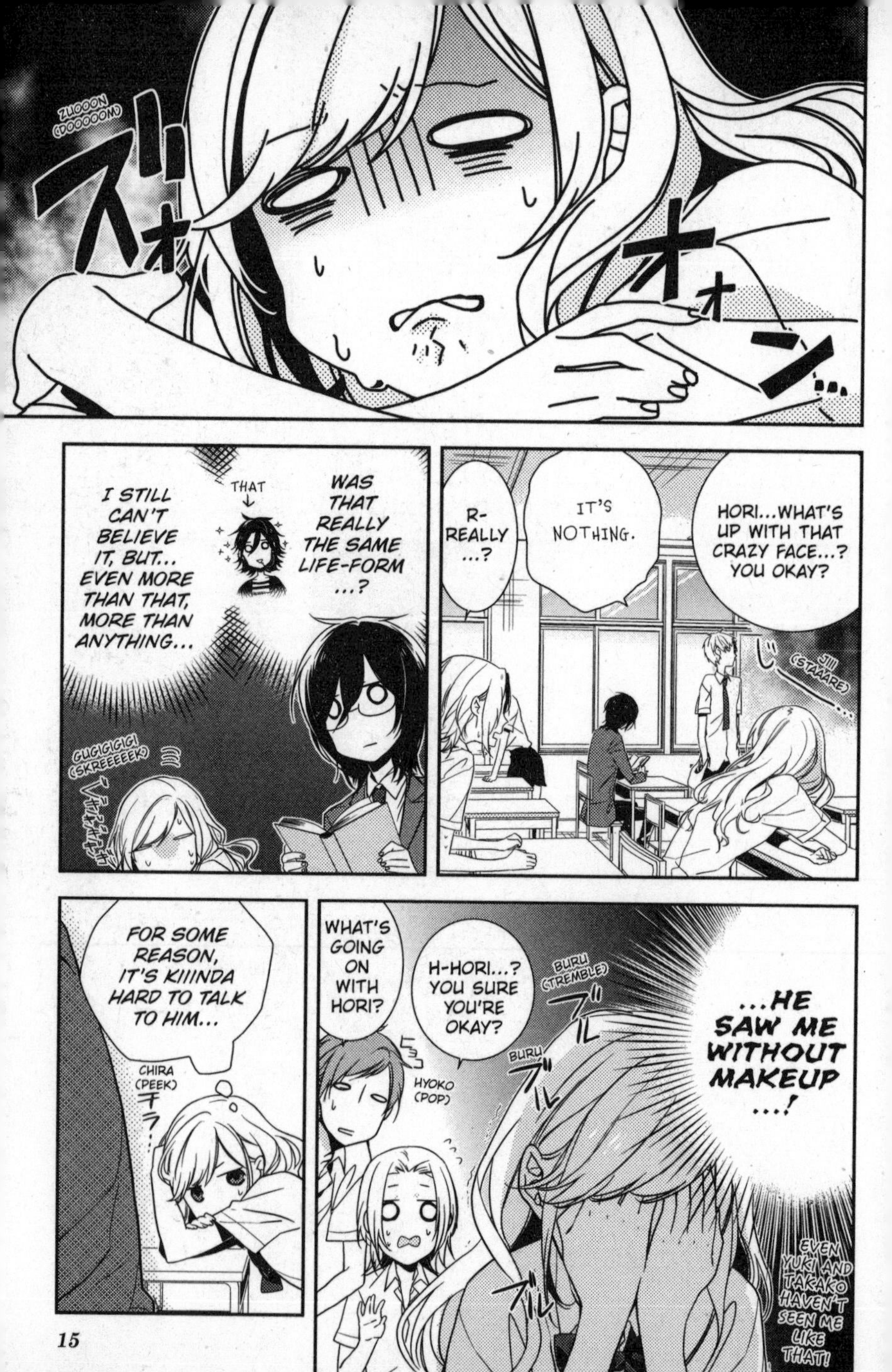
ZUOOON (DOOOOOM)
HORI...WHAT'S UP WITH THAT CRAZY FACE...? YOU OKAY?
IT'S NOTHING.
R-REALLY ...?
JIII (STAAARE)...
WAS THAT REALLY THE SAME LIFE-FORM ...?
THAT
I STILL CAN'T BELIEVE IT, BUT... EVEN MORE THAN THAT, MORE THAN ANYTHING...
GUGIGIGIGI (SKREEEEEK)
...HE SAW ME WITHOUT MAKEUP ...!
BURU (TREMBLE)
BURU
H-HORI...? YOU SURE YOU'RE OKAY?
WHAT'S GOING ON WITH HORI?
HYOKO (POP)
EVEN YUKI AND TAKAKO HAVEN'T SEEN ME LIKE THAT!
FOR SOME REASON, IT'S KIIINDA HARD TO TALK TO HIM...
CHIRA (PEEK)

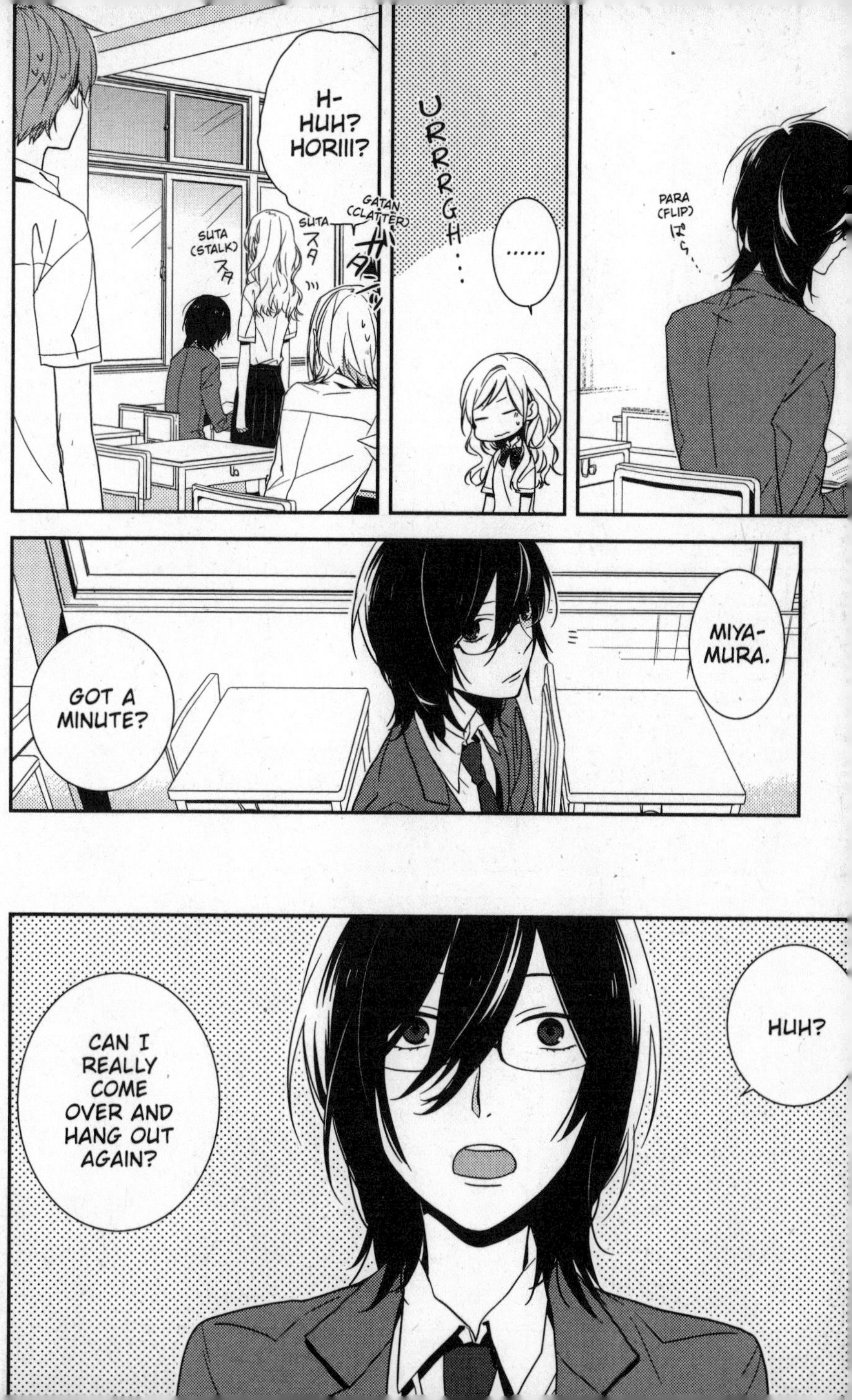
PARA (FLIP)
ぱら
URRRGH...
......
H-HUH? HORIII?
GATAN (CLATTER)
ガタ
SUTA
スタ
SUTA (STALK)
スタ
MIYA-MURA.
GOT A MINUTE?
HUH?
CAN I REALLY COME OVER AND HANG OUT AGAIN?

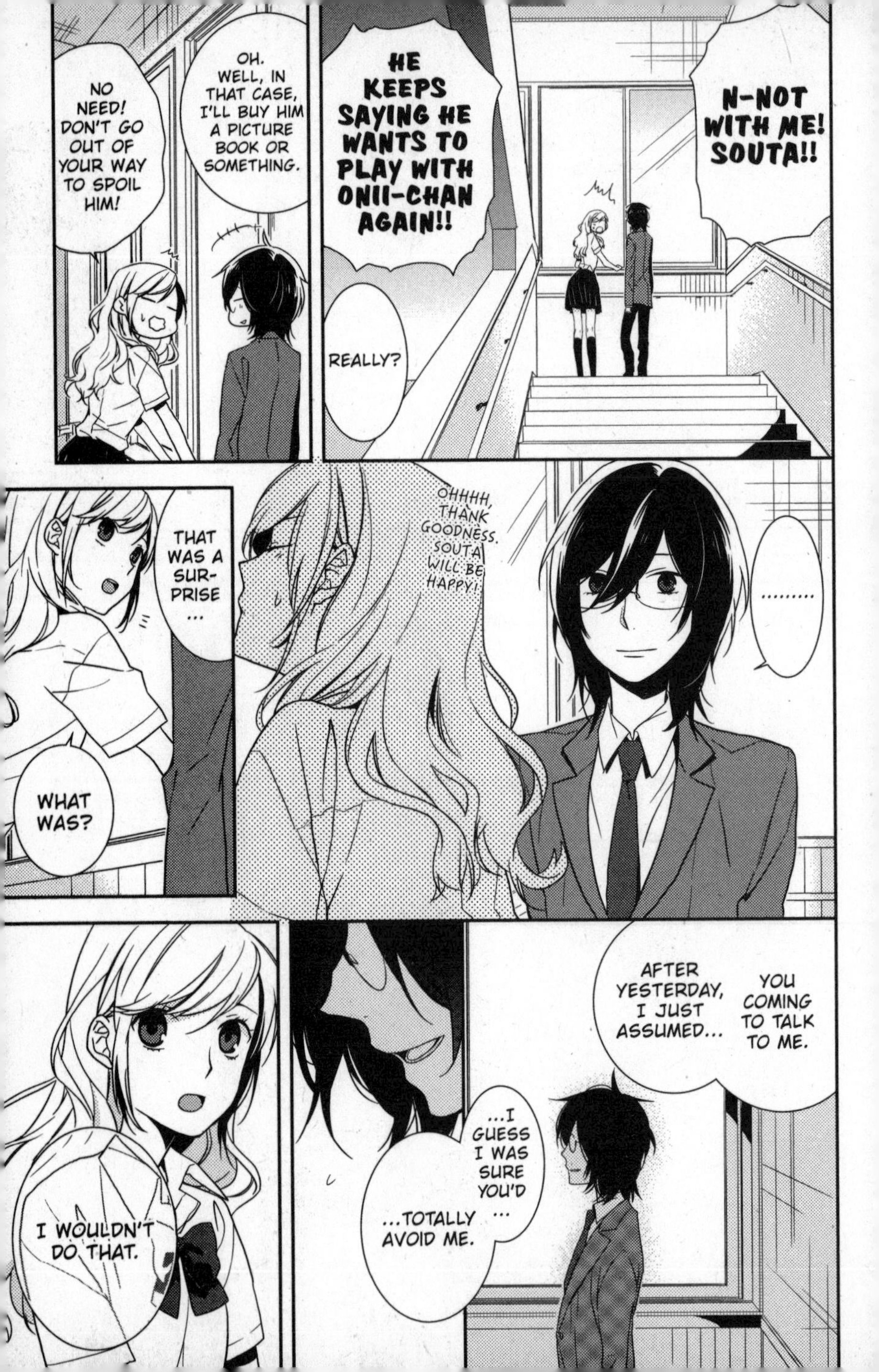
N-NOT WITH ME! SOUTA!!
HE KEEPS SAYING HE WANTS TO PLAY WITH ONII-CHAN AGAIN!!
REALLY?
OH. WELL, IN THAT CASE, I'LL BUY HIM A PICTURE BOOK OR SOMETHING.
NO NEED! DON'T GO OUT OF YOUR WAY TO SPOIL HIM!
....
OHHHH, THANK GOODNESS. SOUTA WILL BE HAPPY!
THAT WAS A SUR-PRISE...
WHAT WAS?
YOU COMING TO TALK TO ME.
AFTER YESTERDAY, I JUST ASSUMED...
...I GUESS I WAS SURE YOU'D...
...TOTALLY AVOID ME.
I WOULDN'T DO THAT.

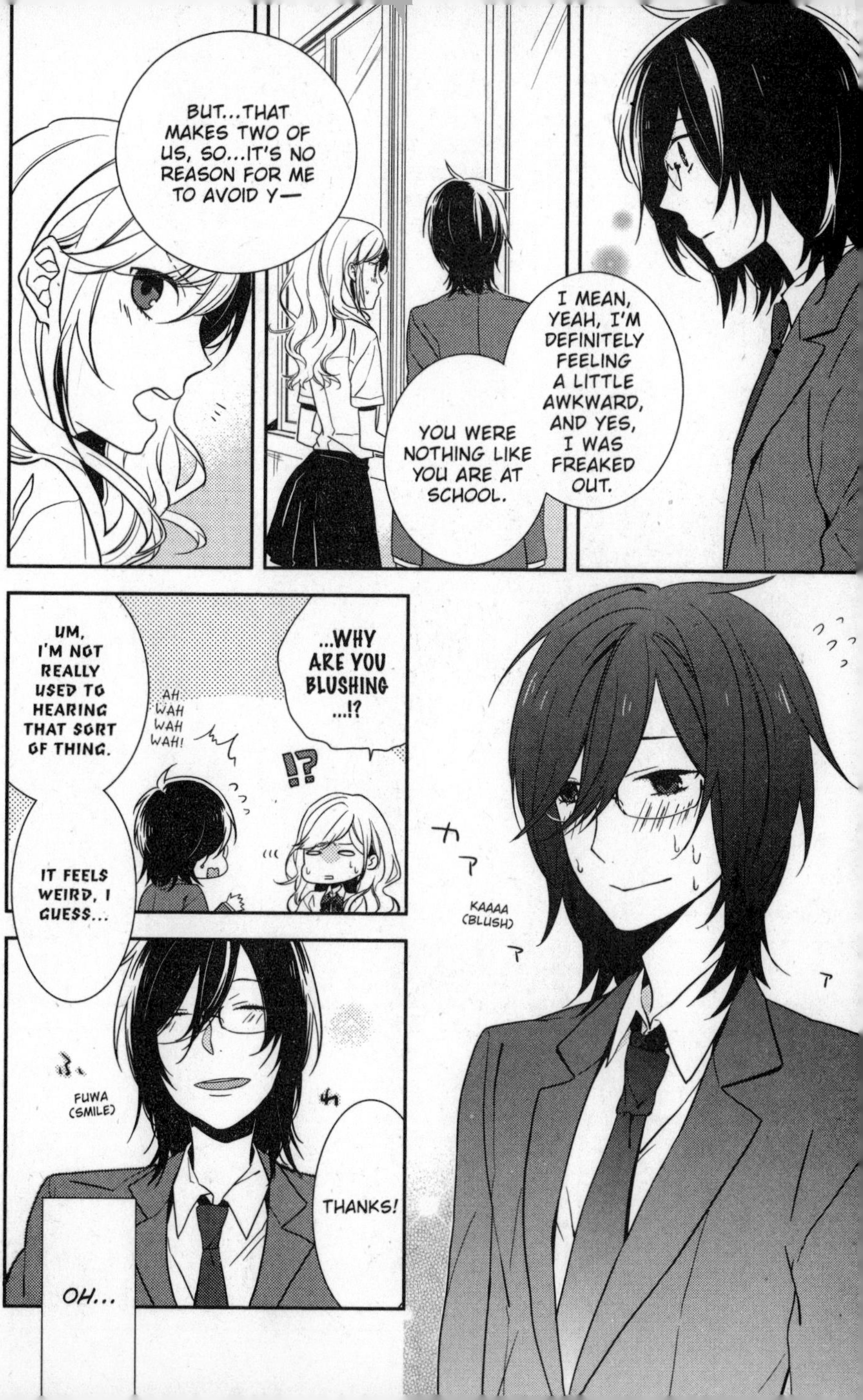
I MEAN, YEAH, I'M DEFINITELY FEELING A LITTLE AWKWARD, AND YES, I WAS FREAKED OUT.
YOU WERE NOTHING LIKE YOU ARE AT SCHOOL.
BUT...THAT MAKES TWO OF US, SO...IT'S NO REASON FOR ME TO AVOID Y—
KAAAA (BLUSH)
...WHY ARE YOU BLUSHING ...!?
!?
UM, I'M NOT REALLY USED TO HEARING THAT SORT OF THING.
AH WAH WAH WAH!
IT FEELS WEIRD, I GUESS...
THANKS!
FUWA (SMILE)
OH...

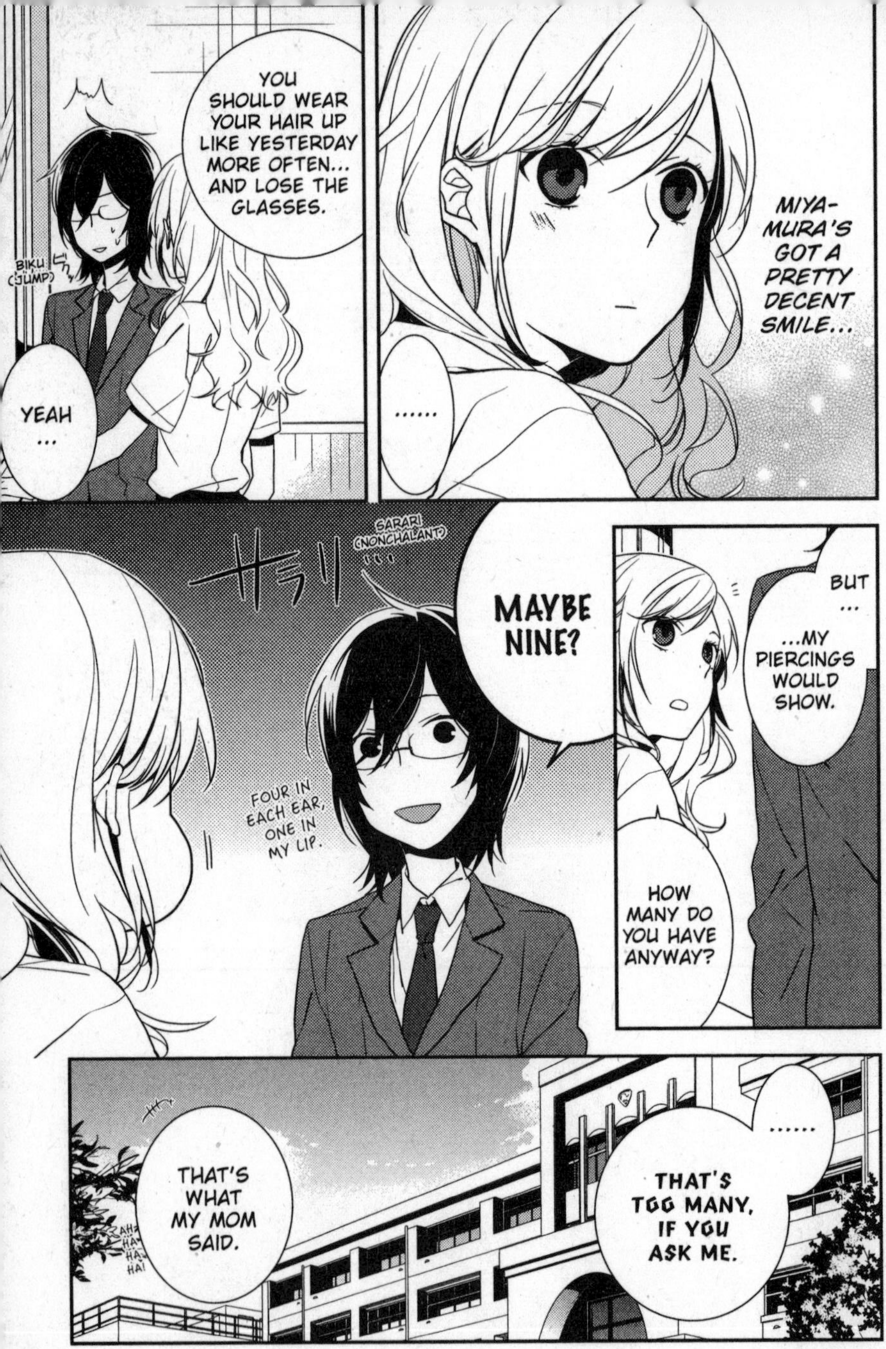
MIYA-MURA'S GOT A PRETTY DECENT SMILE...
......
YOU SHOULD WEAR YOUR HAIR UP LIKE YESTERDAY MORE OFTEN... AND LOSE THE GLASSES.
BIKU (JUMP)
YEAH ...
BUT ...
...MY PIERCINGS WOULD SHOW.
HOW MANY DO YOU HAVE ANYWAY?
MAYBE NINE?
SARARI (NONCHALANT)
FOUR IN EACH EAR, ONE IN MY LIP.
......
THAT'S TOO MANY, IF YOU ASK ME.
THAT'S WHAT MY MOM SAID.
AH HA HA HA

SINCE MIYAMURA STARTED COMING OVER,
I'VE LEARNED A FEW THINGS.

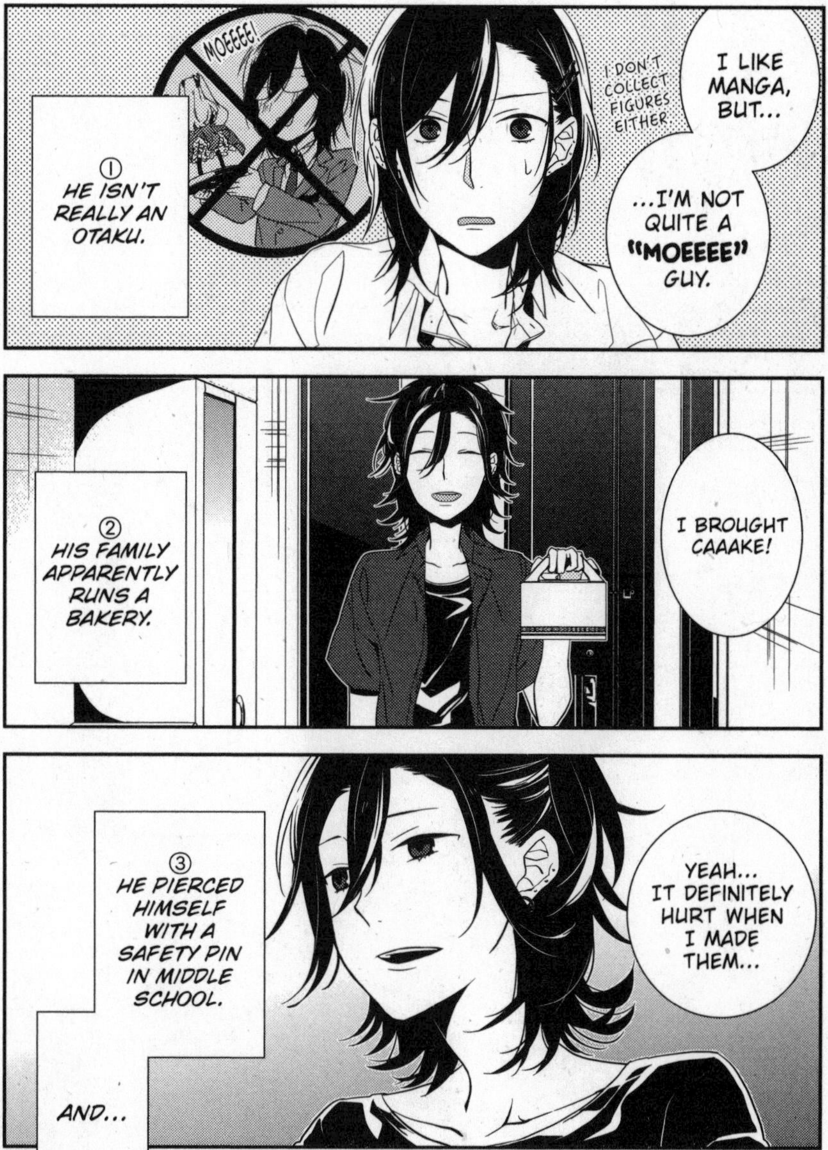
I LIKE MANGA, BUT...
I DON'T COLLECT FIGURES EITHER
...I'M NOT QUITE A "MOEEEE" GUY.
MOEEEE!
① HE ISN'T REALLY AN OTAKU.
I BROUGHT CAAAKE!
② HIS FAMILY APPARENTLY RUNS A BAKERY.
YEAH... IT DEFINITELY HURT WHEN I MADE THEM...
③ HE PIERCED HIMSELF WITH A SAFETY PIN IN MIDDLE SCHOOL.
AND...

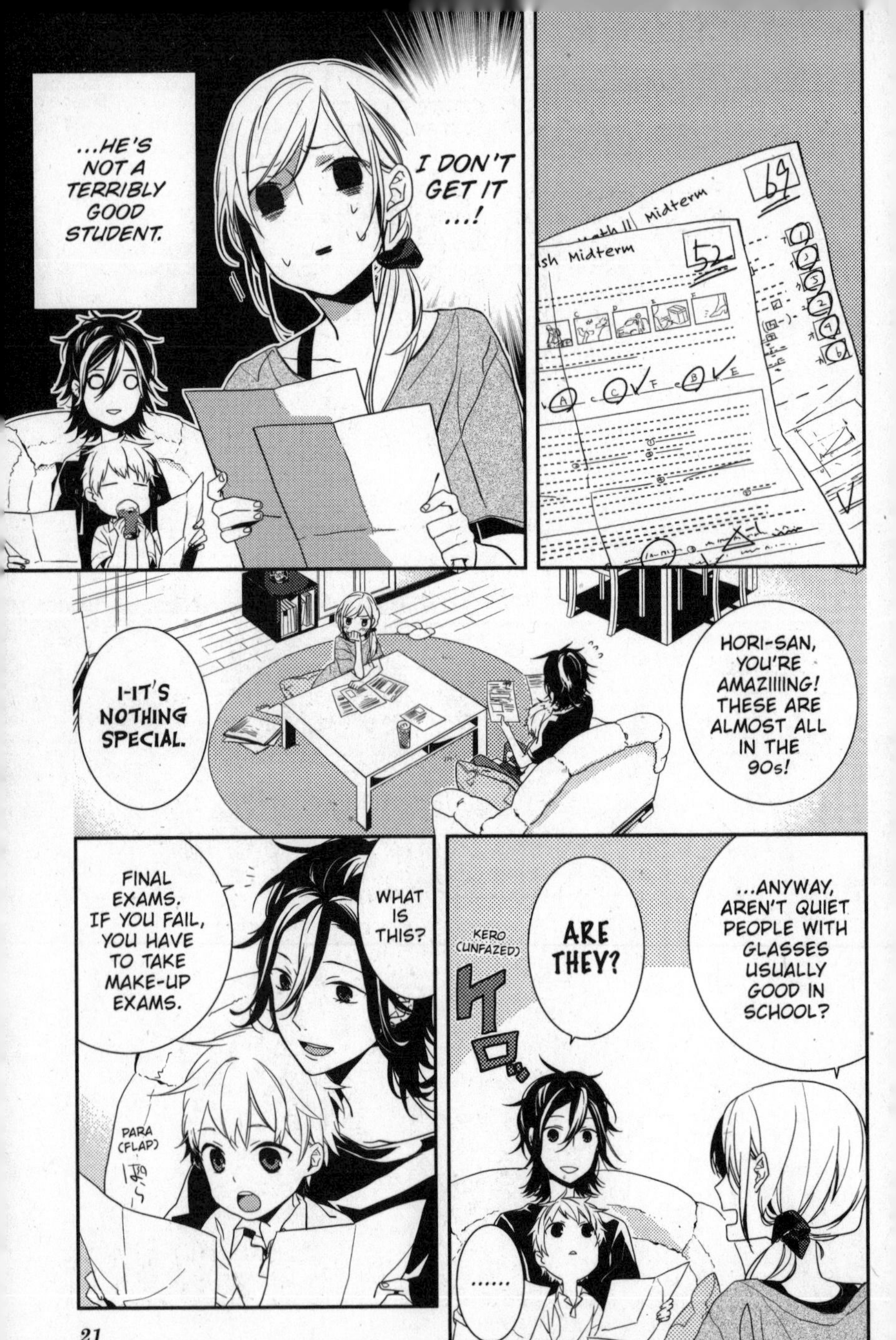
69
52
I DON'T GET IT ...!
...HE'S NOT A TERRIBLY GOOD STUDENT.
HORI-SAN, YOU'RE AMAZIIIING! THESE ARE ALMOST ALL IN THE 90s!
I-IT'S NOTHING SPECIAL.
...ANYWAY, AREN'T QUIET PEOPLE WITH GLASSES USUALLY GOOD IN SCHOOL?
ARE THEY?
KERO (UNFAZED)
......
WHAT IS THIS?
FINAL EXAMS. IF YOU FAIL, YOU HAVE TO TAKE MAKE-UP EXAMS.
PARA (FLAP)

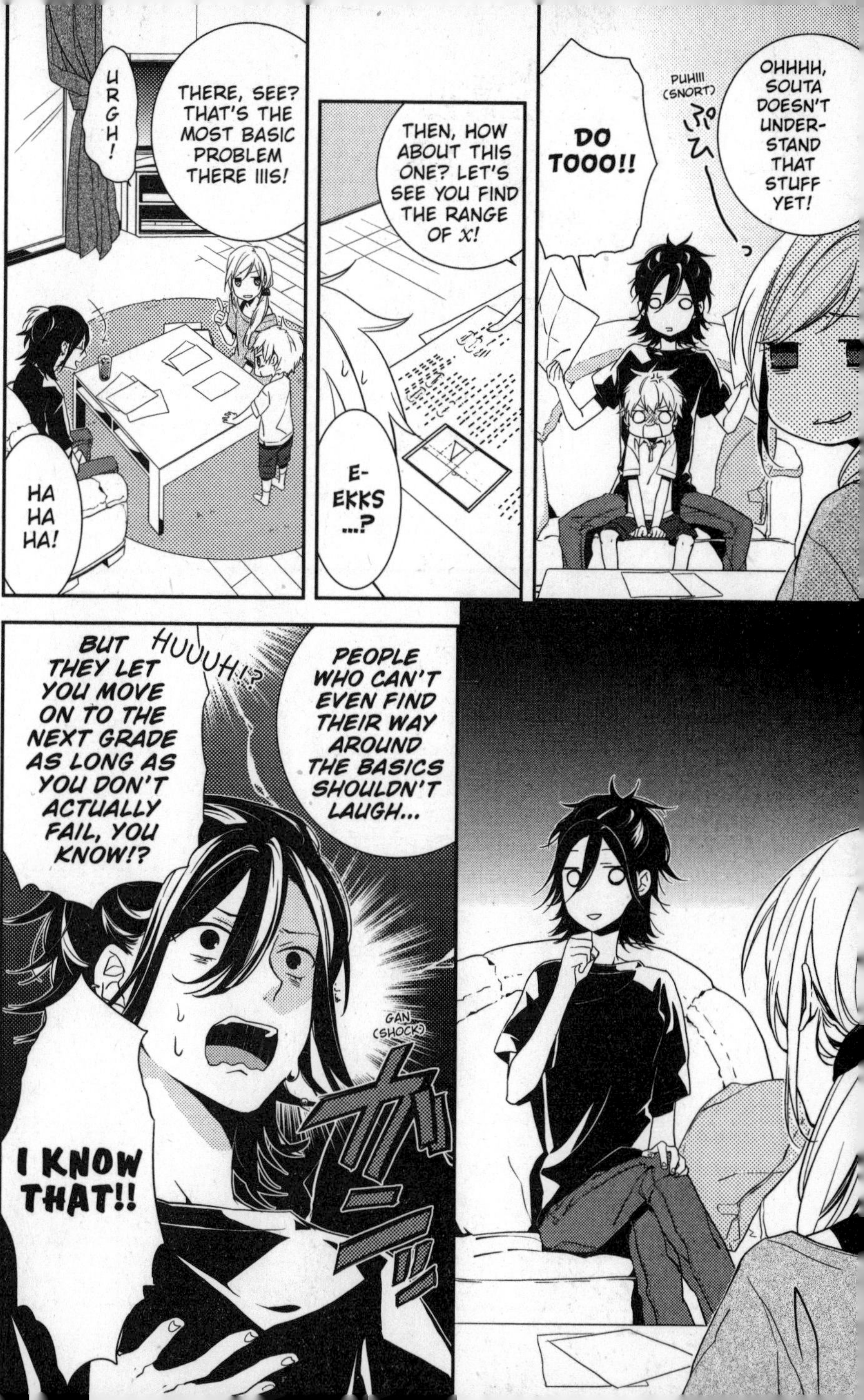
OHHHH, SOUTA DOESN'T UNDER-STAND THAT STUFF YET!
PUHIII (SNORT)
ぷひー
DO TOOO!!
THEN, HOW ABOUT THIS ONE? LET'S SEE YOU FIND THE RANGE OF x!
E-EKKS ...?
THERE, SEE? THAT'S THE MOST BASIC PROBLEM THERE IIIS!
URGH!
HA HA HA!
PEOPLE WHO CAN'T EVEN FIND THEIR WAY AROUND THE BASICS SHOULDN'T LAUGH...
HUUUH!?
BUT THEY LET YOU MOVE ON TO THE NEXT GRADE AS LONG AS YOU DON'T ACTUALLY FAIL, YOU KNOW!?
GAN (SHOCK)
I KNOW THAT!!

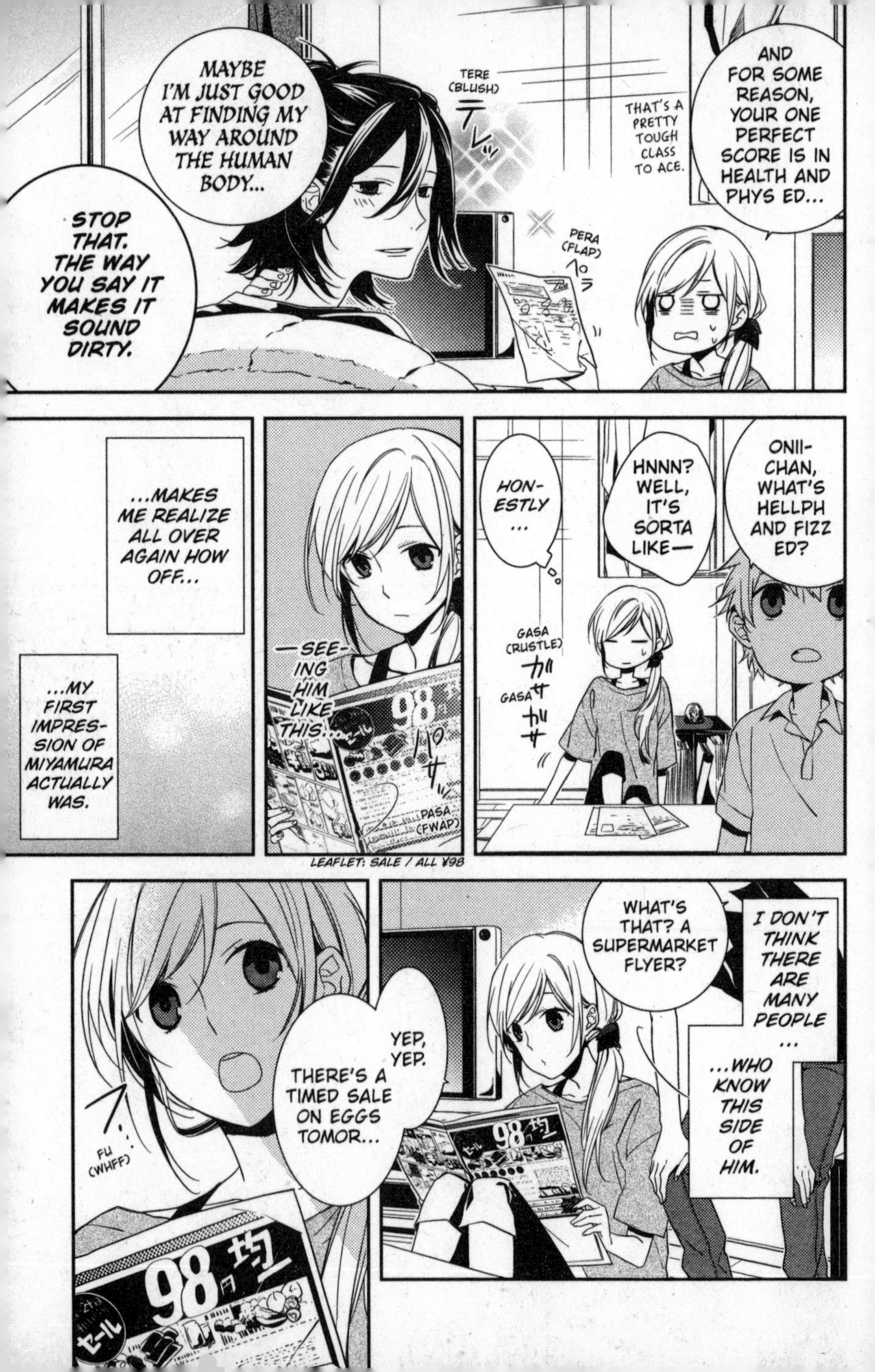

AND FOR SOME REASON, YOUR ONE PERFECT SCORE IS IN HEALTH AND PHYS ED...
THAT'S A PRETTY TOUGH CLASS TO ACE.
TERE (BLUSH)
PERA (FLAP)
MAYBE I'M JUST GOOD AT FINDING MY WAY AROUND THE HUMAN BODY...
STOP THAT. THE WAY YOU SAY IT MAKES IT SOUND DIRTY.
ONII-CHAN, WHAT'S HELLPH AND FIZZ ED?
HNNN? WELL, IT'S SORTA LIKE—
HON-ESTLY...
GASA (RUSTLE)
GASA
—SEE-ING HIM LIKE THIS...
PASA (FWAP)
LEAFLET: SALE / ALL ¥98
...MAKES ME REALIZE ALL OVER AGAIN HOW OFF...
...MY FIRST IMPRESSION OF MIYAMURA ACTUALLY WAS.
I DON'T THINK THERE ARE MANY PEOPLE...
...WHO KNOW THIS SIDE OF HIM.
WHAT'S THAT? A SUPERMARKET FLYER?
YEP, YEP.
THERE'S A TIMED SALE ON EGGS TOMOR...
FU (WHFF)

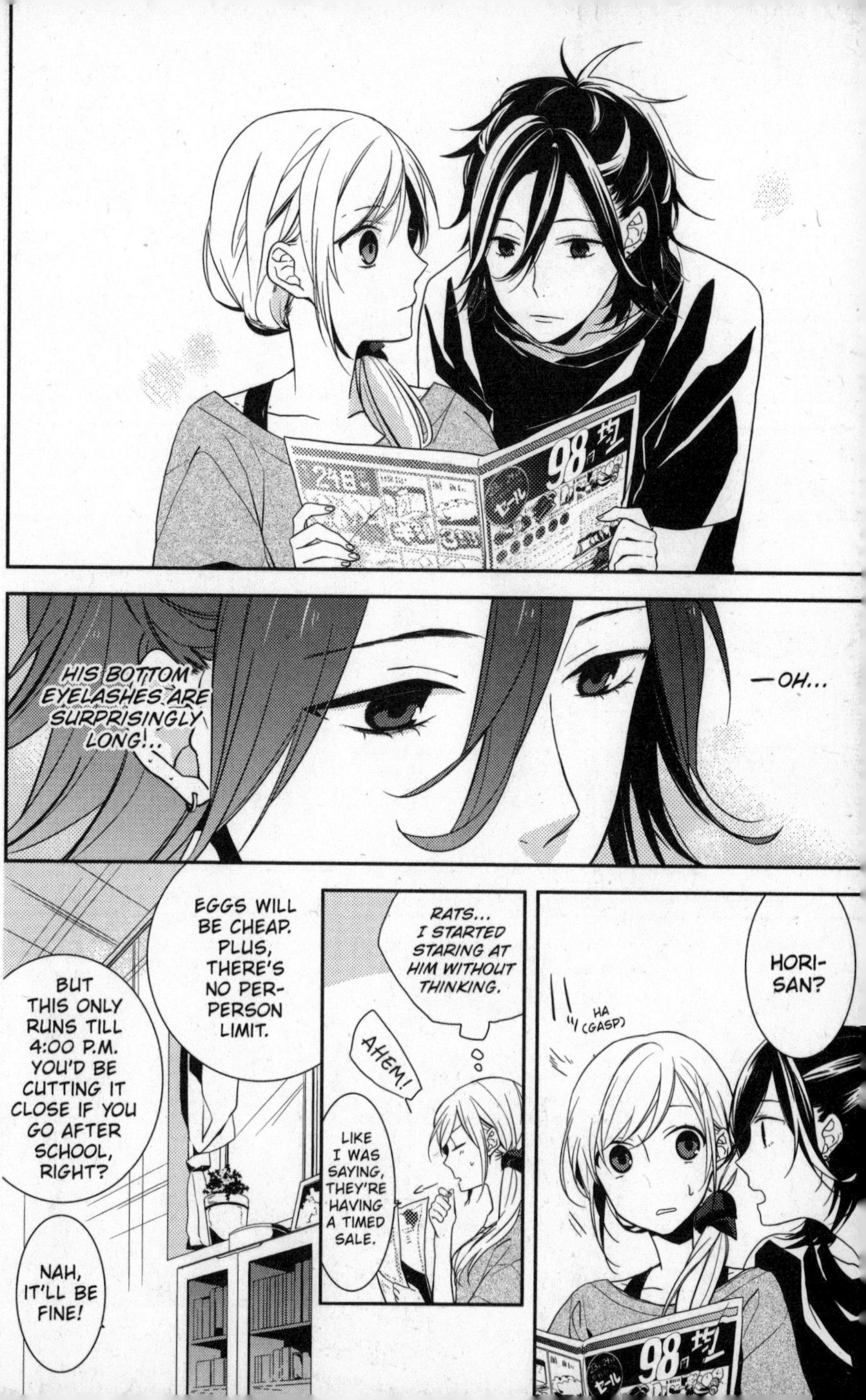
98円
—OH...
HIS BOTTOM EYELASHES ARE SURPRISINGLY LONG!...
HORI-SAN?
HA (GASP)
RATS... I STARTED STARING AT HIM WITHOUT THINKING.
AHEM!
LIKE I WAS SAYING, THEY'RE HAVING A TIMED SALE.
EGGS WILL BE CHEAP. PLUS, THERE'S NO PER-PERSON LIMIT.
BUT THIS ONLY RUNS TILL 4:00 P.M. YOU'D BE CUTTING IT CLOSE IF YOU GO AFTER SCHOOL, RIGHT?
NAH, IT'LL BE FINE!
98円

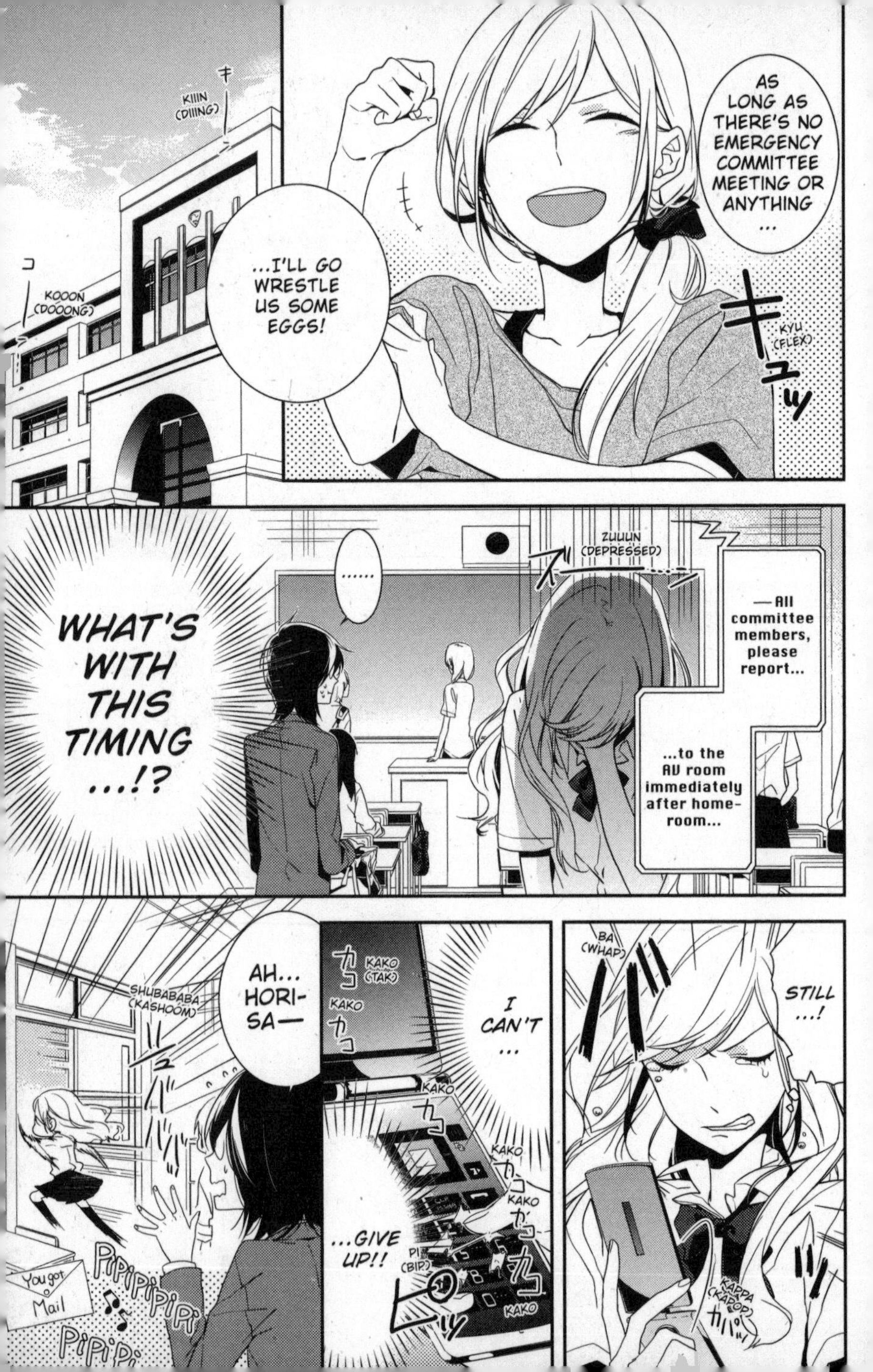
AS LONG AS THERE'S NO EMERGENCY COMMITTEE MEETING OR ANYTHING ...
KYU (FLEX)
...I'LL GO WRESTLE US SOME EGGS!
KIIIN (DIIING)
KOOON (DOOONG)
ZUUUN (DEPRESSED)
—All committee members, please report...
...to the AV room immediately after home-room...
......
WHAT'S WITH THIS TIMING ...!?
BA (WHAP)
STILL ...!
KAPPA (KAPOP)
I CAN'T ...
KAKO (TAK)
KAKO
KAKO
KAKO
KAKO
KAKO
...GIVE UP!!
PI (BIP)
AH... HORI-SA—
SHUBABABA (KASHOOM)
You got Mail
PiPiPiPiPi
PiPiPi

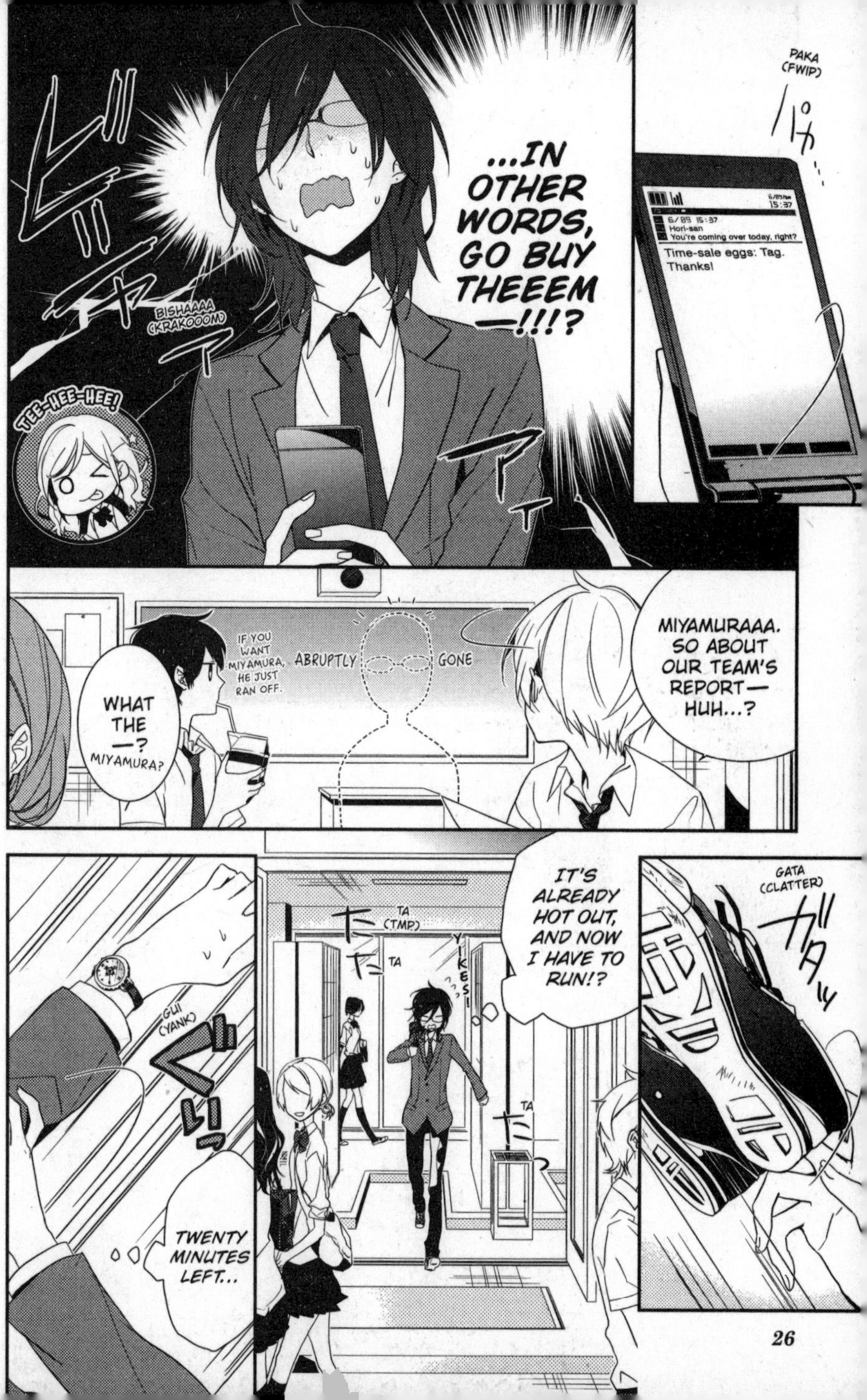

PAKA (FWIP)
6/09 15:37
6/09 15:37
Hori-san
You're coming over today, right?
Time-sale eggs: Tag.
Thanks!
...IN OTHER WORDS, GO BUY THEEEM—!!!?
BISHAAA (KRAKOOOM)
TEE-HEE-HEE!
MIYAMURAAA. SO ABOUT OUR TEAM'S REPORT— HUH...?
ABRUPTLY
GONE
IF YOU WANT MIYAMURA, HE JUST RAN OFF.
WHAT THE—?
MIYAMURA?
GATA (CLATTER)
IT'S ALREADY HOT OUT, AND NOW I HAVE TO RUN!?
TA (TMP)
TA
YIKES!
TA
GUI (YANK)
TWENTY MINUTES LEFT...

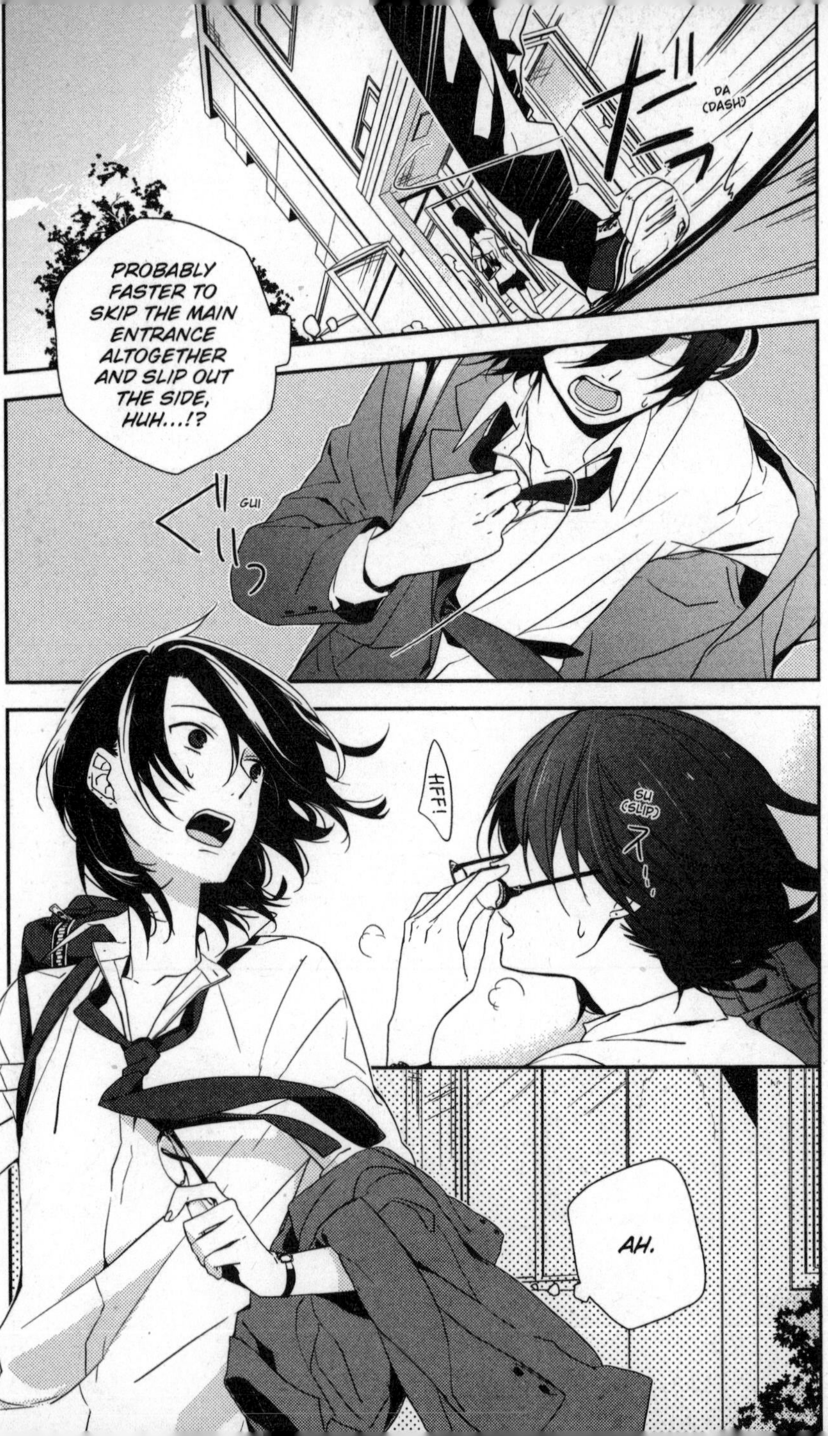
DA (DASH)
PROBABLY FASTER TO SKIP THE MAIN ENTRANCE ALTOGETHER AND SLIP OUT THE SIDE, HUH...!?
GUI
SU (SLIP)
HFF!
AH.

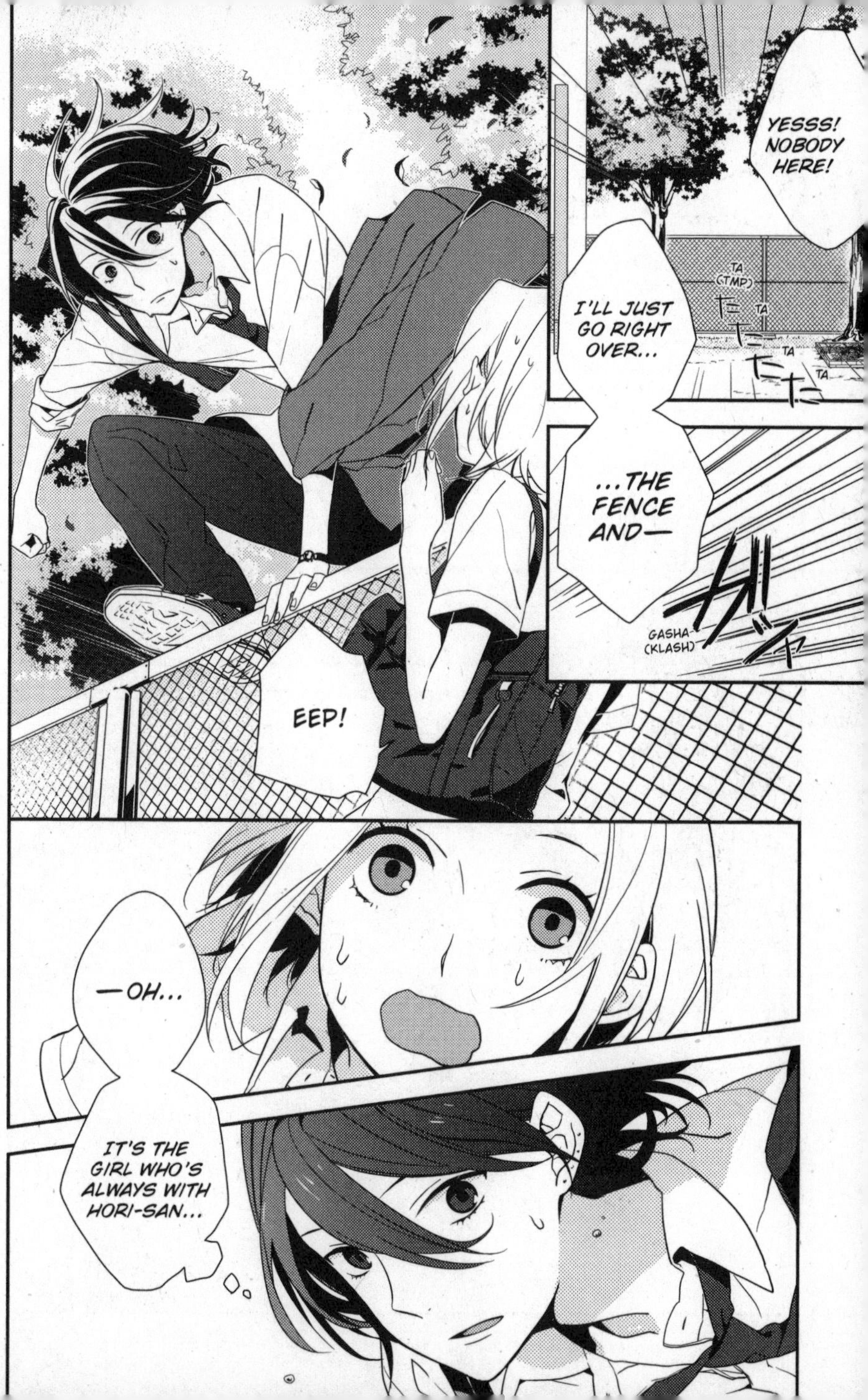
YESSS! NOBODY HERE!
I'LL JUST GO RIGHT OVER...
TA (TMP)
TA
TA
TA
...THE FENCE AND—
GASHA (KLASH)
EEP!
—OH...
IT'S THE GIRL WHO'S ALWAYS WITH HORI-SAN...

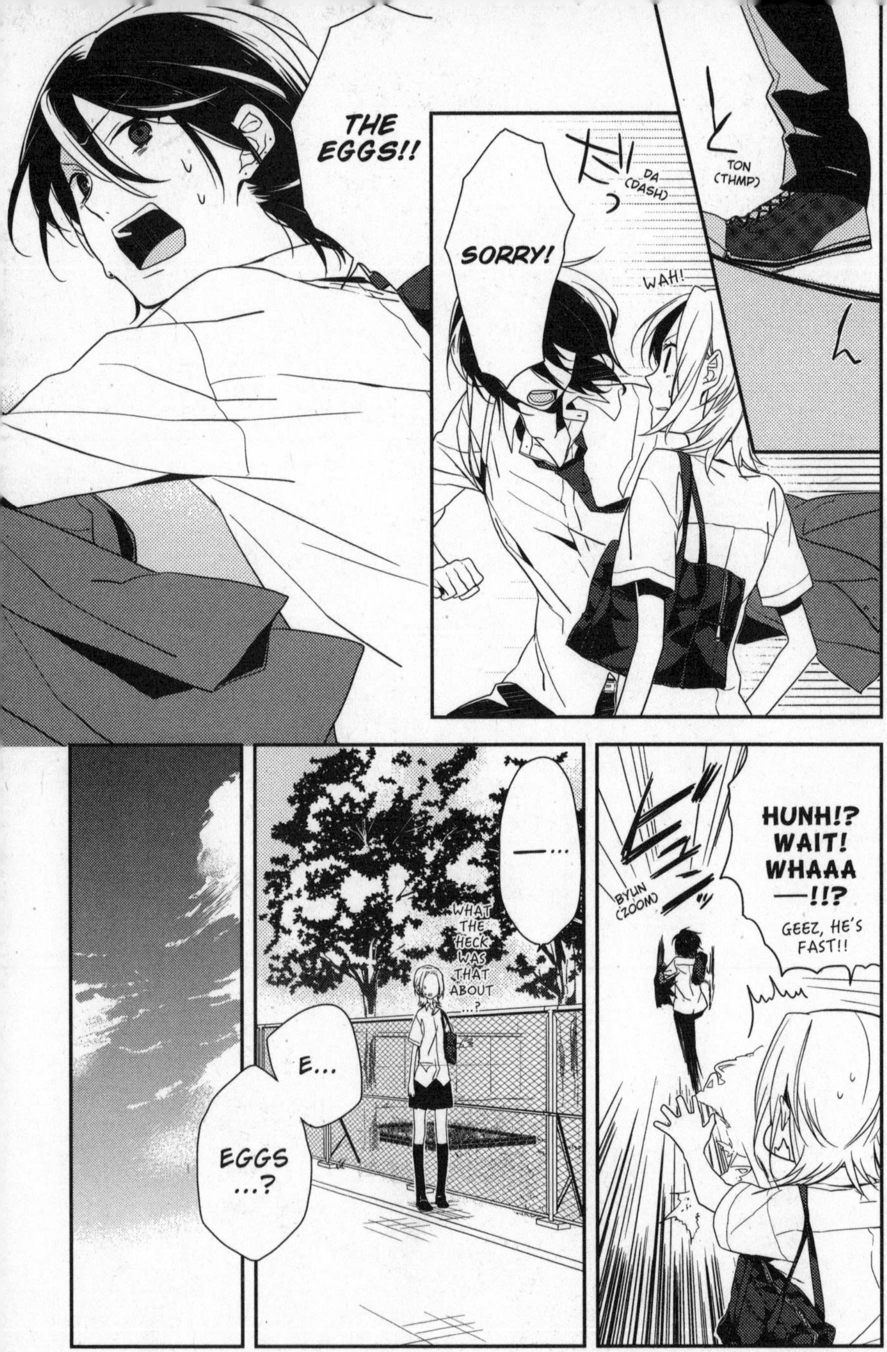
TON (THMP)
DA (DASH)
SORRY!
WAH!
THE EGGS!!
HUNH!? WAIT! WHAAA—!!?
BYUN (ZOOM)
GEEZ, HE'S FAST!!
—...
WHAT THE HECK WAS THAT ABOUT...?
E...
EGGS...?

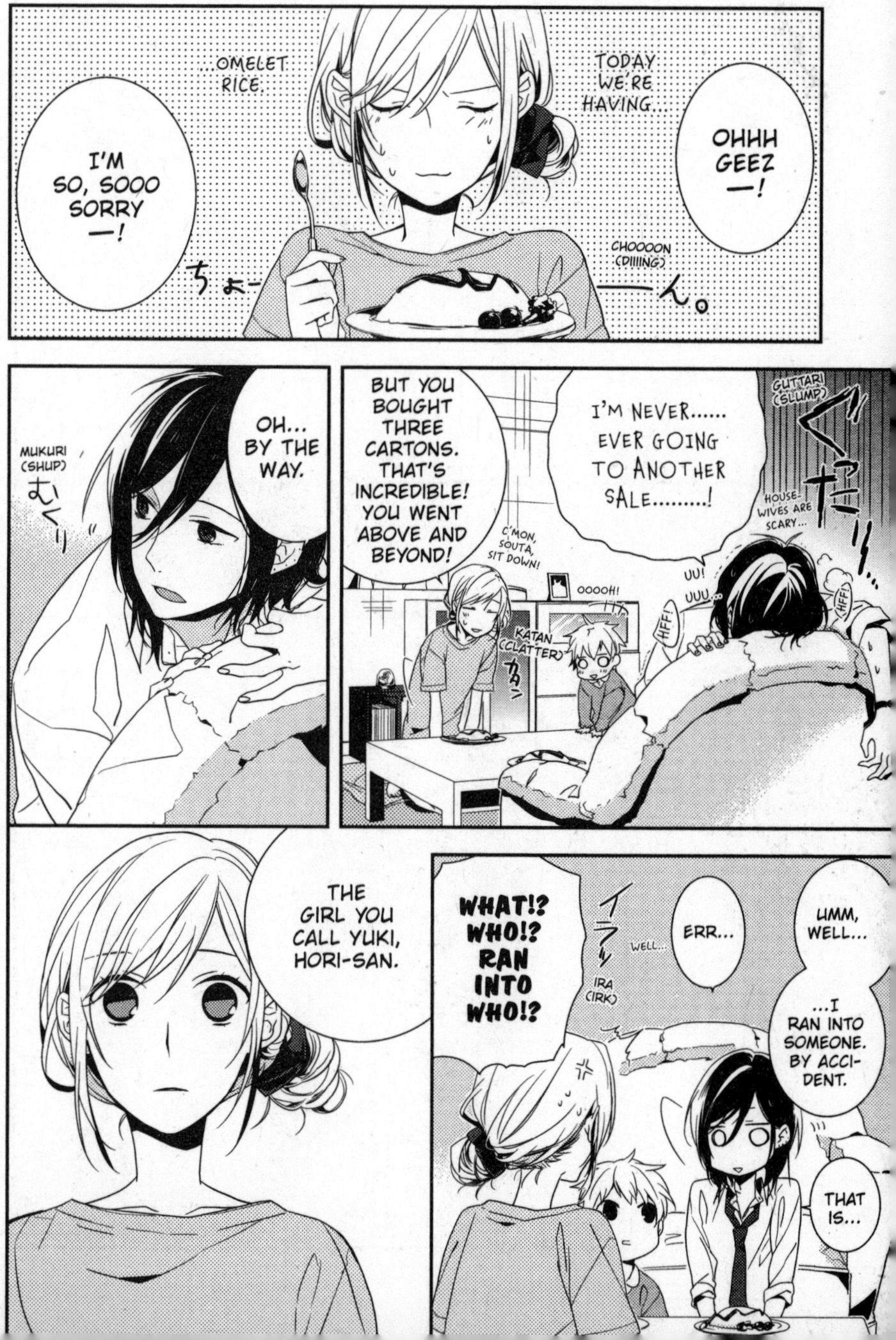
OHHH GEEZ—!
TODAY WE'RE HAVING...
...OMELET RICE.
I'M SO, SOOO SORRY—!
CHOOOON (DIIIING)
ちょーーん。
GUTTARI (SLUMP)
I'M NEVER...... EVER GOING TO ANOTHER SALE.........!
HOUSE-WIVES ARE SCARY...
UU! UUU...
HFF!
HFF!
BUT YOU BOUGHT THREE CARTONS. THAT'S INCREDIBLE! YOU WENT ABOVE AND BEYOND!
C'MON, SOUTA, SIT DOWN!
OOOOH!
KATAN (CLATTER)
OH... BY THE WAY.
MUKURI (SHUP)
UMM, WELL...
...I RAN INTO SOMEONE. BY ACCI-DENT.
ERR...
WELL...
THAT IS...
WHAT!? WHO!? RAN INTO WHO!?
IRA (IRK)
THE GIRL YOU CALL YUKI, HORI-SAN.

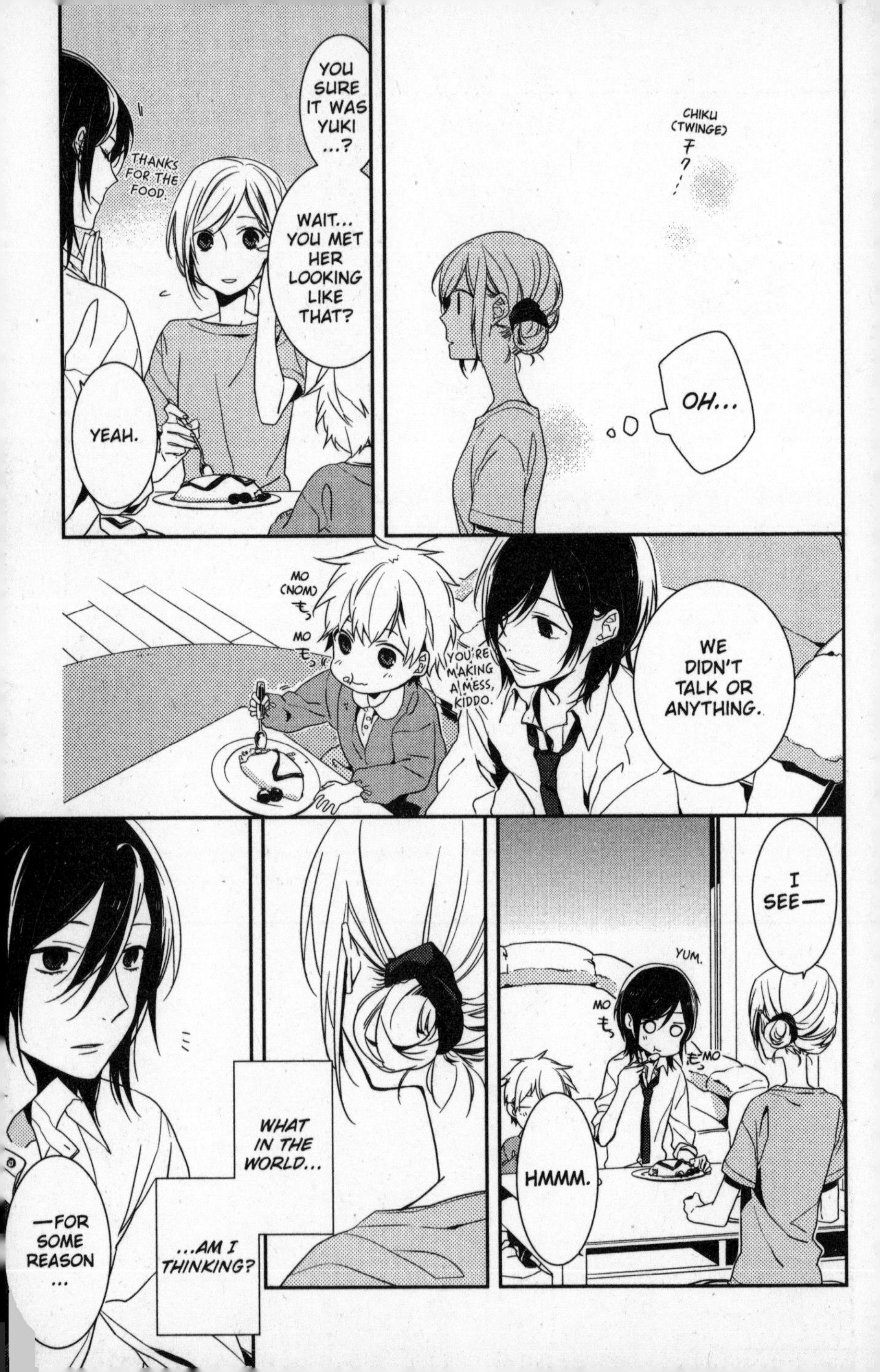
CHIKU (TWINGE)
OH...
YOU SURE IT WAS YUKI ...?
WAIT... YOU MET HER LOOKING LIKE THAT?
THANKS FOR THE FOOD.
YEAH.
WE DIDN'T TALK OR ANYTHING.
YOU'RE MAKING A MESS, KIDDO.
MO (NOM)
MO
I SEE—
YUM.
MO
MO
HMMM.
WHAT IN THE WORLD...
...AM I THINKING?
—FOR SOME REASON ...

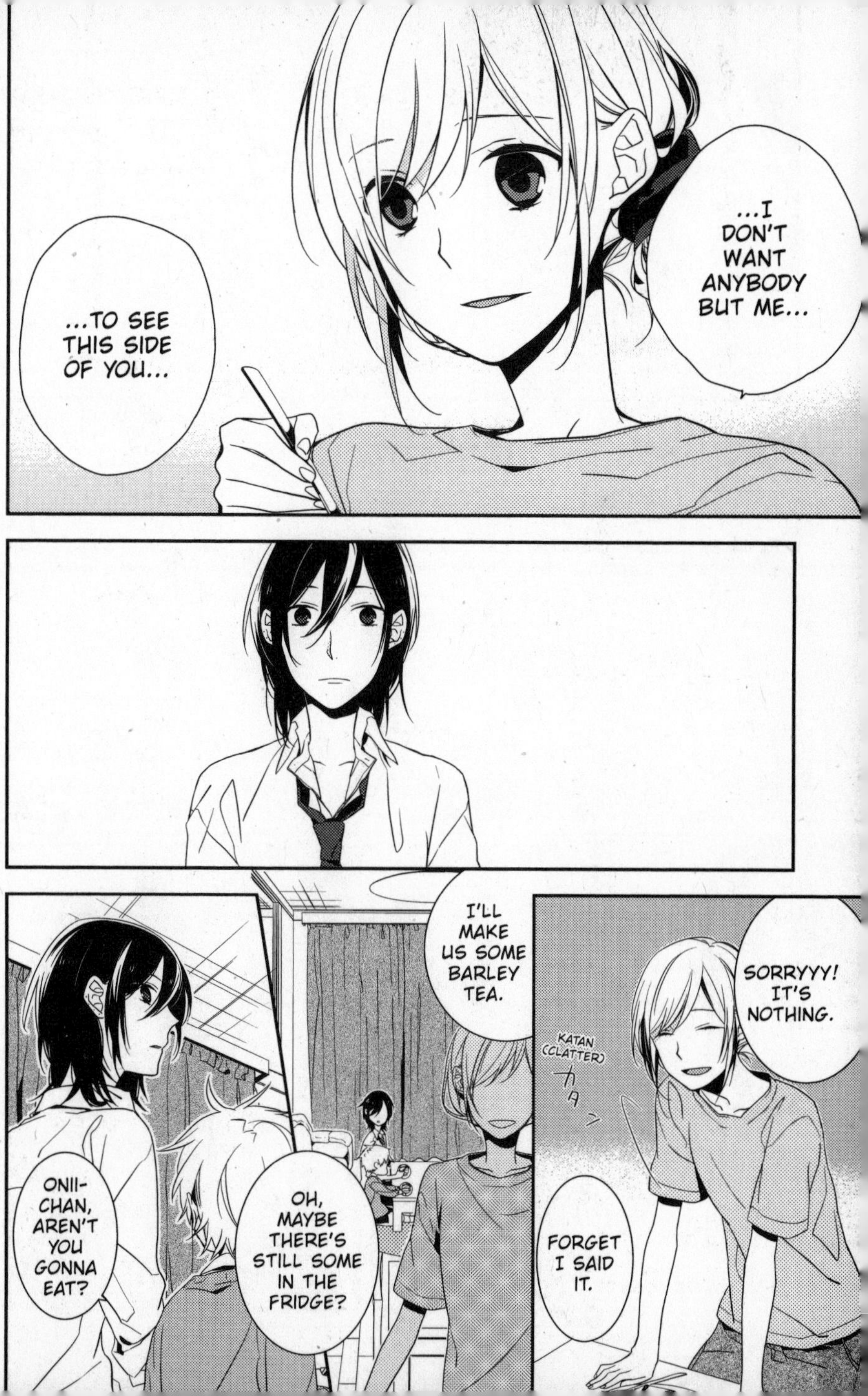
...I DON'T WANT ANYBODY BUT ME...
...TO SEE THIS SIDE OF YOU...
SORRYYY! IT'S NOTHING.
KATAN (CLATTER)
FORGET I SAID IT.
I'LL MAKE US SOME BARLEY TEA.
OH, MAYBE THERE'S STILL SOME IN THE FRIDGE?
ONII-CHAN, AREN'T YOU GONNA EAT?

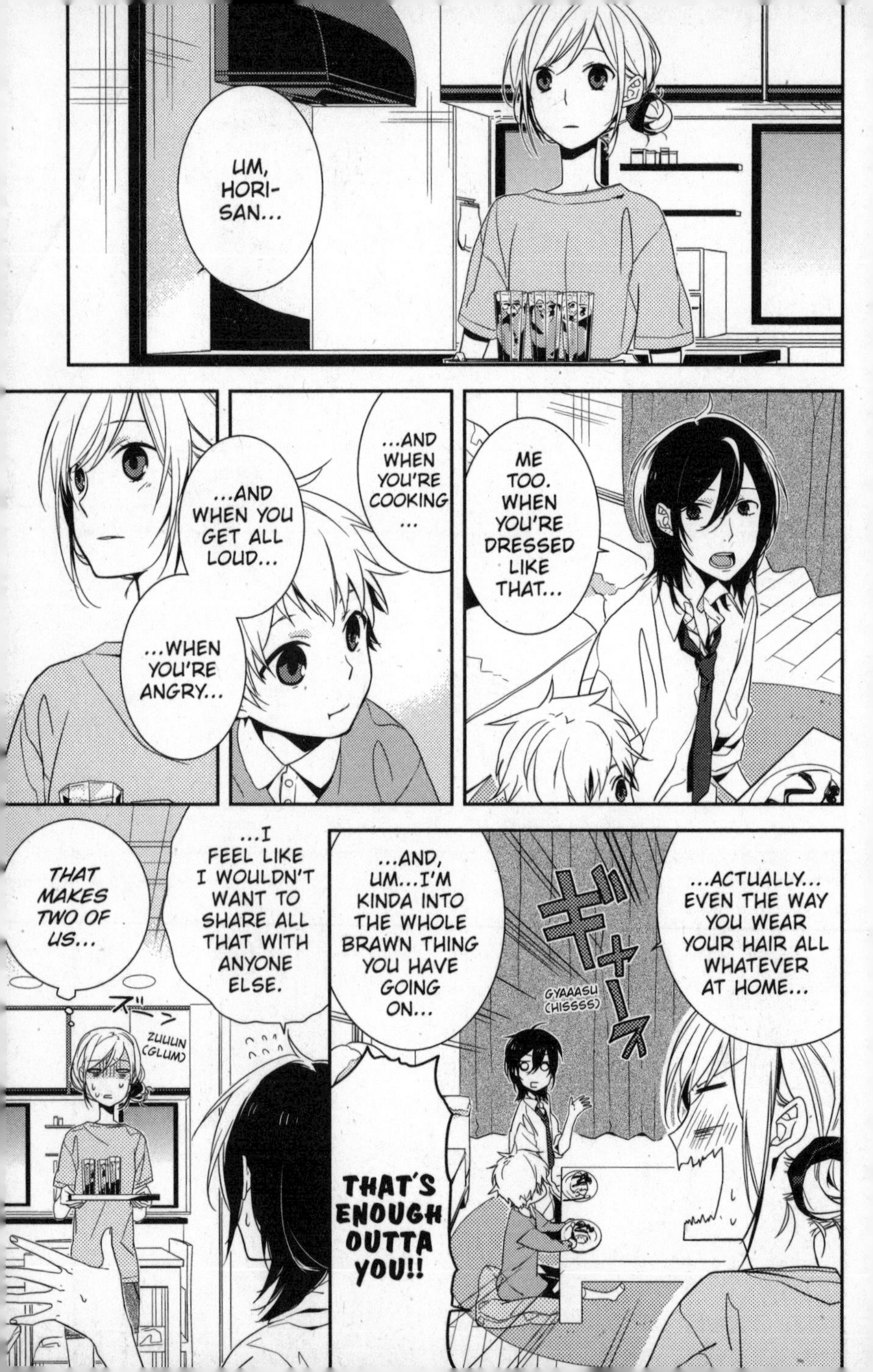
UM, HORI-SAN...
ME TOO. WHEN YOU'RE DRESSED LIKE THAT...
...AND WHEN YOU'RE COOKING ...
...AND WHEN YOU GET ALL LOUD...
...WHEN YOU'RE ANGRY...
...ACTUALLY... EVEN THE WAY YOU WEAR YOUR HAIR ALL WHATEVER AT HOME...
ギャース
GYAAASU (HISSSS)
...AND, UM...I'M KINDA INTO THE WHOLE BRAWN THING YOU HAVE GOING ON...
THAT'S ENOUGH OUTTA YOU!!
...I FEEL LIKE I WOULDN'T WANT TO SHARE ALL THAT WITH ANYONE ELSE.
THAT MAKES TWO OF US...
ズーン
ZUUUN (GLUM)

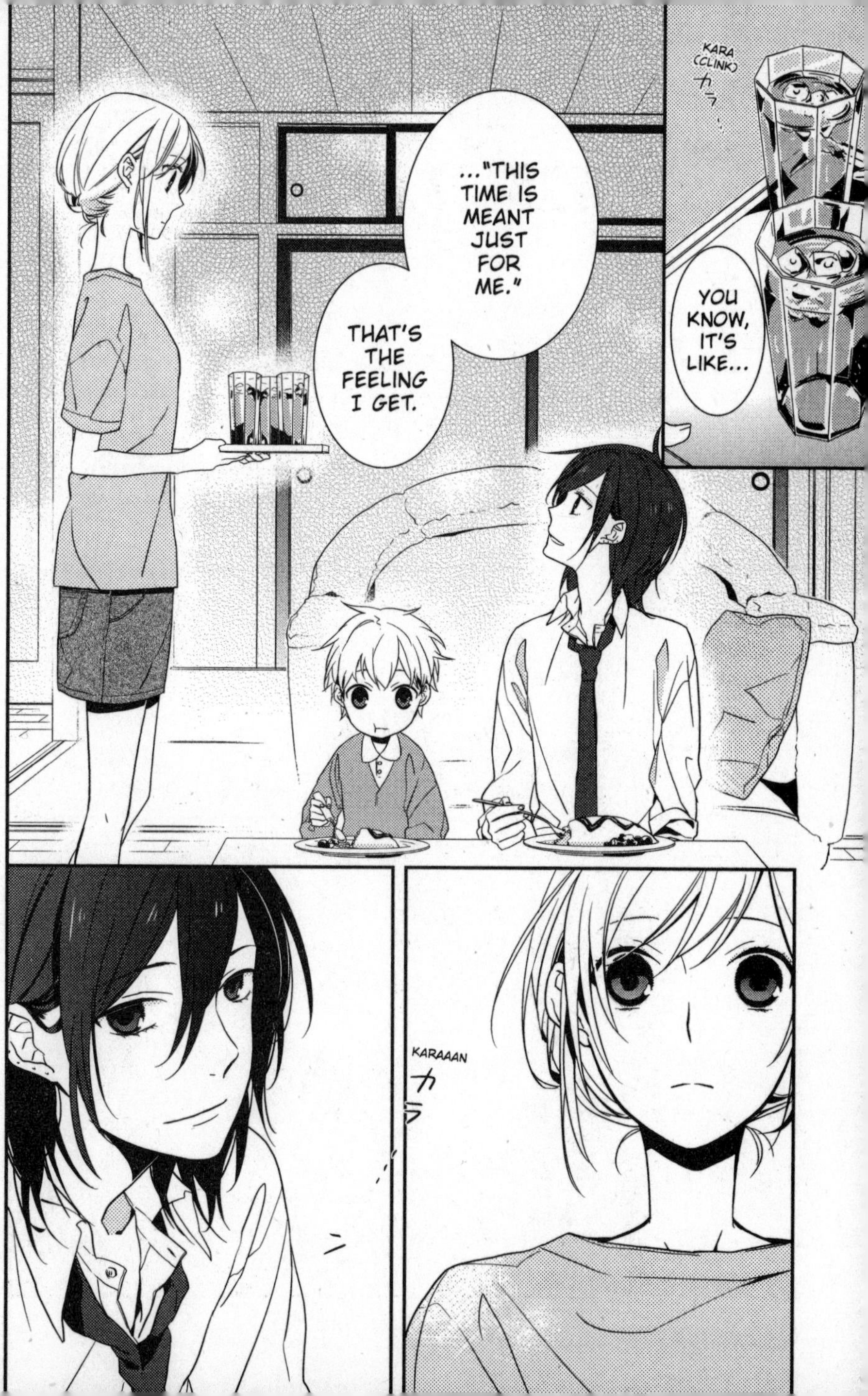
KARA (CLINK)
YOU KNOW, IT'S LIKE...
..."THIS TIME IS MEANT JUST FOR ME."
THAT'S THE FEELING I GET.
KARAAAN

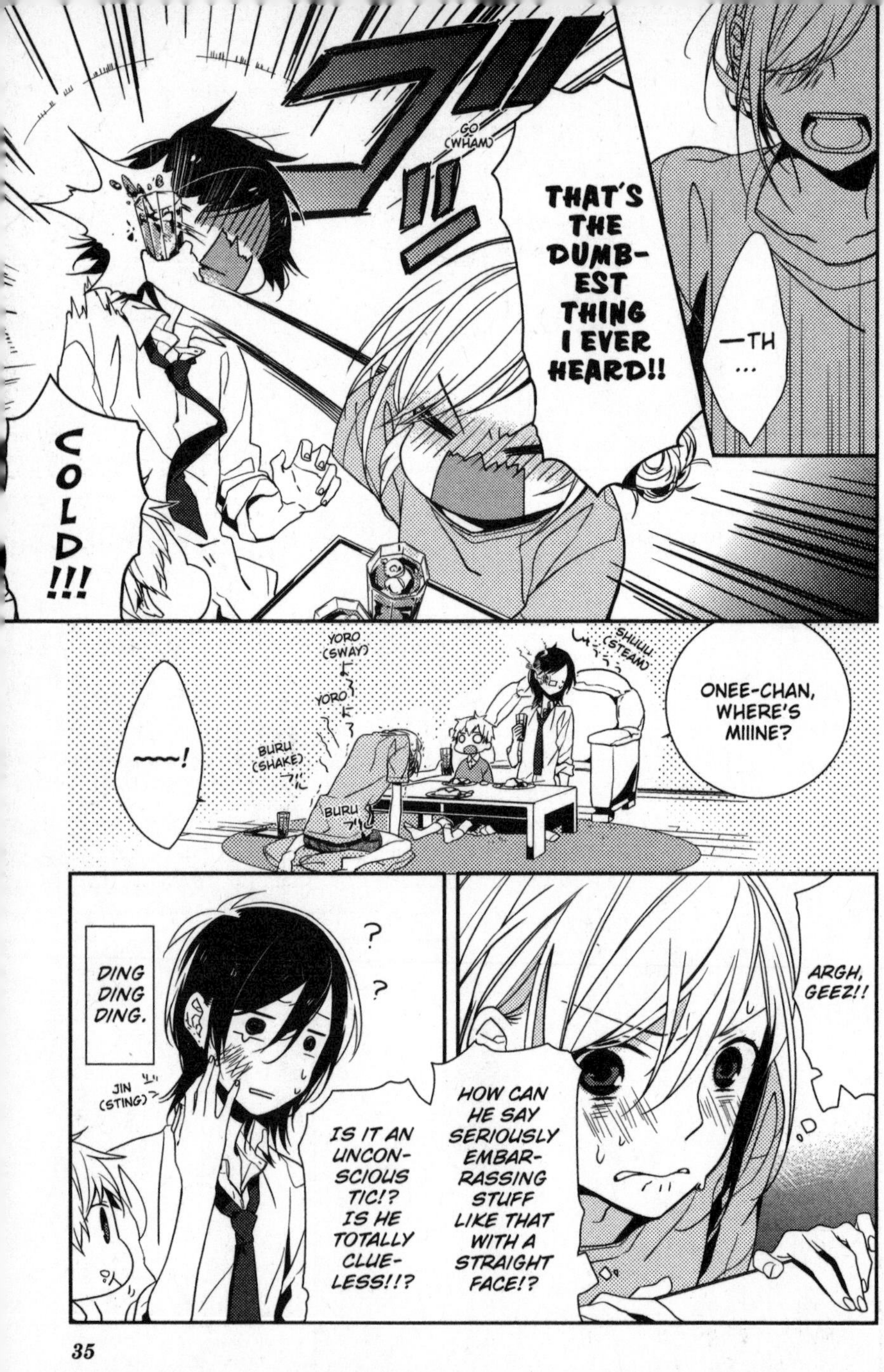
—TH ...
GO (WHAM)
THAT'S THE DUMB-EST THING I EVER HEARD!!
COLD!!!
SHUUU (STEAM)
ONEE-CHAN, WHERE'S MIIINE?
YORO (SWAY)
YORO
BURU (SHAKE)
BURU
~~~!
ARGH, GEEZ!!
HOW CAN HE SAY SERIOUSLY EMBAR-RASSING STUFF LIKE THAT WITH A STRAIGHT FACE!?
IS IT AN UNCON-SCIOUS TIC!? IS HE TOTALLY CLUE-LESS!!?
?
?
DING DING DING.
JIN (STING)
~~~

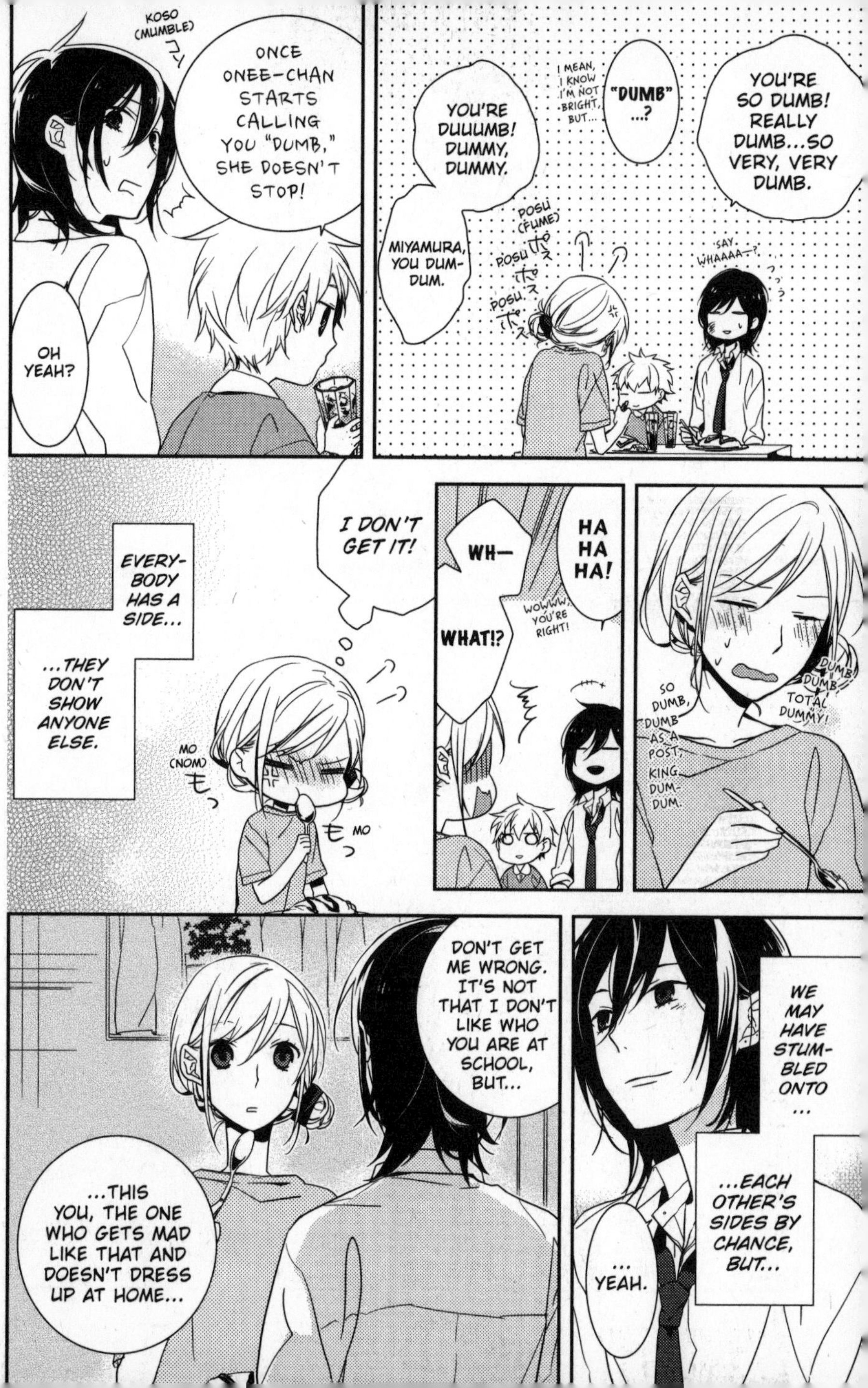
YOU'RE SO DUMB! REALLY DUMB...SO VERY, VERY DUMB.
SAY WHAAAA—?
"DUMB" ...?
I MEAN, I KNOW I'M NOT BRIGHT, BUT...
YOU'RE DUUUMB! DUMMY, DUMMY.
POSU (FUME)
POSU
POSU
MIYAMURA, YOU DUM-DUM.
KOSO (MUMBLE)
ONCE ONEE-CHAN STARTS CALLING YOU "DUMB," SHE DOESN'T STOP!
OH YEAH?
DUMB DUMB TOTAL DUMMY!
SO DUMB, DUMB AS A POST, KING DUM-DUM.
HA HA HA!
WOWWW, YOU'RE RIGHT!
WH—
WHAT!?
I DON'T GET IT!
EVERY-BODY HAS A SIDE...
...THEY DON'T SHOW ANYONE ELSE.
MO (NOM)
MO
WE MAY HAVE STUMBLED ONTO...
...EACH OTHER'S SIDES BY CHANCE, BUT...
...YEAH.
DON'T GET ME WRONG. IT'S NOT THAT I DON'T LIKE WHO YOU ARE AT SCHOOL, BUT...
...THIS YOU, THE ONE WHO GETS MAD LIKE THAT AND DOESN'T DRESS UP AT HOME...

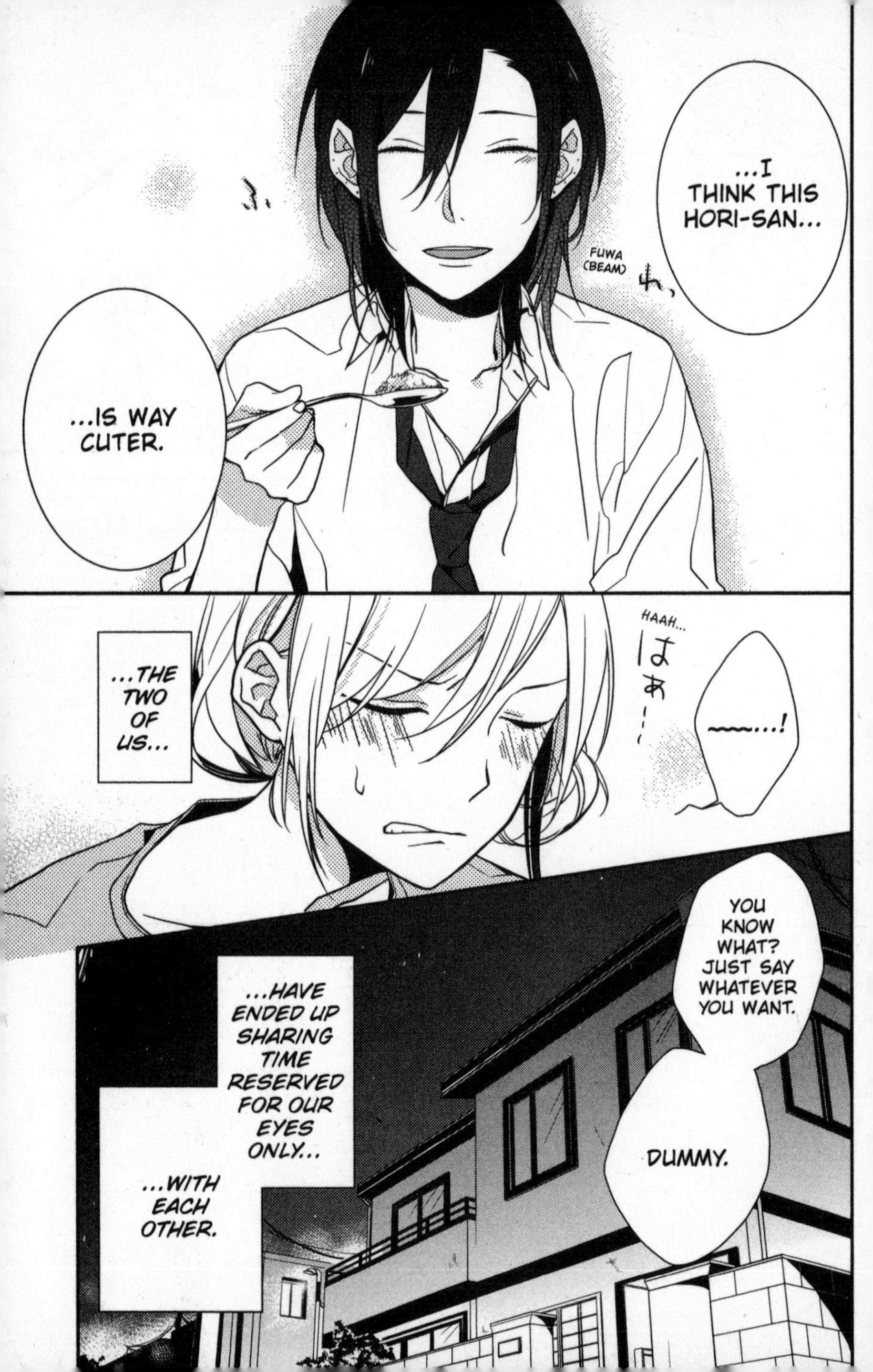
...I THINK THIS HORI-SAN...
FUWA (BEAM)
...IS WAY CUTER.
~~~...!
HAAH...
...THE TWO OF US...
YOU KNOW WHAT? JUST SAY WHATEVER YOU WANT.
DUMMY.
...HAVE ENDED UP SHARING TIME RESERVED FOR OUR EYES ONLY...
...WITH EACH OTHER.
~~~

HORIMIYA

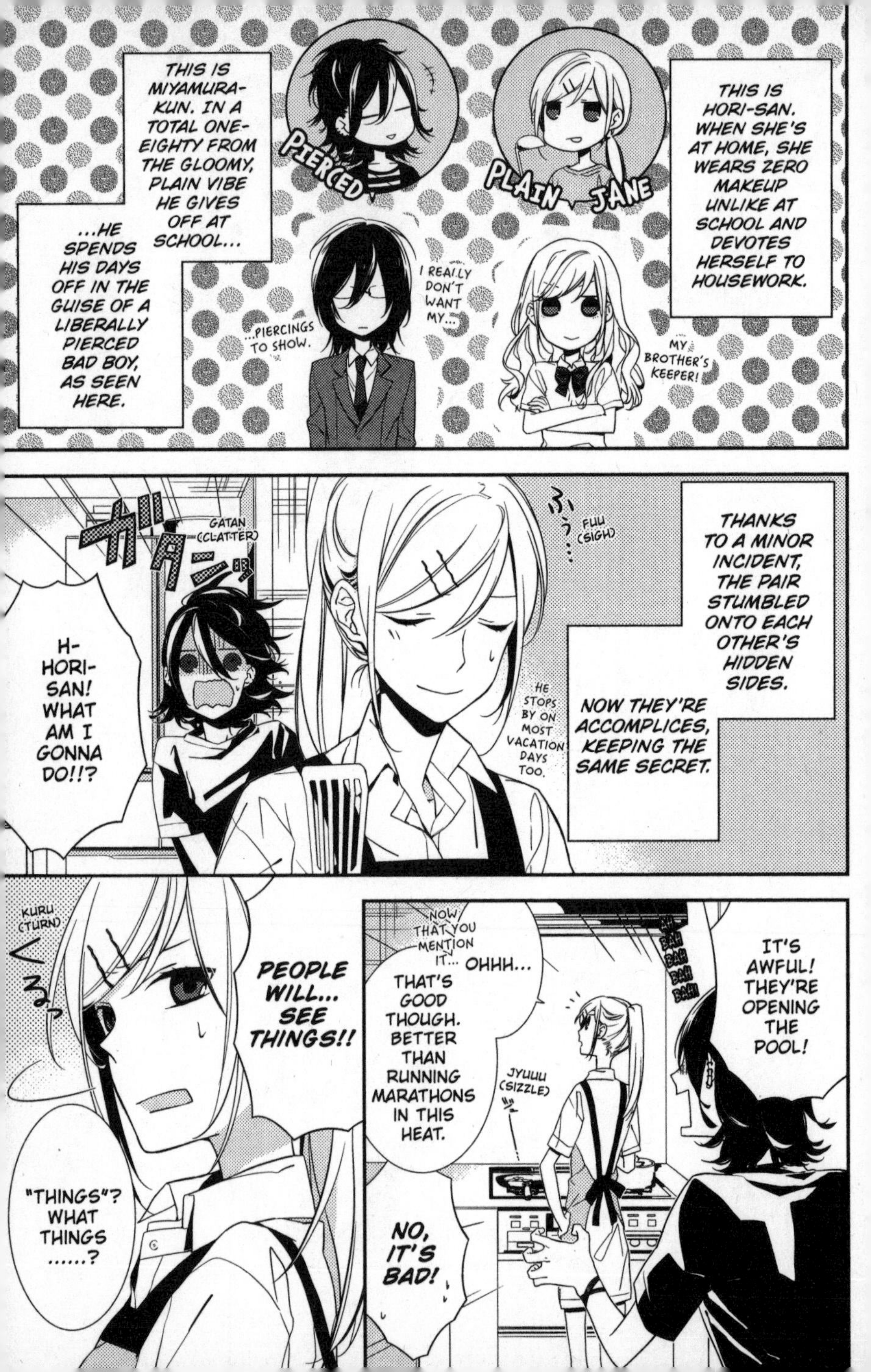
THIS IS HORI-SAN. WHEN SHE'S AT HOME, SHE WEARS ZERO MAKEUP UNLIKE AT SCHOOL AND DEVOTES HERSELF TO HOUSEWORK.
PLAIN JANE
PIERCED
THIS IS MIYAMURA-KUN. IN A TOTAL ONE-EIGHTY FROM THE GLOOMY, PLAIN VIBE HE GIVES OFF AT SCHOOL...
...HE SPENDS HIS DAYS OFF IN THE GUISE OF A LIBERALLY PIERCED BAD BOY, AS SEEN HERE.
MY BROTHER'S KEEPER!
I REALLY DON'T WANT MY...
...PIERCINGS TO SHOW.
THANKS TO A MINOR INCIDENT, THE PAIR STUMBLED ONTO EACH OTHER'S HIDDEN SIDES.
NOW THEY'RE ACCOMPLICES, KEEPING THE SAME SECRET.
FUU (SIGH)
HE STOPS BY ON MOST VACATION DAYS TOO.
GATAN (CLATTER)
H-HORI-SAN! WHAT AM I GONNA DO!!?
IT'S AWFUL! THEY'RE OPENING THE POOL!
NOW THAT YOU MENTION IT... OHHH...
THAT'S GOOD THOUGH. BETTER THAN RUNNING MARATHONS IN THIS HEAT.
JYUUU (SIZZLE)
NO, IT'S BAD!
KURU (TURN)
PEOPLE WILL... SEE THINGS!!
"THINGS"? WHAT THINGS ......?

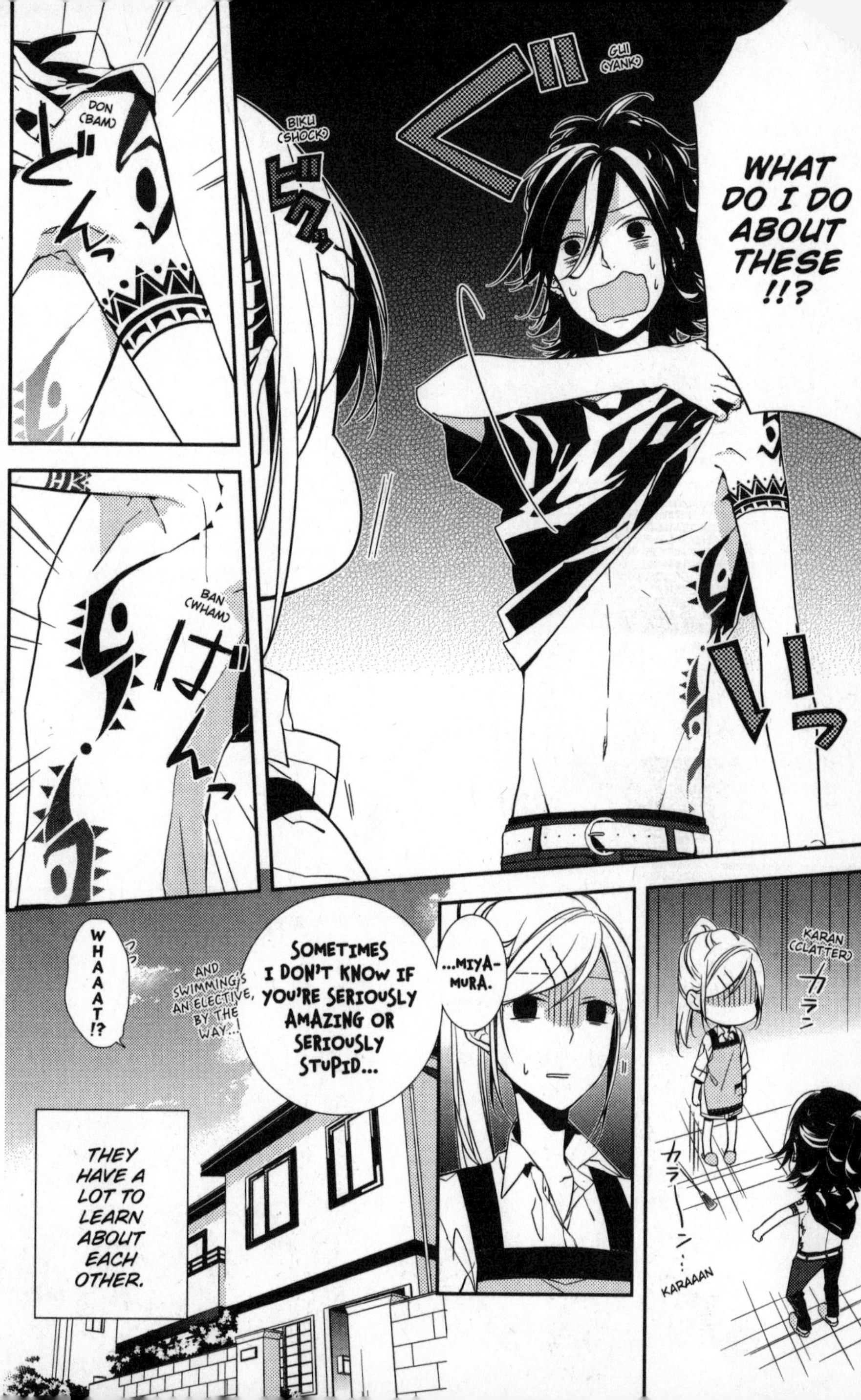
GUI (YANK)
WHAT DO I DO ABOUT THESE!!?
BIKU (SHOCK)
DON (BAM)
BAN (WHAM)
KARAN (CLATTER)
KARAAAN
...MIYA-MURA.
SOMETIMES I DON'T KNOW IF YOU'RE SERIOUSLY AMAZING OR SERIOUSLY STUPID...
AND SWIMMING'S AN ELECTIVE, BY THE WAY...!
WHAAAAT!?
THEY HAVE A LOT TO LEARN ABOUT EACH OTHER.

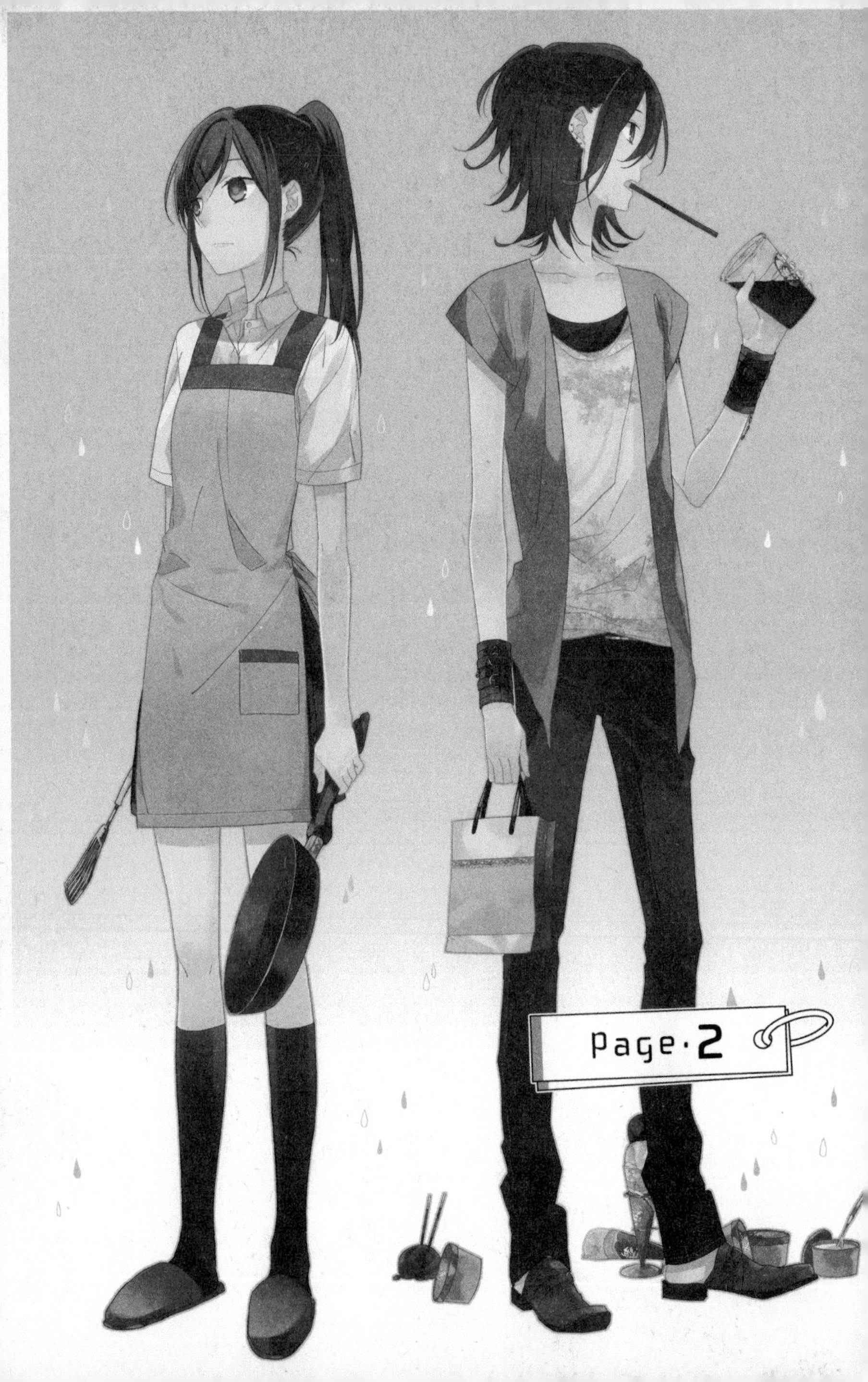
page·2

HORIMIYA

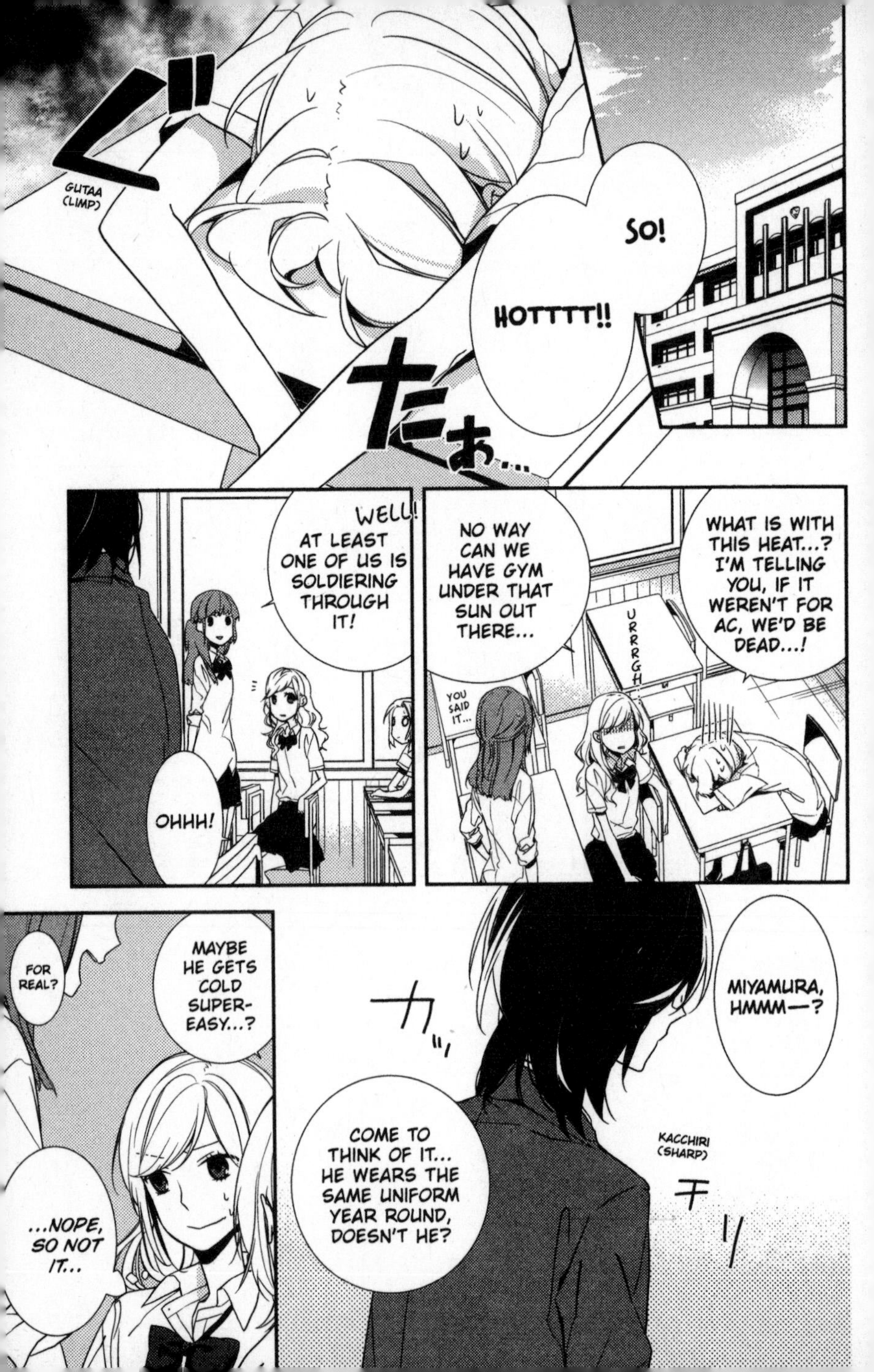
SO!
HOTTTT!!
GUTAA (LIMP)
WHAT IS WITH THIS HEAT...? I'M TELLING YOU, IF IT WEREN'T FOR AC, WE'D BE DEAD...!
NO WAY CAN WE HAVE GYM UNDER THAT SUN OUT THERE...
URRRGH...
YOU SAID IT...
WELL! AT LEAST ONE OF US IS SOLDIERING THROUGH IT!
OHHH!
MIYAMURA, HMMM—?
KACCHIRI (SHARP)
COME TO THINK OF IT... HE WEARS THE SAME UNIFORM YEAR ROUND, DOESN'T HE?
MAYBE HE GETS COLD SUPER-EASY...?
FOR REAL?
...NOPE, SO NOT IT...

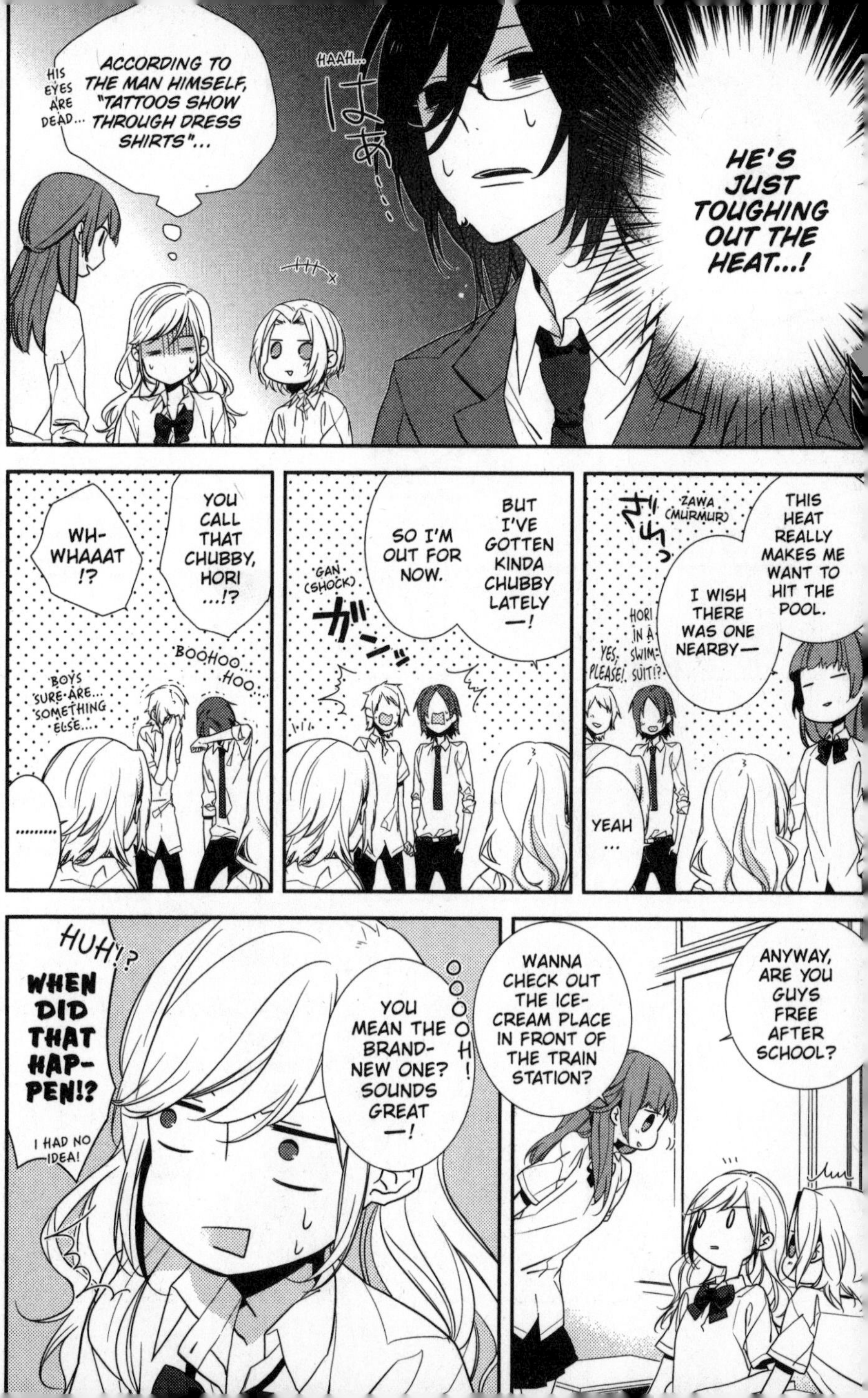
HE'S JUST TOUGHING OUT THE HEAT...!
HAAH...
はあ…
ACCORDING TO THE MAN HIMSELF, "TATTOOS SHOW THROUGH DRESS SHIRTS"...
HIS EYES ARE DEAD...
THIS HEAT REALLY MAKES ME WANT TO HIT THE POOL.
ZAWA (MURMUR)
ざわっ
I WISH THERE WAS ONE NEARBY—
HORI IN A SWIMSUIT!?
YES, PLEASE!
YEAH...
BUT I'VE GOTTEN KINDA CHUBBY LATELY—!
SO I'M OUT FOR NOW.
GAN (SHOCK)
ガーンッ
YOU CALL THAT CHUBBY, HORI...!?
WH-WHAAAT!?
BOOHOO... HOO...
BOYS SURE ARE... SOMETHING ELSE....
....
ANYWAY, ARE YOU GUYS FREE AFTER SCHOOL?
WANNA CHECK OUT THE ICE-CREAM PLACE IN FRONT OF THE TRAIN STATION?
OOOOH!
YOU MEAN THE BRAND-NEW ONE? SOUNDS GREAT—!
HUH!?
WHEN DID THAT HAPPEN!?
I HAD NO IDEA!

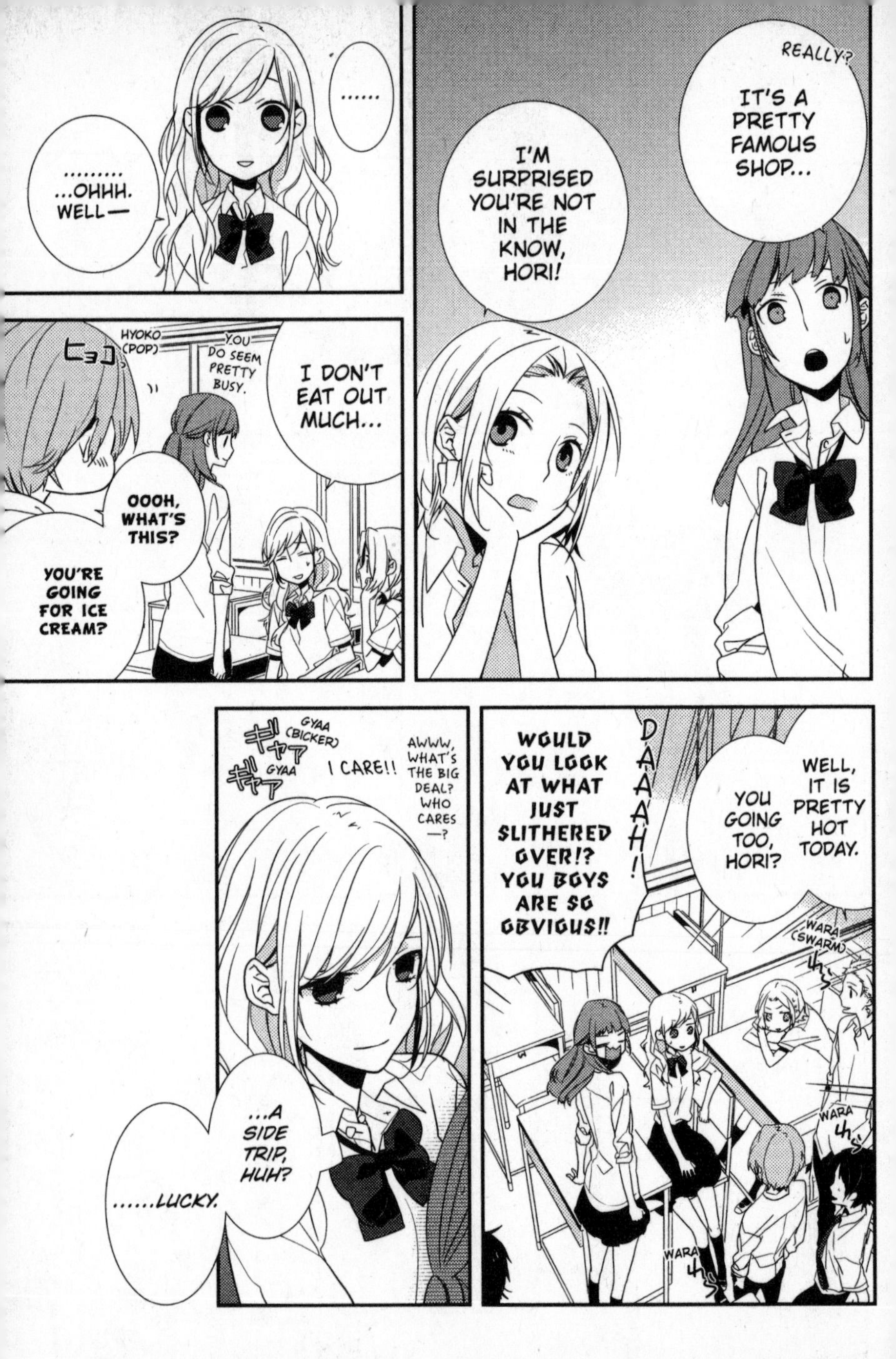
REALLY?
IT'S A PRETTY FAMOUS SHOP...
I'M SURPRISED YOU'RE NOT IN THE KNOW, HORI!
......
....
...OHHH. WELL—
I DON'T EAT OUT MUCH...
YOU DO SEEM PRETTY BUSY.
HYOKO (POP)
OOOH, WHAT'S THIS?
YOU'RE GOING FOR ICE CREAM?
WELL, IT IS PRETTY HOT TODAY.
YOU GOING TOO, HORI?
DAAAAH!
WOULD YOU LOOK AT WHAT JUST SLITHERED OVER!? YOU BOYS ARE SO OBVIOUS!!
WARA (SWARM)
WARA
WARA
AWWW, WHAT'S THE BIG DEAL? WHO CARES—?
I CARE!!
GYAA (BICKER) GYAA
...A SIDE TRIP, HUH?
......LUCKY.

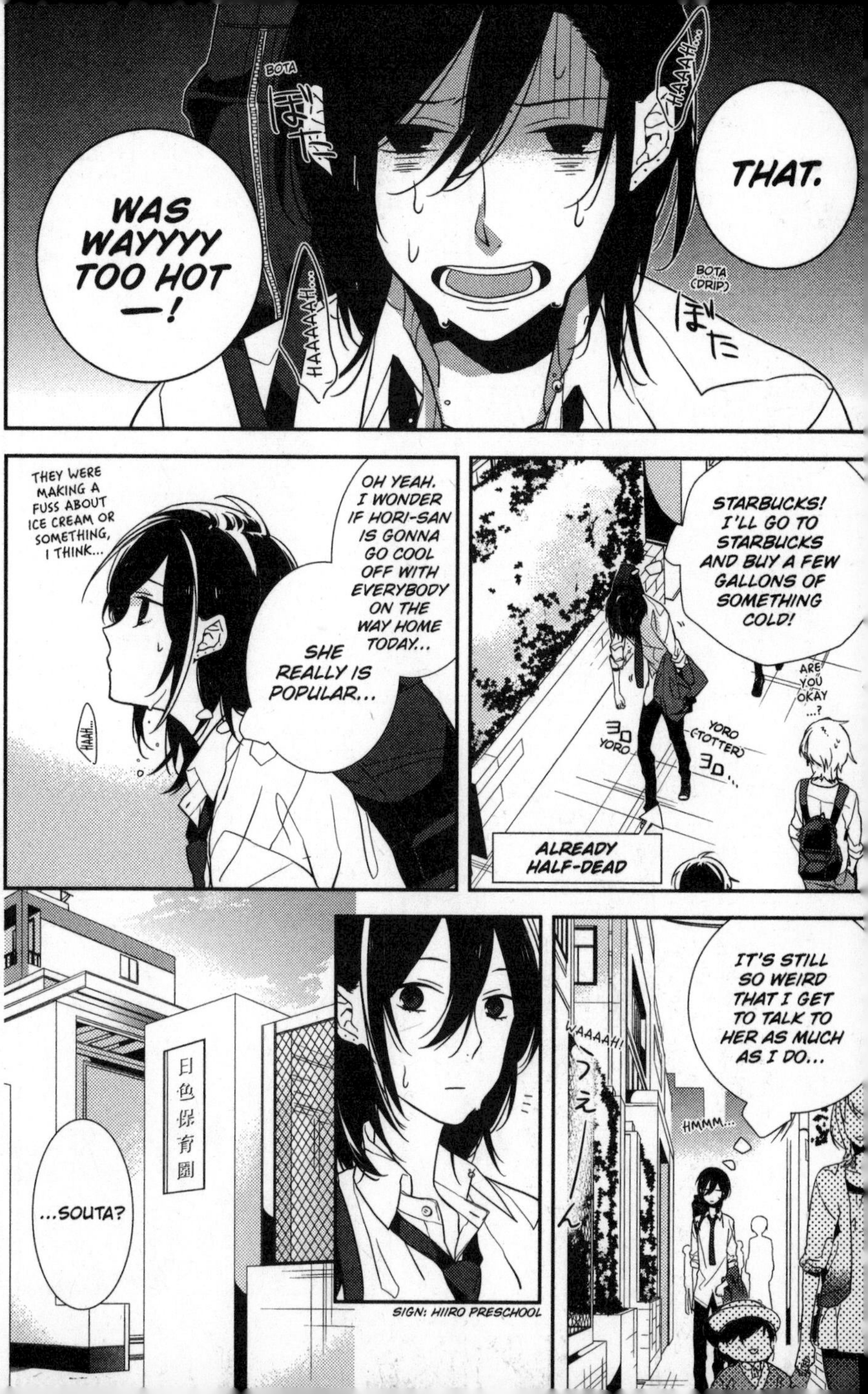
THAT.
HAAAH...
BOTA (DRIP)
ぼた
WAS WAYYYY TOO HOT—!
HAAAAAH...
BOTA
ぼた
STARBUCKS! I'LL GO TO STARBUCKS AND BUY A FEW GALLONS OF SOMETHING COLD!
ARE YOU OKAY...?
YORO (TOTTER)
ヨロ...
ヨロ
YORO
ALREADY HALF-DEAD
OH YEAH. I WONDER IF HORI-SAN IS GONNA GO COOL OFF WITH EVERYBODY ON THE WAY HOME TODAY...
SHE REALLY IS POPULAR...
THEY WERE MAKING A FUSS ABOUT ICE CREAM OR SOMETHING, I THINK...
HAAH...
IT'S STILL SO WEIRD THAT I GET TO TALK TO HER AS MUCH AS I DO...
WAAAAH!
うえーん
HMMM...
日色保育園
...SOUTA?
SIGN: HIIRO PRESCHOOL

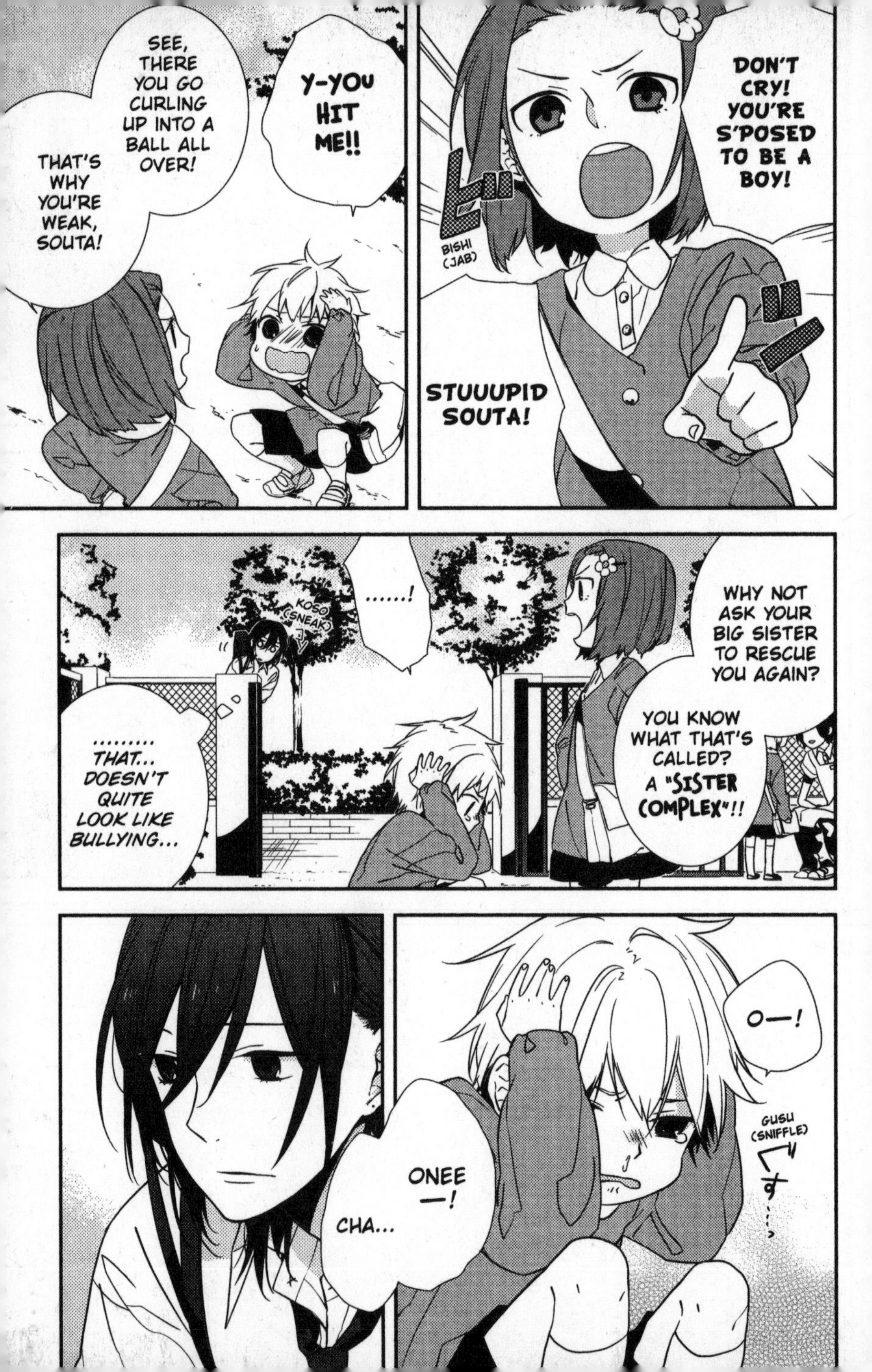
DON'T CRY! YOU'RE S'POSED TO BE A BOY!
BISHI (JAB)
STUUUPID SOUTA!
Y-YOU HIT ME!!
SEE, THERE YOU GO CURLING UP INTO A BALL ALL OVER!
THAT'S WHY YOU'RE WEAK, SOUTA!
WHY NOT ASK YOUR BIG SISTER TO RESCUE YOU AGAIN?
YOU KNOW WHAT THAT'S CALLED? A "SISTER COMPLEX"!!
......!
KOSO (SNEAK)
.... THAT... DOESN'T QUITE LOOK LIKE BULLYING...
O—!
GUSU (SNIFFLE)
ONEE —!
CHA...

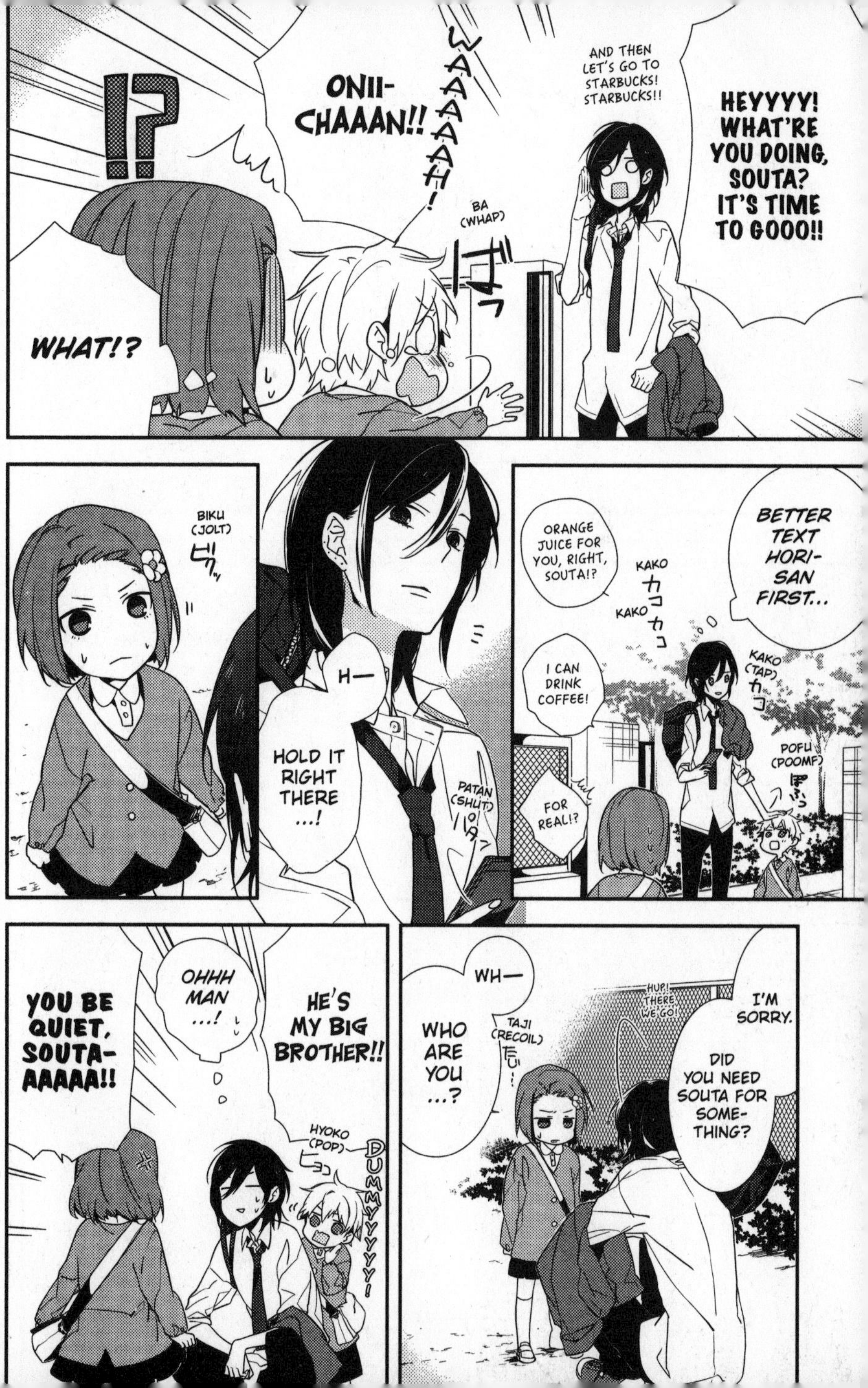
HEYYYY! WHAT'RE YOU DOING, SOUTA? IT'S TIME TO GOOO!!
AND THEN LET'S GO TO STARBUCKS! STARBUCKS!!
WAAAAAAAH!
BA (WHAP)
ONII-CHAAAN!!
!?
WHAT!?
BETTER TEXT HORI-SAN FIRST...
ORANGE JUICE FOR YOU, RIGHT, SOUTA!?
KAKO
KAKO
I CAN DRINK COFFEE!
KAKO (TAP)
POFU (POOMF)
FOR REAL!?
H—
HOLD IT RIGHT THERE ...!
PATAN (SHUT)
BIKU (JOLT)
I'M SORRY.
DID YOU NEED SOUTA FOR SOME-THING?
HUP! THERE WE GO!
WH—
WHO ARE YOU ...?
TAJI (RECOIL)
HE'S MY BIG BROTHER!!
OHHH MAN ...!
YOU BE QUIET, SOUTA-AAAAA!!
HYOKO (POP)
DUMMYYYYY!

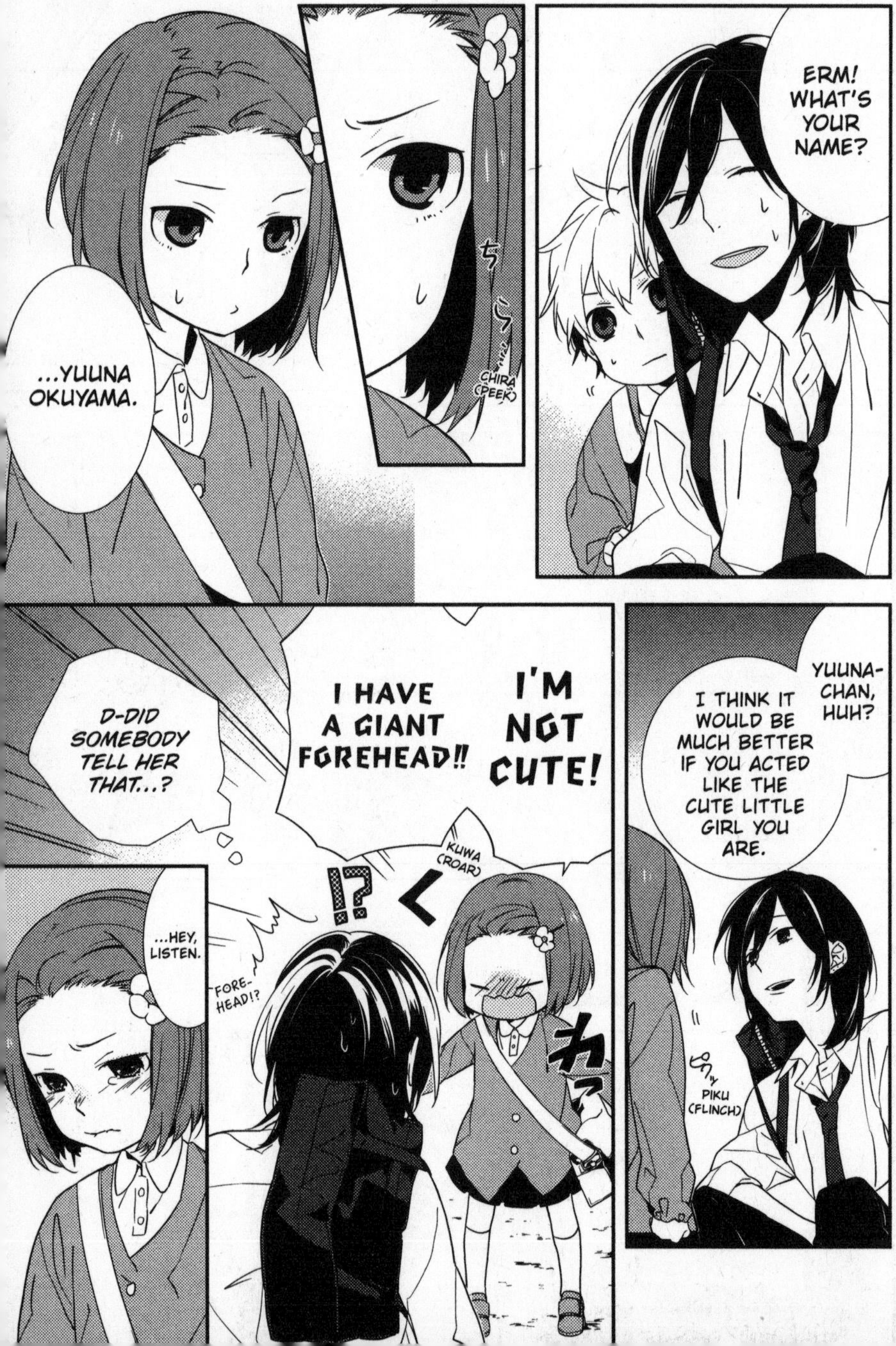
ERM! WHAT'S YOUR NAME?
ちら
CHIRA (PEEK)
...YUUNA OKUYAMA.
YUUNA-CHAN, HUH?
I THINK IT WOULD BE MUCH BETTER IF YOU ACTED LIKE THE CUTE LITTLE GIRL YOU ARE.
PIKU (FLINCH)
I'M NOT CUTE!
I HAVE A GIANT FOREHEAD!!
KUWA (ROAR)
!?
D-DID SOMEBODY TELL HER THAT...?
FORE-HEAD!?
...HEY, LISTEN.

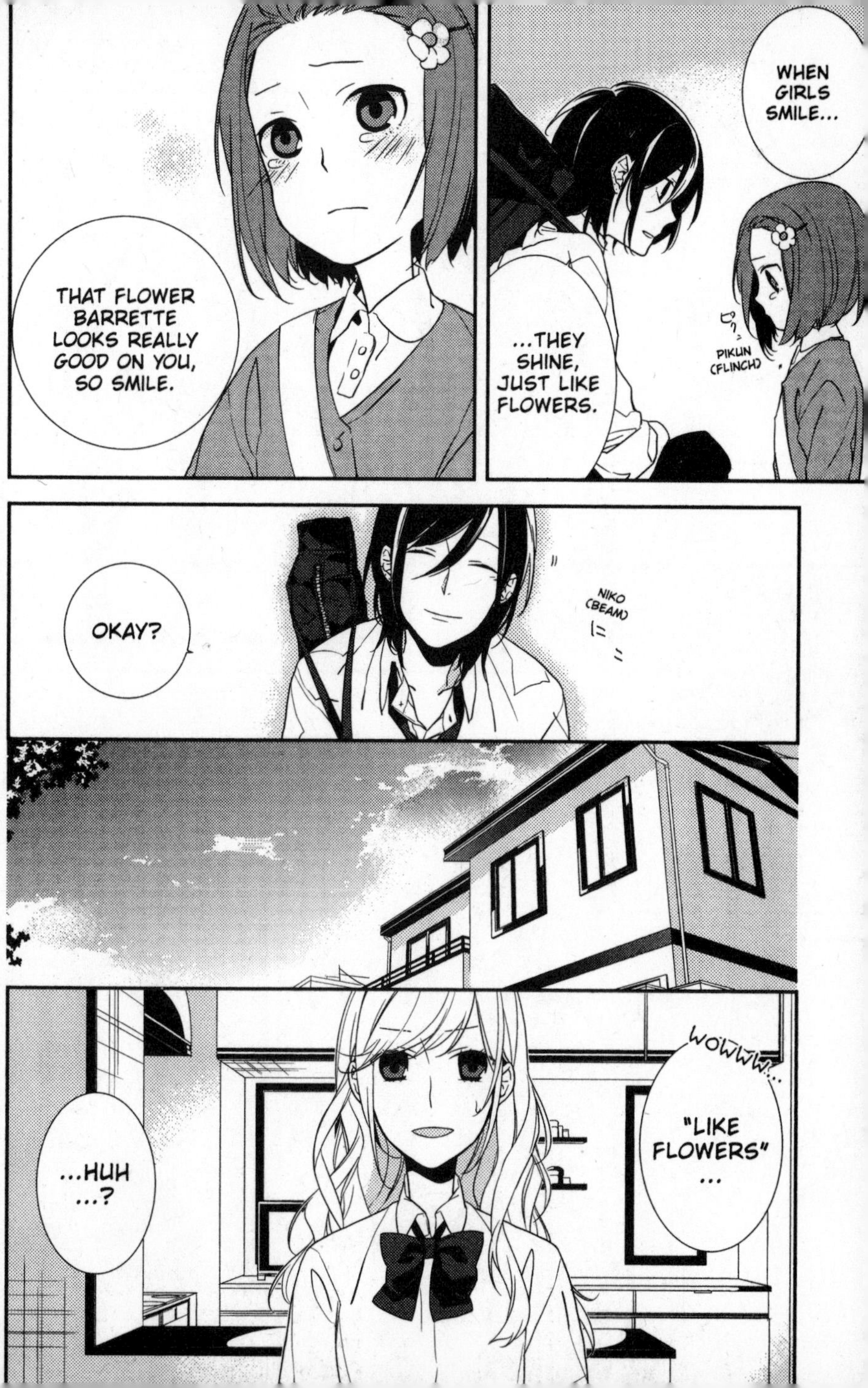

WHEN GIRLS SMILE...
...THEY SHINE, JUST LIKE FLOWERS.
PIKUN (FLINCH)
THAT FLOWER BARRETTE LOOKS REALLY GOOD ON YOU, SO SMILE.
NIKO (BEAM)
OKAY?
WOWWW...
"LIKE FLOWERS" ...
...HUH ...?

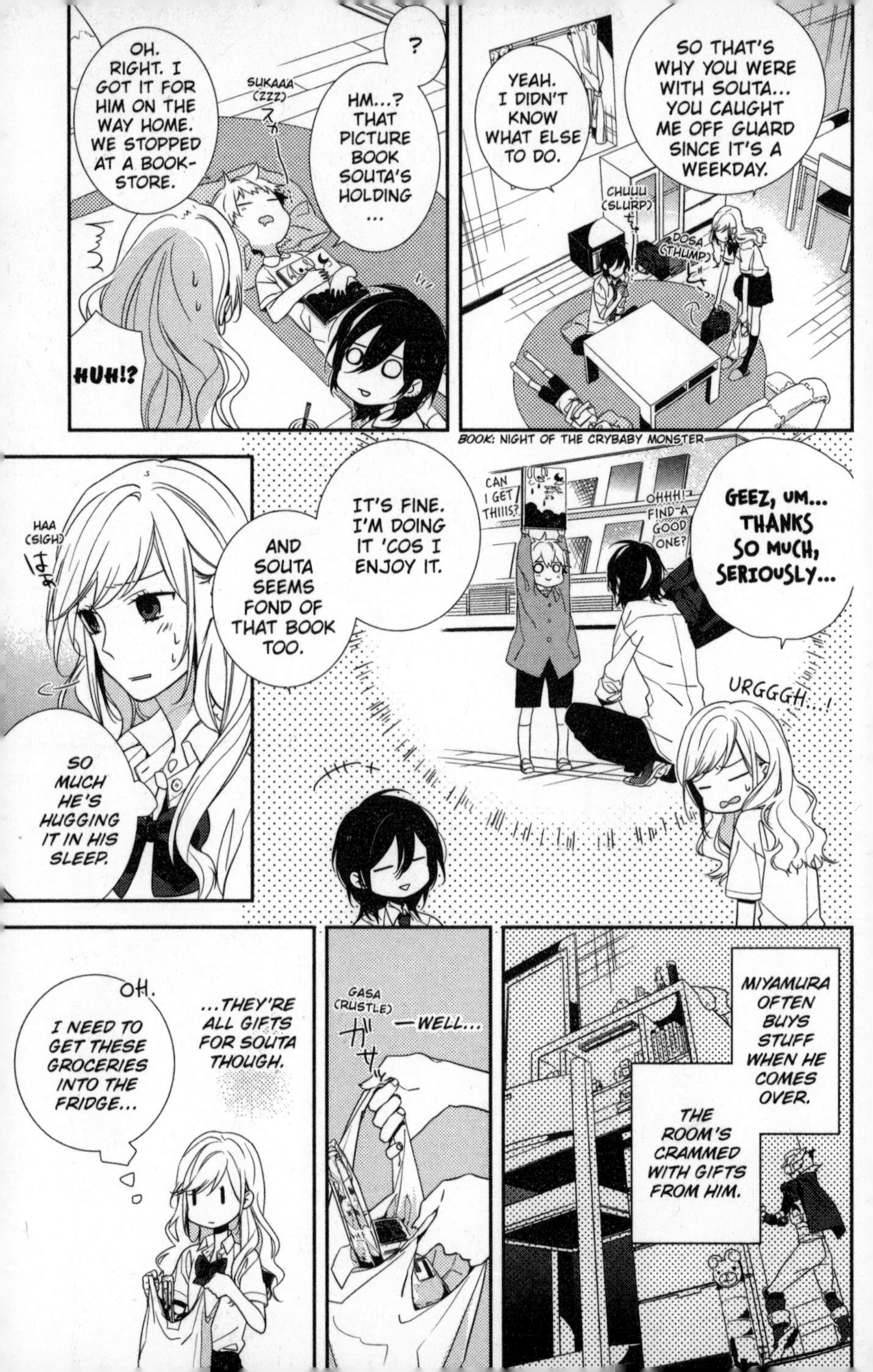
SO THAT'S WHY YOU WERE WITH SOUTA... YOU CAUGHT ME OFF GUARD SINCE IT'S A WEEKDAY.
YEAH. I DIDN'T KNOW WHAT ELSE TO DO.
CHUUU (SLURP)
DOSA (THUMP)
?
HM...? THAT PICTURE BOOK SOUTA'S HOLDING ...
SUKAAA (ZZZ)
OH. RIGHT. I GOT IT FOR HIM ON THE WAY HOME. WE STOPPED AT A BOOK-STORE.
HUH!?
BOOK: NIGHT OF THE CRYBABY MONSTER
GEEZ, UM... THANKS SO MUCH, SERIOUSLY...
OHHH! FIND A GOOD ONE?
CAN I GET THIIIS?
URGGGH...!
IT'S FINE. I'M DOING IT 'COS I ENJOY IT.
AND SOUTA SEEMS FOND OF THAT BOOK TOO.
HAA (SIGH)
SO MUCH HE'S HUGGING IT IN HIS SLEEP.
MIYAMURA OFTEN BUYS STUFF WHEN HE COMES OVER.
THE ROOM'S CRAMMED WITH GIFTS FROM HIM.
GASA (RUSTLE)
—WELL...
...THEY'RE ALL GIFTS FOR SOUTA THOUGH.
OH.
I NEED TO GET THESE GROCERIES INTO THE FRIDGE...

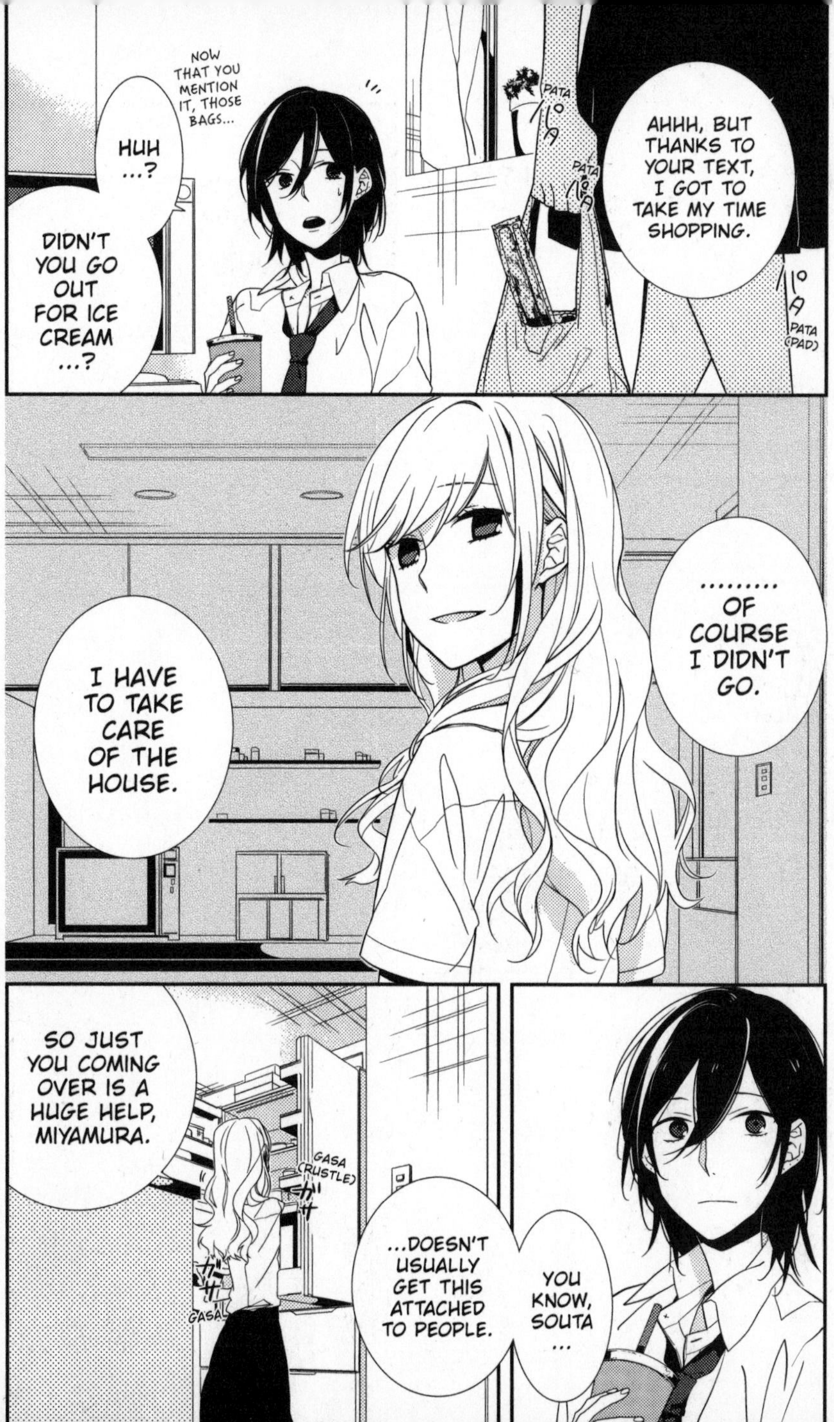

PATA
PATA
AHHH, BUT THANKS TO YOUR TEXT, I GOT TO TAKE MY TIME SHOPPING.
PATA (PAD)
NOW THAT YOU MENTION IT, THOSE BAGS...
HUH ...?
DIDN'T YOU GO OUT FOR ICE CREAM ...?
.... OF COURSE I DIDN'T GO.
I HAVE TO TAKE CARE OF THE HOUSE.
YOU KNOW, SOUTA ...
...DOESN'T USUALLY GET THIS ATTACHED TO PEOPLE.
SO JUST YOU COMING OVER IS A HUGE HELP, MIYAMURA.
GASA (RUSTLE)
GASA

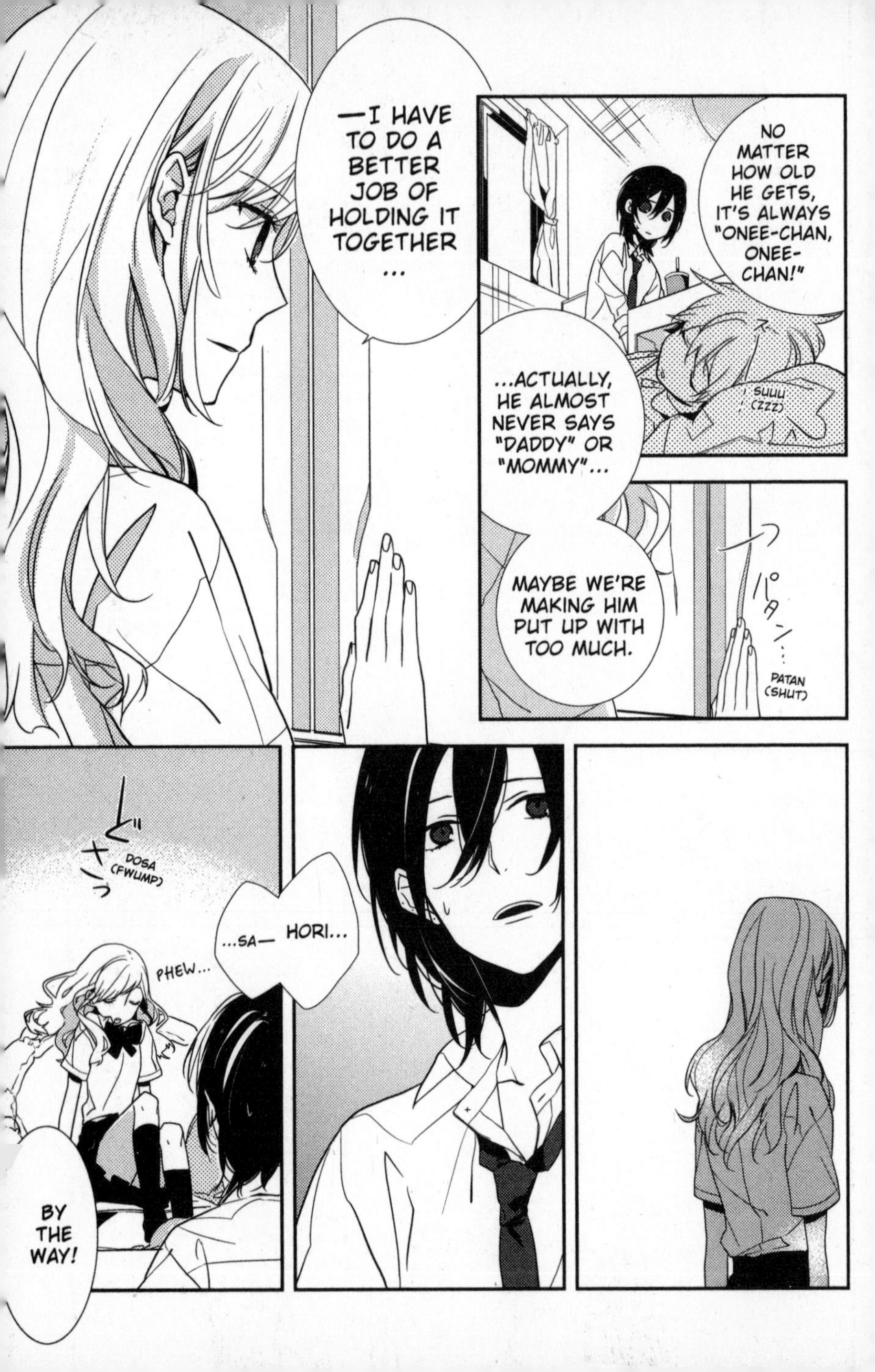
NO MATTER HOW OLD HE GETS, IT'S ALWAYS "ONEE-CHAN, ONEE-CHAN!"
SUUU (ZZZ)
...ACTUALLY, HE ALMOST NEVER SAYS "DADDY" OR "MOMMY"...
MAYBE WE'RE MAKING HIM PUT UP WITH TOO MUCH.
PATAN (SHUT)
—I HAVE TO DO A BETTER JOB OF HOLDING IT TOGETHER ...
...SA— HORI...
DOSA (FWUMP)
PHEW...
BY THE WAY!

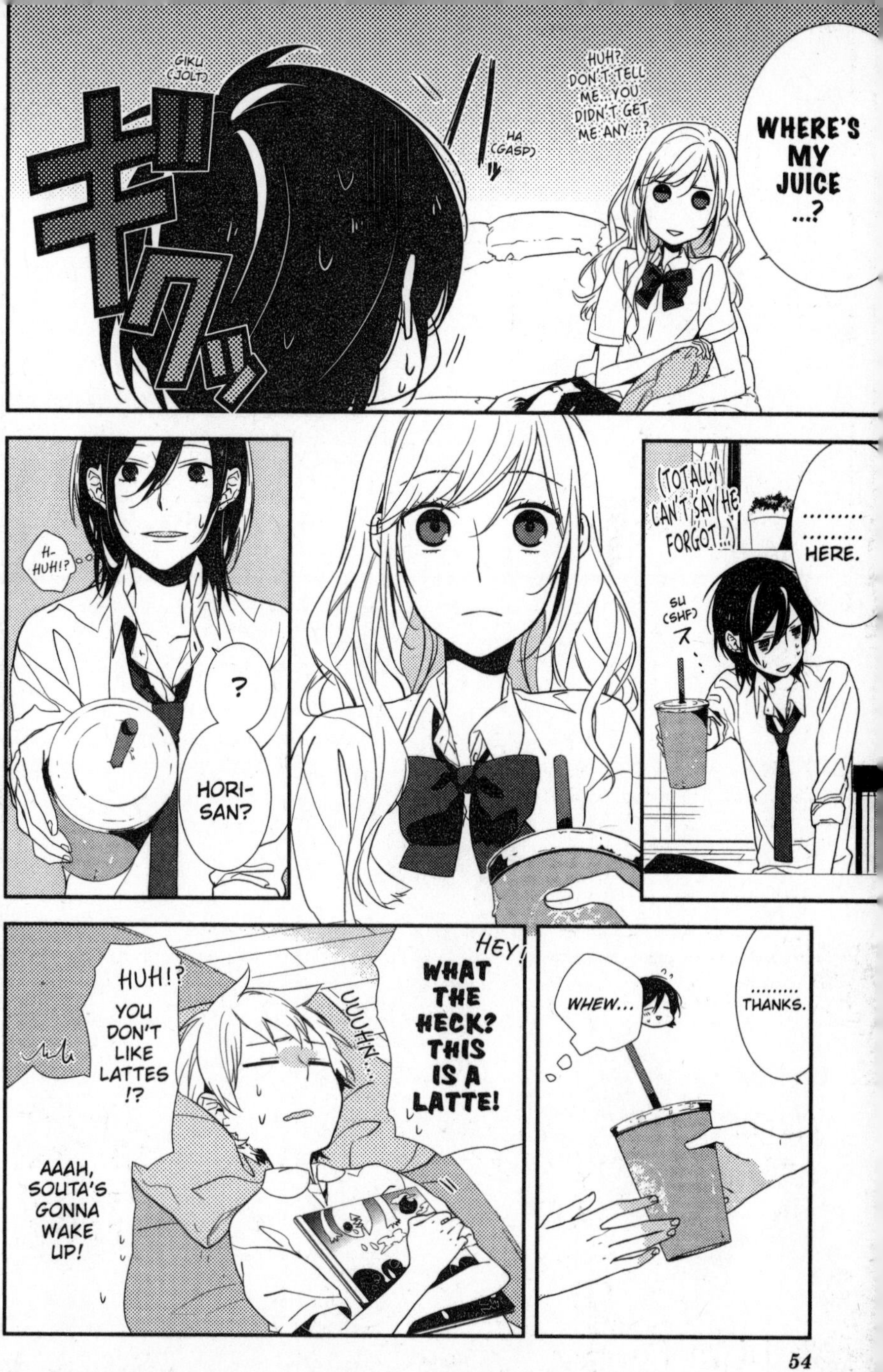
WHERE'S MY JUICE ...?
HUH? DON'T TELL ME.. YOU DIDN'T GET ME ANY...?
HA (GASP)
GIKU (JOLT)
ギクッ
....
.... HERE.
(TOTALLY CAN'T SAY HE FORGOT!!)
SU (SHF)
ス
?
HORI-SAN?
H-HUH!?
....
THANKS.
WHEW...
HEY!
WHAT THE HECK? THIS IS A LATTE!
UUUHN...
HUH!? YOU DON'T LIKE LATTES !?
AAAH, SOUTA'S GONNA WAKE UP!

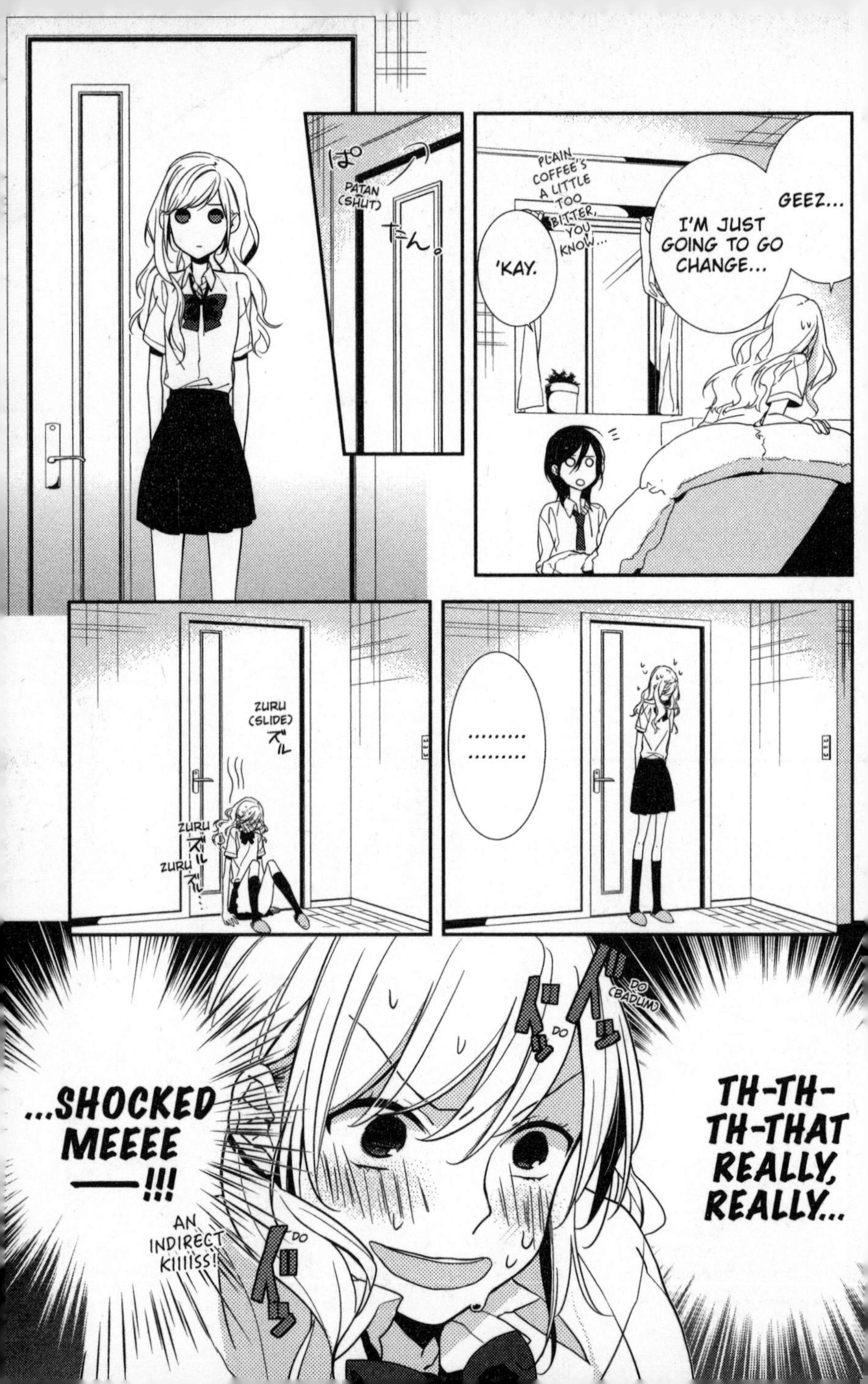
GEEZ...
I'M JUST GOING TO GO CHANGE...
PLAIN COFFEE'S A LITTLE TOO BITTER, YOU KNOW...
'KAY.
ぱたん。
PATAN (SHUT)
....
....
ZURU (SLIDE)
ズル
ZURU
ズル
ZURU
ズル...
TH-TH-TH-THAT REALLY, REALLY...
DO (BADUM)
DO
...SHOCKED MEEEE—!!!
AN INDIRECT KIIIISS!
DO

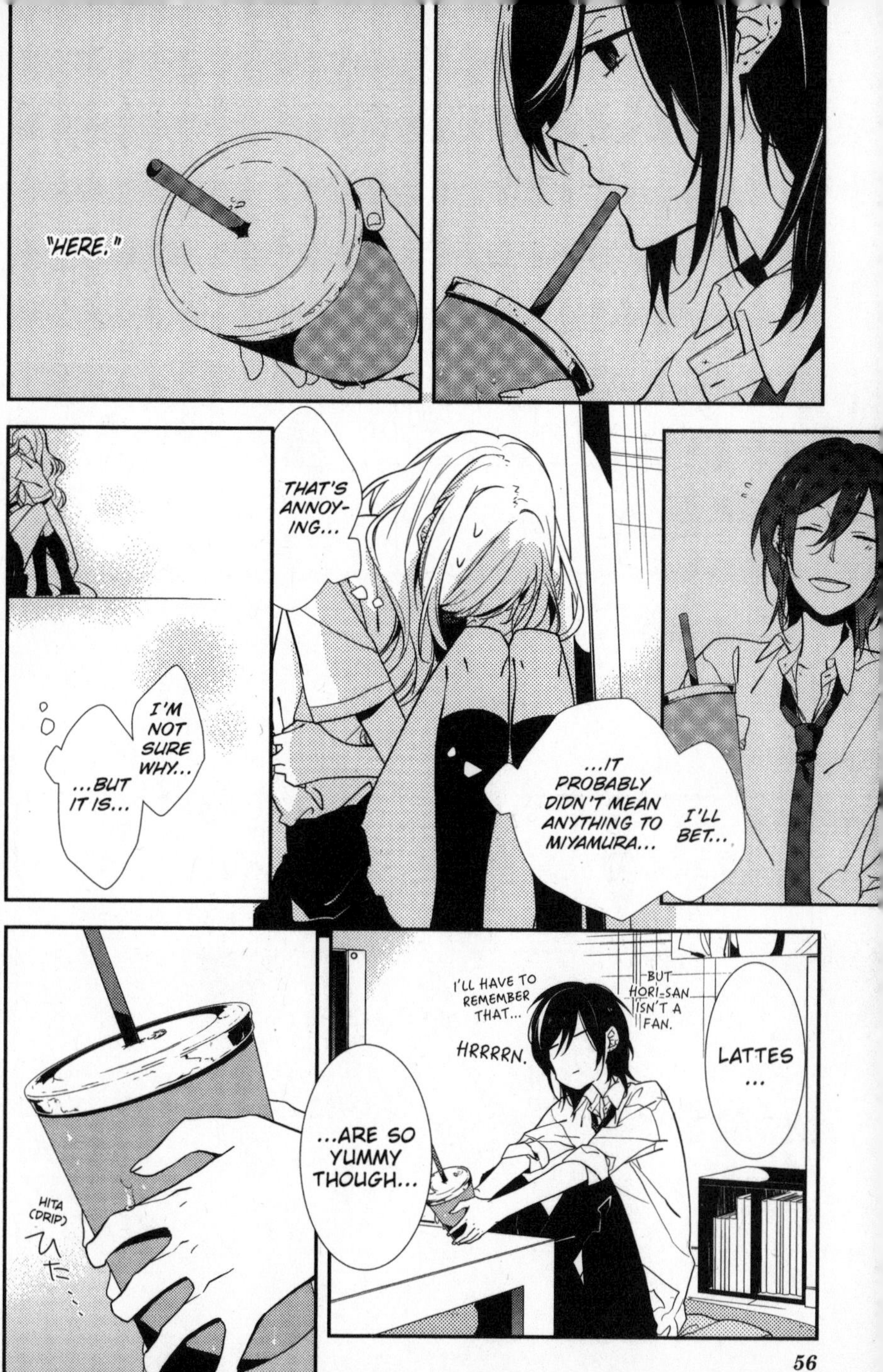
"HERE."
...IT PROBABLY DIDN'T MEAN ANYTHING TO MIYAMURA...
I'LL BET...
THAT'S ANNOYING...
I'M NOT SURE WHY...
...BUT IT IS...
LATTES ...
BUT HORI-SAN ISN'T A FAN.
I'LL HAVE TO REMEMBER THAT...
HRRRRN.
...ARE SO YUMMY THOUGH...
HITA (DRIP)
ひた...

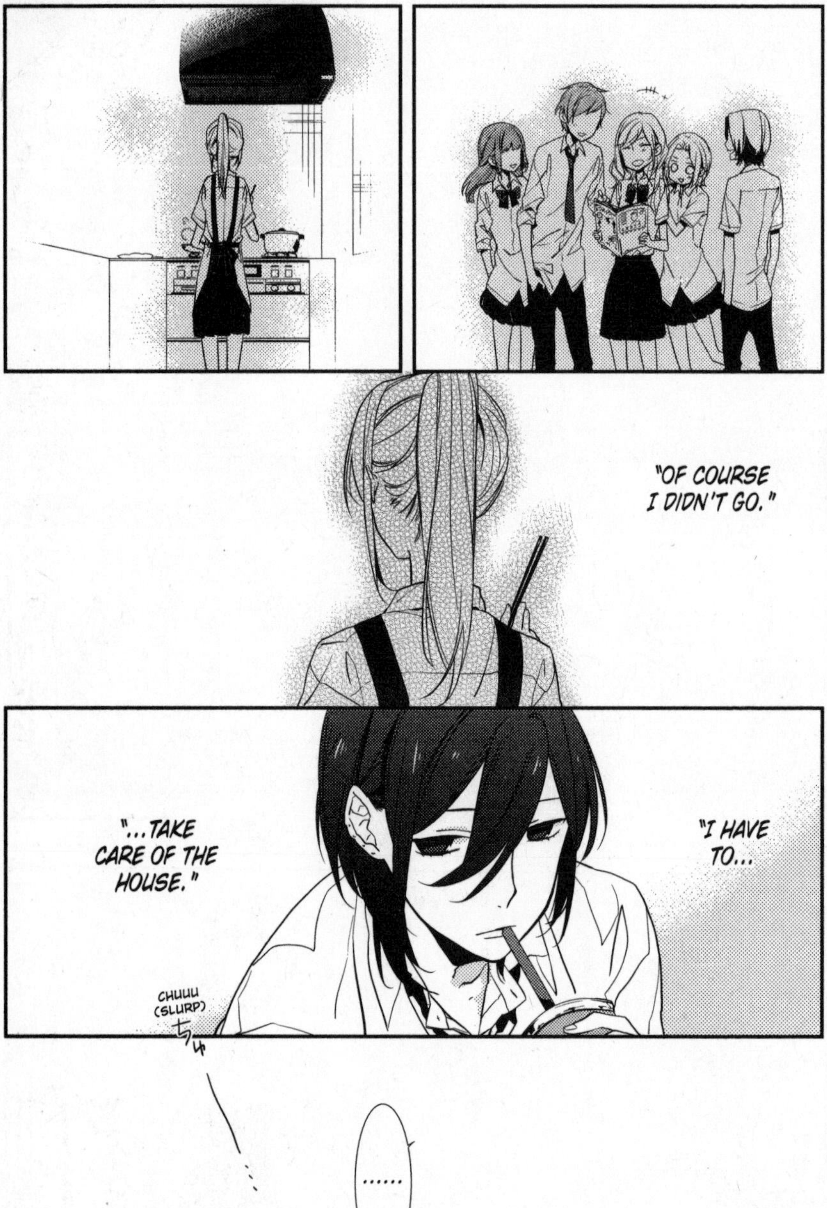
"OF COURSE I DIDN'T GO."
"I HAVE TO...
"...TAKE CARE OF THE HOUSE."
CHUUU (SLURP)
ちゅ
......

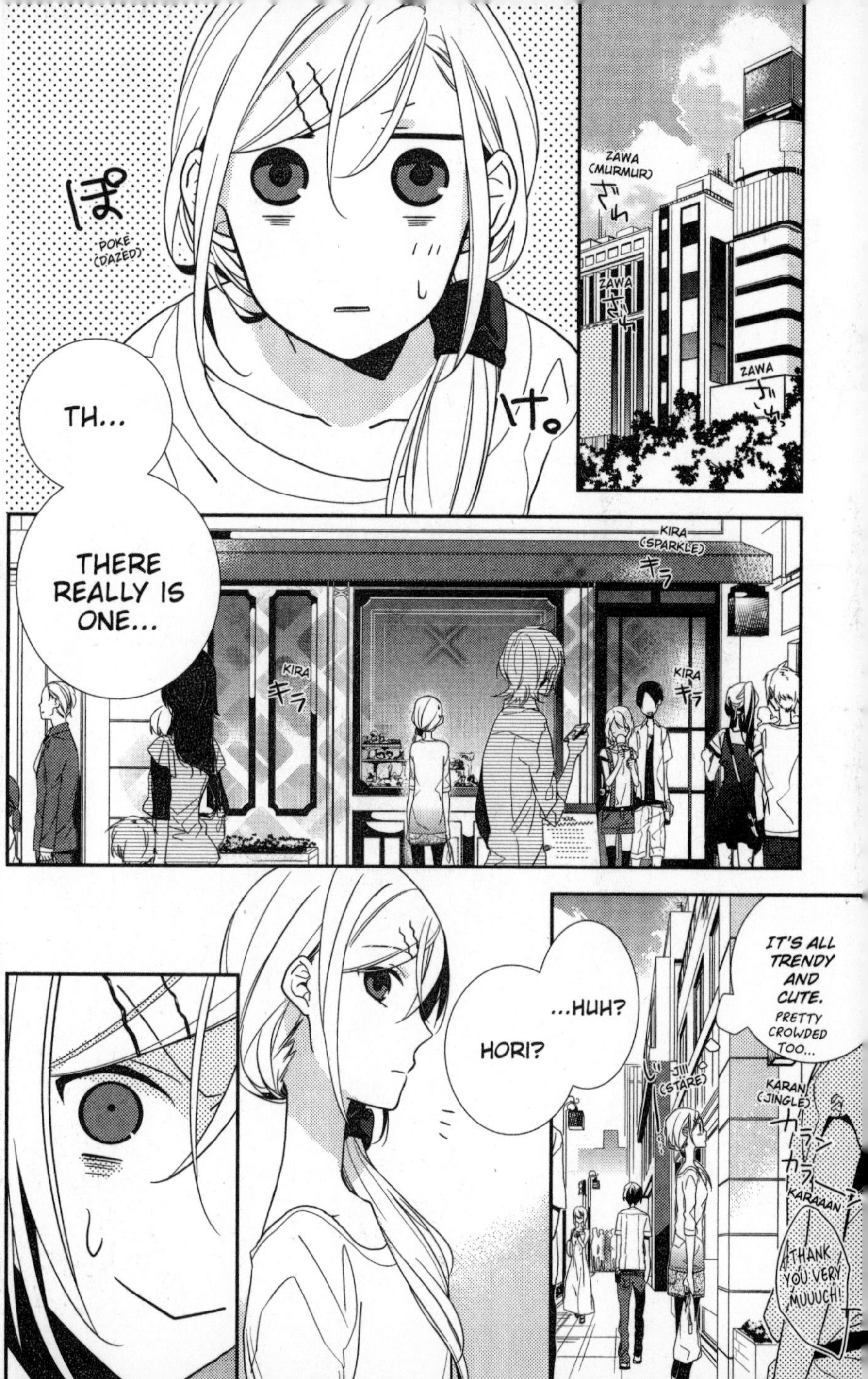

ZAWA (MURMUR)
ざわ
ZAWA
ざわ
ZAWA
ざわ
ぽ
POKE (DAZED)
け。
TH...
THERE REALLY IS ONE...
KIRA (SPARKLE)
キラ
KIRA
キラ
KIRA
キラ
IT'S ALL TRENDY AND CUTE. PRETTY CROWDED TOO...
JII (STARE)
じ
KARAN (JINGLE)
カラン
カラ
KARAAAN
THANK YOU VERY MUUUCH!
...HUH?
HORI?

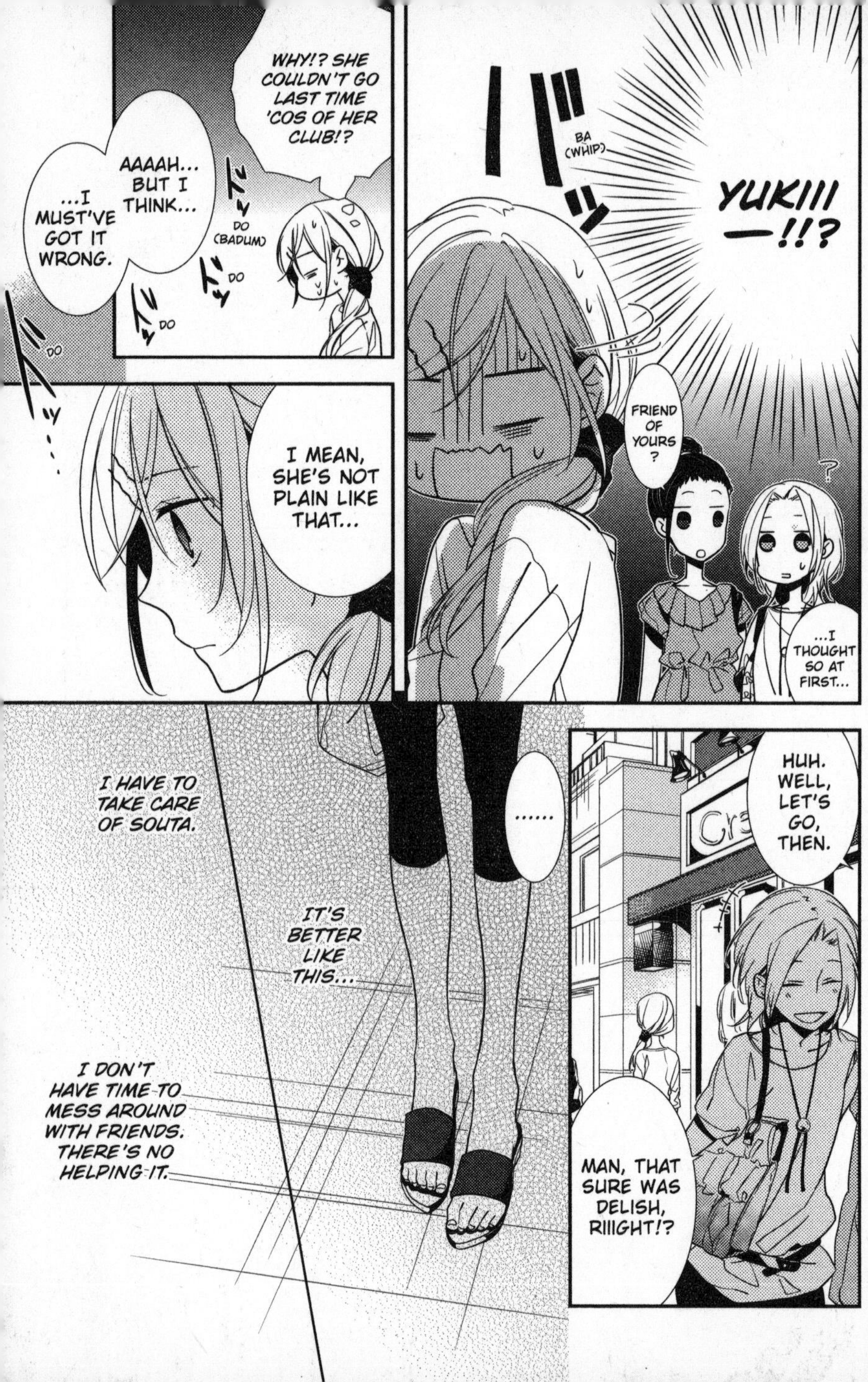
BA (WHIP)
YUKIIII—!!?
FRIEND OF YOURS?
...I THOUGHT SO AT FIRST...
WHY!? SHE COULDN'T GO LAST TIME 'COS OF HER CLUB!?
AAAAH... BUT I THINK...
...I MUST'VE GOT IT WRONG.
DO (BADUM)
DO
DO
DO
I MEAN, SHE'S NOT PLAIN LIKE THAT...
HUH. WELL, LET'S GO, THEN.
MAN, THAT SURE WAS DELISH, RIIIGHT!?
......
I HAVE TO TAKE CARE OF SOUTA.
IT'S BETTER LIKE THIS...
I DON'T HAVE TIME TO MESS AROUND WITH FRIENDS. THERE'S NO HELPING IT.

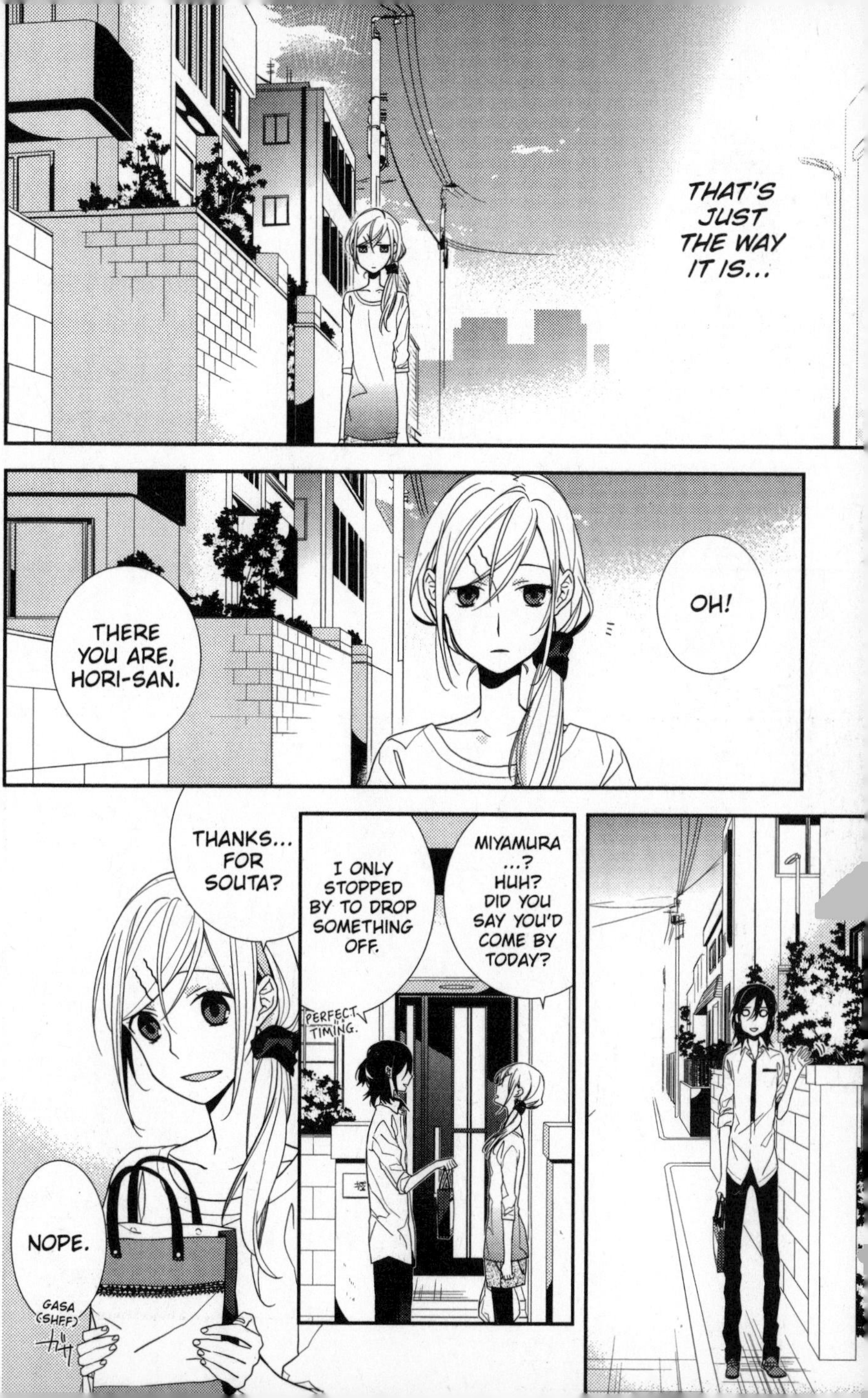
THAT'S JUST THE WAY IT IS...
OH!
THERE YOU ARE, HORI-SAN.
MIYAMURA ...? HUH? DID YOU SAY YOU'D COME BY TODAY?
I ONLY STOPPED BY TO DROP SOMETHING OFF.
PERFECT TIMING.
THANKS... FOR SOUTA?
NOPE.
GASA (SHFF)

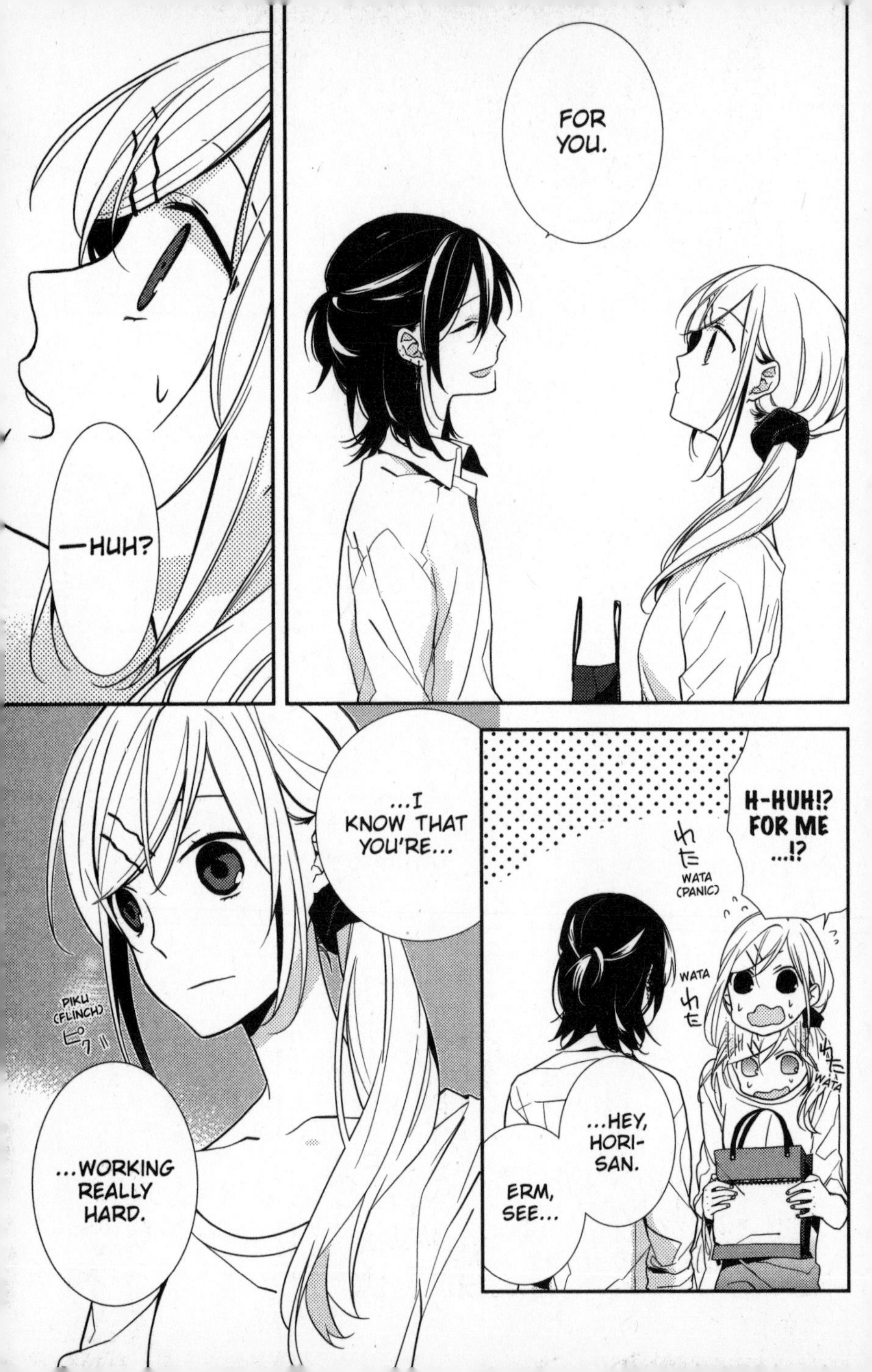

FOR YOU.
—HUH?
H-HUH!? FOR ME ...!?
わた
WATA (PANIC)
WATA
わた
わた
WATA
...HEY, HORI-SAN.
ERM, SEE...
...I KNOW THAT YOU'RE...
PIKU (FLINCH)
ピクッ
...WORKING REALLY HARD.

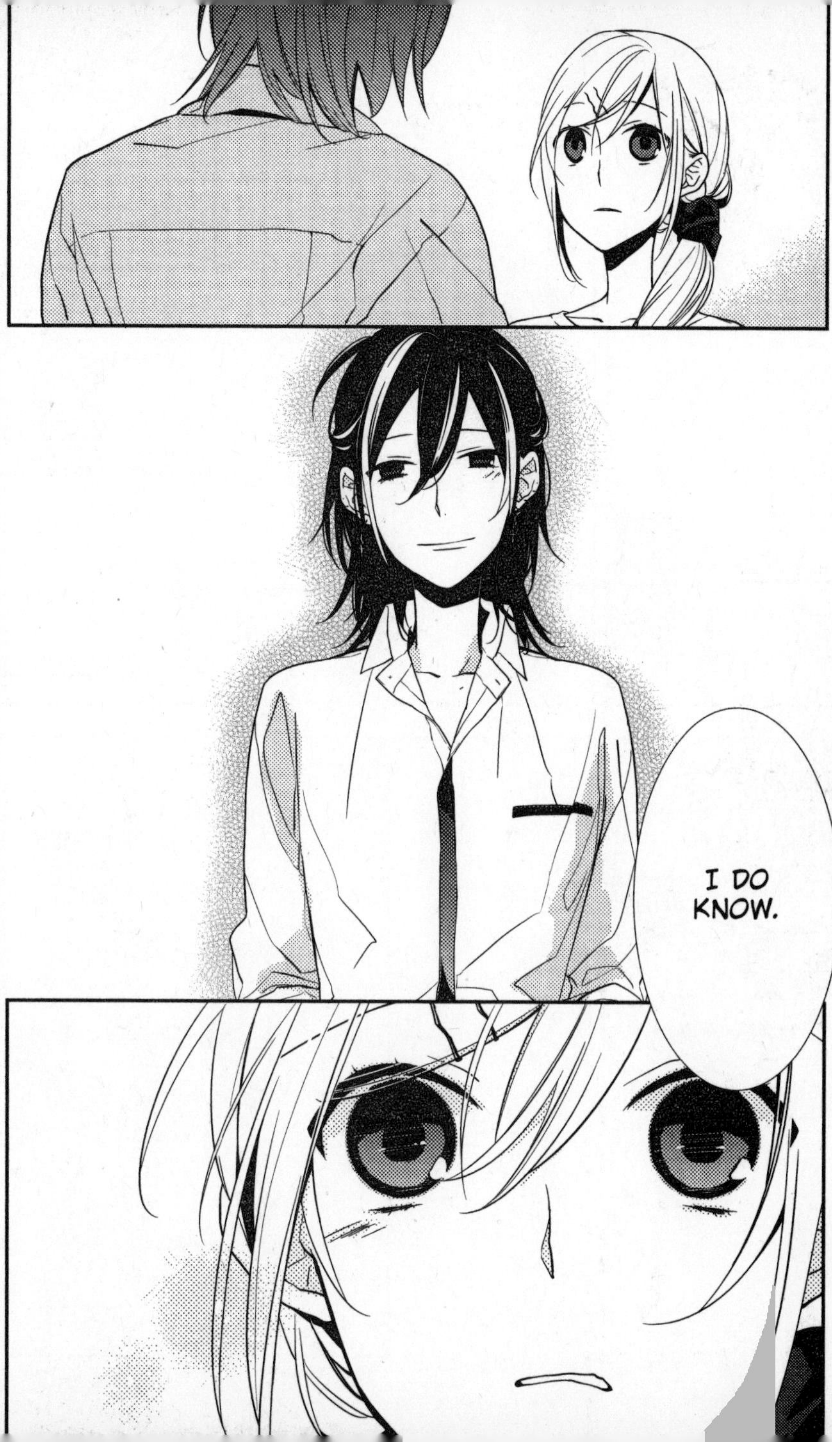
I DO KNOW.

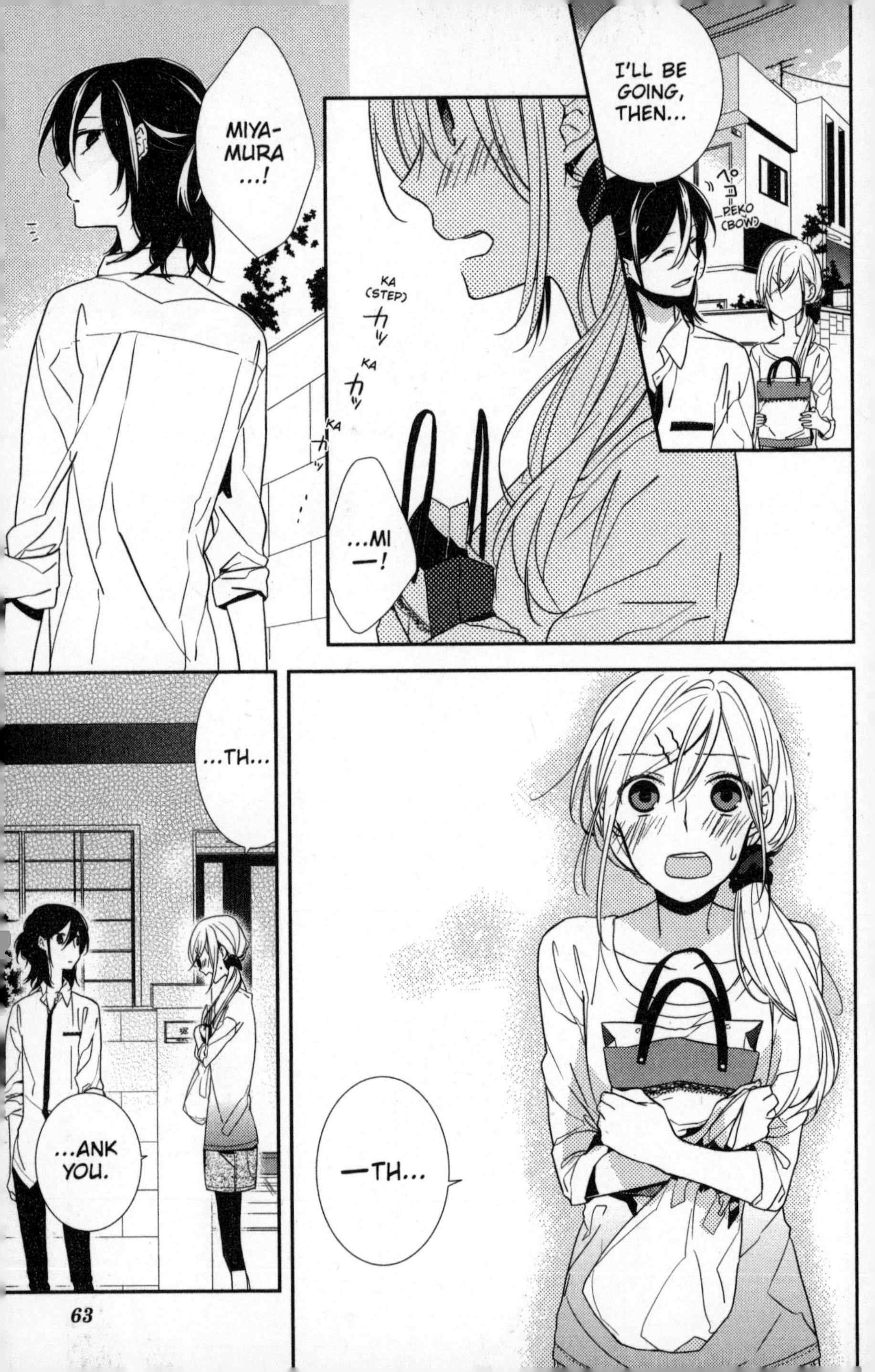
I'LL BE GOING, THEN...
PEKO (BOW)
KA (STEP)
KA
KA
...MI—!
MIYA-MURA ...!
—TH...
...TH...
...ANK YOU.

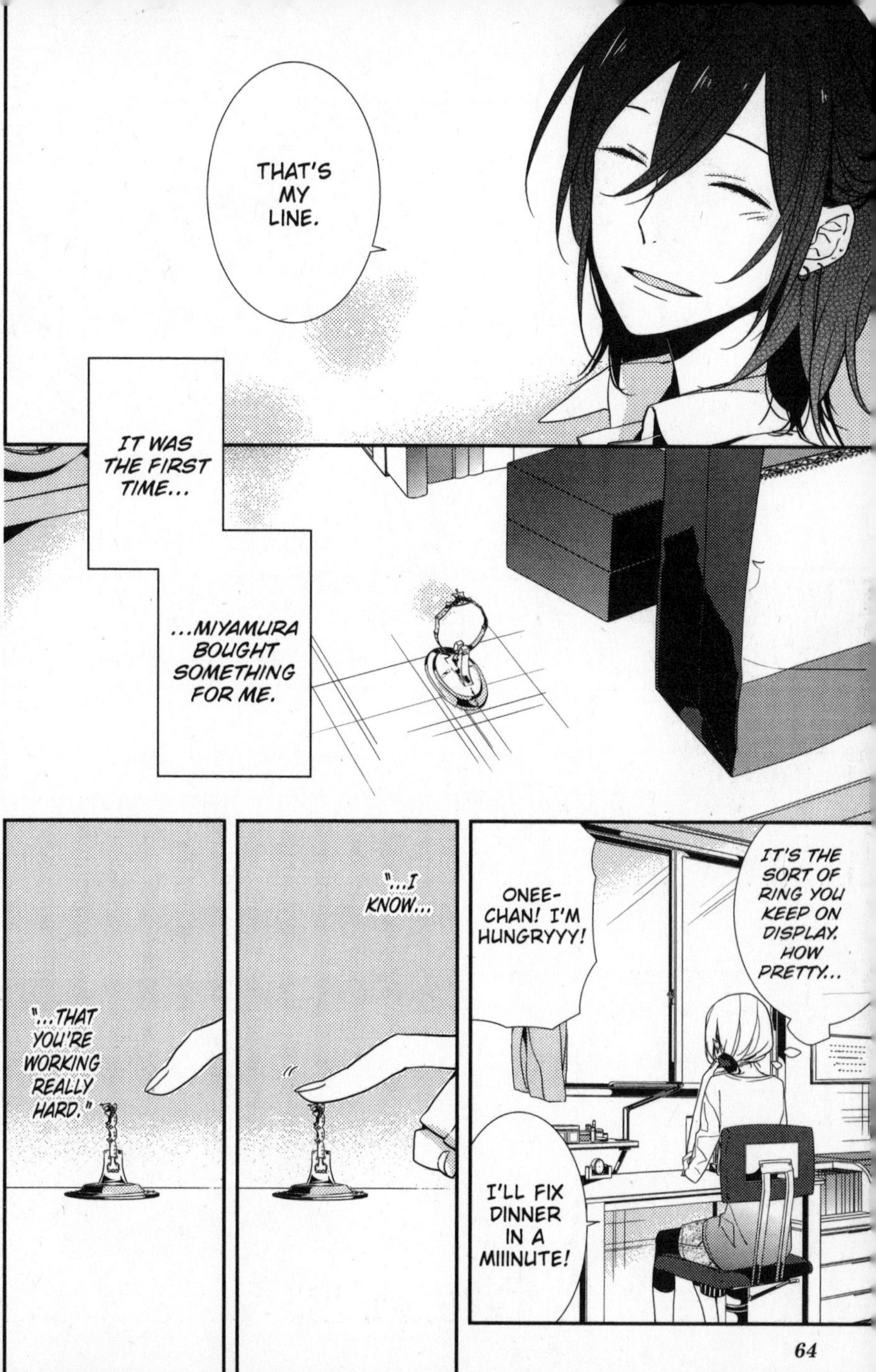
THAT'S MY LINE.
IT WAS THE FIRST TIME...
...MIYAMURA BOUGHT SOMETHING FOR ME.
IT'S THE SORT OF RING YOU KEEP ON DISPLAY. HOW PRETTY...
ONEE-CHAN! I'M HUNGRYYY!
I'LL FIX DINNER IN A MIIINUTE!
"...I KNOW...
"...THAT YOU'RE WORKING REALLY HARD."

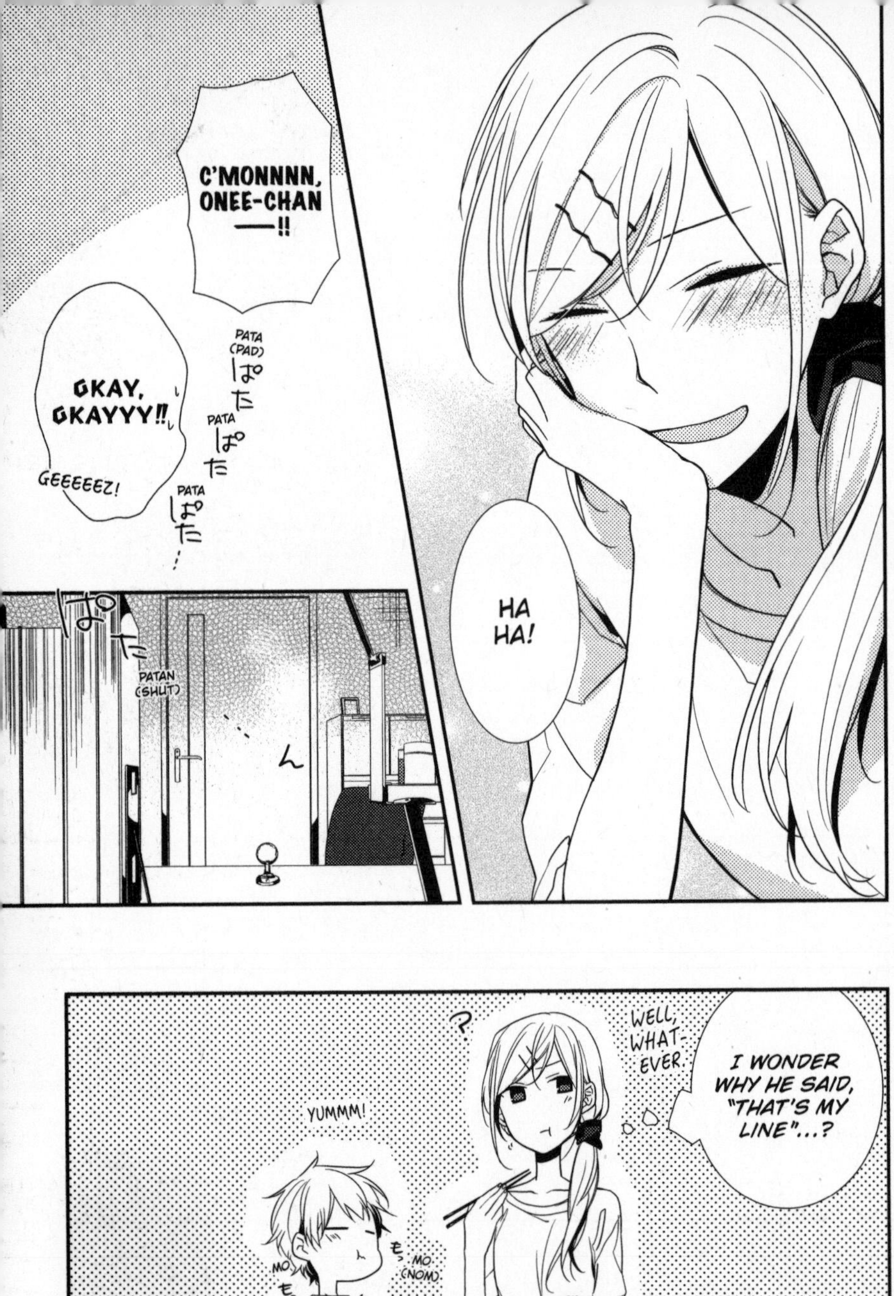
HA HA!
C'MONNNN, ONEE-CHAN—!!
OKAY, OKAYYY!!
GEEEEEZ!
PATA (PAD) ぱた
PATA ぱた
PATA ぱた
ぱたん
PATAN (SHUT)
...ん
I WONDER WHY HE SAID, "THAT'S MY LINE"...?
WELL, WHATEVER.
?
YUMMM!
MO (NOM) も
MO も

HORIMIYA

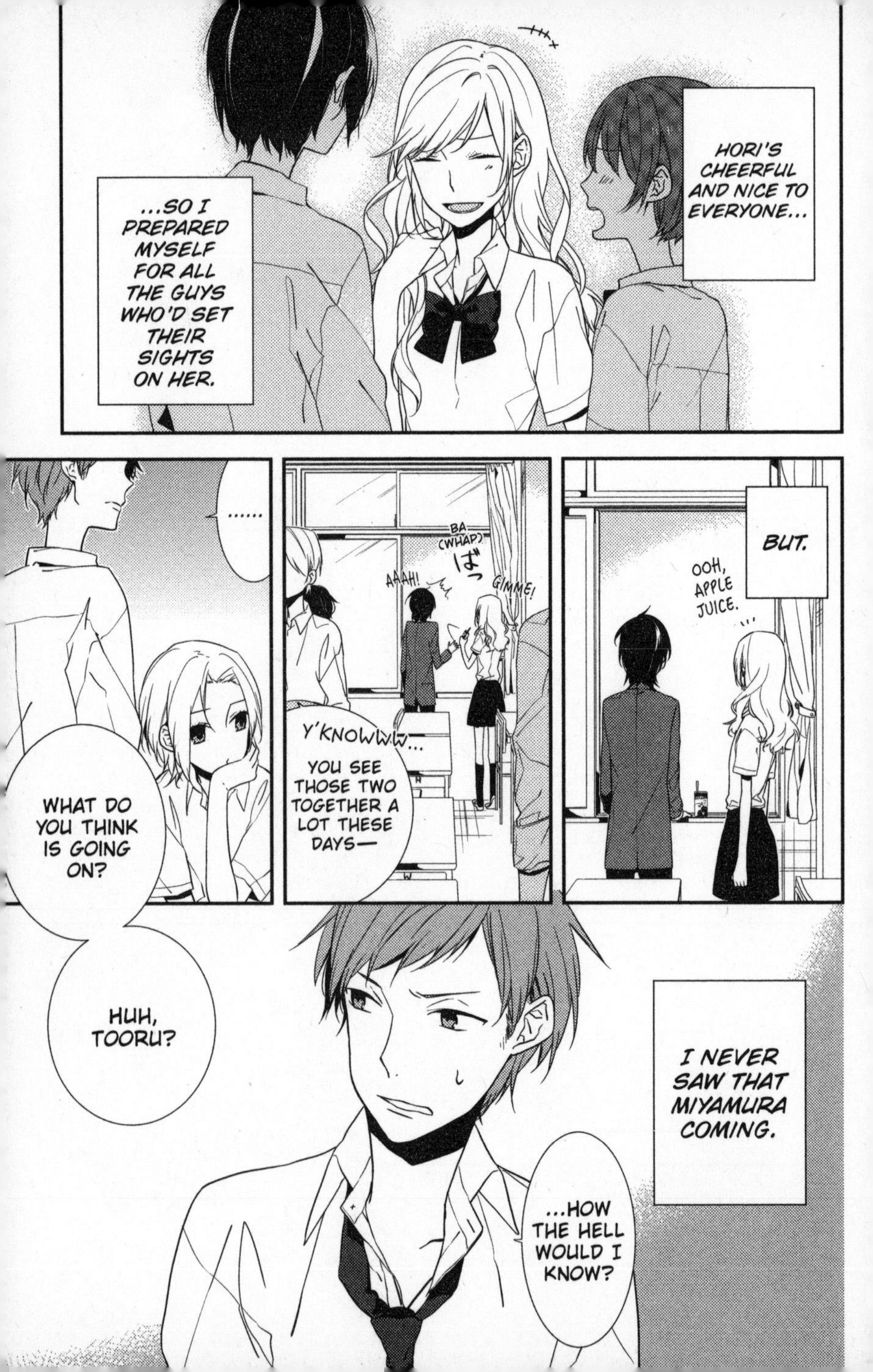
HORI'S CHEERFUL AND NICE TO EVERYONE...
...SO I PREPARED MYSELF FOR ALL THE GUYS WHO'D SET THEIR SIGHTS ON HER.
BUT.
OOH, APPLE JUICE.
BA (WHAP) ばっ
GIMME!
AAAH!
Y'KNOWWW...
YOU SEE THOSE TWO TOGETHER A LOT THESE DAYS—
......
WHAT DO YOU THINK IS GOING ON?
I NEVER SAW THAT MIYAMURA COMING.
HUH, TOORU?
...HOW THE HELL WOULD I KNOW?

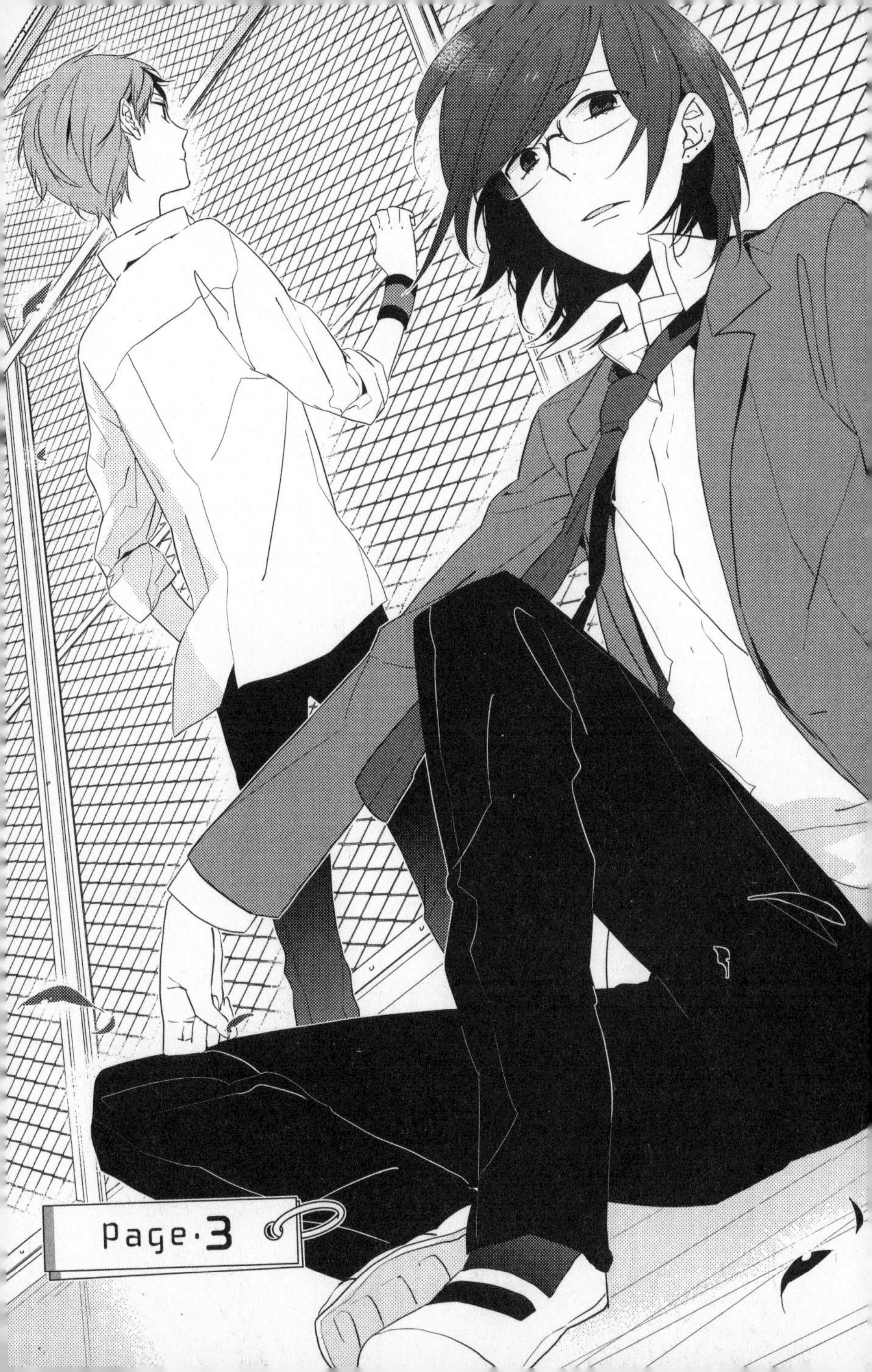

page·3

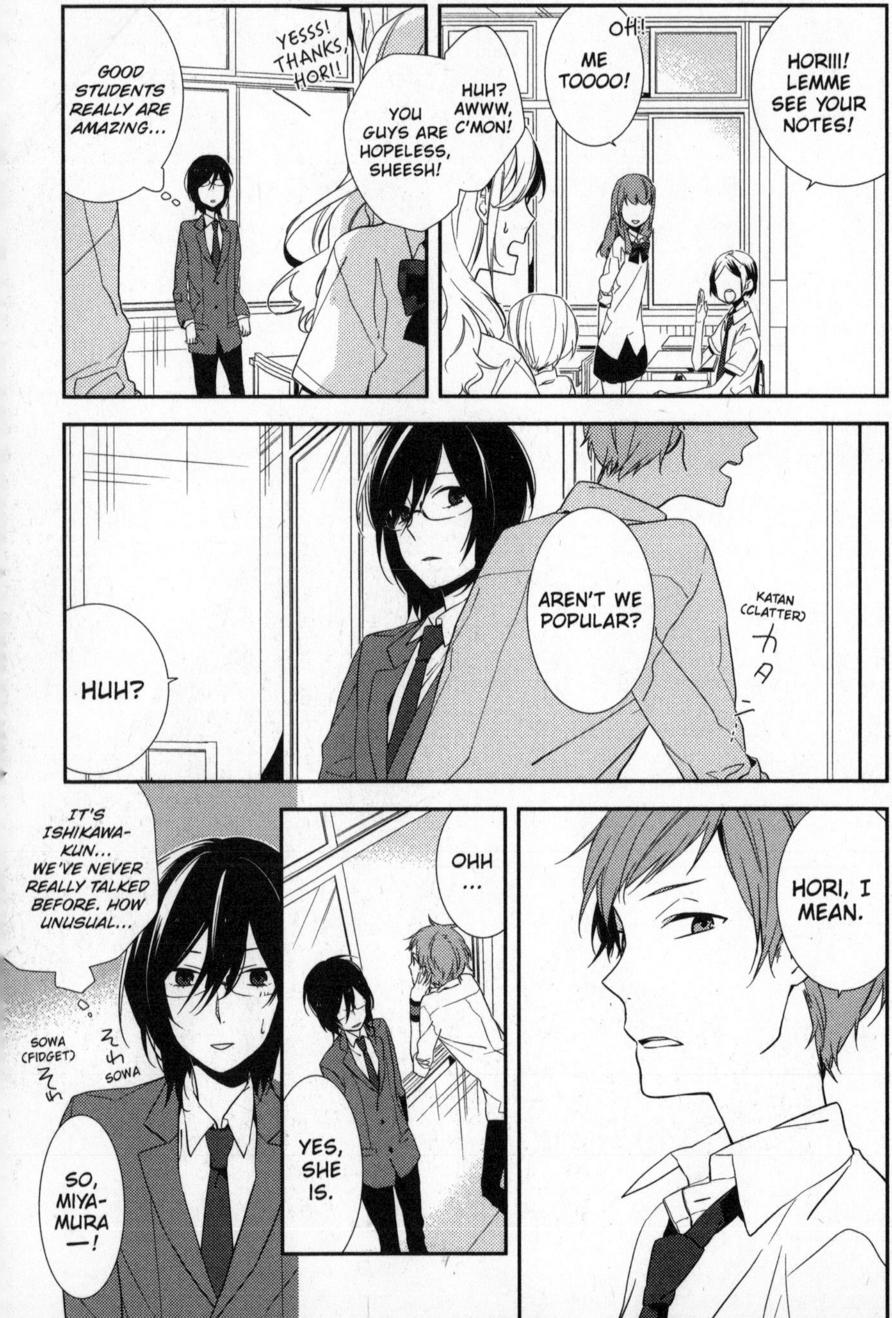
HORIII! LEMME SEE YOUR NOTES!
OH!
ME TOOOO!
HUH? AWWW, C'MON!
YOU GUYS ARE HOPELESS, SHEESH!
YESSS! THANKS, HORI!
GOOD STUDENTS REALLY ARE AMAZING...
KATAN (CLATTER)
AREN'T WE POPULAR?
HUH?
HORI, I MEAN.
OHH ...
YES, SHE IS.
IT'S ISHIKAWA-KUN... WE'VE NEVER REALLY TALKED BEFORE. HOW UNUSUAL...
SOWA (FIDGET) SOWA
SO, MIYAMURA—!

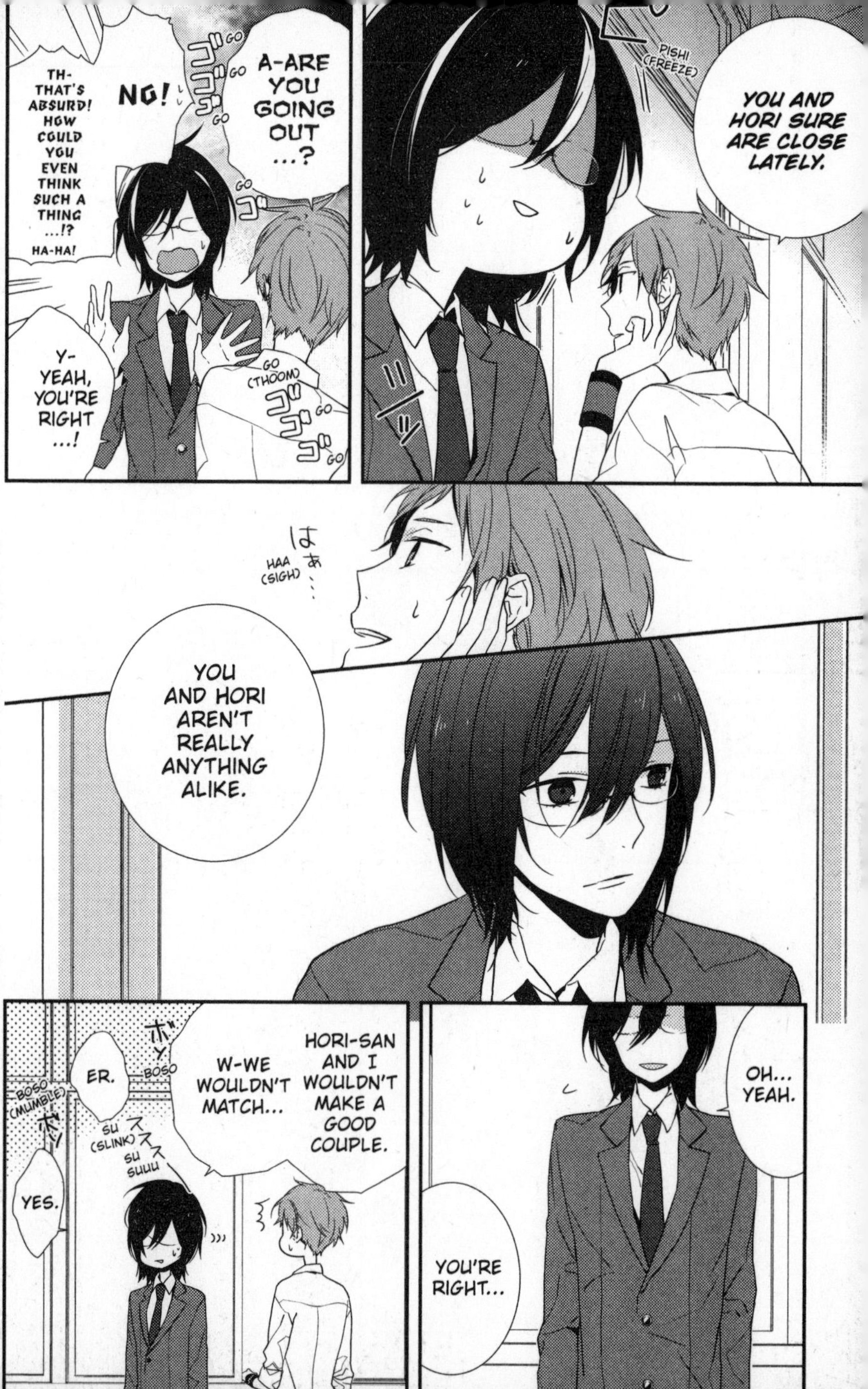
PISHI (FREEZE)
YOU AND HORI SURE ARE CLOSE LATELY.
A-ARE YOU GOING OUT ...?
GO GO GO GO
NG!
TH-THAT'S ABSURD! HOW COULD YOU EVEN THINK SUCH A THING ...!? HA-HA!
GO (THOOM) GO GO
Y-YEAH, YOU'RE RIGHT ...!
HAA (SIGH)
YOU AND HORI AREN'T REALLY ANYTHING ALIKE.
OH... YEAH.
YOU'RE RIGHT...
HORI-SAN AND I WOULDN'T MAKE A GOOD COUPLE.
W-WE WOULDN'T MATCH...
BOSO
ER.
BOSO (MUMBLE)
SU (SLINK) SU SUUU
YES.

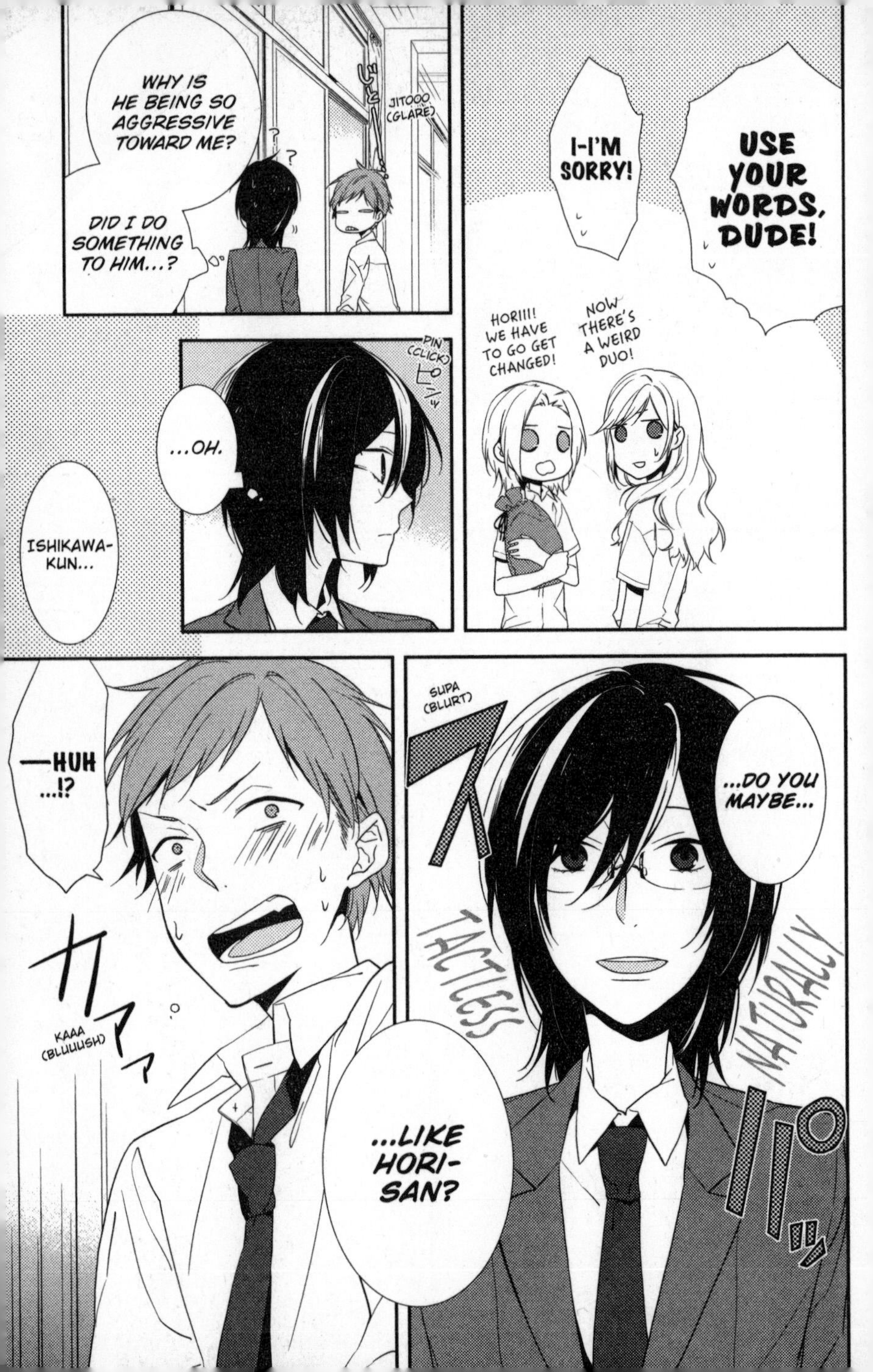
USE YOUR WORDS, DUDE!
I-I'M SORRY!
NOW THERE'S A WEIRD DUO!
HORIIII! WE HAVE TO GO GET CHANGED!
JITOOO (GLARE)
WHY IS HE BEING SO AGGRESSIVE TOWARD ME?
DID I DO SOMETHING TO HIM...?
PIN (CLICK)
...OH.
ISHIKAWA-KUN...
SUPA (BLURT)
...DO YOU MAYBE...
NATURALLY
TACTLESS
...LIKE HORI-SAN?
—HUH ...!?
KAAA (BLUUUSH)

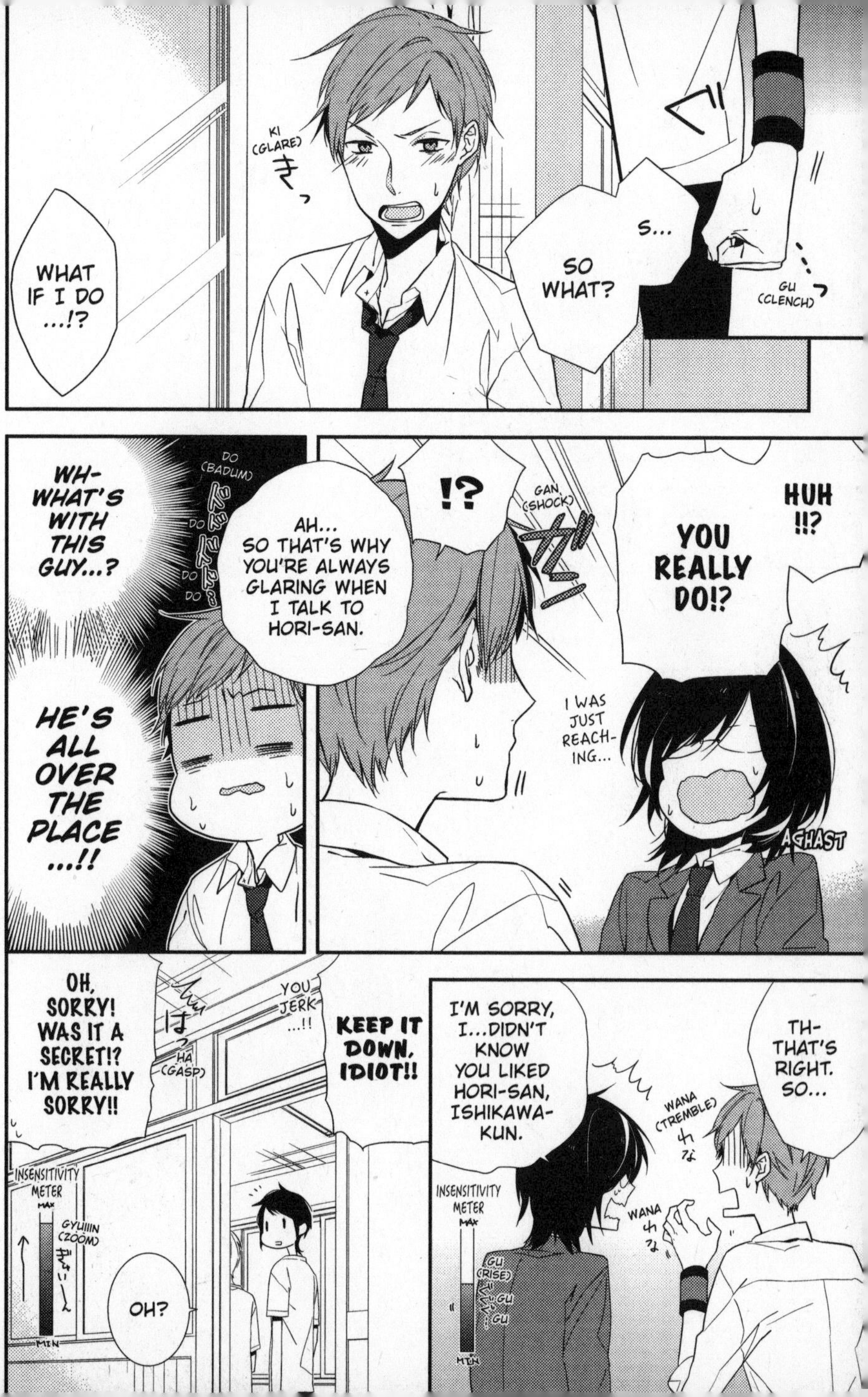
S...
SO WHAT?
GU (CLENCH)
KI (GLARE)
WHAT IF I DO ...!?
HUH !!?
YOU REALLY DO!?
I WAS JUST REACHING...
AGHAST
GAN (SHOCK)
!?
AH... SO THAT'S WHY YOU'RE ALWAYS GLARING WHEN I TALK TO HORI-SAN.
DO (BADUM) DO DO DO
WH-WHAT'S WITH THIS GUY...?
HE'S ALL OVER THE PLACE...!!
TH-THAT'S RIGHT. SO...
I'M SORRY, I...DIDN'T KNOW YOU LIKED HORI-SAN, ISHIKAWA-KUN.
WANA (TREMBLE)
WANA
INSENSITIVITY METER
MAX
MIN
GU (RISE) GU GU
KEEP IT DOWN, IDIOT!!
YOU JERK...!!
HA (GASP)
OH, SORRY! WAS IT A SECRET!? I'M REALLY SORRY!!
INSENSITIVITY METER
MAX
MIN
GYUIIIN (ZOOM)
OH?

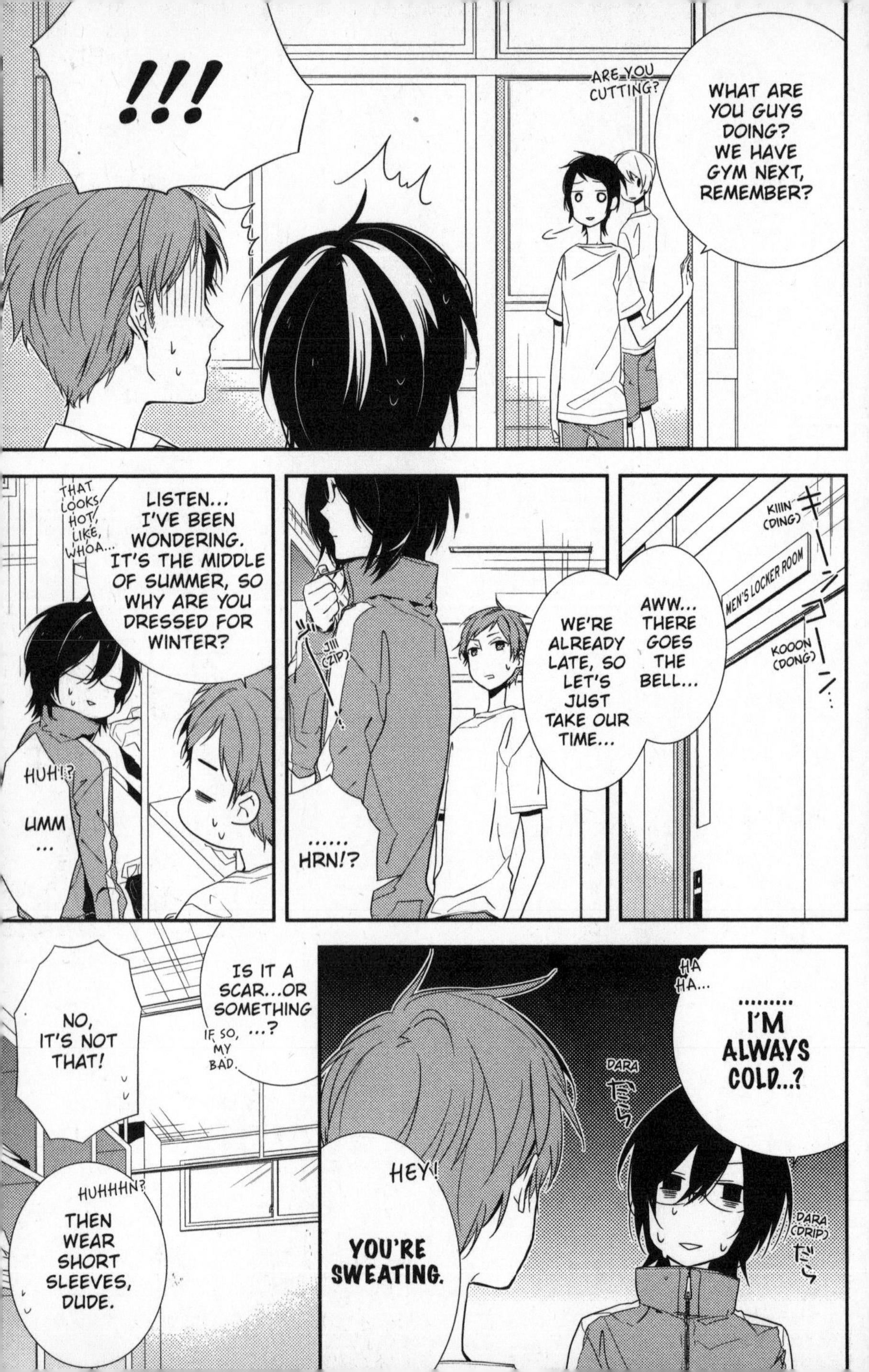
WHAT ARE YOU GUYS DOING? WE HAVE GYM NEXT, REMEMBER?
ARE YOU CUTTING?
!!!
KIIIN (DING)
MEN'S LOCKER ROOM
KOOON (DONG)
AWW... THERE GOES THE BELL... WE'RE ALREADY LATE, SO LET'S JUST TAKE OUR TIME...
JIII (ZIP)
......HRN!?
LISTEN... I'VE BEEN WONDERING. IT'S THE MIDDLE OF SUMMER, SO WHY ARE YOU DRESSED FOR WINTER?
THAT LOOKS HOT, LIKE, WHOA...
HUH!?
UMM...
HA HA...
.... I'M ALWAYS COLD...?
DARA
DARA (DRIP)
HEY!
YOU'RE SWEATING.
IS IT A SCAR...OR SOMETHING...?
IF SO, MY BAD.
NO, IT'S NOT THAT!
HUHHHN?
THEN WEAR SHORT SLEEVES, DUDE.

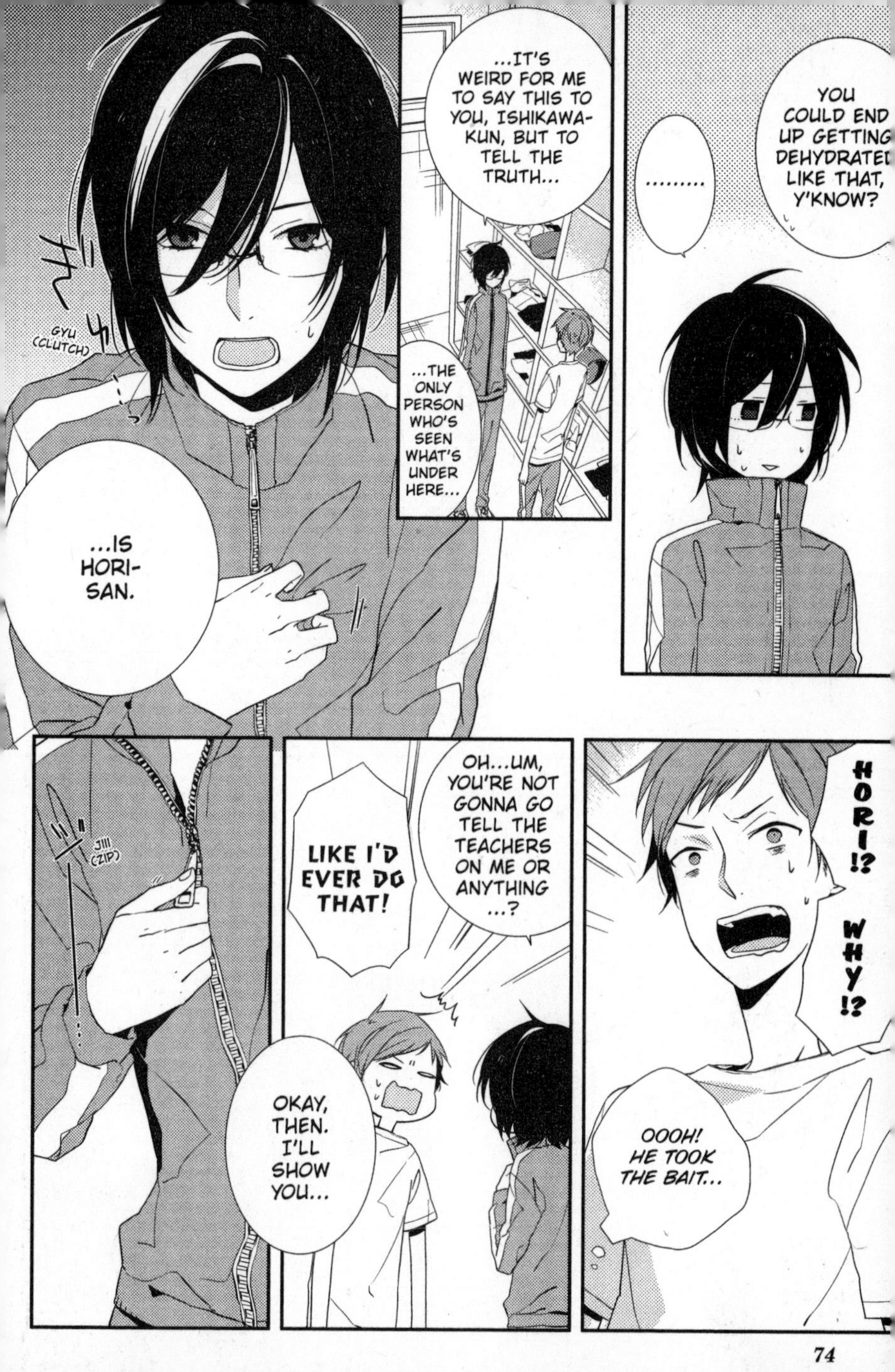
YOU COULD END UP GETTING DEHYDRATED LIKE THAT, Y'KNOW?
....
...IT'S WEIRD FOR ME TO SAY THIS TO YOU, ISHIKAWA-KUN, BUT TO TELL THE TRUTH...
...THE ONLY PERSON WHO'S SEEN WHAT'S UNDER HERE...
GYU (CLUTCH)
...IS HORI-SAN.
HORI!? WHY!?
OOOH! HE TOOK THE BAIT...
OH...UM, YOU'RE NOT GONNA GO TELL THE TEACHERS ON ME OR ANYTHING ...?
LIKE I'D EVER DO THAT!
OKAY, THEN. I'LL SHOW YOU...
JIII (ZIP)

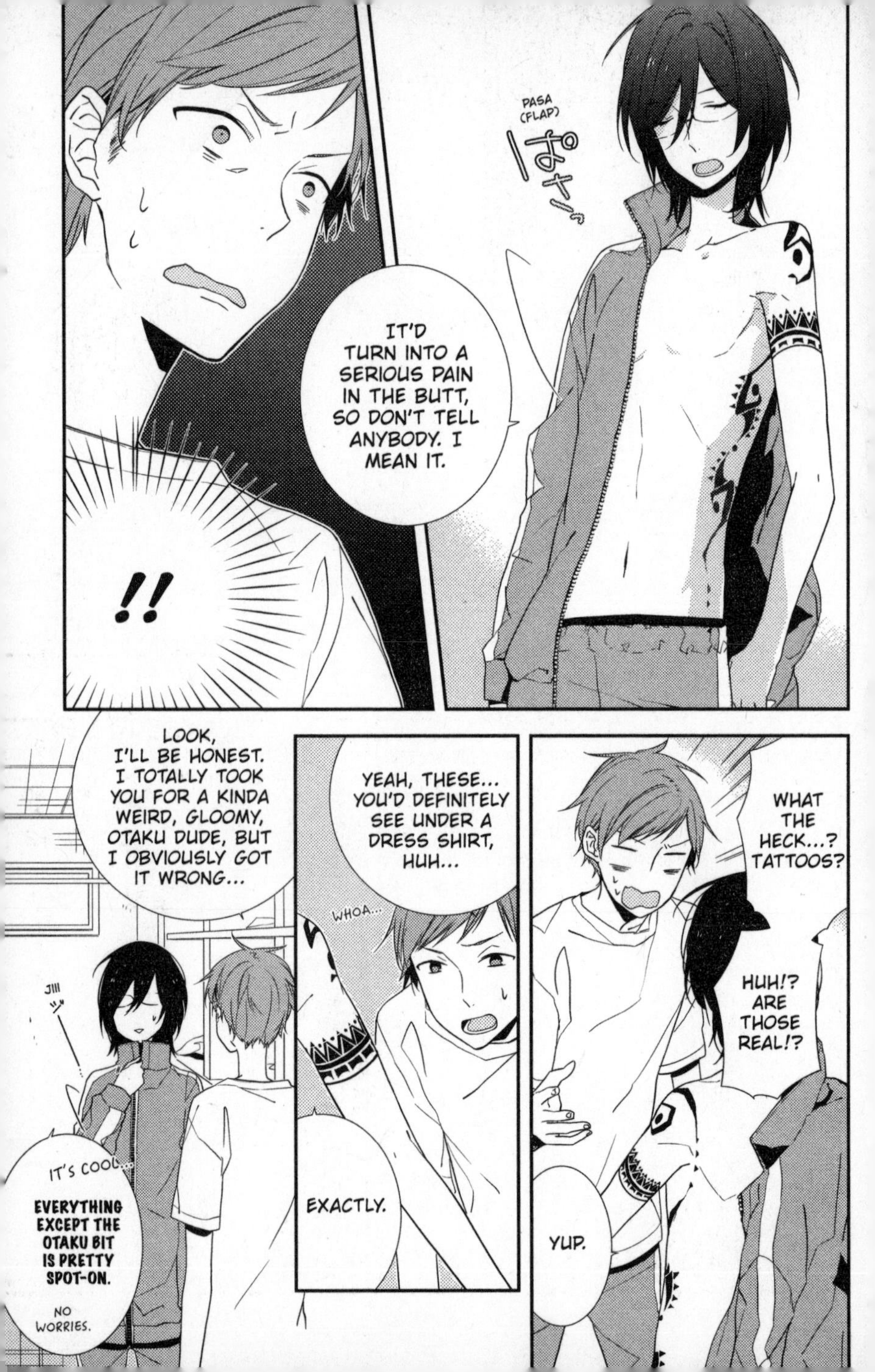
PASA (FLAP)
IT'D TURN INTO A SERIOUS PAIN IN THE BUTT, SO DON'T TELL ANYBODY. I MEAN IT.
!!
WHAT THE HECK...? TATTOOS?
HUH!? ARE THOSE REAL!?
YUP.
WHOA...
YEAH, THESE... YOU'D DEFINITELY SEE UNDER A DRESS SHIRT, HUH...
EXACTLY.
LOOK, I'LL BE HONEST. I TOTALLY TOOK YOU FOR A KINDA WEIRD, GLOOMY, OTAKU DUDE, BUT I OBVIOUSLY GOT IT WRONG...
JIII
IT'S COOL...
EVERYTHING EXCEPT THE OTAKU BIT IS PRETTY SPOT-ON.
NO WORRIES.

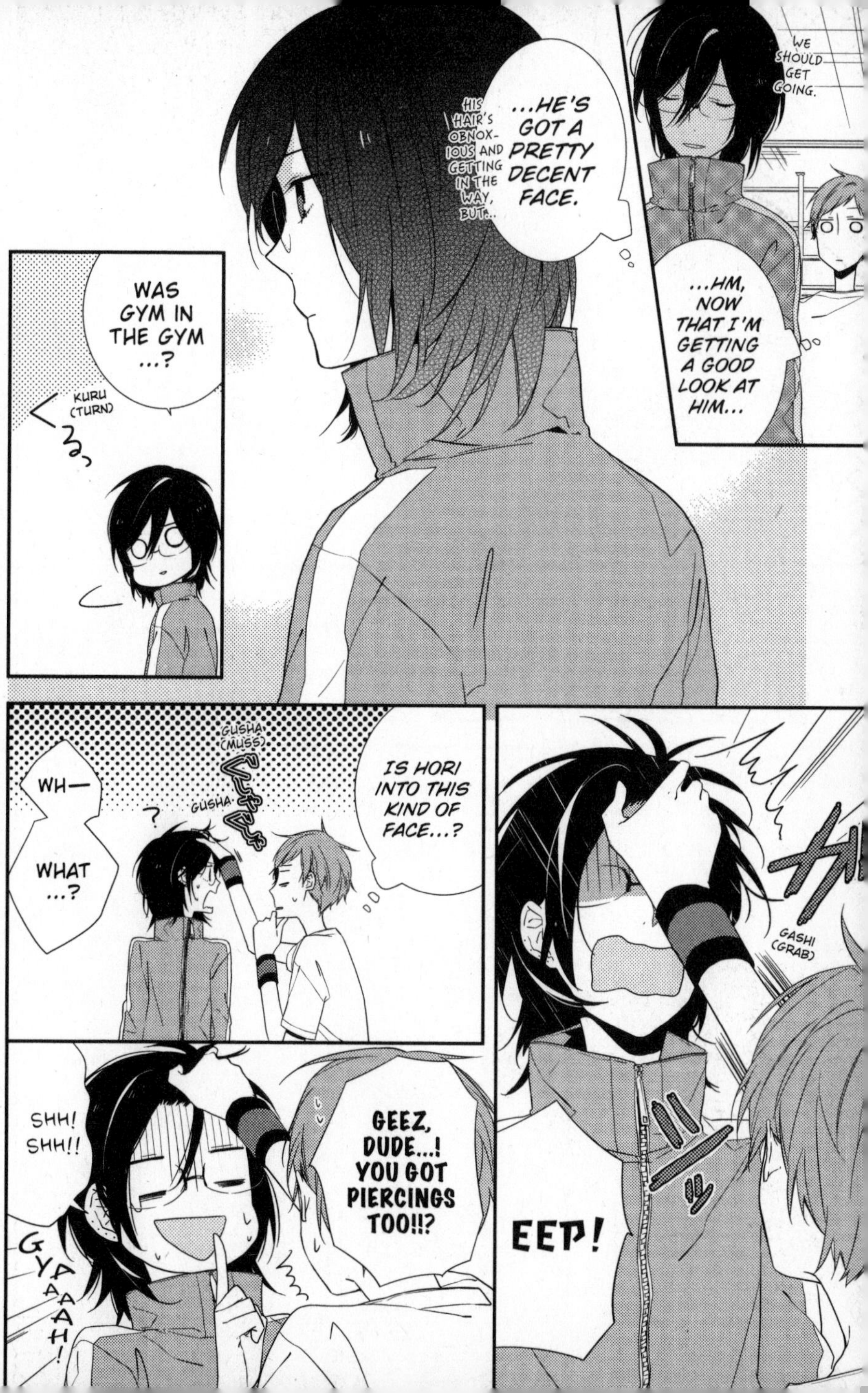
WE SHOULD GET GOING.
...HM, NOW THAT I'M GETTING A GOOD LOOK AT HIM...
HIS HAIR'S OBNOXIOUS AND GETTING IN THE WAY, BUT...
...HE'S GOT A PRETTY DECENT FACE.
WAS GYM IN THE GYM ...?
KURU (TURN)
GASHI (GRAB)
EEP!
IS HORI INTO THIS KIND OF FACE...?
GUSHA (MUSS)
GUSHA
?
WH—
WHAT ...?
GEEZ, DUDE...! YOU GOT PIERCINGS TOO!!?
SHH! SHH!!
GYAAAAH!

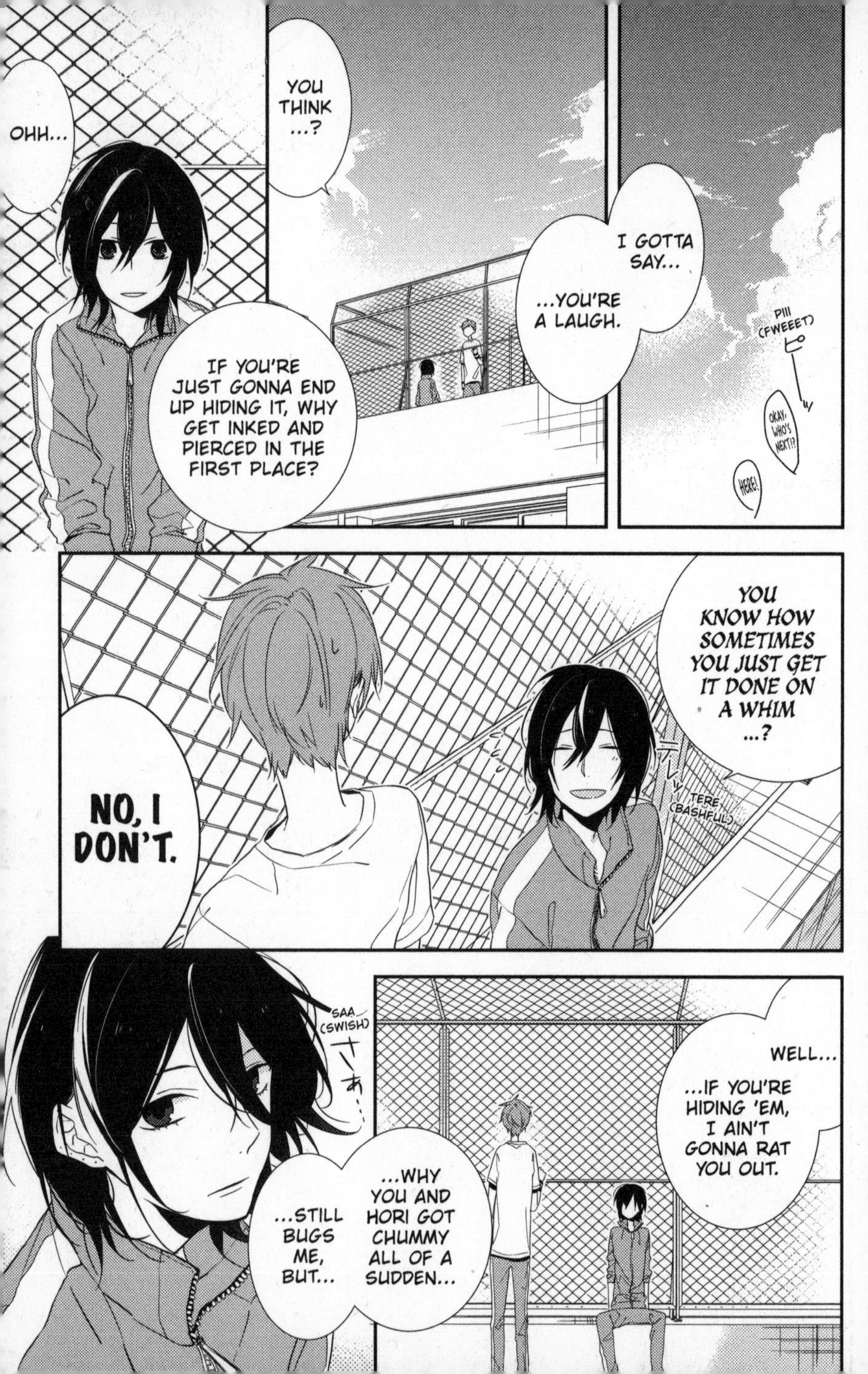
I GOTTA SAY...
...YOU'RE A LAUGH.
PIII (FWEEET)
OKAY, WHO'S NEXT!?
HERE!
YOU THINK ...?
OHH...
IF YOU'RE JUST GONNA END UP HIDING IT, WHY GET INKED AND PIERCED IN THE FIRST PLACE?
YOU KNOW HOW SOMETIMES YOU JUST GET IT DONE ON A WHIM ...?
TERE (BASHFUL)
NO, I DON'T.
WELL...
...IF YOU'RE HIDING 'EM, I AIN'T GONNA RAT YOU OUT.
SAA (SWISH)
...WHY YOU AND HORI GOT CHUMMY ALL OF A SUDDEN...
...STILL BUGS ME, BUT...

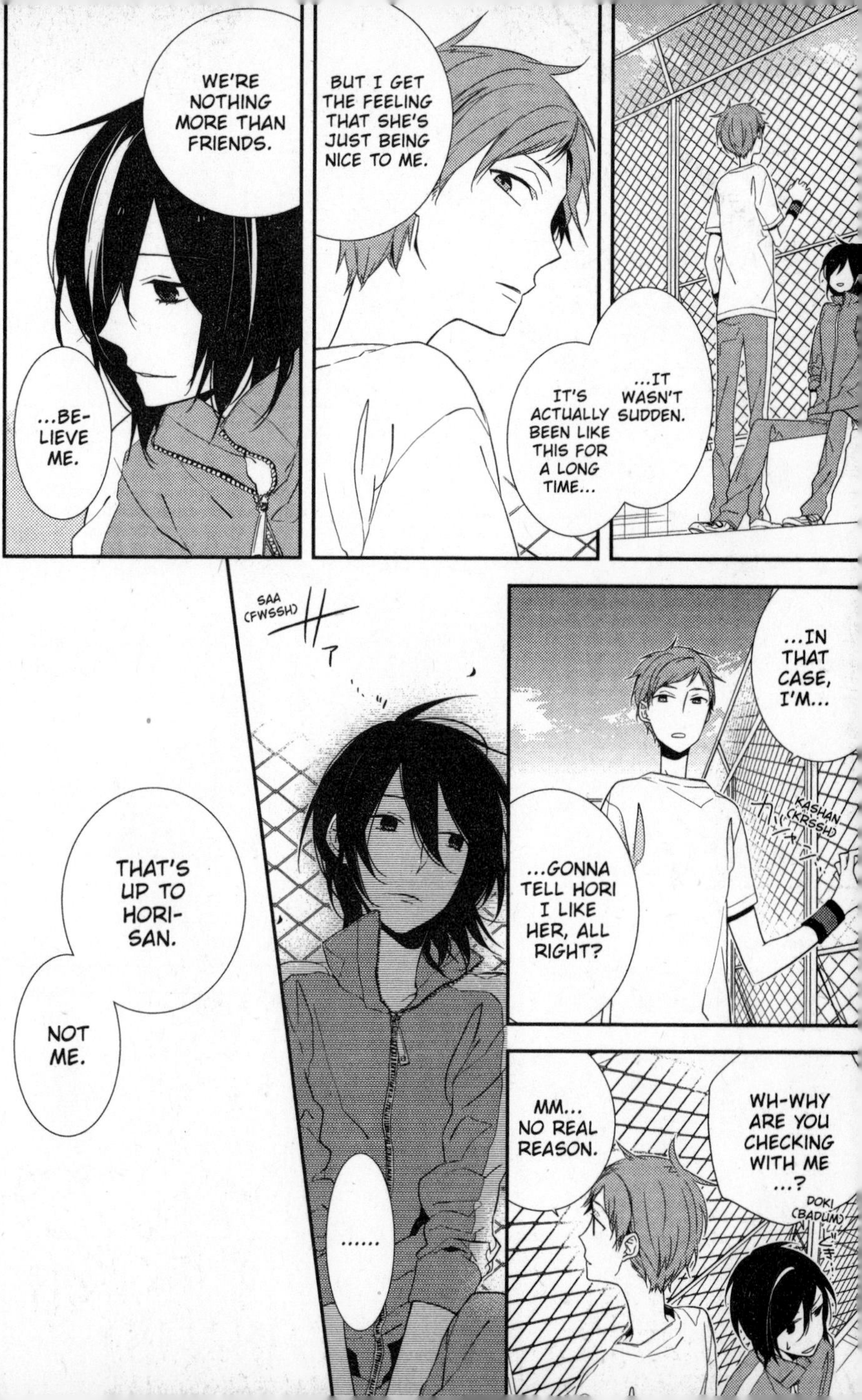
...IT WASN'T SUDDEN.
IT'S ACTUALLY BEEN LIKE THIS FOR A LONG TIME...
BUT I GET THE FEELING THAT SHE'S JUST BEING NICE TO ME.
WE'RE NOTHING MORE THAN FRIENDS.
...BE-LIEVE ME.
...IN THAT CASE, I'M...
KASHAN (KRSSH)
...GONNA TELL HORI I LIKE HER, ALL RIGHT?
WH-WHY ARE YOU CHECKING WITH ME ...?
DOKI (BADUM)
MM... NO REAL REASON.
SAA (FWSSH)
......
THAT'S UP TO HORI-SAN.
NOT ME.

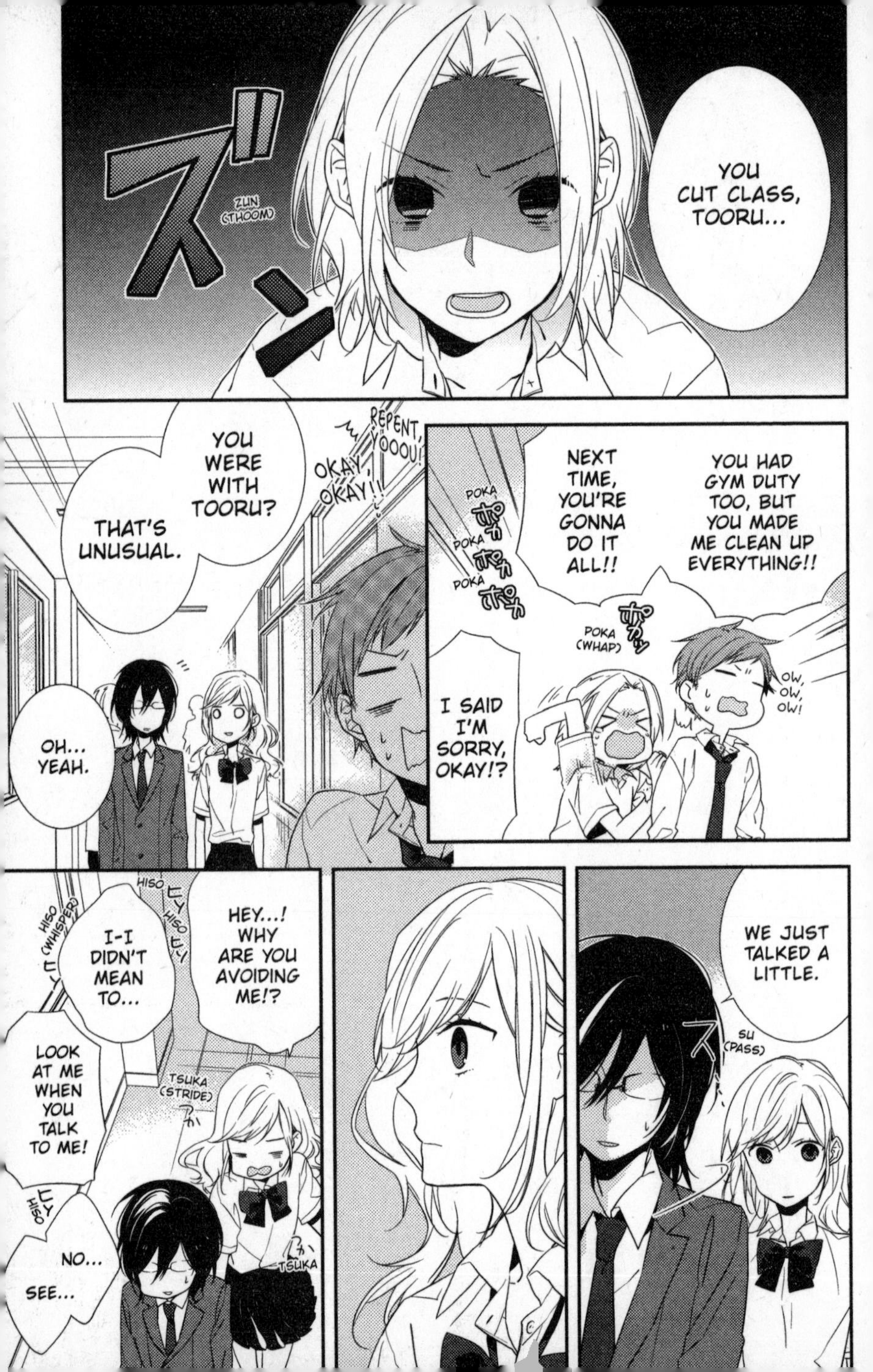
ZUN (THOOM)
YOU CUT CLASS, TOORU...
YOU HAD GYM DUTY TOO, BUT YOU MADE ME CLEAN UP EVERYTHING!!
NEXT TIME, YOU'RE GONNA DO IT ALL!!
POKA
POKA
POKA
POKA (WHAP)
OW, OW, OW!
I SAID I'M SORRY, OKAY!?
REPENT, YOOOU!
OKAY, OKAY!!
YOU WERE WITH TOORU?
THAT'S UNUSUAL.
OH... YEAH.
WE JUST TALKED A LITTLE.
SU (PASS)
HEY...! WHY ARE YOU AVOIDING ME!?
HISO
HISO
I-I DIDN'T MEAN TO...
HISO (WHISPER)
LOOK AT ME WHEN YOU TALK TO ME!
TSUKA (STRIDE)
TSUKA
HISO
NO... SEE...

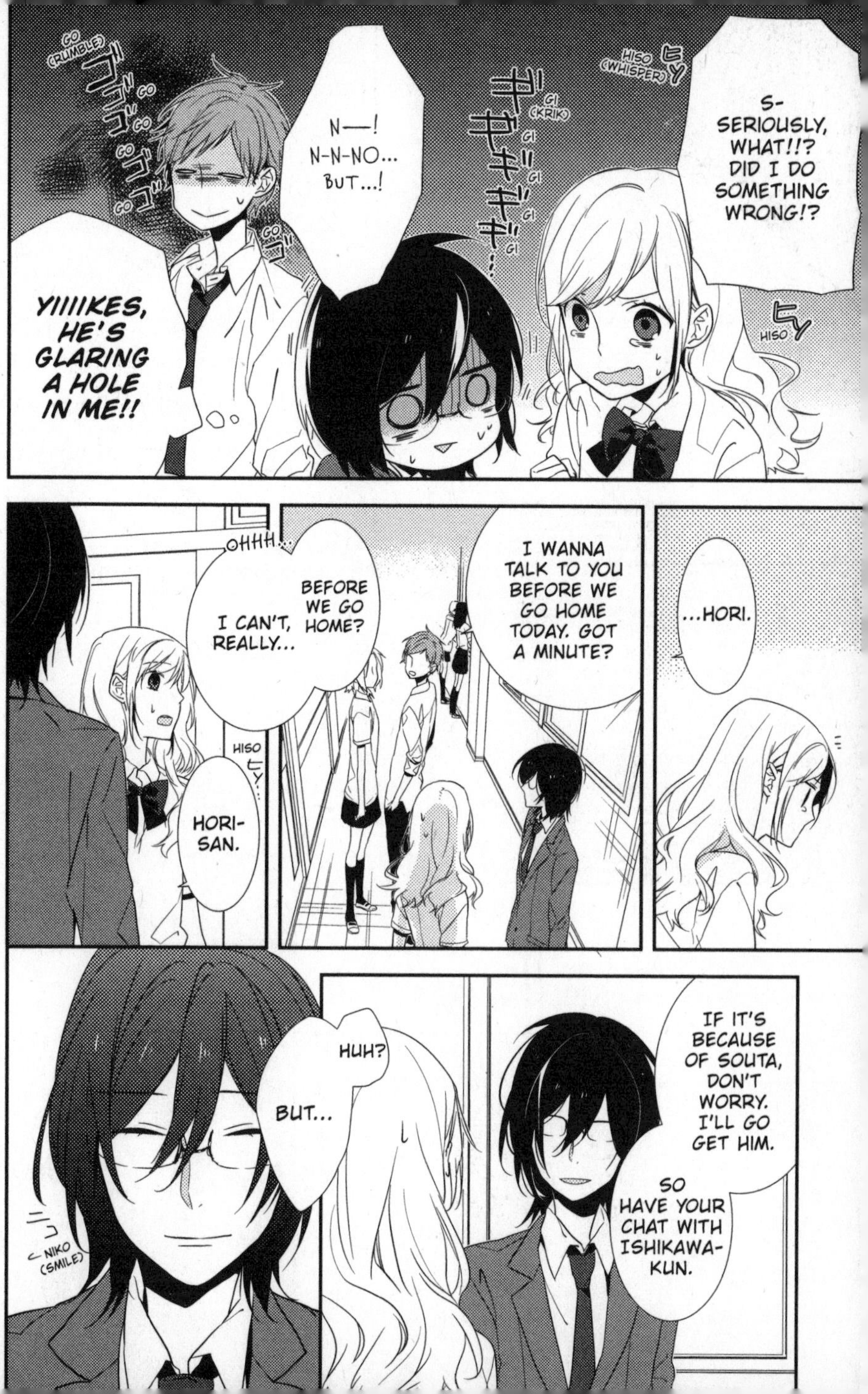
S-SERIOUSLY, WHAT!!? DID I DO SOMETHING WRONG!?
HISO (WHISPER)
HISO
GI (KRIK) GI GI GI GI
N—! N-N-NO... BUT...!
GO (RUMBLE) GO GO GO GO GO
YIIIIKES, HE'S GLARING A HOLE IN ME!!
...HORI.
I WANNA TALK TO YOU BEFORE WE GO HOME TODAY. GOT A MINUTE?
OHHH...
BEFORE WE GO HOME?
I CAN'T, REALLY...
HISO
HORI-SAN.
IF IT'S BECAUSE OF SOUTA, DON'T WORRY. I'LL GO GET HIM.
SO HAVE YOUR CHAT WITH ISHIKAWA-KUN.
HUH?
BUT...
NIKO (SMILE)

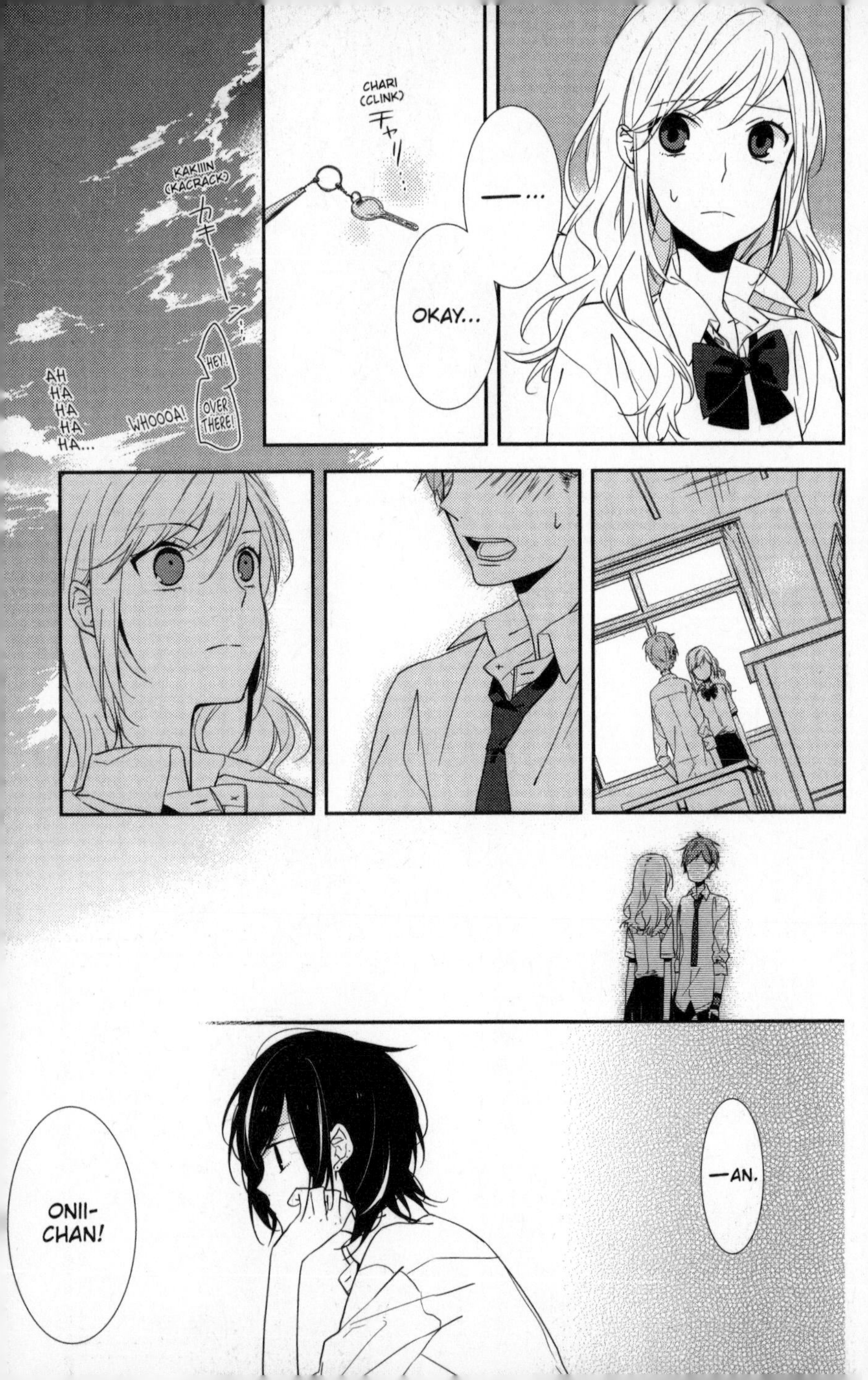
—...
OKAY...
CHARI (CLINK)
チャリ...
KAKIIIN (KACRACK)
カキーン...
HEY! OVER THERE!
WHOOOA!
AH HA HA HA HA...
—AN.
ONII-CHAN!

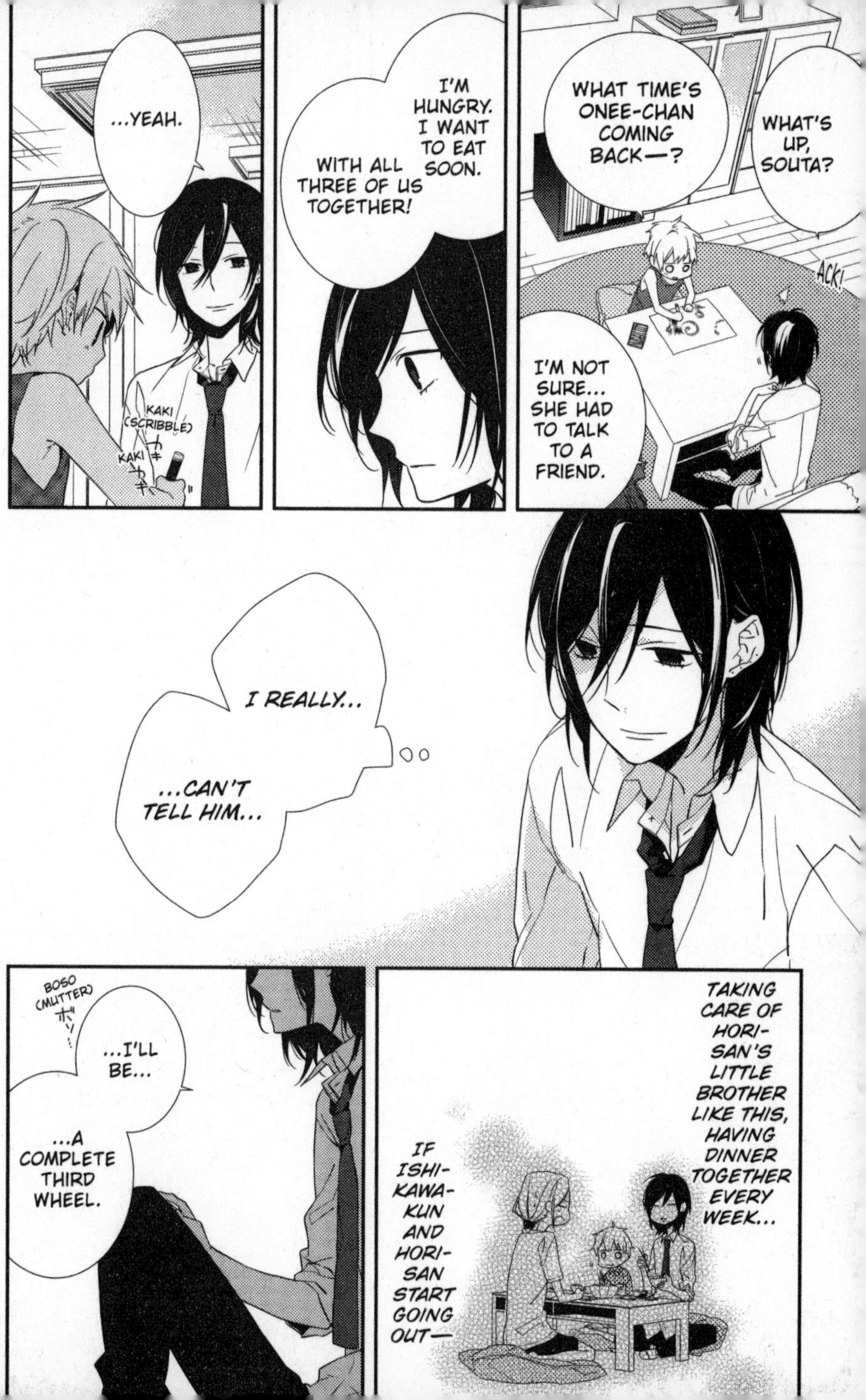
WHAT'S UP, SOUTA?
WHAT TIME'S ONEE-CHAN COMING BACK—?
ACK!
I'M NOT SURE... SHE HAD TO TALK TO A FRIEND.
I'M HUNGRY. I WANT TO EAT SOON.
WITH ALL THREE OF US TOGETHER!
...YEAH.
KAKI (SCRIBBLE)
KAKI
I REALLY...
...CAN'T TELL HIM...
TAKING CARE OF HORI-SAN'S LITTLE BROTHER LIKE THIS, HAVING DINNER TOGETHER EVERY WEEK...
IF ISHI-KAWA-KUN AND HORI-SAN START GOING OUT—
BOSO (MUTTER)
...I'LL BE...
...A COMPLETE THIRD WHEEL.

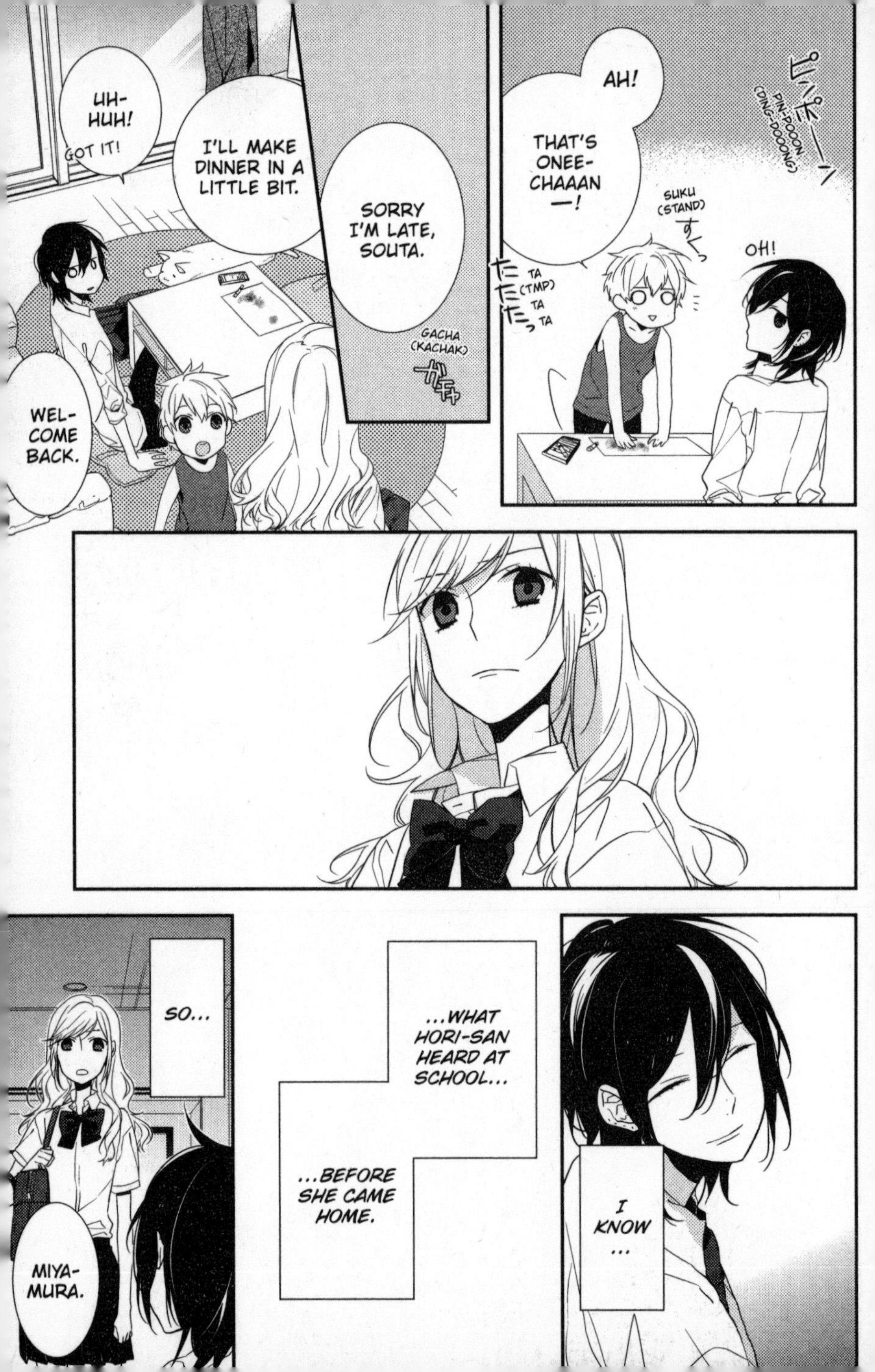
ピンポーン
PIN-POOON (DING-DOOONG)
AH!
THAT'S ONEE-CHAAAN—!
SUKU (STAND)
すくっ
OH!
たたたっ
TA (TMP) TA TA
SORRY I'M LATE, SOUTA.
GACHA (KACHAK)
ガチャ
I'LL MAKE DINNER IN A LITTLE BIT.
UH-HUH! GOT IT!
WEL-COME BACK.
I KNOW ...
...WHAT HORI-SAN HEARD AT SCHOOL...
...BEFORE SHE CAME HOME.
SO...
MIYA-MURA.

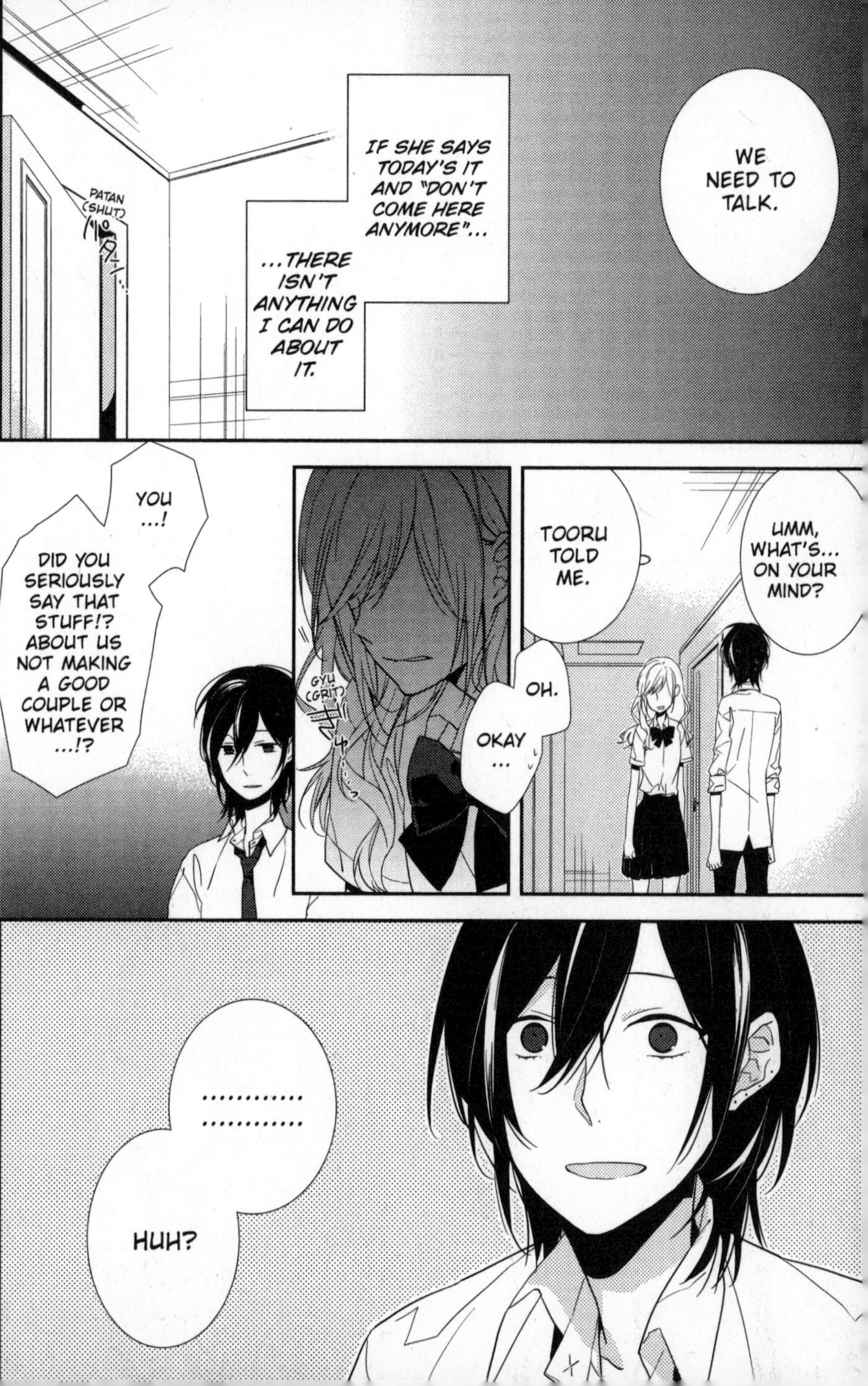
WE NEED TO TALK.
IF SHE SAYS TODAY'S IT AND "DON'T COME HERE ANYMORE"...
...THERE ISN'T ANYTHING I CAN DO ABOUT IT.
PATAN (SHUT)
UMM, WHAT'S... ON YOUR MIND?
TOORU TOLD ME.
OH.
OKAY ...
GYU (GRIT)
YOU ...!
DID YOU SERIOUSLY SAY THAT STUFF!? ABOUT US NOT MAKING A GOOD COUPLE OR WHATEVER ...!?
....
HUH?

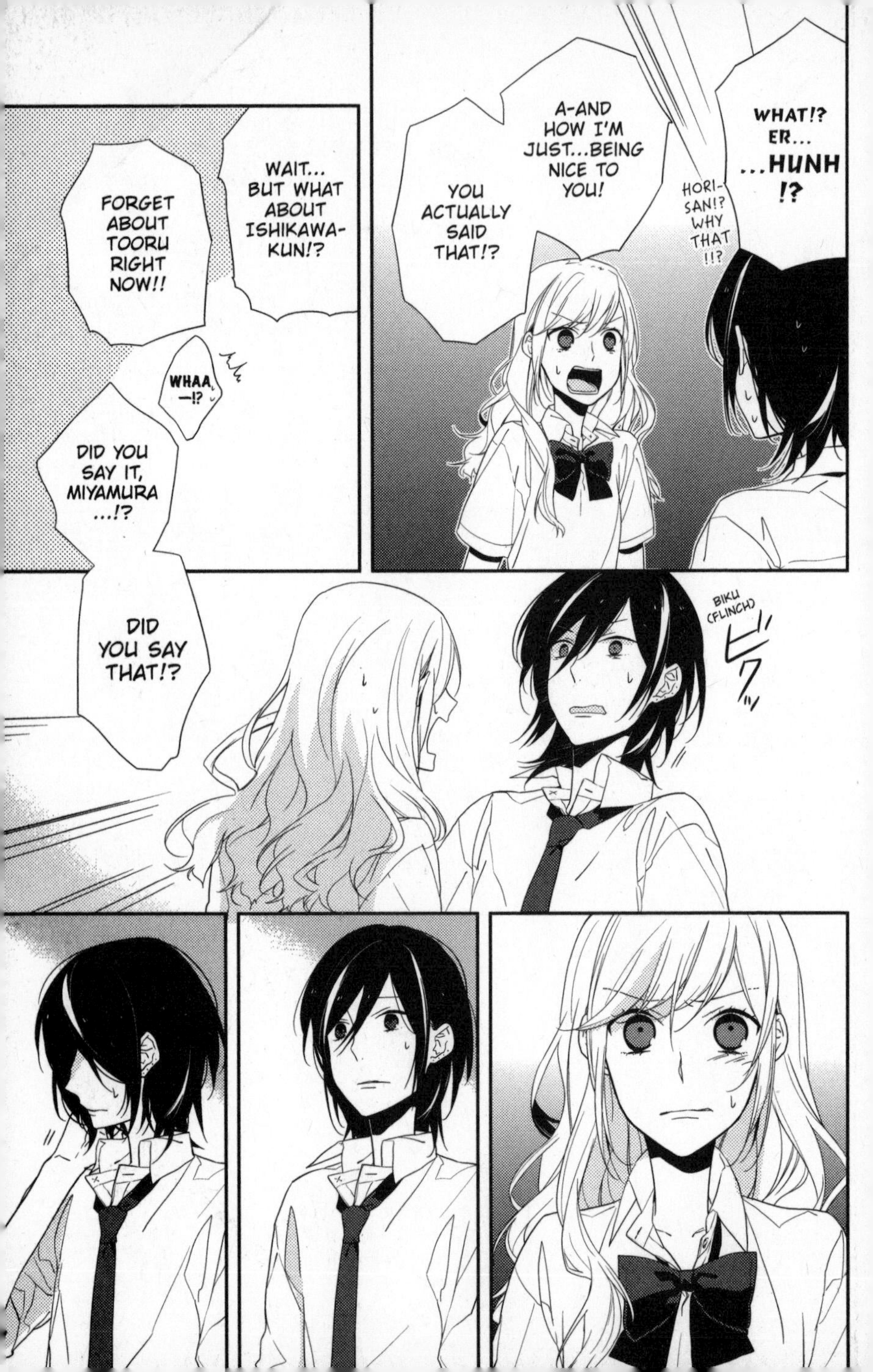
WHAT!? ER... ...HUNH !?
A-AND HOW I'M JUST...BEING NICE TO YOU!
HORI-SAN!? WHY THAT !!?
YOU ACTUALLY SAID THAT!?
WAIT... BUT WHAT ABOUT ISHIKAWA-KUN!?
FORGET ABOUT TOORU RIGHT NOW!!
WHAA —!?
DID YOU SAY IT, MIYAMURA ...!?
BIKU (FLINCH)
DID YOU SAY THAT!?

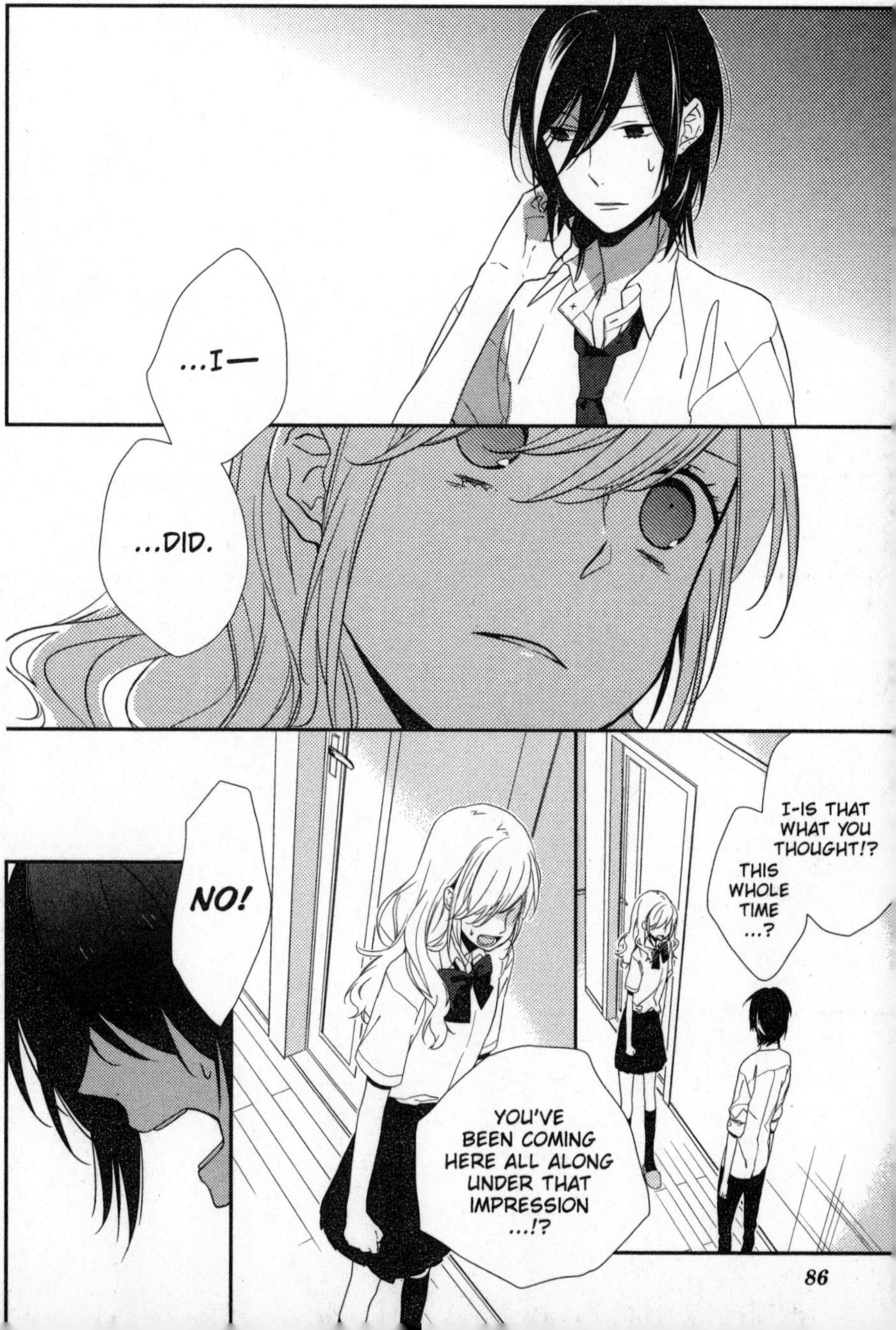
...I—
...DID.
I-IS THAT WHAT YOU THOUGHT!? THIS WHOLE TIME ...?
YOU'VE BEEN COMING HERE ALL ALONG UNDER THAT IMPRESSION ...!?
NO!

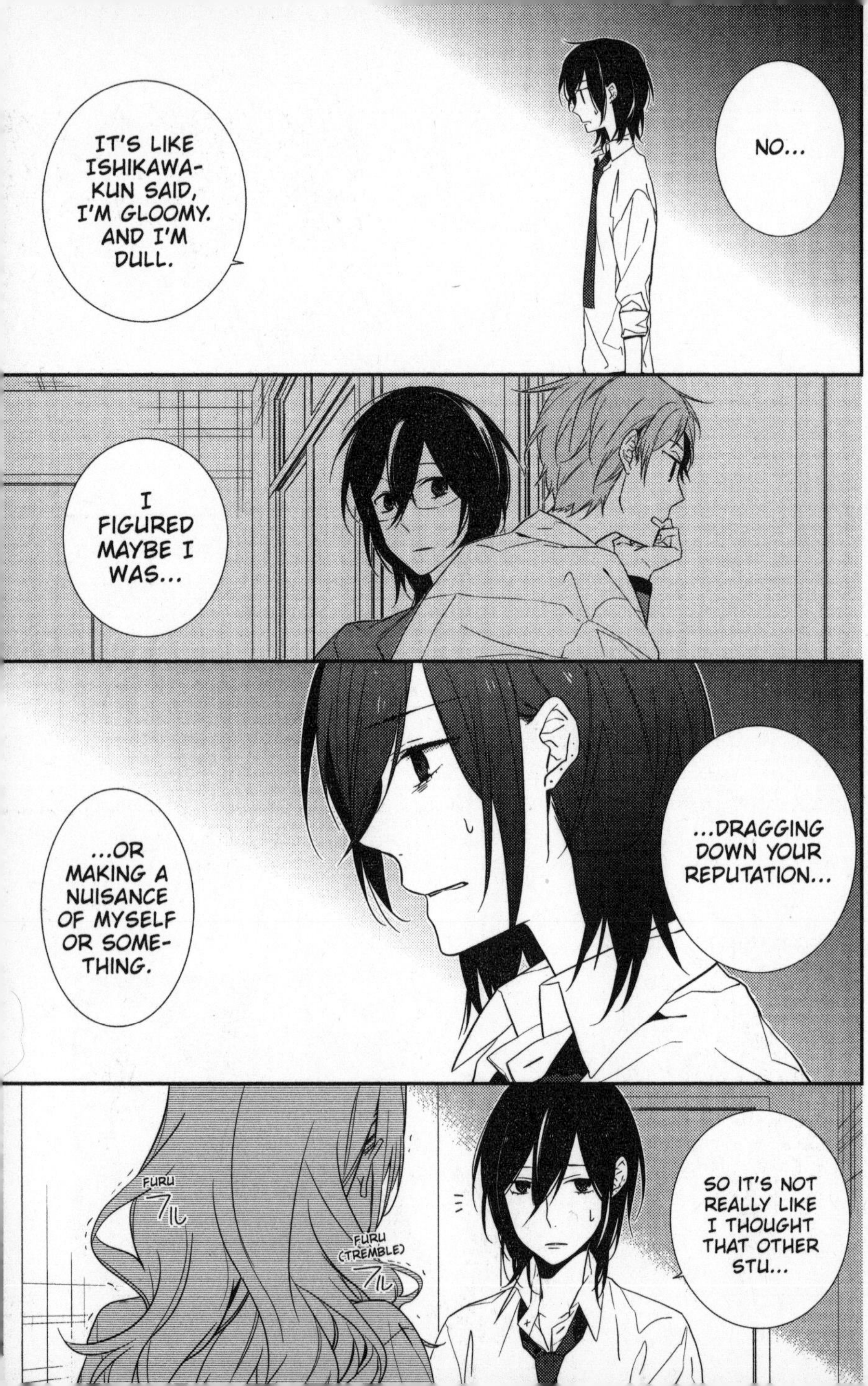
NO...
IT'S LIKE ISHIKAWA-KUN SAID, I'M GLOOMY. AND I'M DULL.
I FIGURED MAYBE I WAS...
...DRAGGING DOWN YOUR REPUTATION...
...OR MAKING A NUISANCE OF MYSELF OR SOME-THING.
SO IT'S NOT REALLY LIKE I THOUGHT THAT OTHER STU...
FURU (TREMBLE) フル
FURU フル

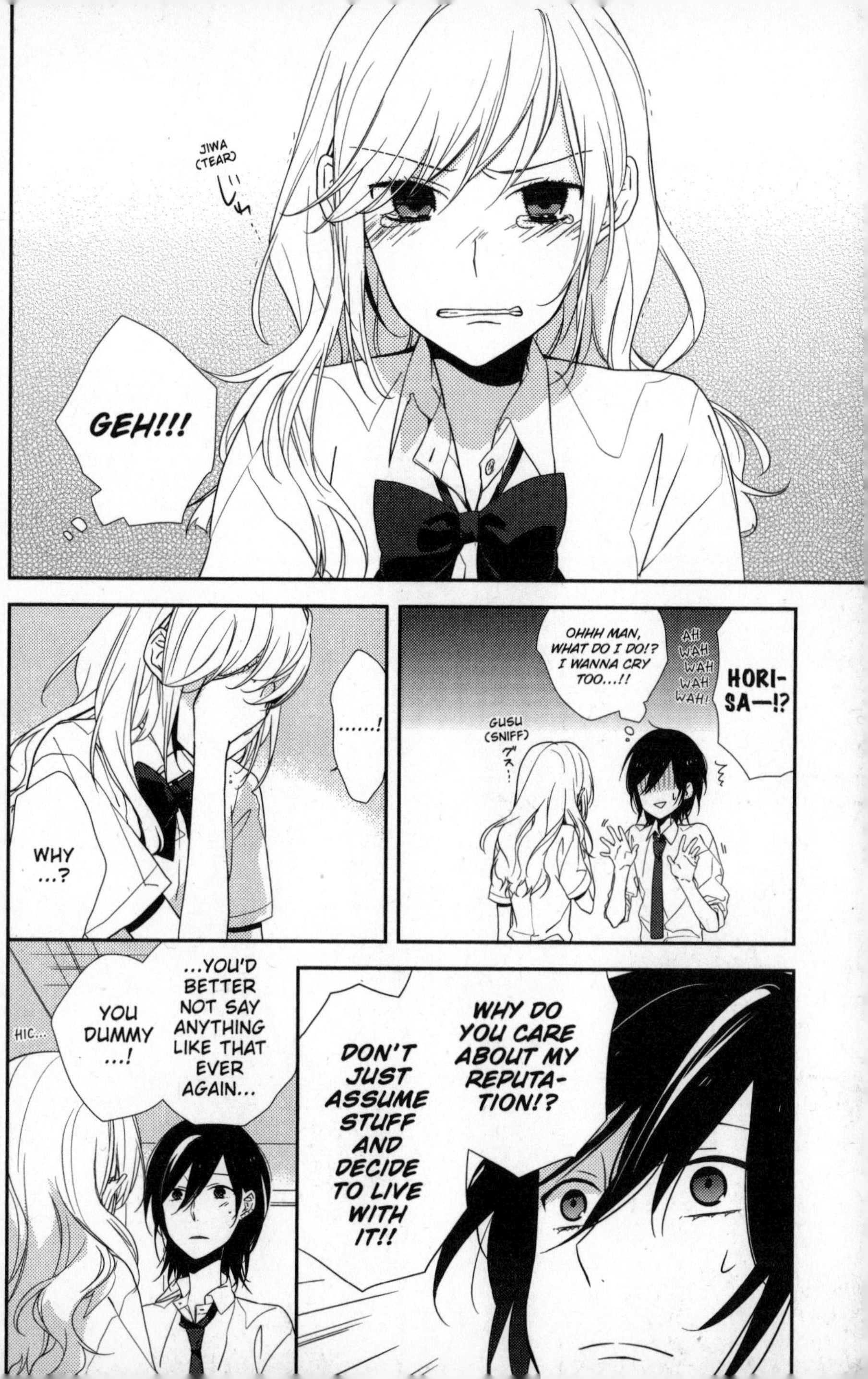
JIWA (TEAR)
じわ…
GEH!!!
HORI-SA—!?
AH WAH WAH WAH WAH!
OHHH MAN, WHAT DO I DO!? I WANNA CRY TOO...!!
GUSU (SNIFF)
グス…
......!
WHY ...?
WHY DO YOU CARE ABOUT MY REPUTATION!?
DON'T JUST ASSUME STUFF AND DECIDE TO LIVE WITH IT!!
...YOU'D BETTER NOT SAY ANYTHING LIKE THAT EVER AGAIN...
YOU DUMMY ...!
HIC...

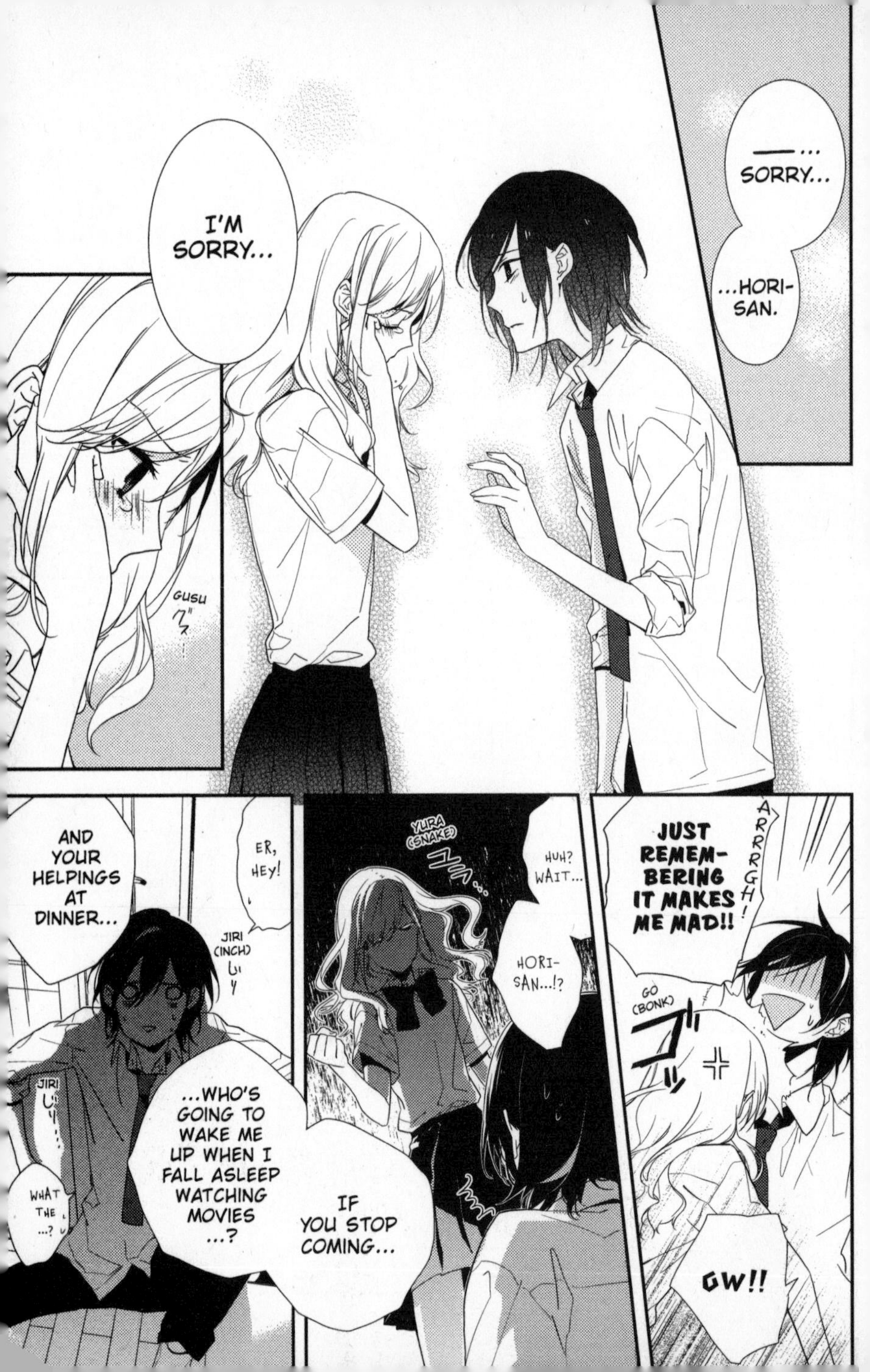
——... SORRY...
...HORI-SAN.
I'M SORRY...
GUSU
ARRRGH!
JUST REMEMBERING IT MAKES ME MAD!!
GO (BONK)
GW!!
YURA (SNAKE)
HUH? WAIT...
HORI-SAN...!?
ER, HEY!
AND YOUR HELPINGS AT DINNER...
JIRI (INCH)
JIRI
...WHO'S GOING TO WAKE ME UP WHEN I FALL ASLEEP WATCHING MOVIES ...?
IF YOU STOP COMING...
WHAT THE ...?

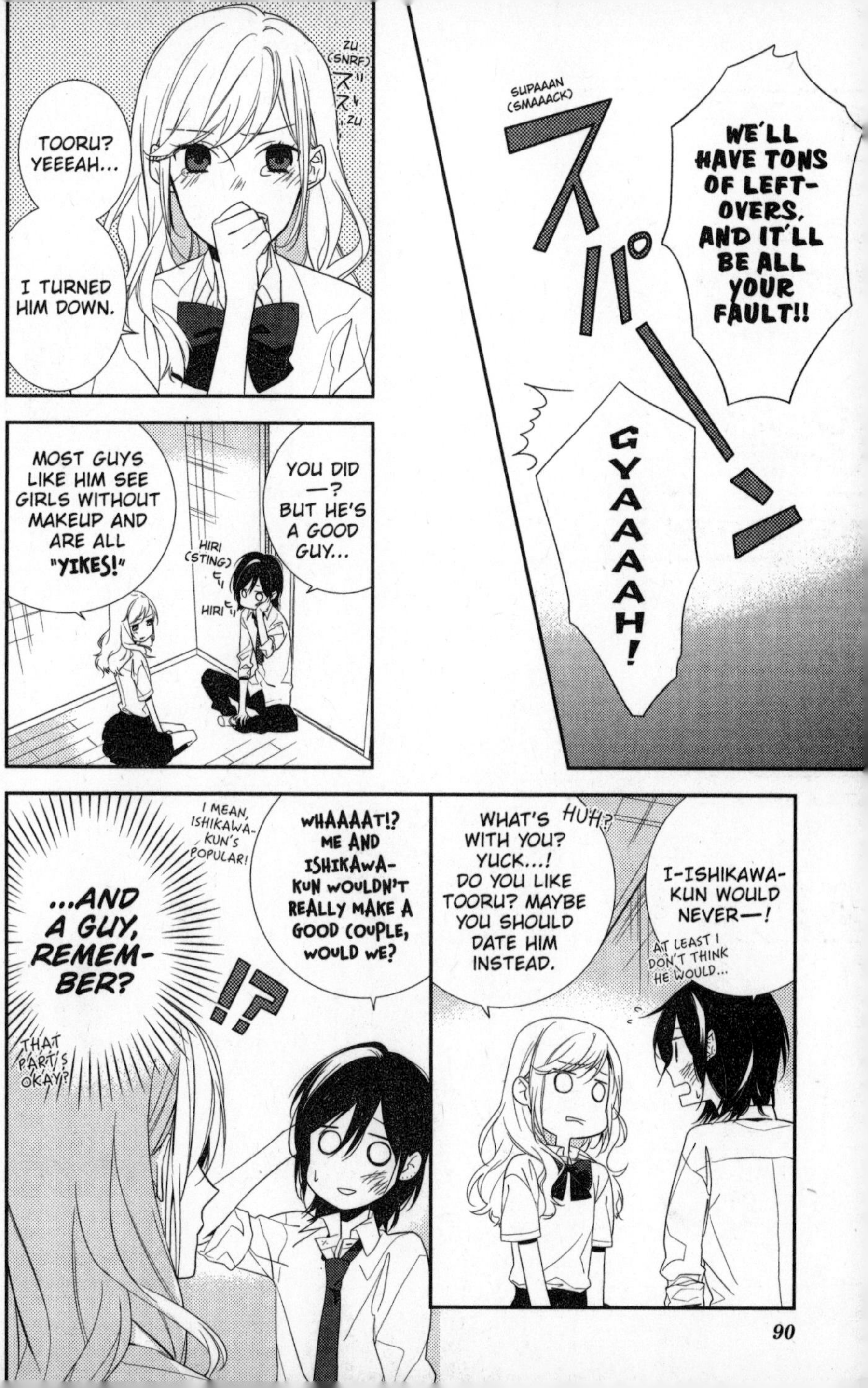
WE'LL HAVE TONS OF LEFT-OVERS, AND IT'LL BE ALL YOUR FAULT!!
SUPAAAN (SMAAACK)
GYAAAAH!
ZU (SNRF) ZU
TOORU? YEEEAH...
I TURNED HIM DOWN.
YOU DID—? BUT HE'S A GOOD GUY...
HIRI (STING) HIRI
MOST GUYS LIKE HIM SEE GIRLS WITHOUT MAKEUP AND ARE ALL "YIKES!"
I-ISHIKAWA-KUN WOULD NEVER—!
AT LEAST I DON'T THINK HE WOULD...
HUH?
WHAT'S WITH YOU? YUCK...! DO YOU LIKE TOORU? MAYBE YOU SHOULD DATE HIM INSTEAD.
WHAAAAT!? ME AND ISHIKAWA-KUN WOULDN'T REALLY MAKE A GOOD COUPLE, WOULD WE?
I MEAN, ISHIKAWA-KUN'S POPULAR!
!?
...AND A GUY, REMEMBER?
THAT PART'S OKAY?

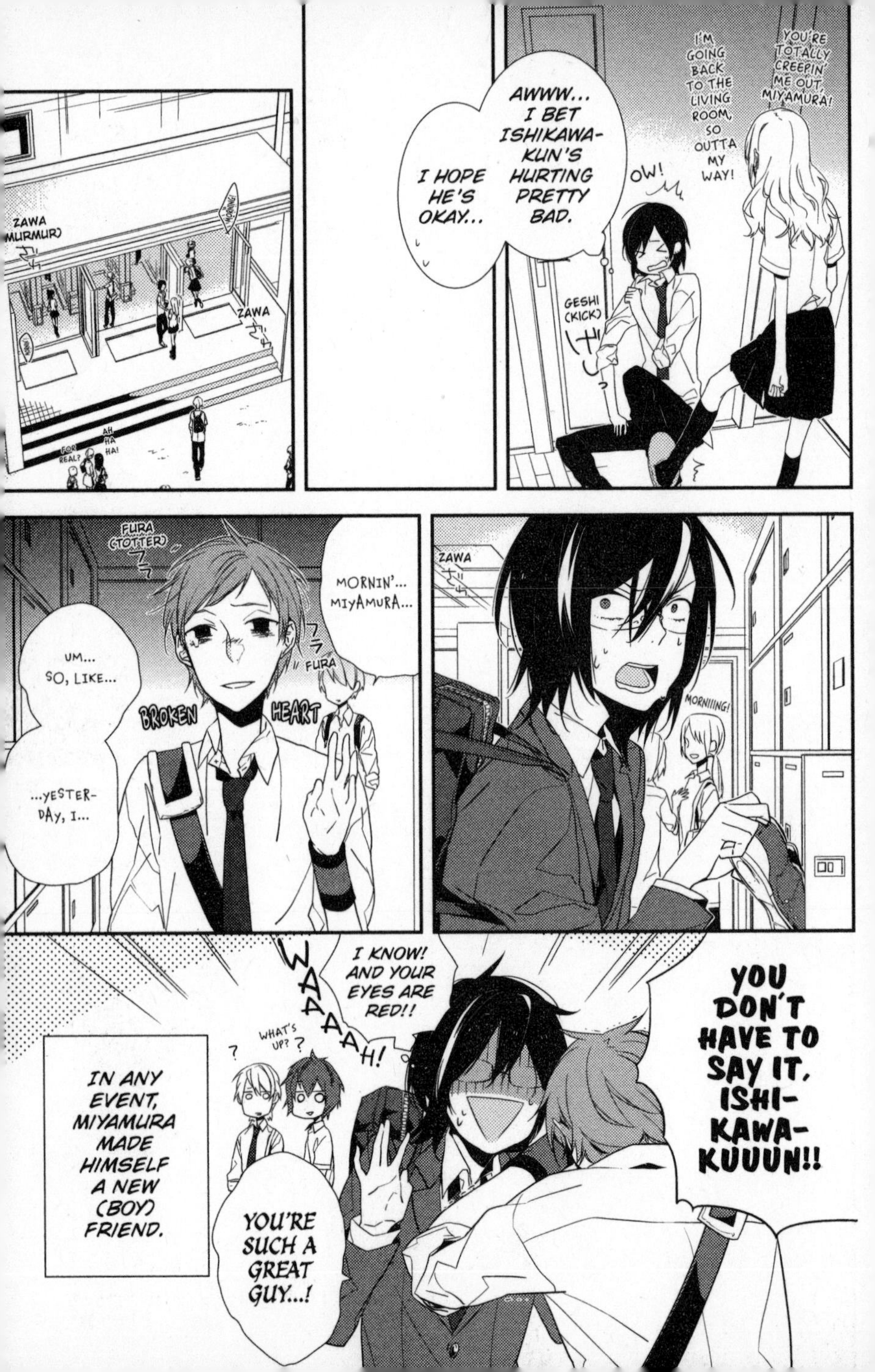
YOU'RE TOTALLY CREEPIN' ME OUT, MIYAMURA!
I'M GOING BACK TO THE LIVING ROOM, SO OUTTA MY WAY!
OW!
GESHI (KICK)
AWWW... I BET ISHIKAWA-KUN'S HURTING PRETTY BAD.
I HOPE HE'S OKAY...
MORNIN'!
ZAWA (MURMUR)
ZAWA
AH HA HA!
FOR REAL?
ZAWA
MORNIIING!
FURA (TOTTER)
MORNIN'... MIYAMURA...
FURA
UM... SO, LIKE...
BROKEN HEART
...YESTER-DAY, I...
YOU DON'T HAVE TO SAY IT, ISHI-KAWA-KUUUN!!
I KNOW! AND YOUR EYES ARE RED!!
WAAAAAH!
WHAT'S UP?
?
?
YOU'RE SUCH A GREAT GUY...!
IN ANY EVENT, MIYAMURA MADE HIMSELF A NEW (BOY) FRIEND.

HORIMIYA

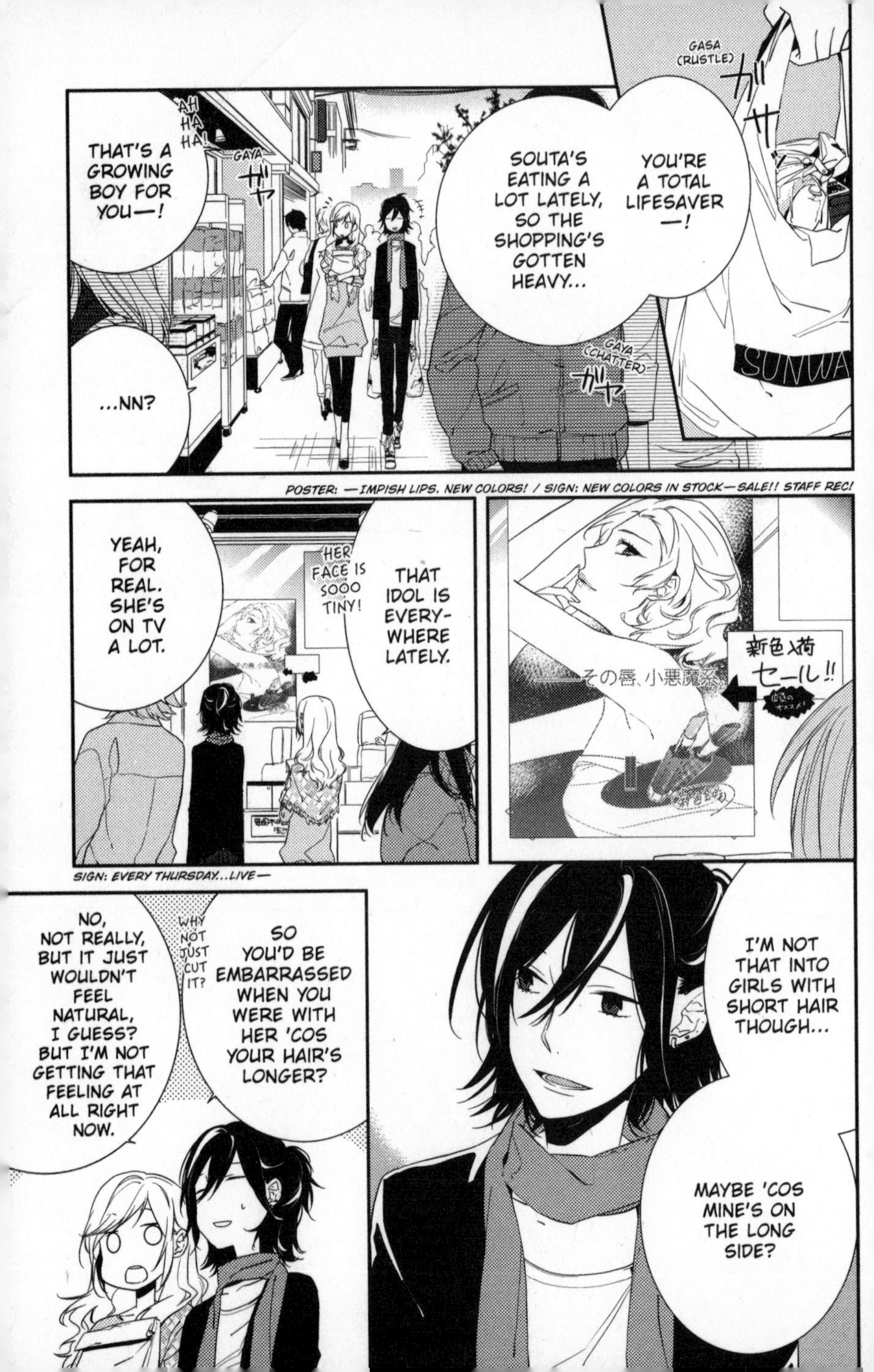
GASA (RUSTLE)
YOU'RE A TOTAL LIFESAVER—!
SOUTA'S EATING A LOT LATELY, SO THE SHOPPING'S GOTTEN HEAVY...
GAYA (CHATTER)
AH HA HA!
GAYA
THAT'S A GROWING BOY FOR YOU—!
...NN?
新色入荷 セール!!
店員のオススメ!
——その唇、小悪魔系
HER FACE IS SOOO TINY!
THAT IDOL IS EVERYWHERE LATELY.
YEAH, FOR REAL. SHE'S ON TV A LOT.
I'M NOT THAT INTO GIRLS WITH SHORT HAIR THOUGH...
MAYBE 'COS MINE'S ON THE LONG SIDE?
SO YOU'D BE EMBARRASSED WHEN YOU WERE WITH HER 'COS YOUR HAIR'S LONGER?
WHY NOT JUST CUT IT?
NO, NOT REALLY, BUT IT JUST WOULDN'T FEEL NATURAL, I GUESS? BUT I'M NOT GETTING THAT FEELING AT ALL RIGHT NOW.

POSTER: —IMPISH LIPS. NEW COLORS! / SIGN: NEW COLORS IN STOCK—SALE!! STAFF REC!

SIGN: EVERY THURSDAY...LIVE—

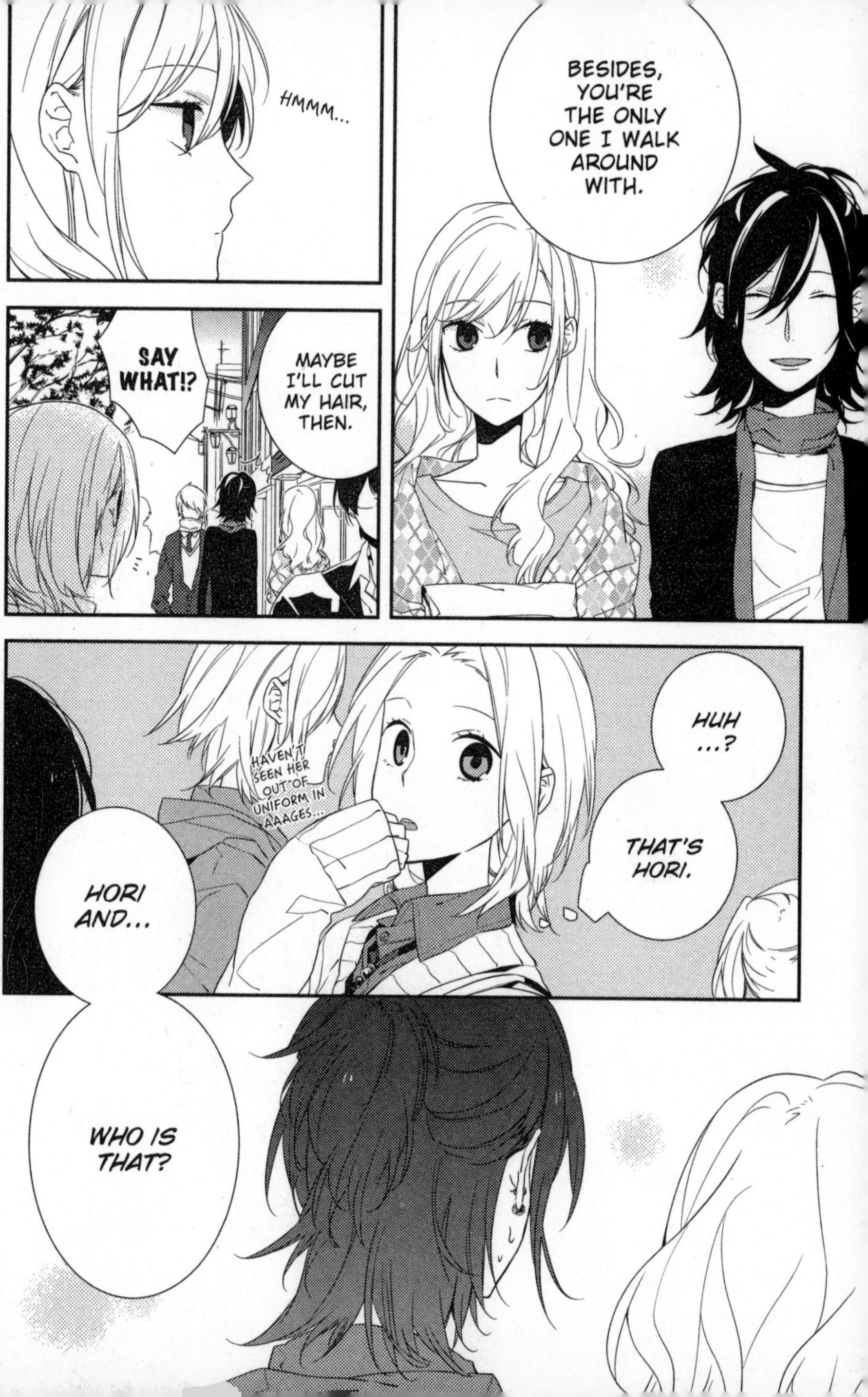
BESIDES, YOU'RE THE ONLY ONE I WALK AROUND WITH.
HMMM...
MAYBE I'LL CUT MY HAIR, THEN.
SAY WHAT!?
HUH ...?
THAT'S HORI.
HAVEN'T SEEN HER OUT OF UNIFORM IN AAAGES...
HORI AND...
WHO IS THAT?

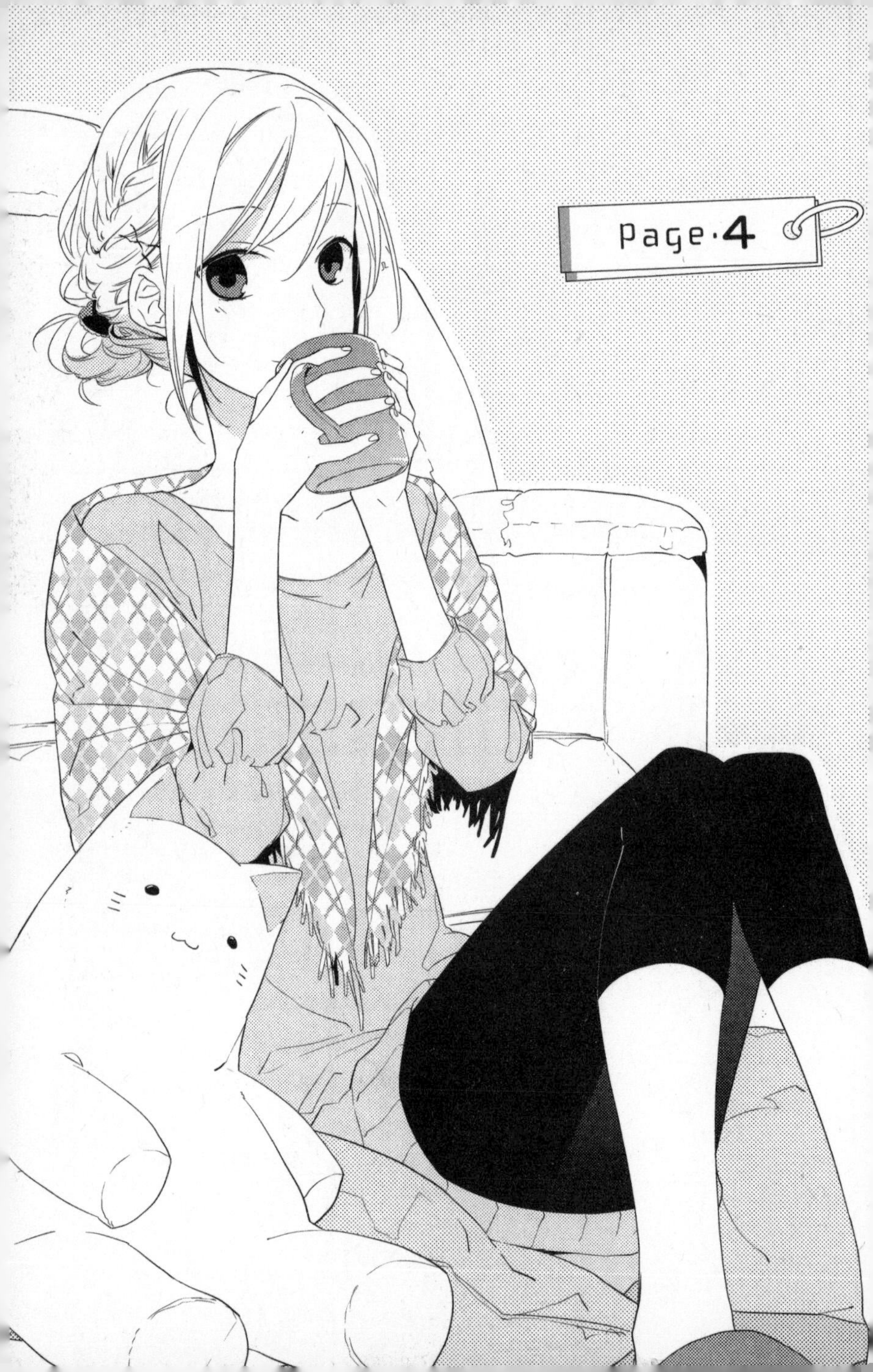
page·4

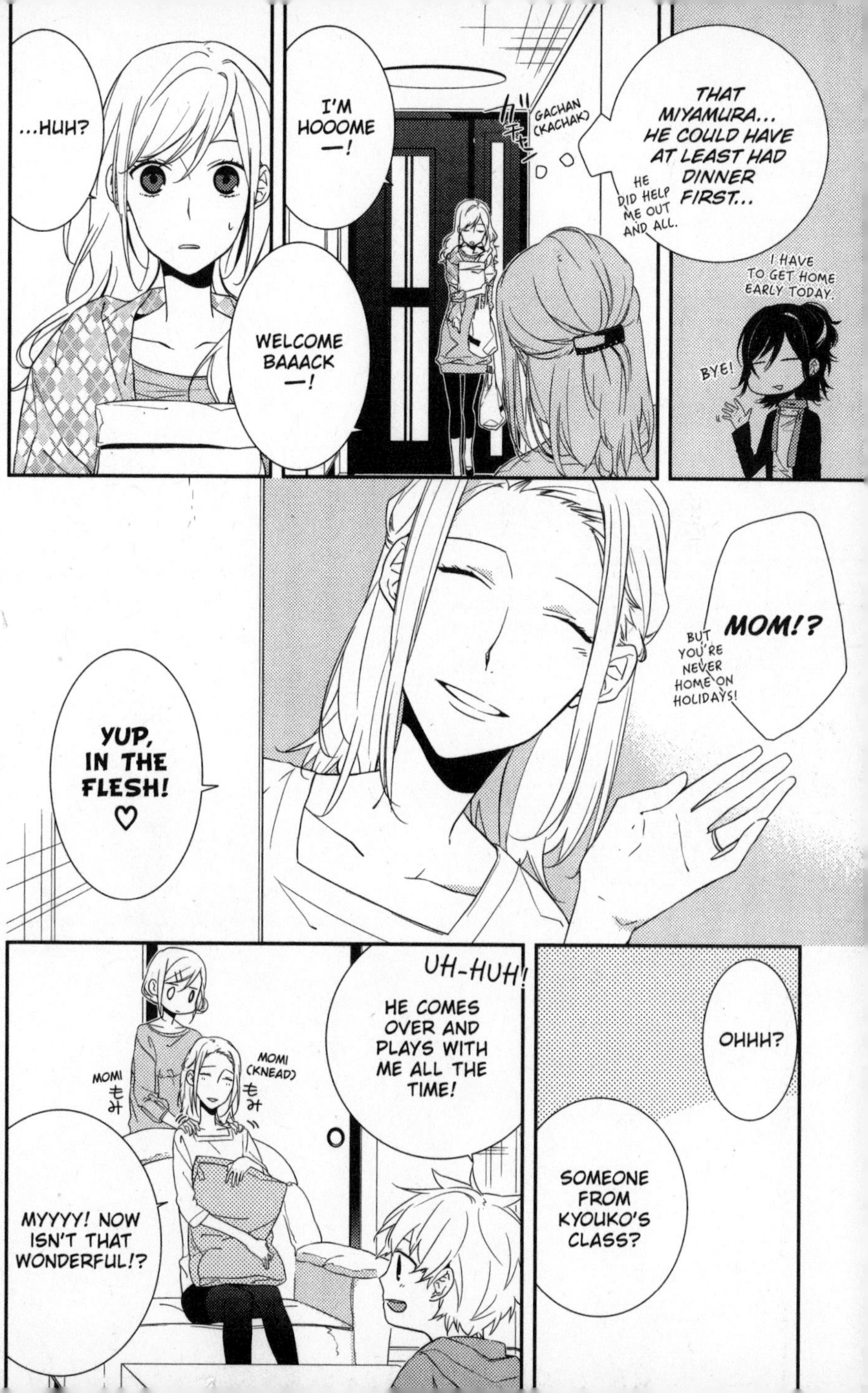
THAT MIYAMURA... HE COULD HAVE AT LEAST HAD DINNER FIRST...
HE DID HELP ME OUT AND ALL.
I HAVE TO GET HOME EARLY TODAY.
BYE!
カチャン
GACHAN (KACHAK)
I'M HOOOME—!
WELCOME BAAACK—!
...HUH?
MOM!?
BUT YOU'RE NEVER HOME ON HOLIDAYS!
YUP, IN THE FLESH! ♡
OHHH?
SOMEONE FROM KYOUKO'S CLASS?
UH-HUH!
HE COMES OVER AND PLAYS WITH ME ALL THE TIME!
もみ
MOMI (KNEAD)
もみ
MOMI
MYYYY! NOW ISN'T THAT WONDERFUL!?

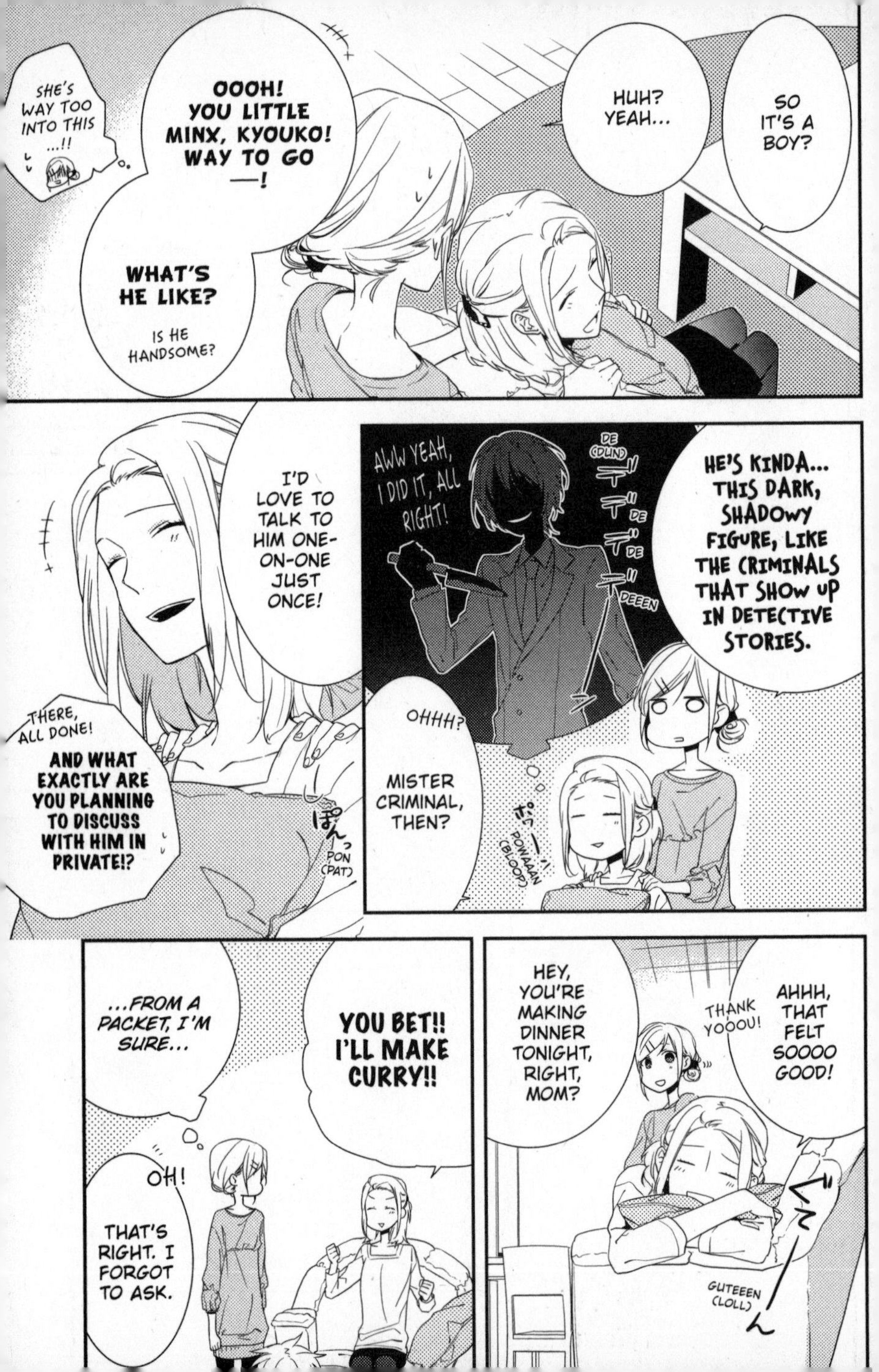
SO IT'S A BOY?
HUH? YEAH...
OOOH! YOU LITTLE MINX, KYOUKO! WAY TO GO—!
SHE'S WAY TOO INTO THIS ...!!
WHAT'S HE LIKE?
IS HE HANDSOME?
HE'S KINDA... THIS DARK, SHADOWY FIGURE, LIKE THE CRIMINALS THAT SHOW UP IN DETECTIVE STORIES.
DE (DUN) DE DE DEEEN
AWW YEAH, I DID IT, ALL RIGHT!
OHHH?
MISTER CRIMINAL, THEN?
POWAAAN (BLOOP)
I'D LOVE TO TALK TO HIM ONE-ON-ONE JUST ONCE!
PON (PAT)
THERE, ALL DONE!
AND WHAT EXACTLY ARE YOU PLANNING TO DISCUSS WITH HIM IN PRIVATE!?
AHHH, THAT FELT SOOOO GOOD!
THANK YOOOU!
HEY, YOU'RE MAKING DINNER TONIGHT, RIGHT, MOM?
GUTEEEN (LOLL)
YOU BET!! I'LL MAKE CURRY!!
...FROM A PACKET, I'M SURE...
OH!
THAT'S RIGHT. I FORGOT TO ASK.

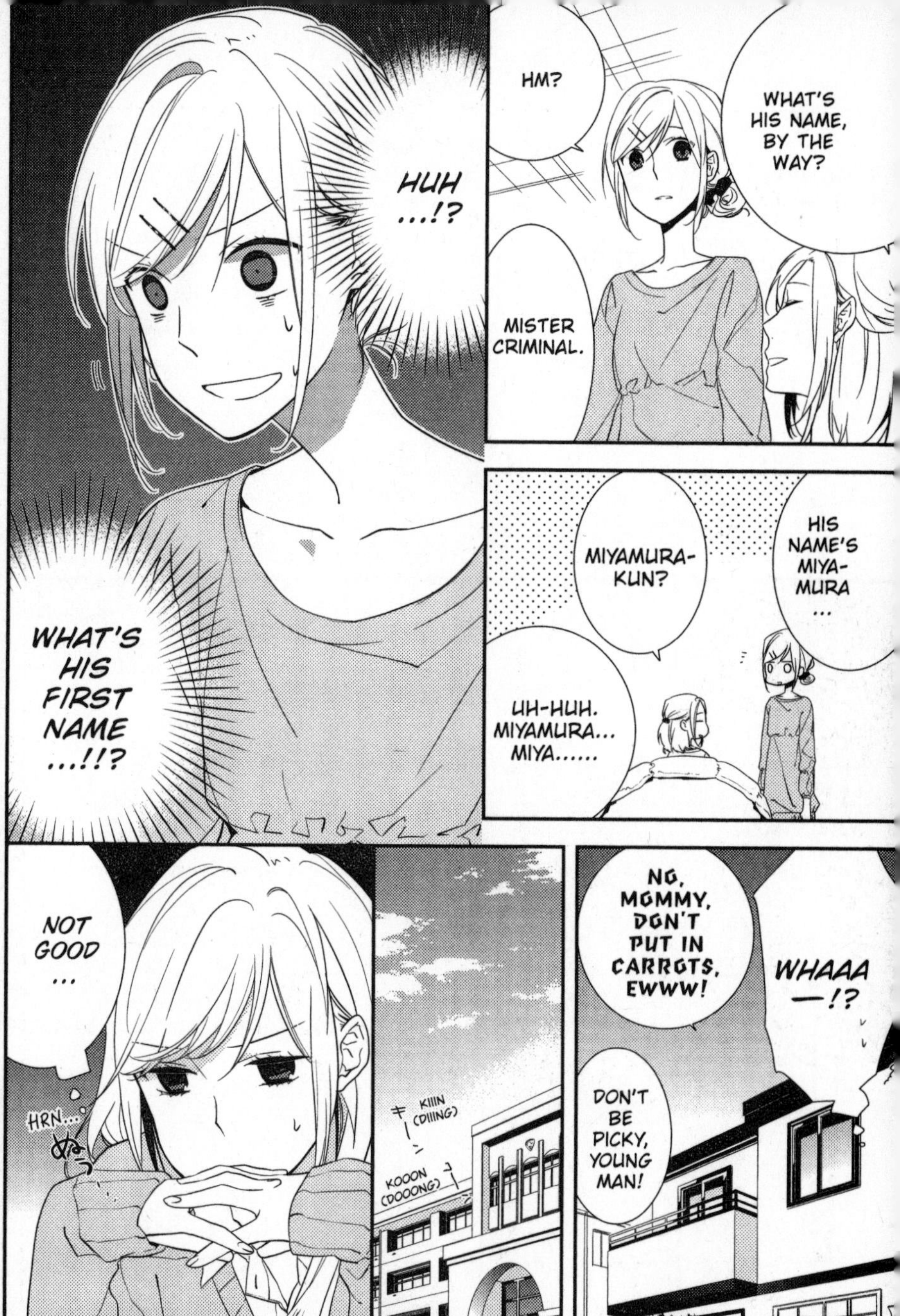
WHAT'S HIS NAME, BY THE WAY?
HM?
MISTER CRIMINAL.
HIS NAME'S MIYA-MURA ...
MIYAMURA-KUN?
UH-HUH. MIYAMURA... MIYA......
HUH ...!?
WHAT'S HIS FIRST NAME ...!!?
WHAAA —!?
NO, MOMMY, DON'T PUT IN CARROTS, EWWW!
DON'T BE PICKY, YOUNG MAN!
KIIIN (DIIING)
KOOON (DOOONG)
NOT GOOD ...
HRN...

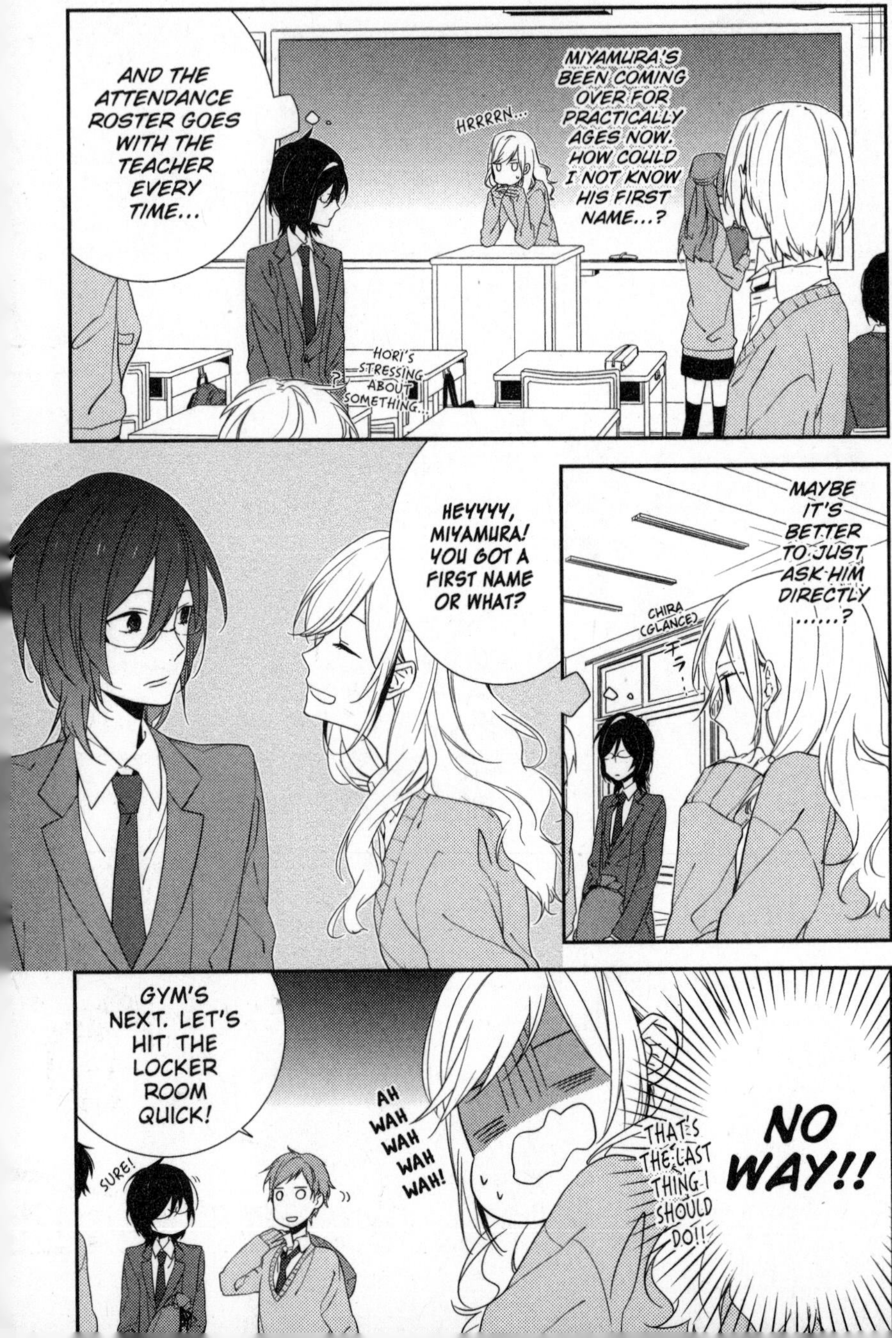
MIYAMURA'S BEEN COMING OVER FOR PRACTICALLY AGES NOW. HOW COULD I NOT KNOW HIS FIRST NAME...?
HRRRRN...
AND THE ATTENDANCE ROSTER GOES WITH THE TEACHER EVERY TIME...
HORI'S STRESSING ABOUT SOMETHING...
MAYBE IT'S BETTER TO JUST ASK HIM DIRECTLY......?
CHIRA (GLANCE)
HEYYYY, MIYAMURA! YOU GOT A FIRST NAME OR WHAT?
NO WAY!!
THAT'S THE LAST THING I SHOULD DO!!
AH WAH WAH WAH WAH!
GYM'S NEXT. LET'S HIT THE LOCKER ROOM QUICK!
SURE!

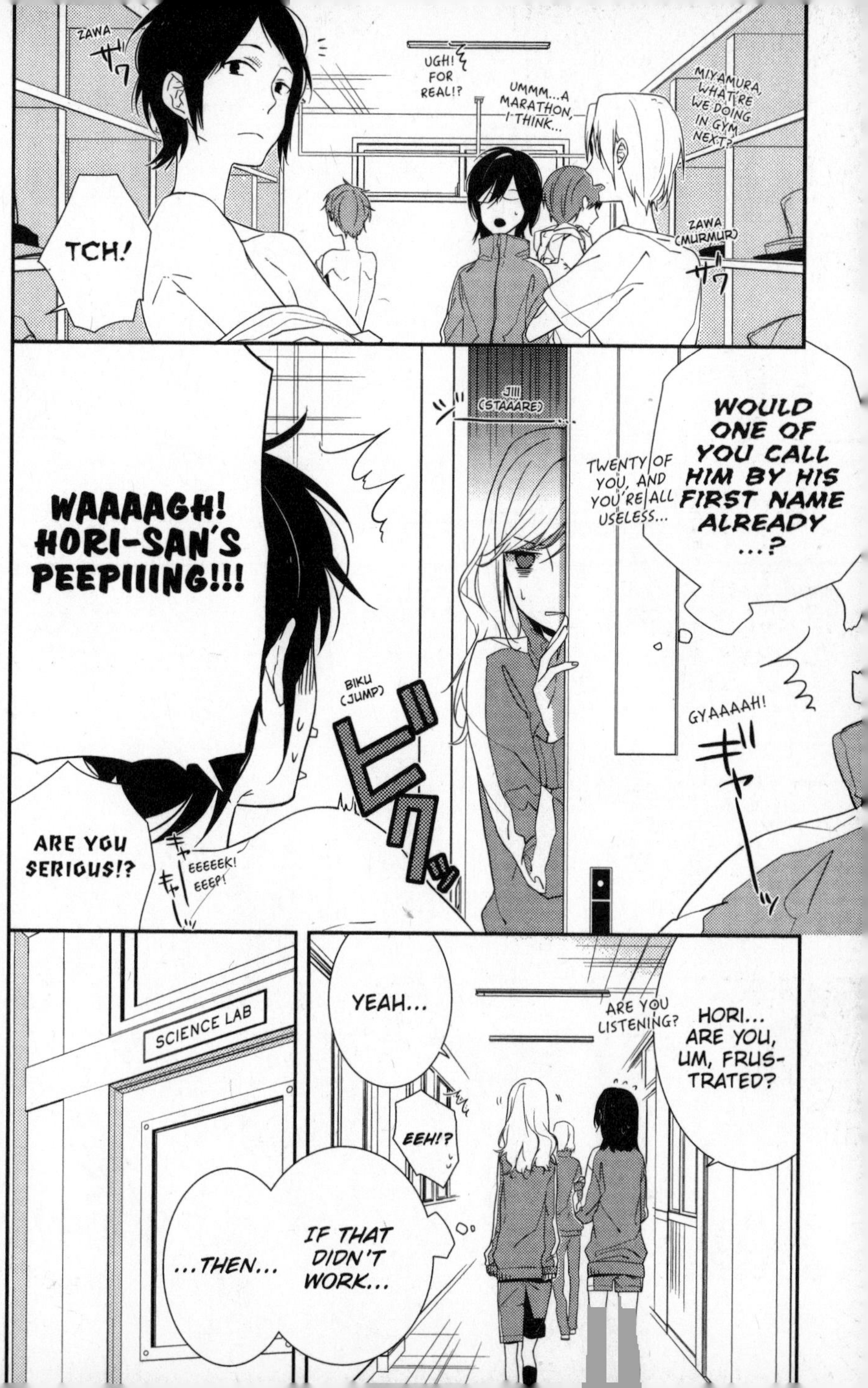
MIYAMURA, WHAT'RE WE DOING IN GYM NEXT?
UMMM...A MARATHON, I THINK...
UGH! FOR REAL!?
ZAWA (MURMUR)
ZAWA
TCH!
WOULD ONE OF YOU CALL HIM BY HIS FIRST NAME ALREADY...?
TWENTY OF YOU, AND YOU'RE ALL USELESS...
JIII (STAAARE)
GYAAAAH!
WAAAAGH! HORI-SAN'S PEEPIIING!!!
BIKU (JUMP)
ARE YOU SERIOUS!?
EEEEEK! EEEP!
HORI... ARE YOU, UM, FRUS-TRATED?
ARE YOU LISTENING?
YEAH...
EEH!?
IF THAT DIDN'T WORK...
...THEN...
SCIENCE LAB

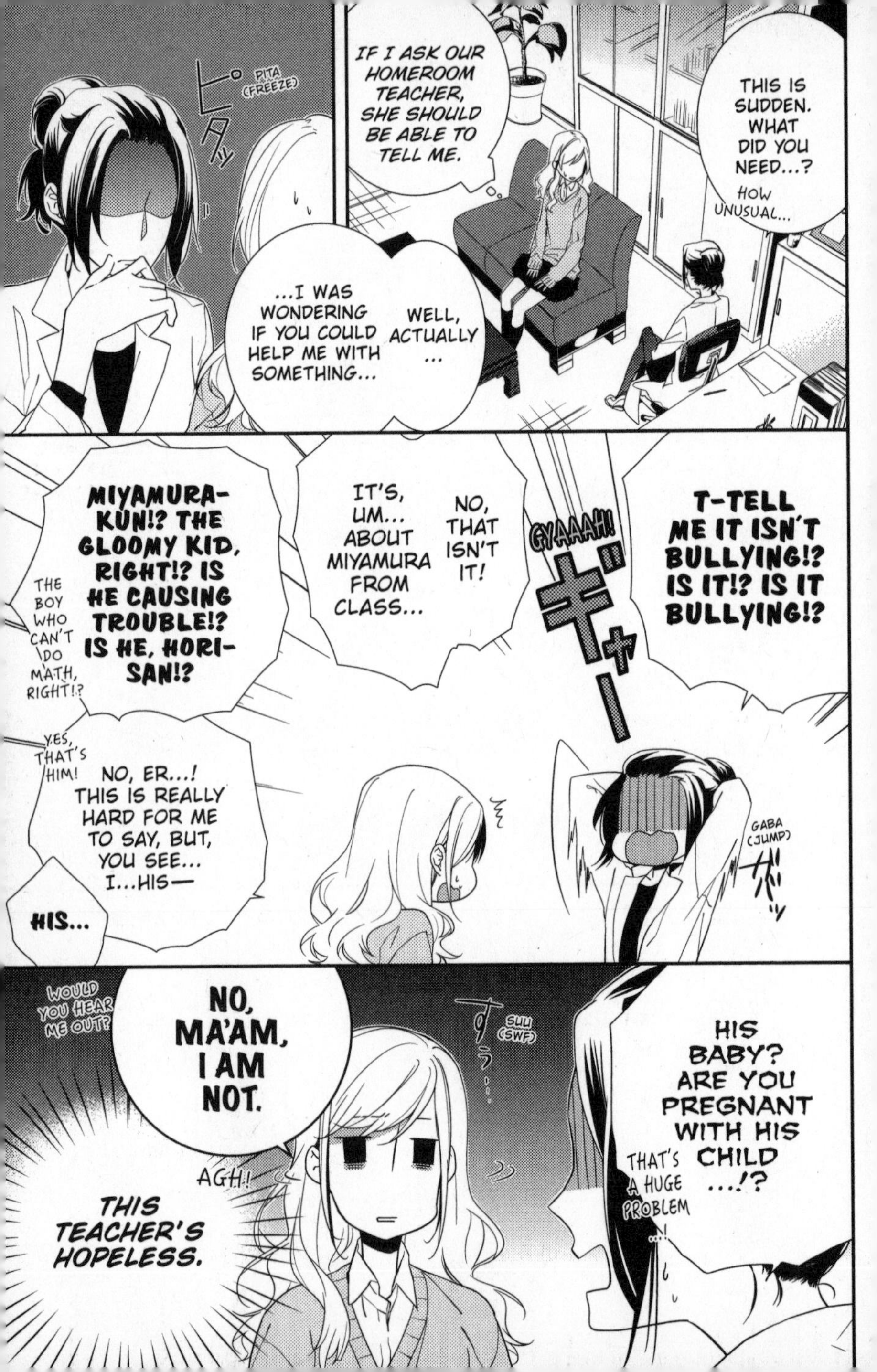
THIS IS SUDDEN. WHAT DID YOU NEED...?
HOW UNUSUAL...
IF I ASK OUR HOMEROOM TEACHER, SHE SHOULD BE ABLE TO TELL ME.
WELL, ACTUALLY...
...I WAS WONDERING IF YOU COULD HELP ME WITH SOMETHING...
PITA (FREEZE)
T-TELL ME IT ISN'T BULLYING!? IS IT!? IS IT BULLYING!?
GYAAAH!
NO, THAT ISN'T IT!
IT'S, UM... ABOUT MIYAMURA FROM CLASS...
MIYAMURA-KUN!? THE GLOOMY KID, RIGHT!? IS HE CAUSING TROUBLE!? IS HE, HORI-SAN!?
THE BOY WHO CAN'T DO MATH, RIGHT!?
GABA (JUMP)
YES, THAT'S HIM!
NO, ER...! THIS IS REALLY HARD FOR ME TO SAY, BUT, YOU SEE... I...HIS—
HIS...
HIS BABY? ARE YOU PREGNANT WITH HIS CHILD...!?
THAT'S A HUGE PROBLEM...!
SUU (SWF)
NO, MA'AM, I AM NOT.
WOULD YOU HEAR ME OUT?
AGH!
THIS TEACHER'S HOPELESS.

HORI? HEADING HOME ALREADY?

YORO (TOTTER)

I NEVER THOUGHT FINDING OUT A SINGLE NAME COULD BE THIS EXHAUSTING...

I WANTED TO ASK YOU SOMETHING ABOUT MIYAMU...

TOORU...! GREAT TIMING.

HEY...!

DA (DASH)

REJECTED → HIM

USELESS!!

MY HEART IS CURRENTLY BROKEN!!!

BWAH!

GOT → REJECTED

DON (BUMP)

SOMETHIN' ON YOUR MIND!?

IF ONLY HE WAS SMART...!

IF...

HIGH

	CLASS	NAME
1	3	SENGO
2	4	TACHI
3	6	KOBAY
4	1	SATOU
5	2	ISHIDA
6	4	KURO
7	1	HORI,
8	5	YAMAD

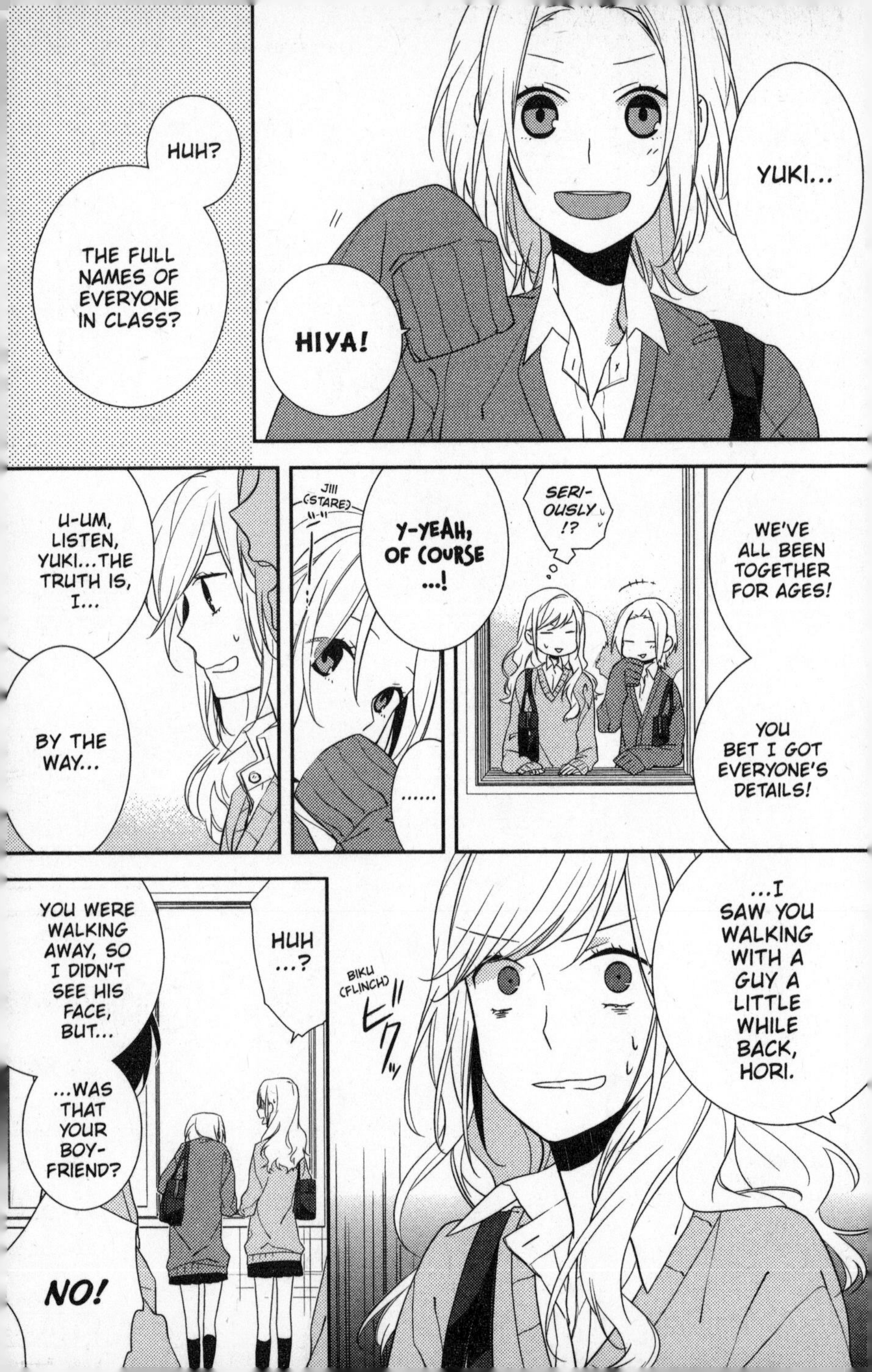
YUKI...
HIYA!
HUH?
THE FULL NAMES OF EVERYONE IN CLASS?
WE'VE ALL BEEN TOGETHER FOR AGES!
SERI-OUSLY!?
YOU BET I GOT EVERYONE'S DETAILS!
JIII (STARE)
Y-YEAH, OF COURSE ...!
......
U-UM, LISTEN, YUKI...THE TRUTH IS, I...
BY THE WAY...
...I SAW YOU WALKING WITH A GUY A LITTLE WHILE BACK, HORI.
BIKU (FLINCH)
HUH ...?
YOU WERE WALKING AWAY, SO I DIDN'T SEE HIS FACE, BUT...
...WAS THAT YOUR BOY-FRIEND?
NO!

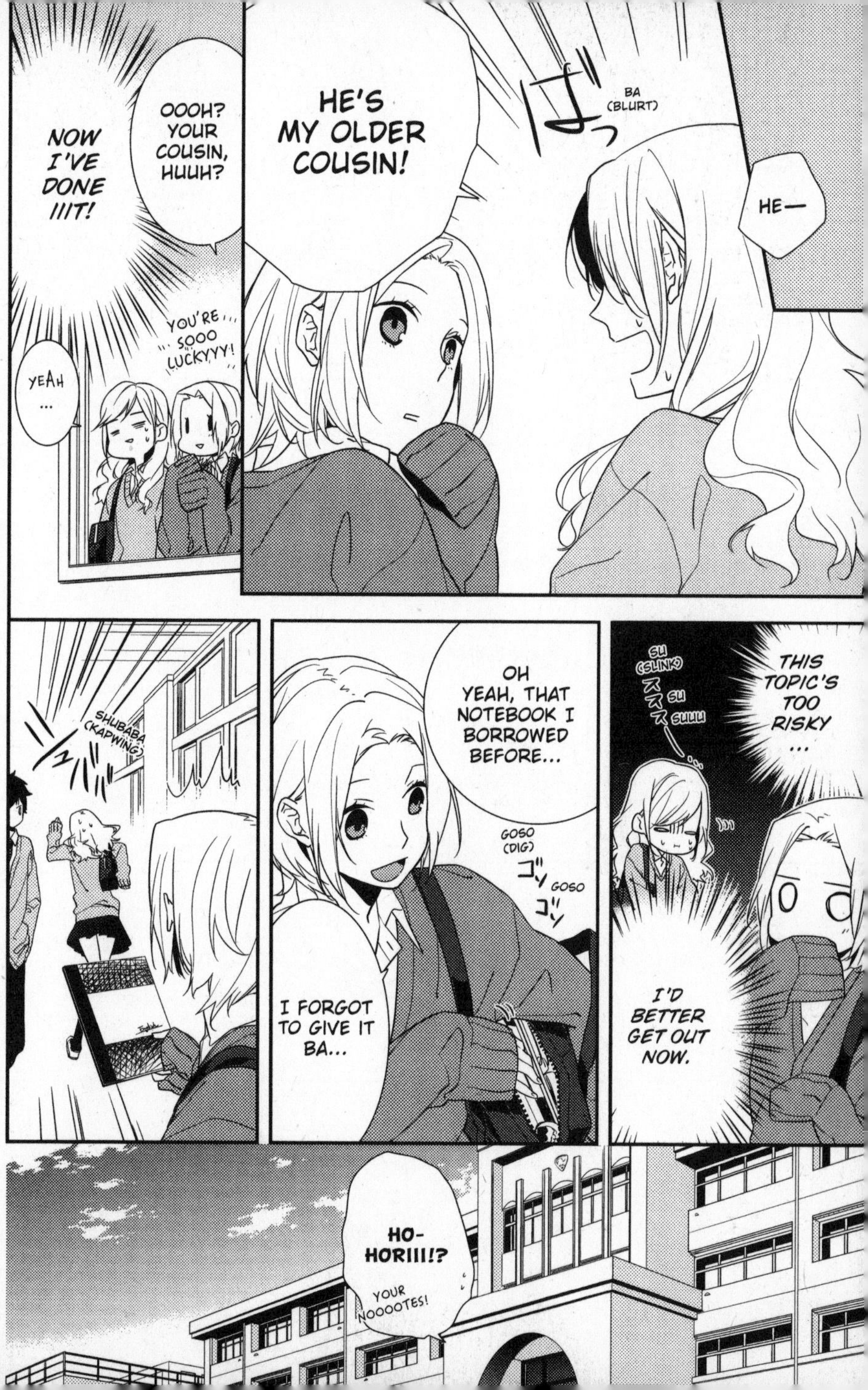
HE—
BA (BLURT)
HE'S MY OLDER COUSIN!
OOOH? YOUR COUSIN, HUUH?
NOW I'VE DONE IIIT!
YOU'RE... SOOO LUCKYYY!
YEAH...
THIS TOPIC'S TOO RISKY...
SU (SLINK) SU SUUU
I'D BETTER GET OUT NOW.
OH YEAH, THAT NOTEBOOK I BORROWED BEFORE...
GOSO (DIG) GOSO
I FORGOT TO GIVE IT BA...
SHUBABA (KAPWING)
HO-HORIII!?
YOUR NOOOOTES!

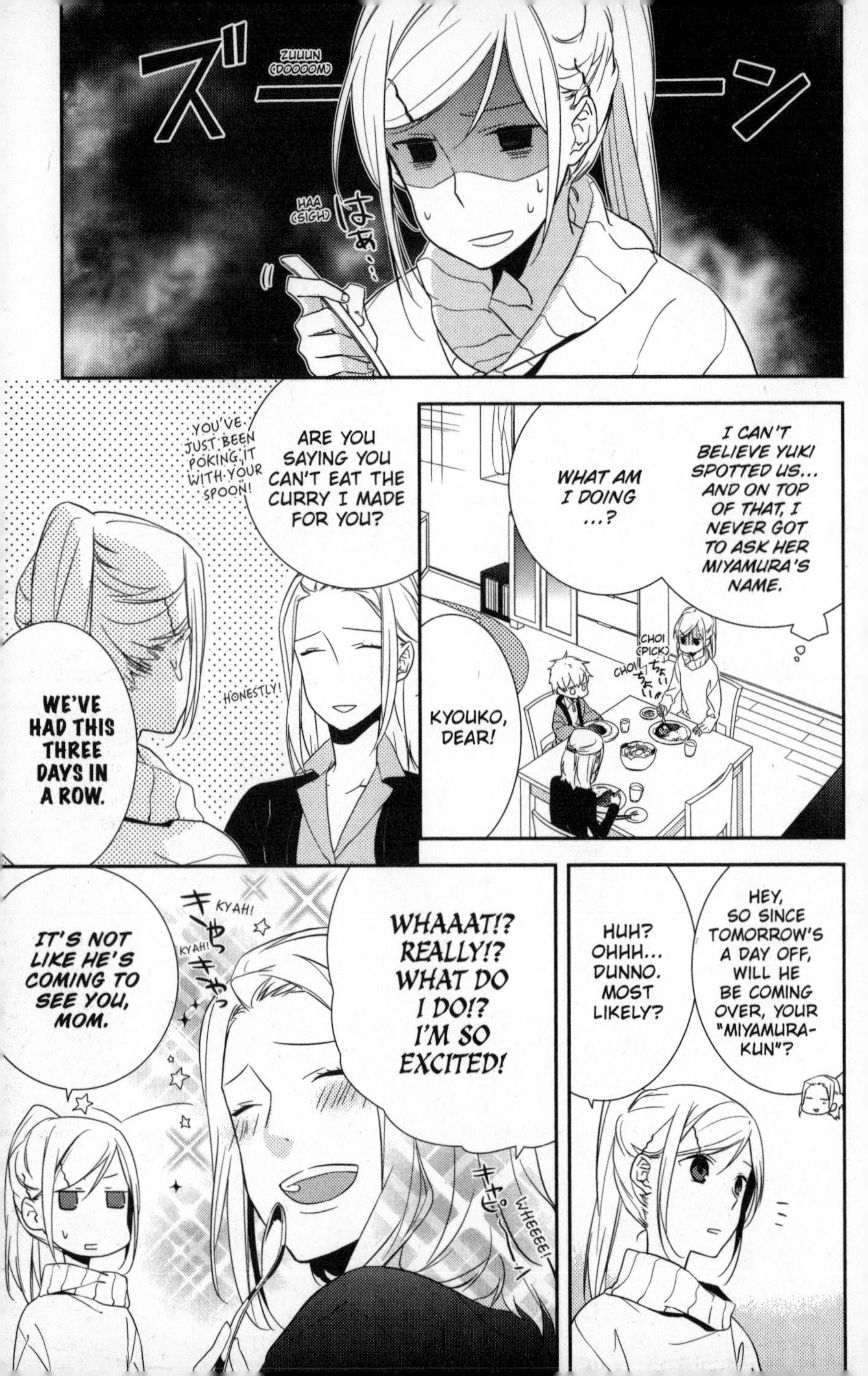
ZUUUN (DOOOOM)
HAA (SIGH)
I CAN'T BELIEVE YUKI SPOTTED US... AND ON TOP OF THAT, I NEVER GOT TO ASK HER MIYAMURA'S NAME.
WHAT AM I DOING ...?
CHOI (PICK)
CHOI
KYOUKO, DEAR!
ARE YOU SAYING YOU CAN'T EAT THE CURRY I MADE FOR YOU?
YOU'VE JUST BEEN POKING IT WITH YOUR SPOON!
HONESTLY!
WE'VE HAD THIS THREE DAYS IN A ROW.
HEY, SO SINCE TOMORROW'S A DAY OFF, WILL HE BE COMING OVER, YOUR "MIYAMURA-KUN"?
HUH? OHHH... DUNNO. MOST LIKELY?
WHAAAT!? REALLY!? WHAT DO I DO!? I'M SO EXCITED!
KYAH!
KYAH!
WHEEEEE!
IT'S NOT LIKE HE'S COMING TO SEE YOU, MOM.

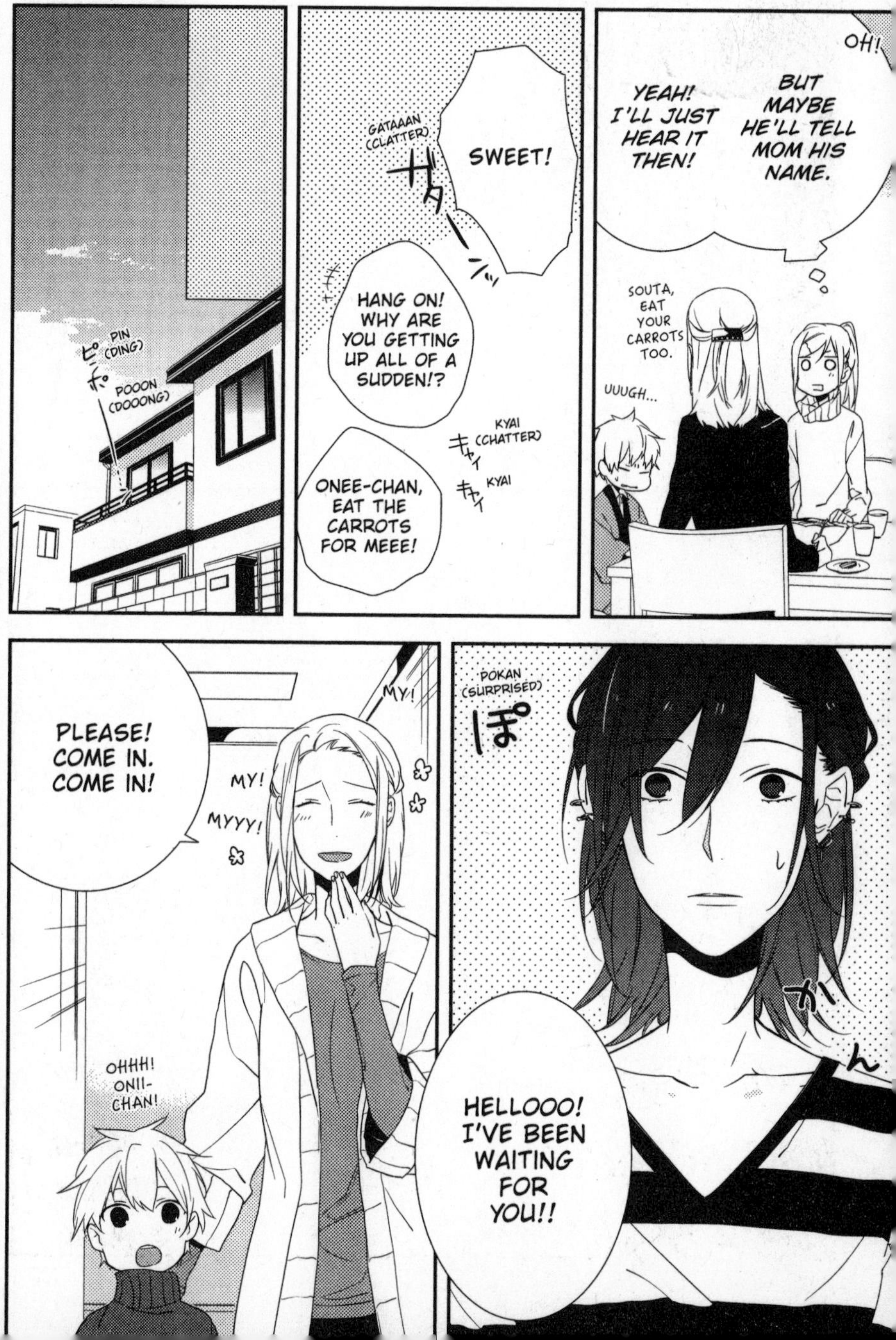
OH!
BUT MAYBE HE'LL TELL MOM HIS NAME.
YEAH! I'LL JUST HEAR IT THEN!
SOUTA, EAT YOUR CARROTS TOO.
UUUGH...
SWEET!
GATAAAN (CLATTER)
HANG ON! WHY ARE YOU GETTING UP ALL OF A SUDDEN!?
KYAI (CHATTER)
KYAI
ONEE-CHAN, EAT THE CARROTS FOR MEEE!
PIN (DING)
POOON (DOOONG)
POKAN (SURPRISED)
HELLOOO! I'VE BEEN WAITING FOR YOU!!
MY!
PLEASE! COME IN. COME IN!
MY!
MYYY!
OHHH! ONII-CHAN!

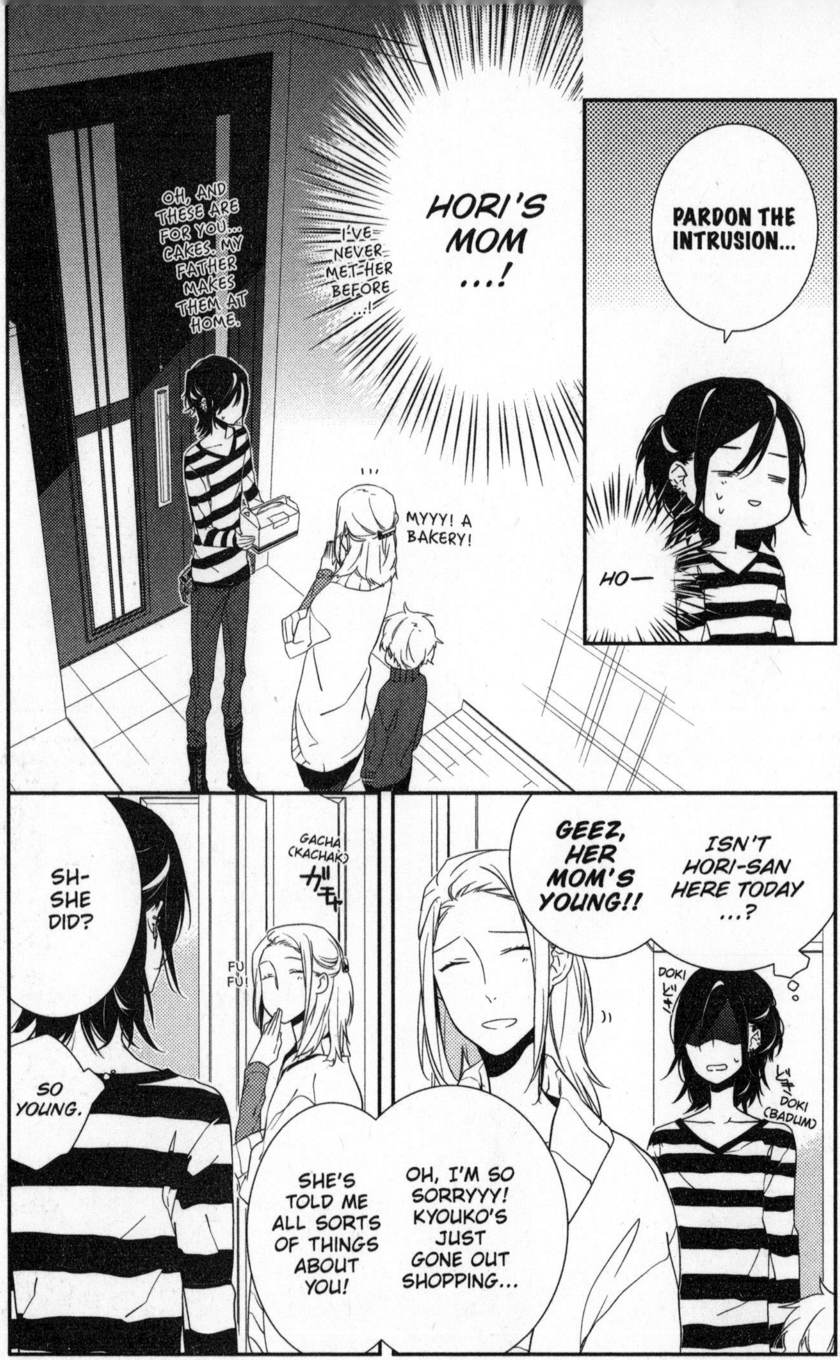
PARDON THE INTRUSION...
HO—
HORI'S MOM ...!
I'VE NEVER MET HER BEFORE ...!
OH, AND THESE ARE FOR YOU... CAKES. MY FATHER MAKES THEM AT HOME.
MYYY! A BAKERY!
GEEZ, HER MOM'S YOUNG!!
ISN'T HORI-SAN HERE TODAY ...?
DOKI
DOKI (BADUM)
OH, I'M SO SORRYYY! KYOUKO'S JUST GONE OUT SHOPPING...
SHE'S TOLD ME ALL SORTS OF THINGS ABOUT YOU!
GACHA (KACHAK)
FU FU!
SH-SHE DID?
SO YOUNG.

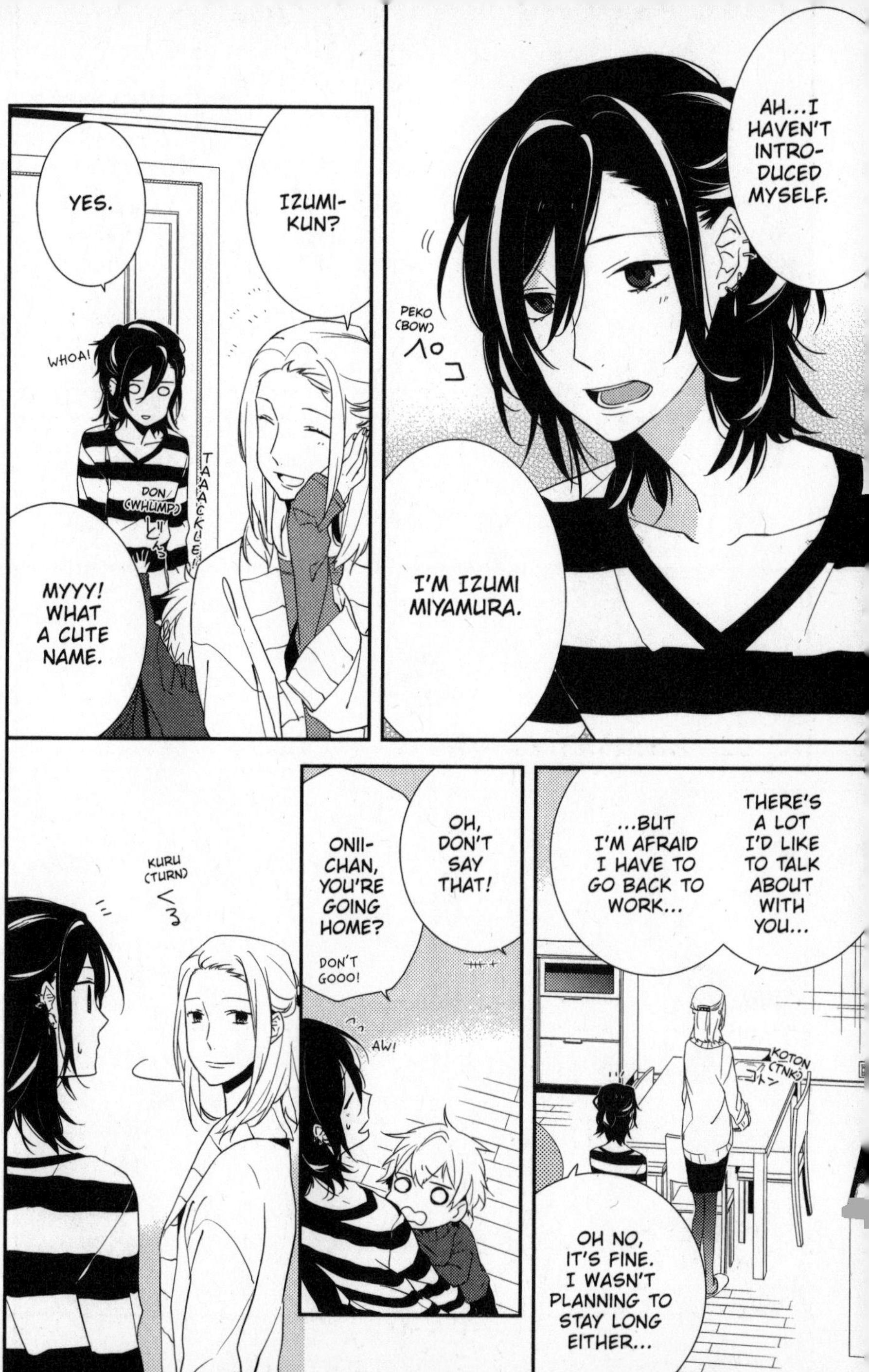
AH...I HAVEN'T INTRO-DUCED MYSELF.
PEKO (BOW)
I'M IZUMI MIYAMURA.
IZUMI-KUN?
YES.
WHOA!
TAAACKLE!
DON (WHUMP)
MYYY! WHAT A CUTE NAME.
THERE'S A LOT I'D LIKE TO TALK ABOUT WITH YOU...
...BUT I'M AFRAID I HAVE TO GO BACK TO WORK...
KOTON (TNK)
OH NO, IT'S FINE. I WASN'T PLANNING TO STAY LONG EITHER...
OH, DON'T SAY THAT!
ONII-CHAN, YOU'RE GOING HOME?
DON'T GOOO!
AW!
KURU (TURN)

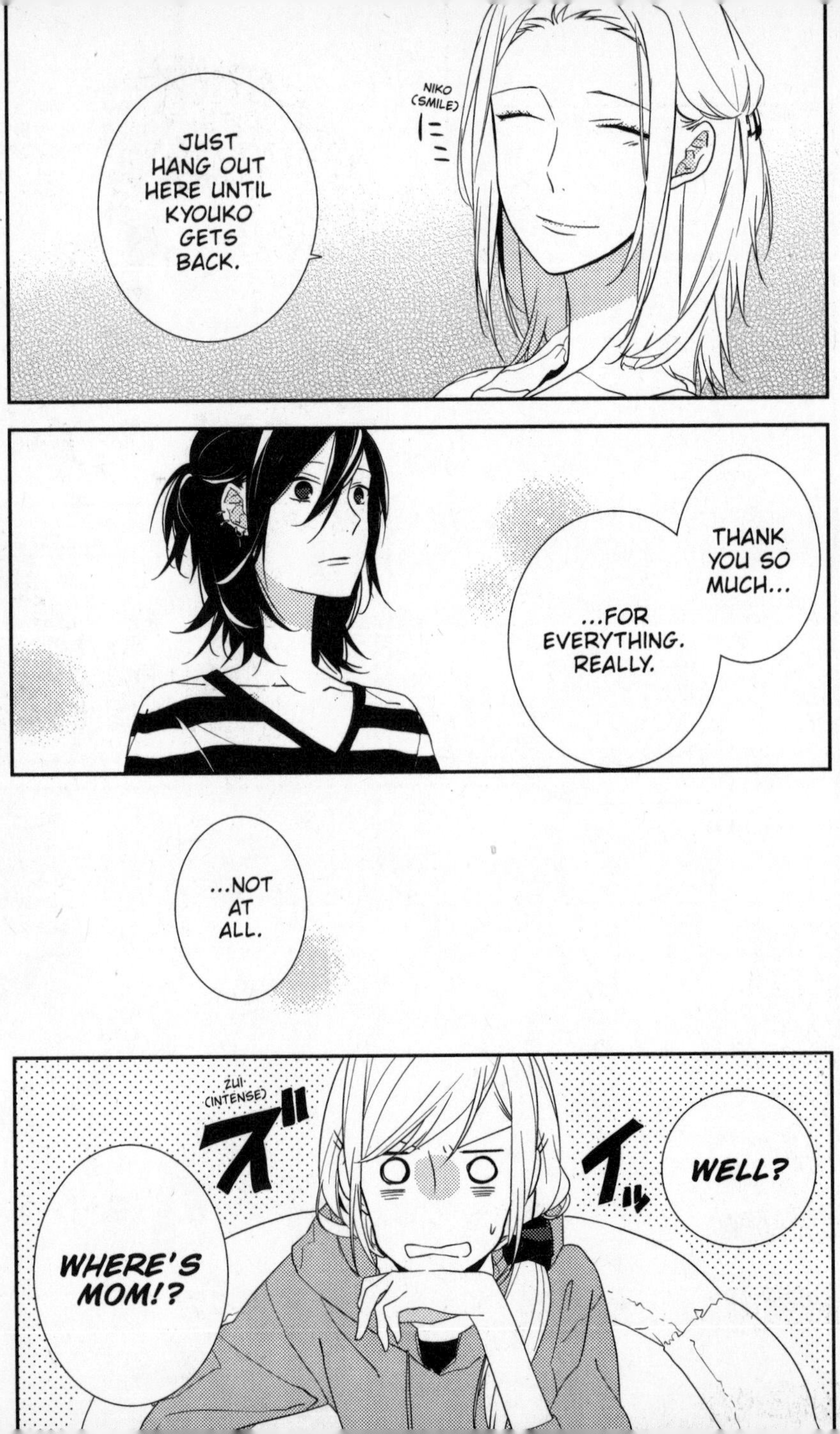
NIKO (SMILE)
JUST HANG OUT HERE UNTIL KYOUKO GETS BACK.
THANK YOU SO MUCH...
...FOR EVERYTHING. REALLY.
...NOT AT ALL.
WELL?
ZUI (INTENSE)
WHERE'S MOM!?

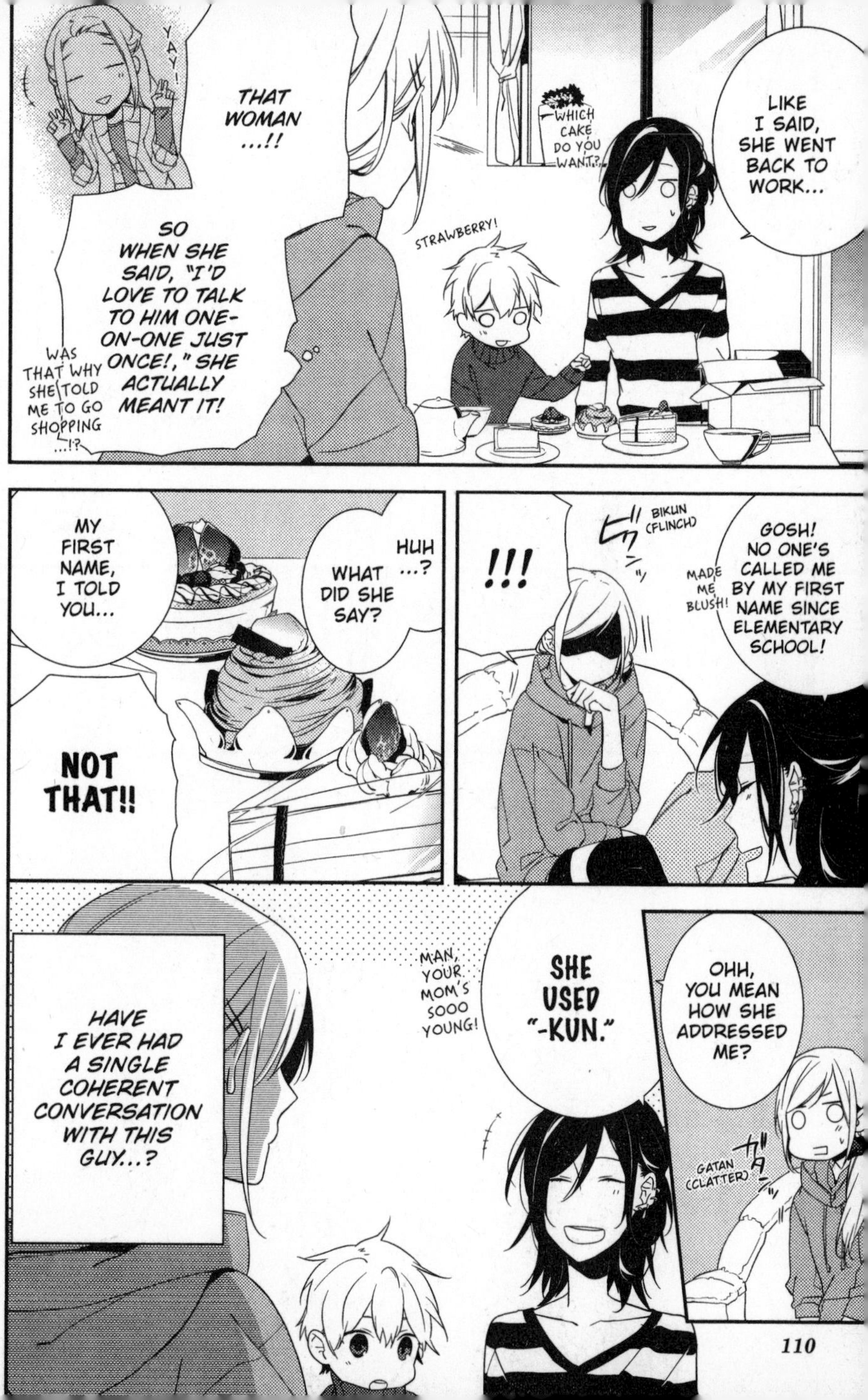
LIKE I SAID, SHE WENT BACK TO WORK...
WHICH CAKE DO YOU WANT?
STRAWBERRY!
YAY!
THAT WOMAN ...!!
SO WHEN SHE SAID, "I'D LOVE TO TALK TO HIM ONE-ON-ONE JUST ONCE!," SHE ACTUALLY MEANT IT!
WAS THAT WHY SHE TOLD ME TO GO SHOPPING ...!?
GOSH! NO ONE'S CALLED ME BY MY FIRST NAME SINCE ELEMENTARY SCHOOL!
MADE ME BLUSH!
BIKUN (FLINCH)
!!!
HUH ...?
WHAT DID SHE SAY?
MY FIRST NAME, I TOLD YOU...
NOT THAT!!
OHH, YOU MEAN HOW SHE ADDRESSED ME?
GATAN (CLATTER)
SHE USED "-KUN."
MAN, YOUR MOM'S SOOO YOUNG!
HAVE I EVER HAD A SINGLE COHERENT CONVERSATION WITH THIS GUY...?

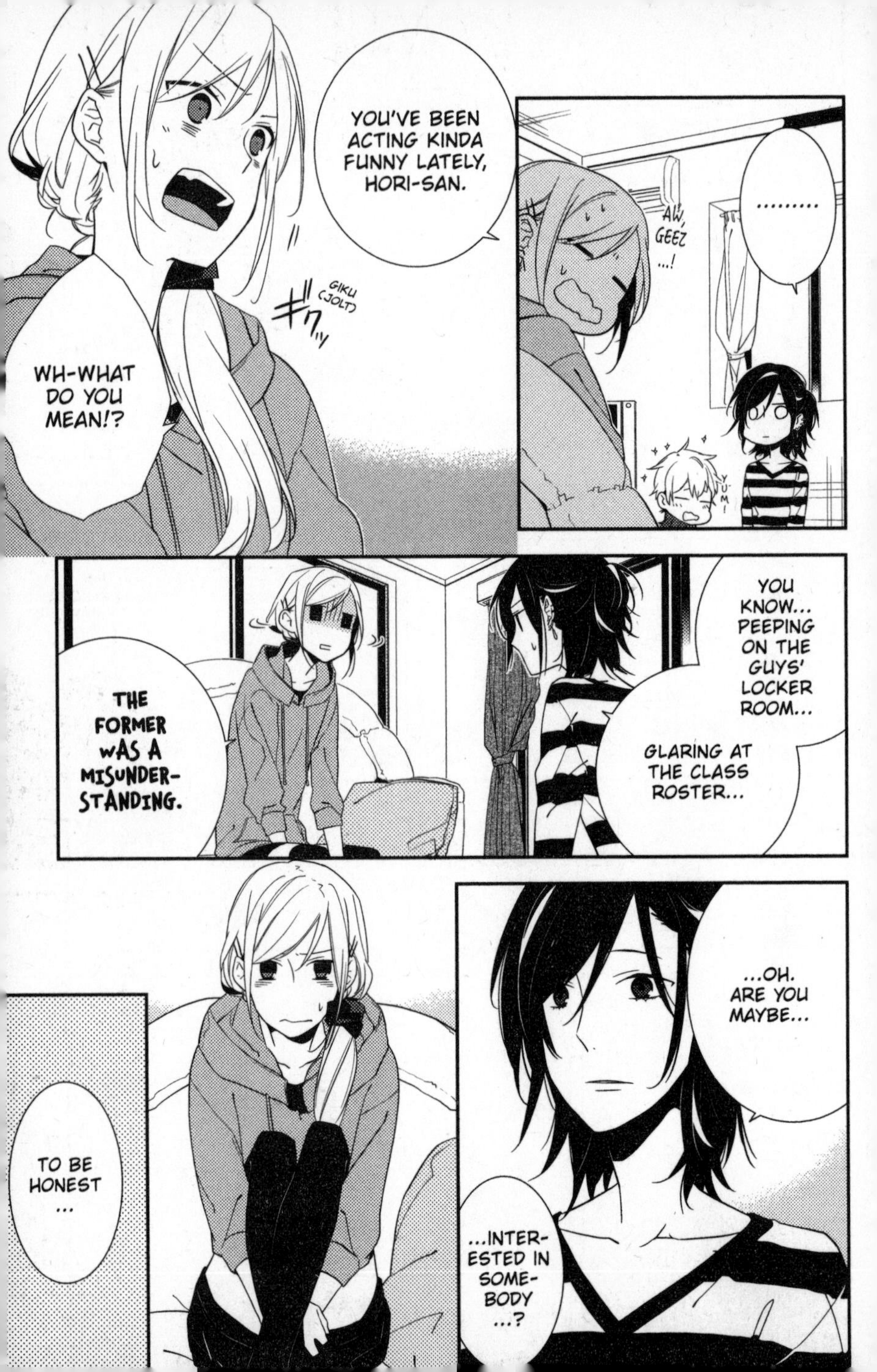
....
AW, GEEZ ...!
YUM!
YOU'VE BEEN ACTING KINDA FUNNY LATELY, HORI-SAN.
ギクッ
GIKU (JOLT)
WH-WHAT DO YOU MEAN!?
YOU KNOW... PEEPING ON THE GUYS' LOCKER ROOM...
GLARING AT THE CLASS ROSTER...
THE FORMER WAS A MISUNDER-STANDING.
...OH. ARE YOU MAYBE...
...INTER-ESTED IN SOME-BODY ...?
TO BE HONEST ...

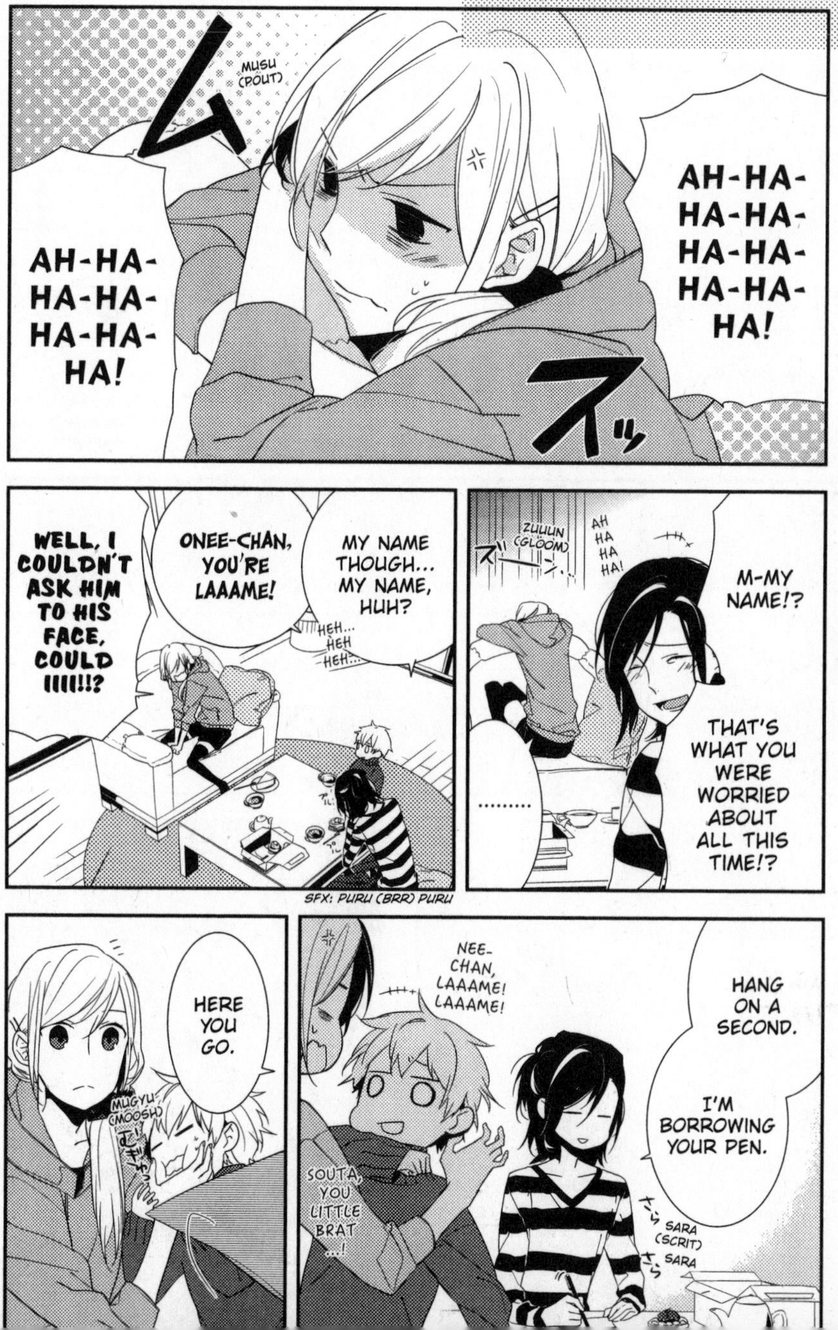

AH-HA-HA-HA-HA-HA-HA-HA-HA!
MUSU (POUT)
AH-HA-HA-HA-HA-HA-HA!
AH HA HA HA!
ZUUUN (GLOOM)
M-MY NAME!?
THAT'S WHAT YOU WERE WORRIED ABOUT ALL THIS TIME!?
....
MY NAME THOUGH... MY NAME, HUH?
ONEE-CHAN, YOU'RE LAAAME!
HEH... HEH HEH...
WELL, I COULDN'T ASK HIM TO HIS FACE, COULD IIIII!!?
SFX: PURU (BRR) PURU
HANG ON A SECOND.
I'M BORROWING YOUR PEN.
NEE-CHAN, LAAAME! LAAAME!
SARA (SCRIT) SARA
SOUTA, YOU LITTLE BRAT...!
HERE YOU GO.
MUGYU (MOOSH)

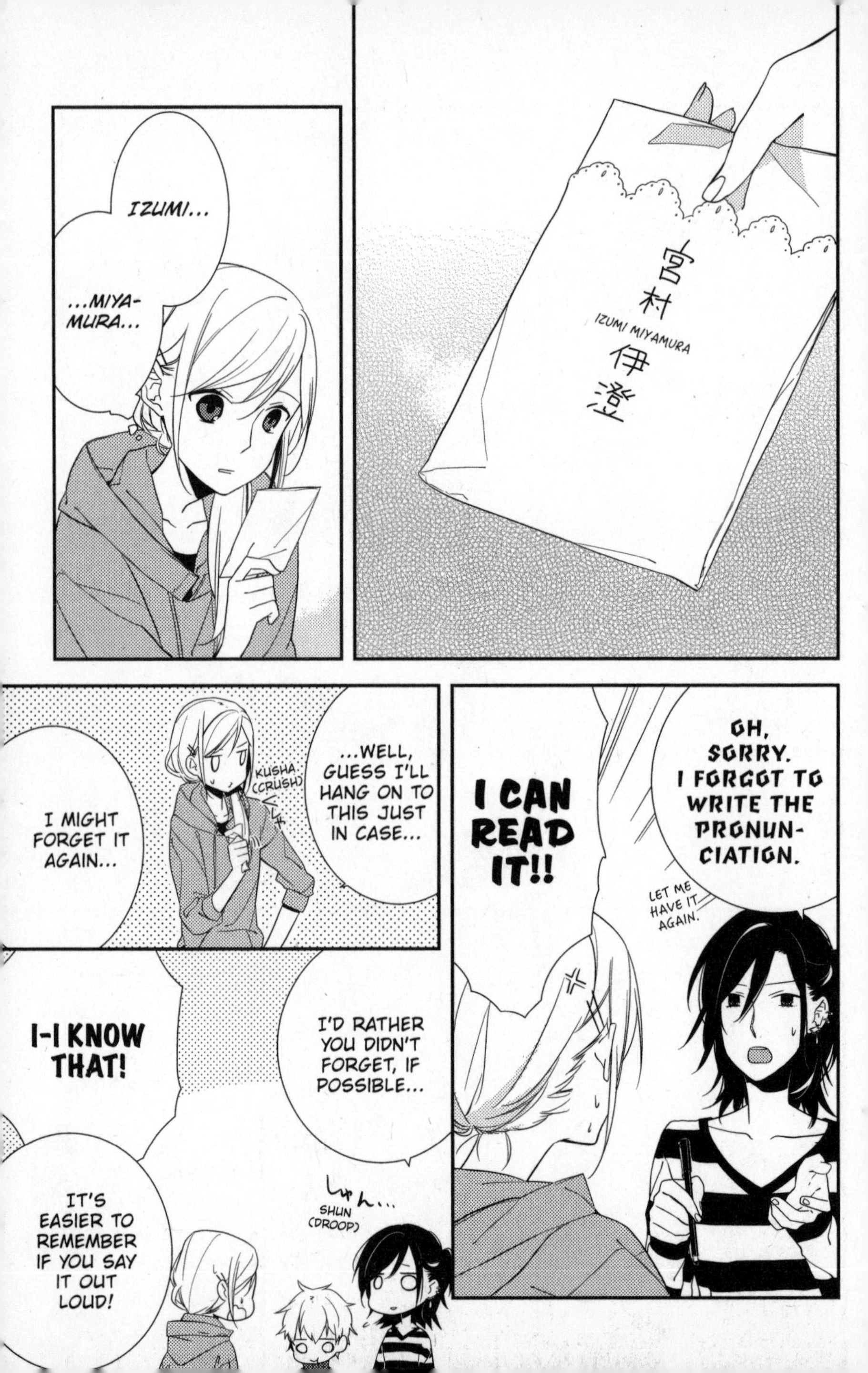
宮村
伊澄
IZUMI MIYAMURA
IZUMI...
...MIYA-MURA...
OH, SORRY. I FORGOT TO WRITE THE PRONUN-CIATION.
LET ME HAVE IT AGAIN.
I CAN READ IT!!
...WELL, GUESS I'LL HANG ON TO THIS JUST IN CASE...
KUSHA (CRUSH)
I MIGHT FORGET IT AGAIN...
I'D RATHER YOU DIDN'T FORGET, IF POSSIBLE...
I-I KNOW THAT!
しゅん...
SHUN (DROOP)
IT'S EASIER TO REMEMBER IF YOU SAY IT OUT LOUD!

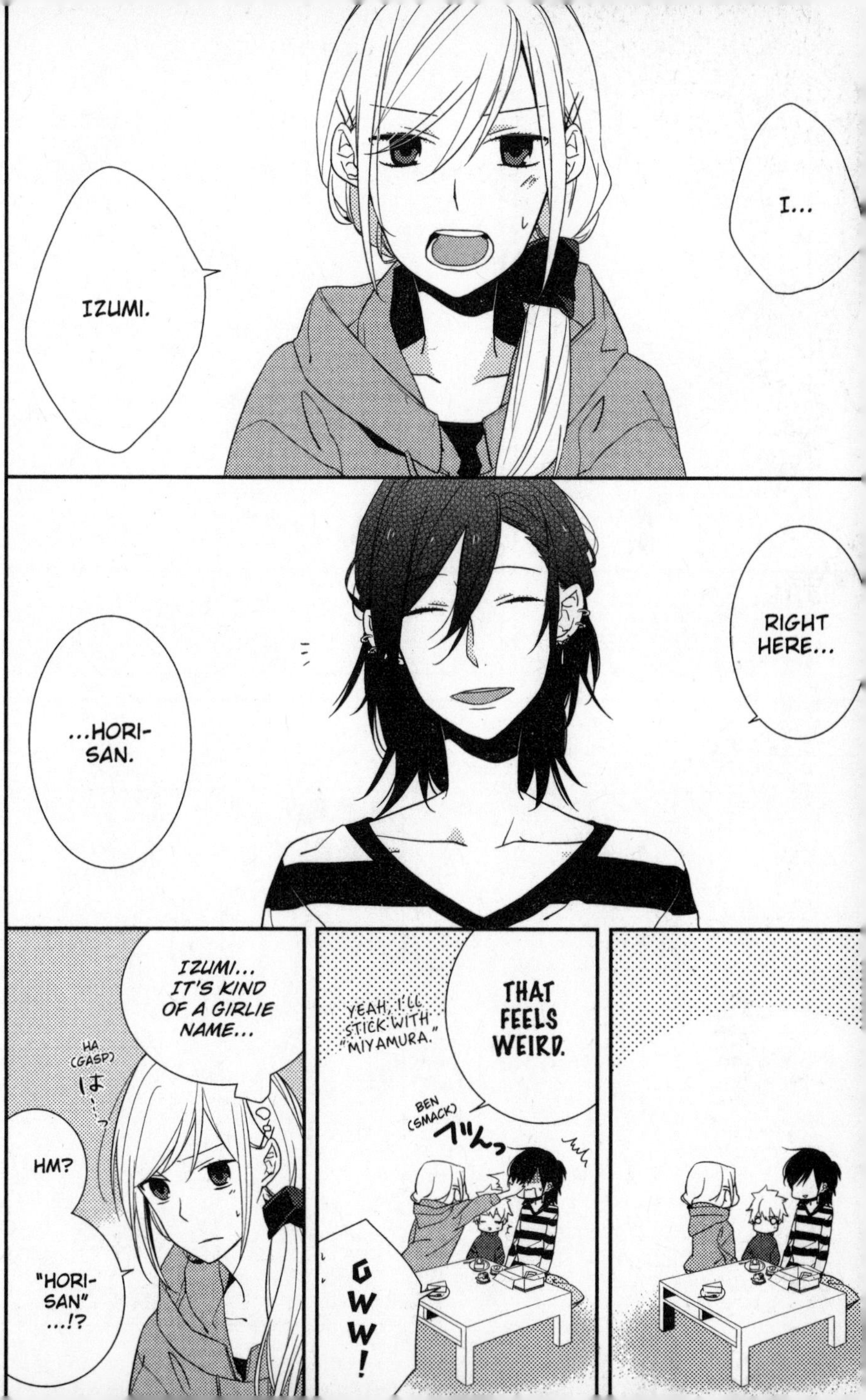
I...
IZUMI.
RIGHT HERE...
...HORI-SAN.
THAT FEELS WEIRD.
YEAH, I'LL STICK WITH "MIYAMURA."
BEN (SMACK)
GWW!
IZUMI... IT'S KIND OF A GIRLIE NAME...
HA (GASP)
HM?
"HORI-SAN" ...!?

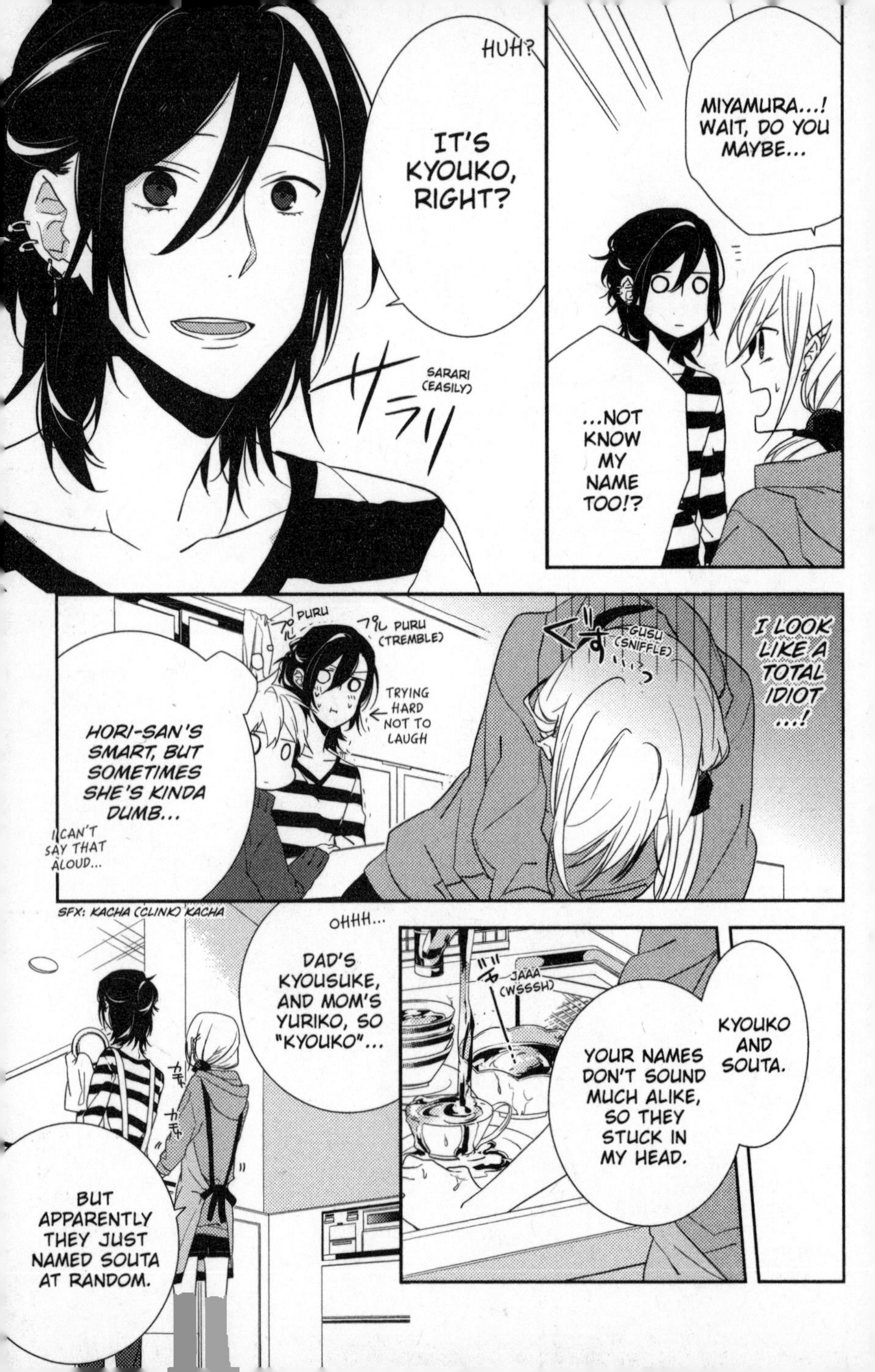
MIYAMURA...! WAIT, DO YOU MAYBE...
...NOT KNOW MY NAME TOO!?
HUH?
IT'S KYOUKO, RIGHT?
SARARI (EASILY)
I LOOK LIKE A TOTAL IDIOT...!
GUSU (SNIFFLE)
PURU PURU (TREMBLE)
TRYING HARD NOT TO LAUGH
HORI-SAN'S SMART, BUT SOMETIMES SHE'S KINDA DUMB...
I CAN'T SAY THAT ALOUD...
KYOUKO AND SOUTA.
YOUR NAMES DON'T SOUND MUCH ALIKE, SO THEY STUCK IN MY HEAD.
JAAA (WSSSH)
OHHH...
DAD'S KYOUSUKE, AND MOM'S YURIKO, SO "KYOUKO"...
SFX: KACHA (CLINK) KACHA
BUT APPARENTLY THEY JUST NAMED SOUTA AT RANDOM.

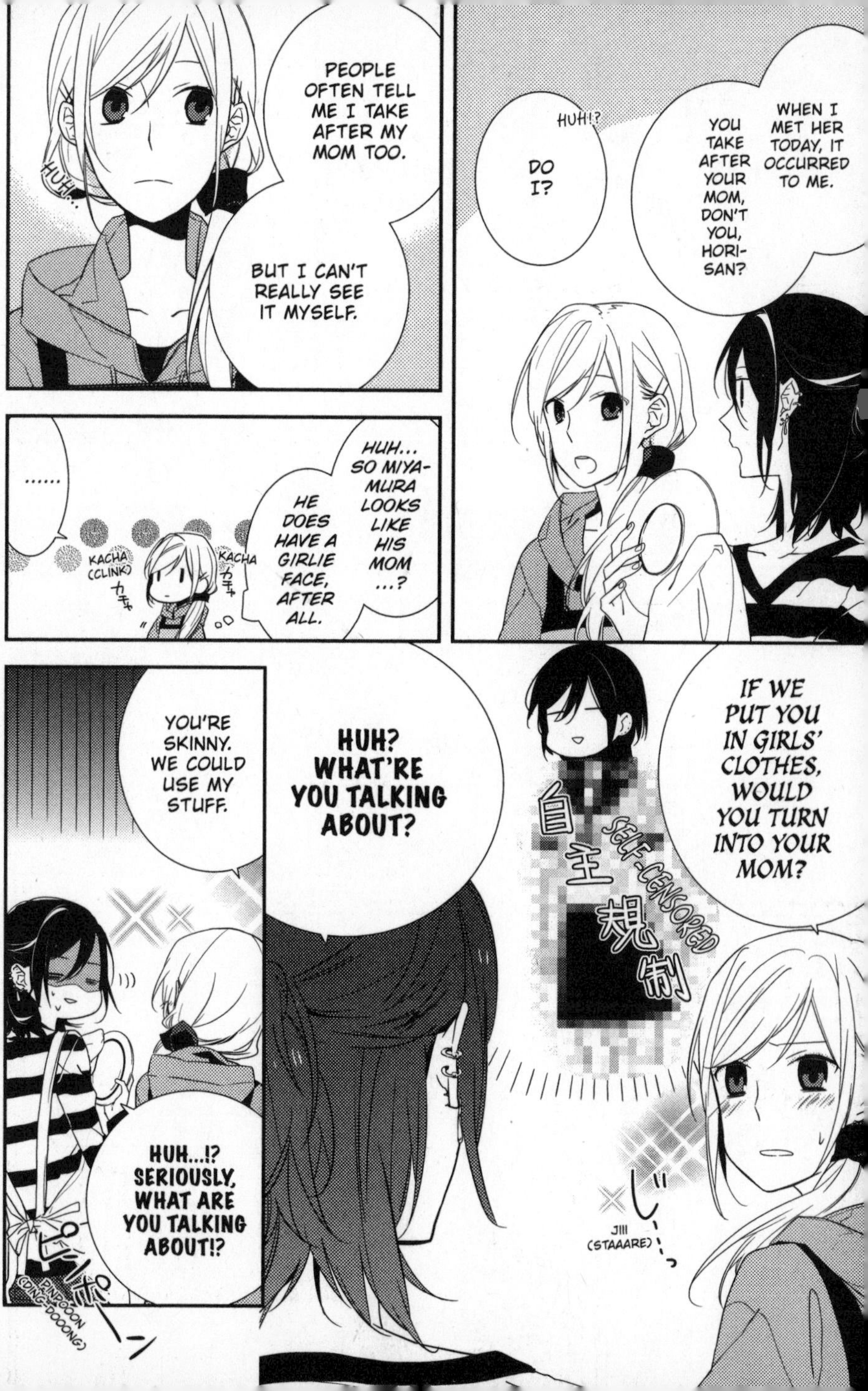
WHEN I MET HER TODAY, IT OCCURRED TO ME.
YOU TAKE AFTER YOUR MOM, DON'T YOU, HORI-SAN?
HUH!?
DO I?
PEOPLE OFTEN TELL ME I TAKE AFTER MY MOM TOO.
HUH...
BUT I CAN'T REALLY SEE IT MYSELF.
HUH... SO MIYAMURA LOOKS LIKE HIS MOM ...?
HE DOES HAVE A GIRLIE FACE, AFTER ALL.
KACHA
カチャ
KACHA (CLINK)
カチャ
......
IF WE PUT YOU IN GIRLS' CLOTHES, WOULD YOU TURN INTO YOUR MOM?
自主規制
SELF-CENSORED
じー
JIII (STAAARE)
HUH? WHAT'RE YOU TALKING ABOUT?
YOU'RE SKINNY. WE COULD USE MY STUFF.
HUH...!? SERIOUSLY, WHAT ARE YOU TALKING ABOUT!?
ピンポーン
PINPOOON (DING-DOOONG)

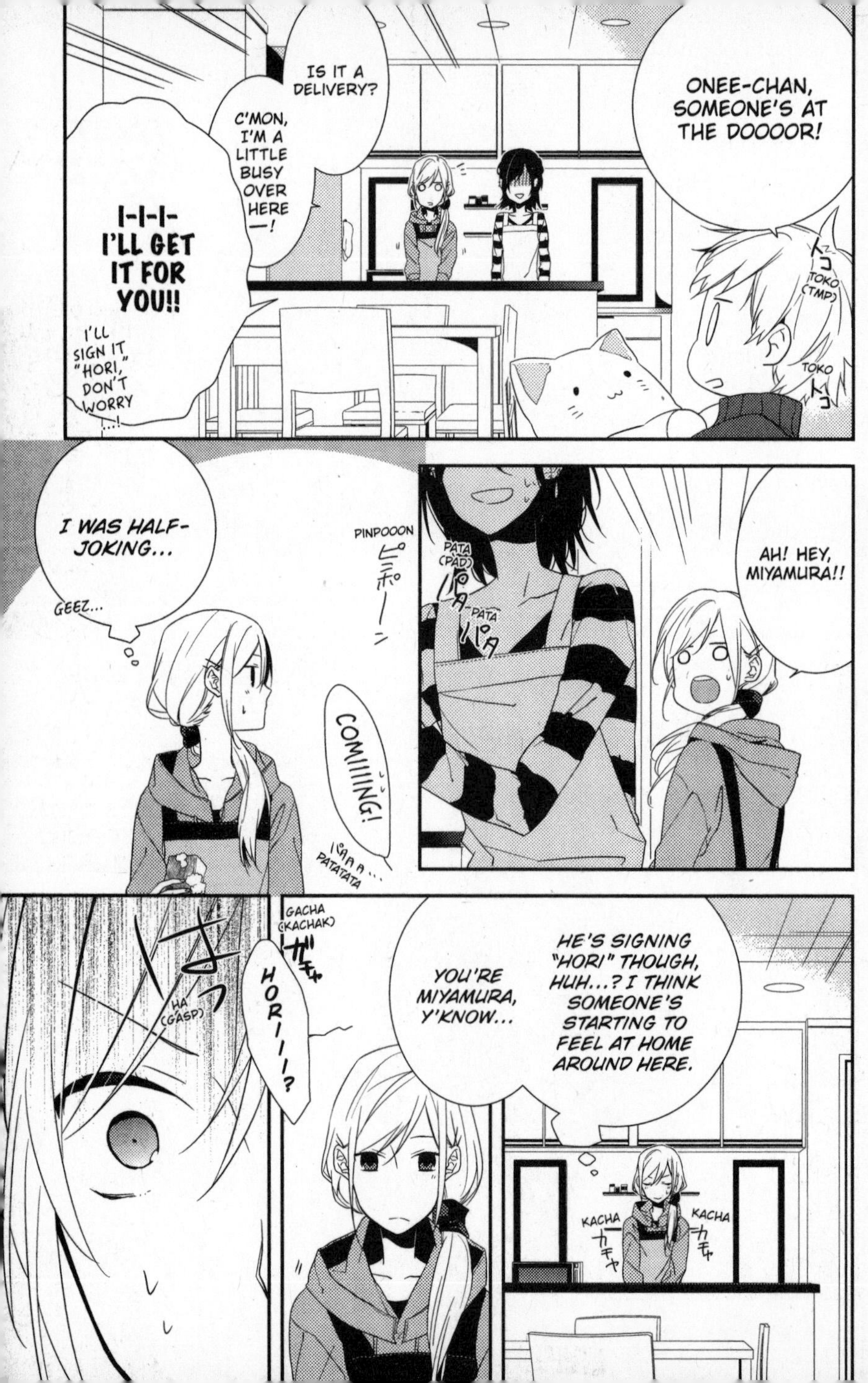

ONEE-CHAN, SOMEONE'S AT THE DOOOOR!
TOKO (TMP)
TOKO
IS IT A DELIVERY?
C'MON, I'M A LITTLE BUSY OVER HERE—!
I-I-I-I'LL GET IT FOR YOU!!
I'LL SIGN IT "HORI," DON'T WORRY...!
AH! HEY, MIYAMURA!!
PATA (PAD)
PATA
PINPOOON
COMIIIING!
PATATATA
I WAS HALF-JOKING...
GEEZ...
HE'S SIGNING "HORI" THOUGH, HUH...? I THINK SOMEONE'S STARTING TO FEEL AT HOME AROUND HERE.
YOU'RE MIYAMURA, Y'KNOW...
KACHA
KACHA
GACHA (KACHAK)
HORIIII?
HA (GASP)

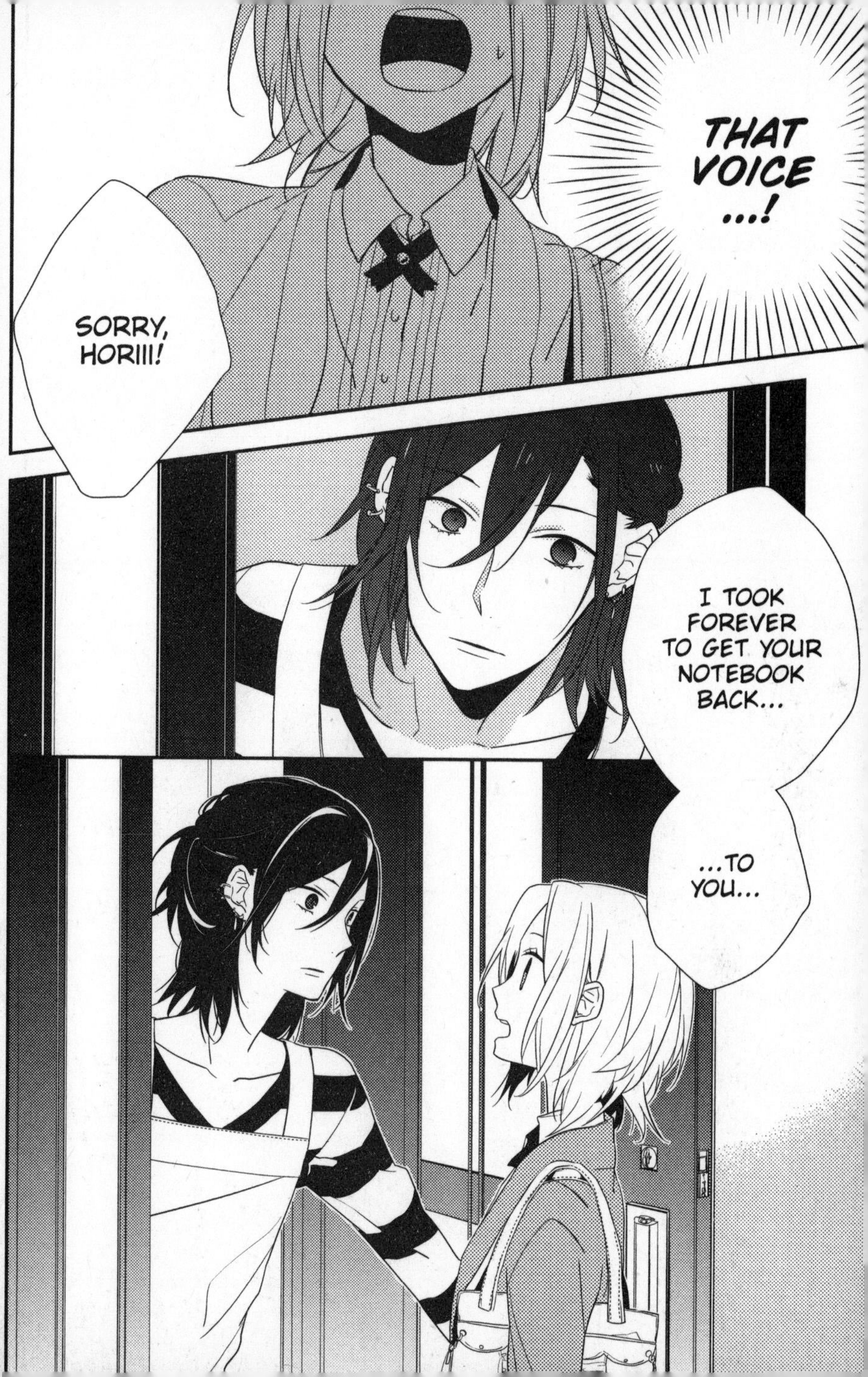
THAT VOICE ...!
SORRY, HORIII!
I TOOK FOREVER TO GET YOUR NOTEBOOK BACK...
...TO YOU...

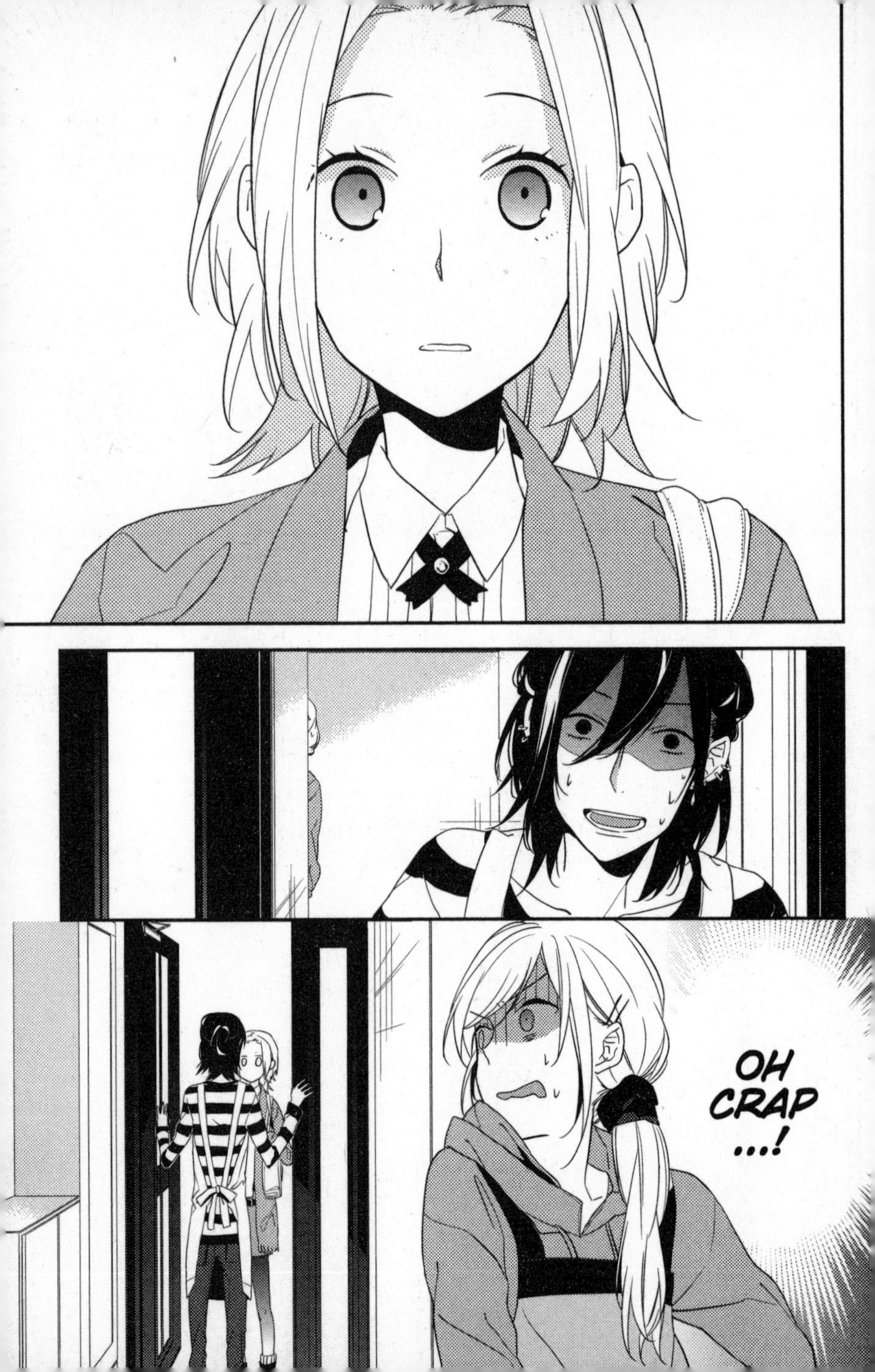
OH CRAP ...!

HORIMIYA

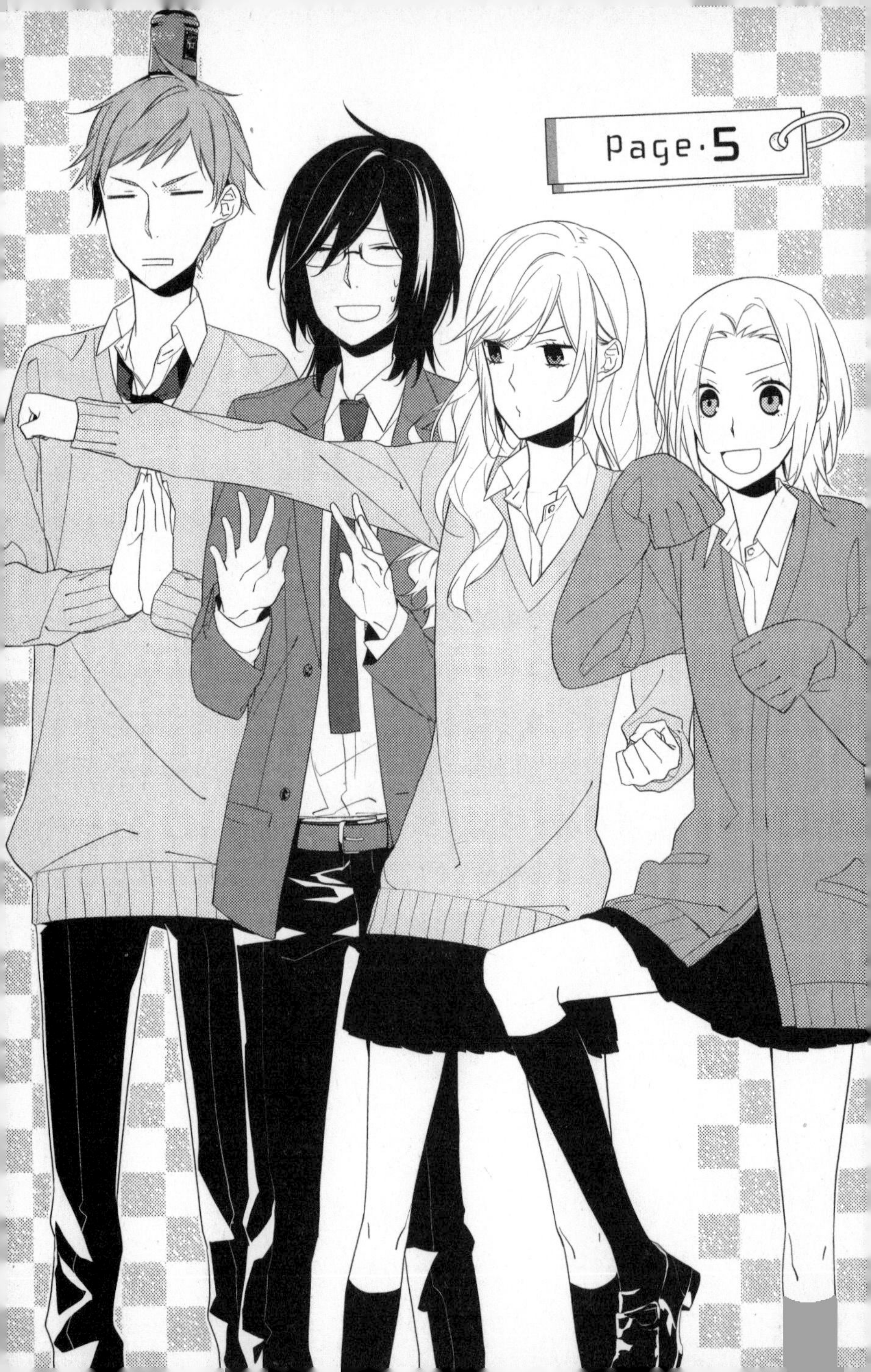
page·5

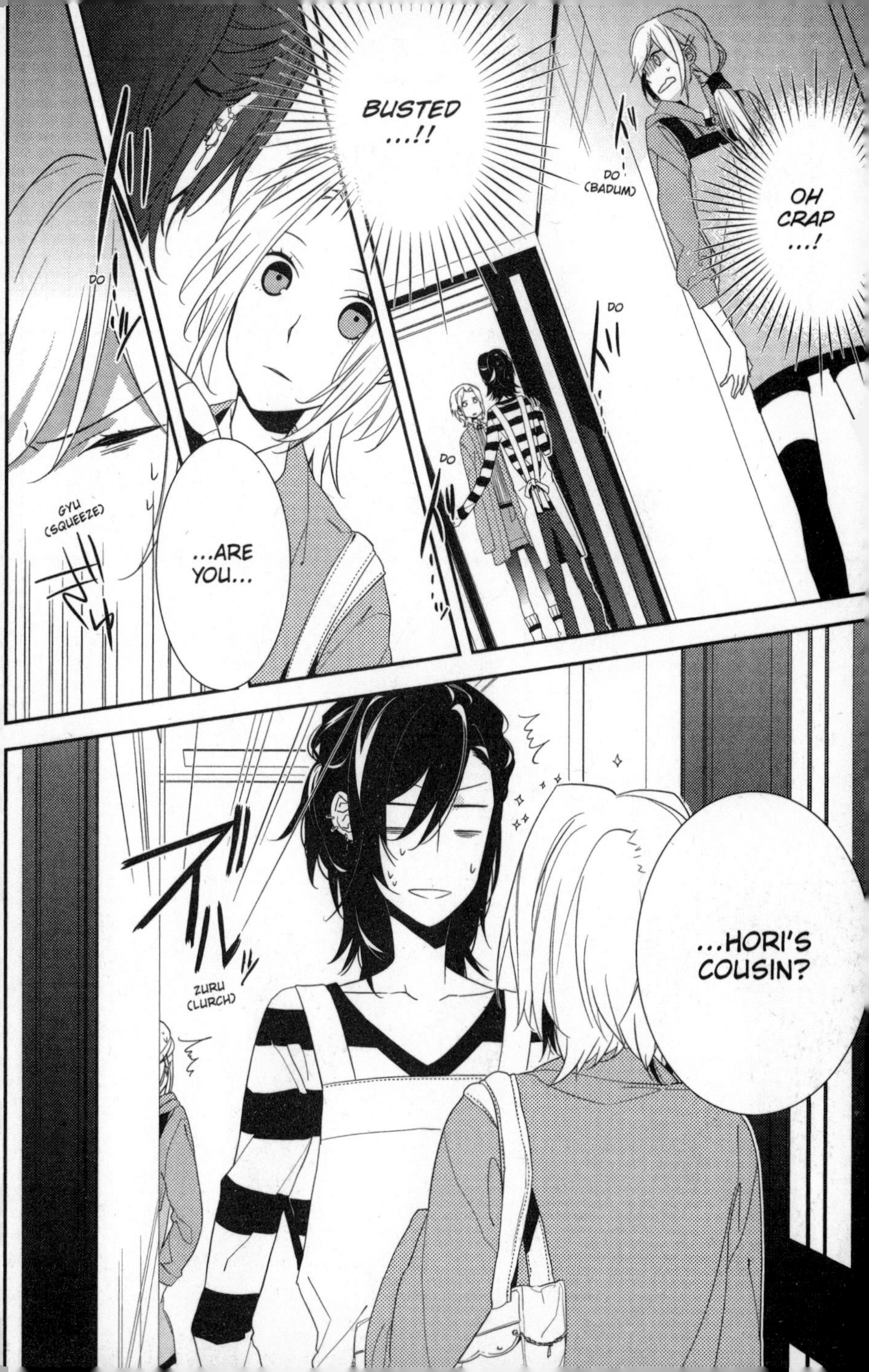
OH CRAP ...!
DO (BADUM)
DO
DO
BUSTED ...!!
DO
GYU (SQUEEZE)
...ARE YOU...
...HORI'S COUSIN?
ZURU (LURCH)

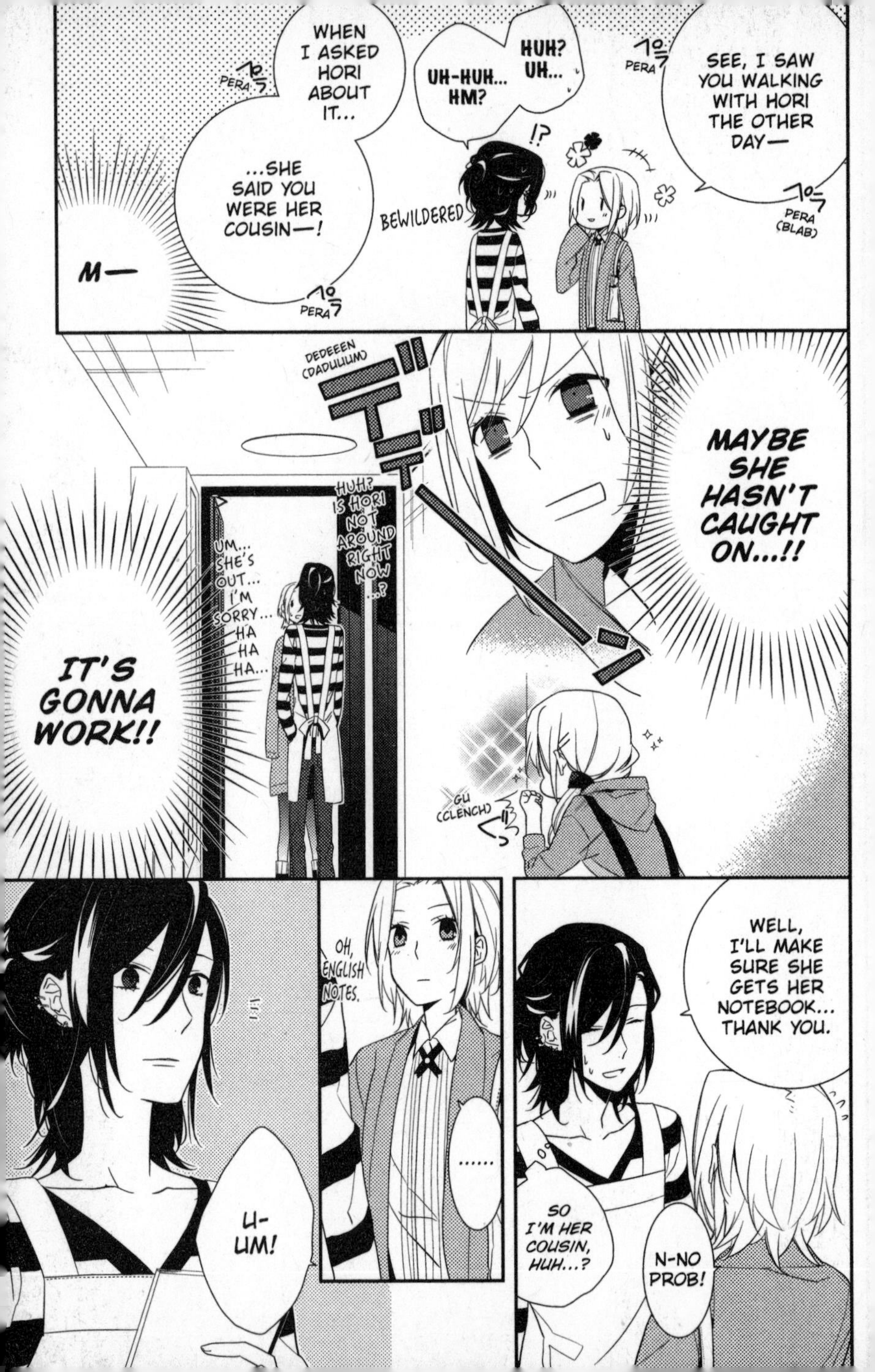
PERA
SEE, I SAW YOU WALKING WITH HORI THE OTHER DAY—
PERA (BLAB)
HUH? UH...
UH-HUH... HM?
!?
PERA
WHEN I ASKED HORI ABOUT IT...
...SHE SAID YOU WERE HER COUSIN—!
PERA
BEWILDERED
M—
DEDEEEN (DADUUUM)
MAYBE SHE HASN'T CAUGHT ON...!!
GU (CLENCH)
HUH? IS HORI NOT AROUND RIGHT NOW...?
UM... SHE'S OUT... I'M SORRY... HA HA HA...
IT'S GONNA WORK!!
WELL, I'LL MAKE SURE SHE GETS HER NOTEBOOK... THANK YOU.
N-NO PROB!
SO I'M HER COUSIN, HUH...?
OH, ENGLISH NOTES.
......
U-UM!

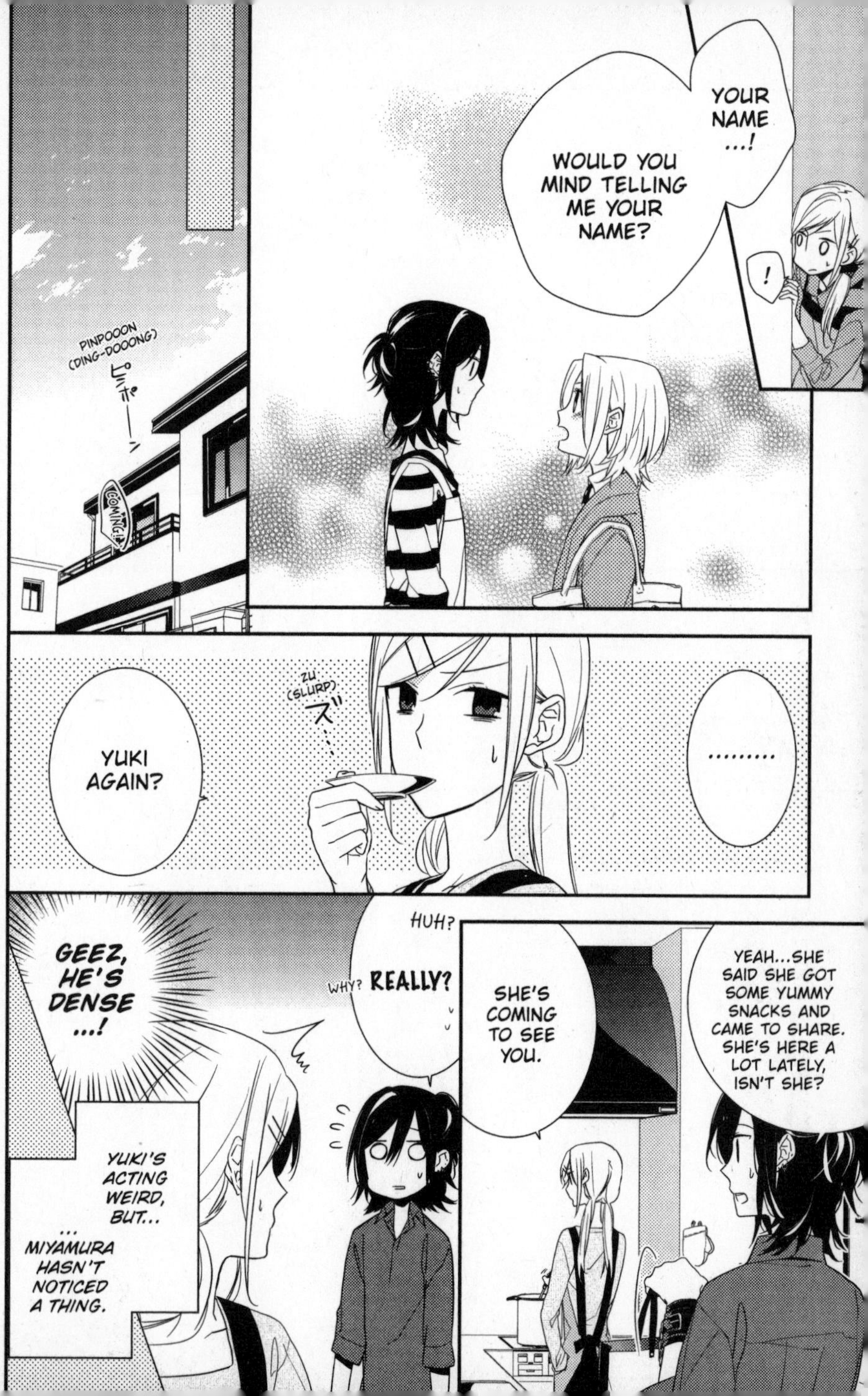
YOUR NAME ...!
WOULD YOU MIND TELLING ME YOUR NAME?
!
PINPOOON (DING-DOOONG)
ピンポーン
COMING!!
....
ZU (SLURP)
ズ…
YUKI AGAIN?
YEAH...SHE SAID SHE GOT SOME YUMMY SNACKS AND CAME TO SHARE. SHE'S HERE A LOT LATELY, ISN'T SHE?
SHE'S COMING TO SEE YOU.
HUH?
WHY? REALLY?
GEEZ, HE'S DENSE ...!
YUKI'S ACTING WEIRD, BUT...
... MIYAMURA HASN'T NOTICED A THING.

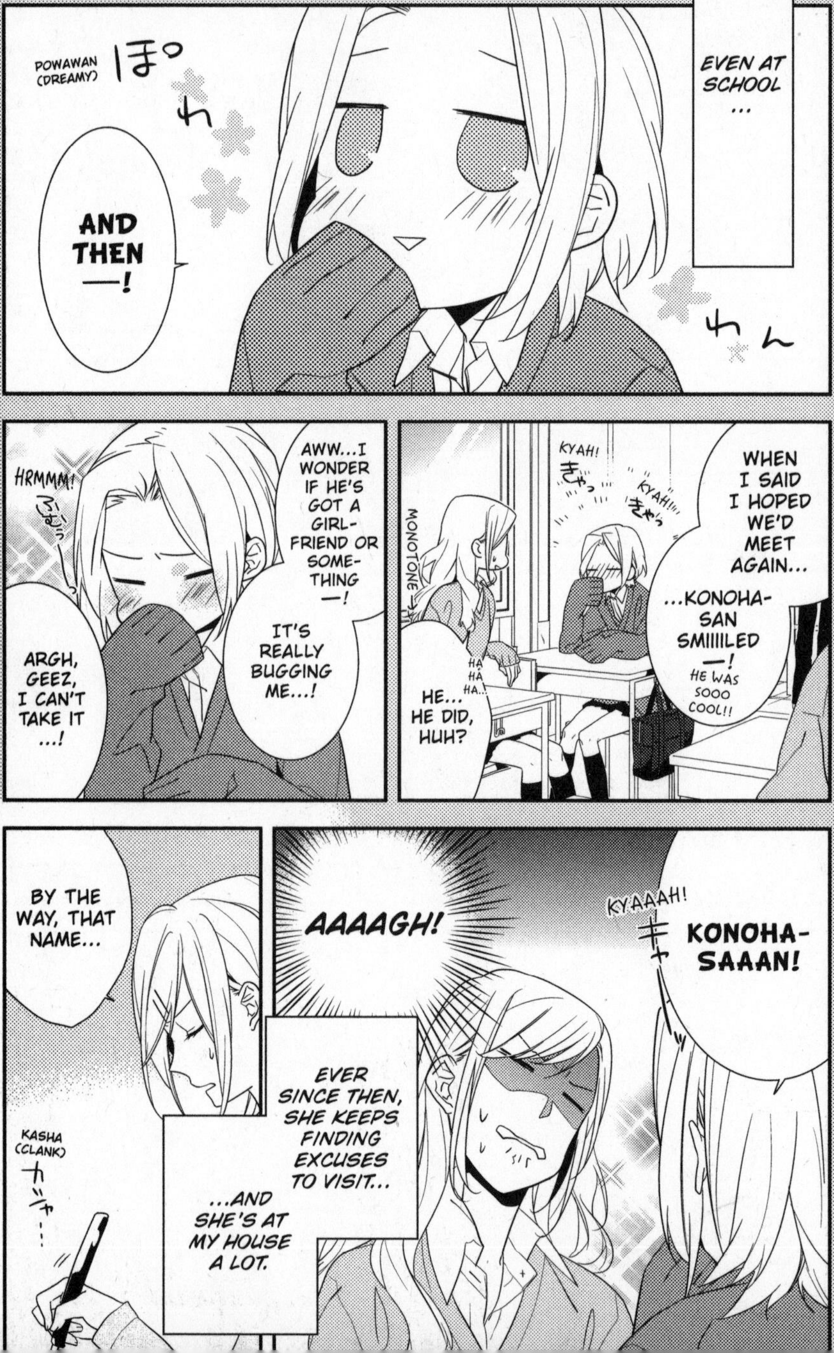
EVEN AT SCHOOL...
POWAWAN (DREAMY) ぽわ
AND THEN—!
わん
KYAH! きゃっ
KYAH!!! きゃっ
WHEN I SAID I HOPED WE'D MEET AGAIN...
...KONOHA-SAN SMIIIILED—!
HE WAS SOOO COOL!!
MONOTONE→
HA HA HA...
HE... HE DID, HUH?
AWW...I WONDER IF HE'S GOT A GIRLFRIEND OR SOMETHING—!
IT'S REALLY BUGGING ME...!
HRMMM! ふむっ
ARGH, GEEZ, I CAN'T TAKE IT...!
KYAAAH! キャー
KONOHA-SAAAN!
AAAAGH!
EVER SINCE THEN, SHE KEEPS FINDING EXCUSES TO VISIT...
...AND SHE'S AT MY HOUSE A LOT.
BY THE WAY, THAT NAME...
KASHA (CLANK) カシャ...

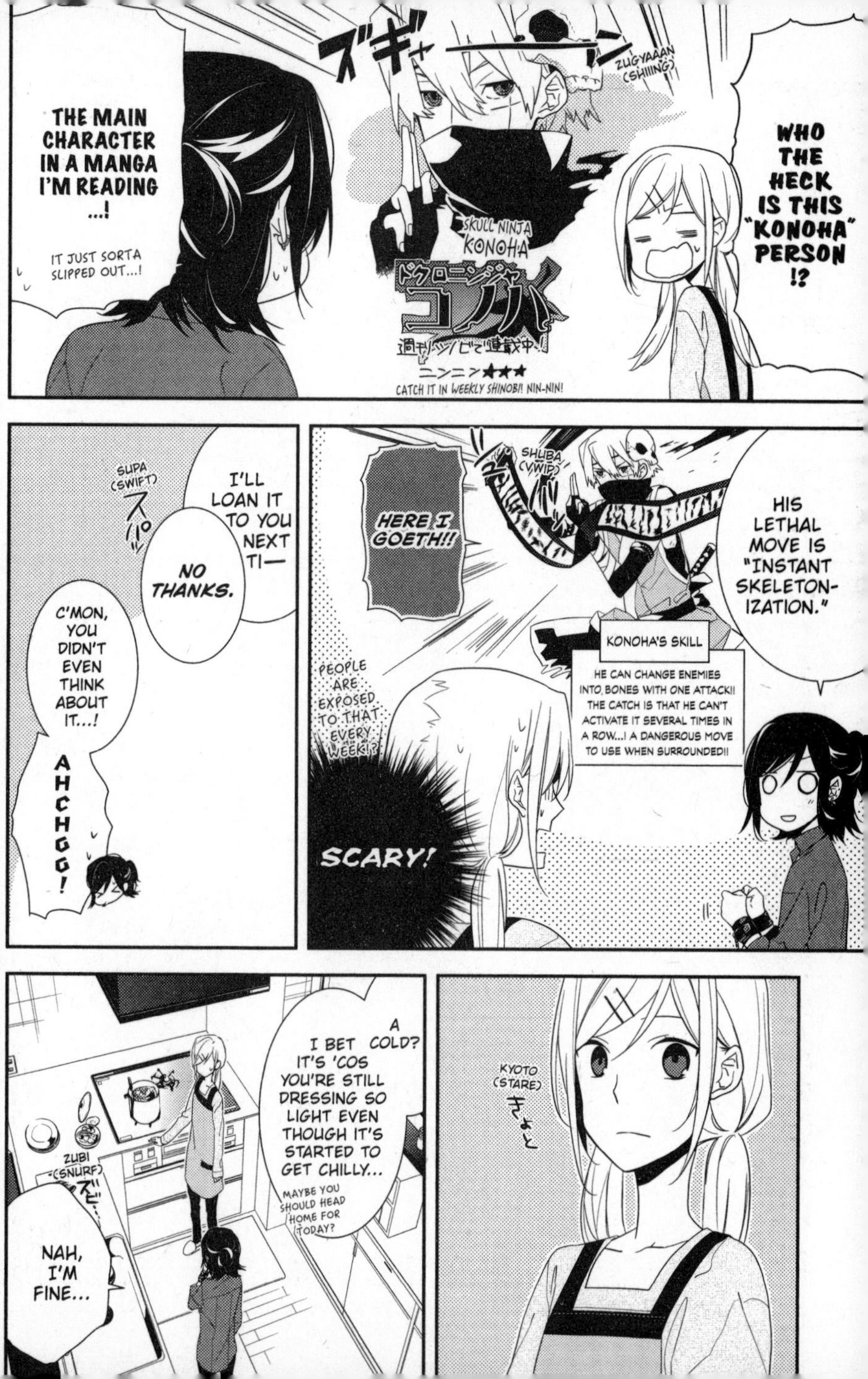

WHO THE HECK IS THIS "KONOHA" PERSON!?
ZUGYAAAN (SHIIING)
SKULL NINJA KONOHA
ドクロニンジャ コノハ
週刊シノビで連載中!
ニンニン★★★
CATCH IT IN WEEKLY SHINOBI!! NIN-NIN!
THE MAIN CHARACTER IN A MANGA I'M READING ...!
IT JUST SORTA SLIPPED OUT...!
HIS LETHAL MOVE IS "INSTANT SKELETON-IZATION."
SHUBA (VWIP)
HERE I GOETH!!
KONOHA'S SKILL
HE CAN CHANGE ENEMIES INTO BONES WITH ONE ATTACK!! THE CATCH IS THAT HE CAN'T ACTIVATE IT SEVERAL TIMES IN A ROW...! A DANGEROUS MOVE TO USE WHEN SURROUNDED!!
PEOPLE ARE EXPOSED TO THAT EVERY WEEK!?
SCARY!
I'LL LOAN IT TO YOU NEXT TI—
SUPA (SWIFT)
NO THANKS.
C'MON, YOU DIDN'T EVEN THINK ABOUT IT...!
AHCHGG!
KYOTO (STARE)
A COLD?
I BET IT'S 'COS YOU'RE STILL DRESSING SO LIGHT EVEN THOUGH IT'S STARTED TO GET CHILLY...
MAYBE YOU SHOULD HEAD HOME FOR TODAY?
ZUBI (SNURF)
NAH, I'M FINE...

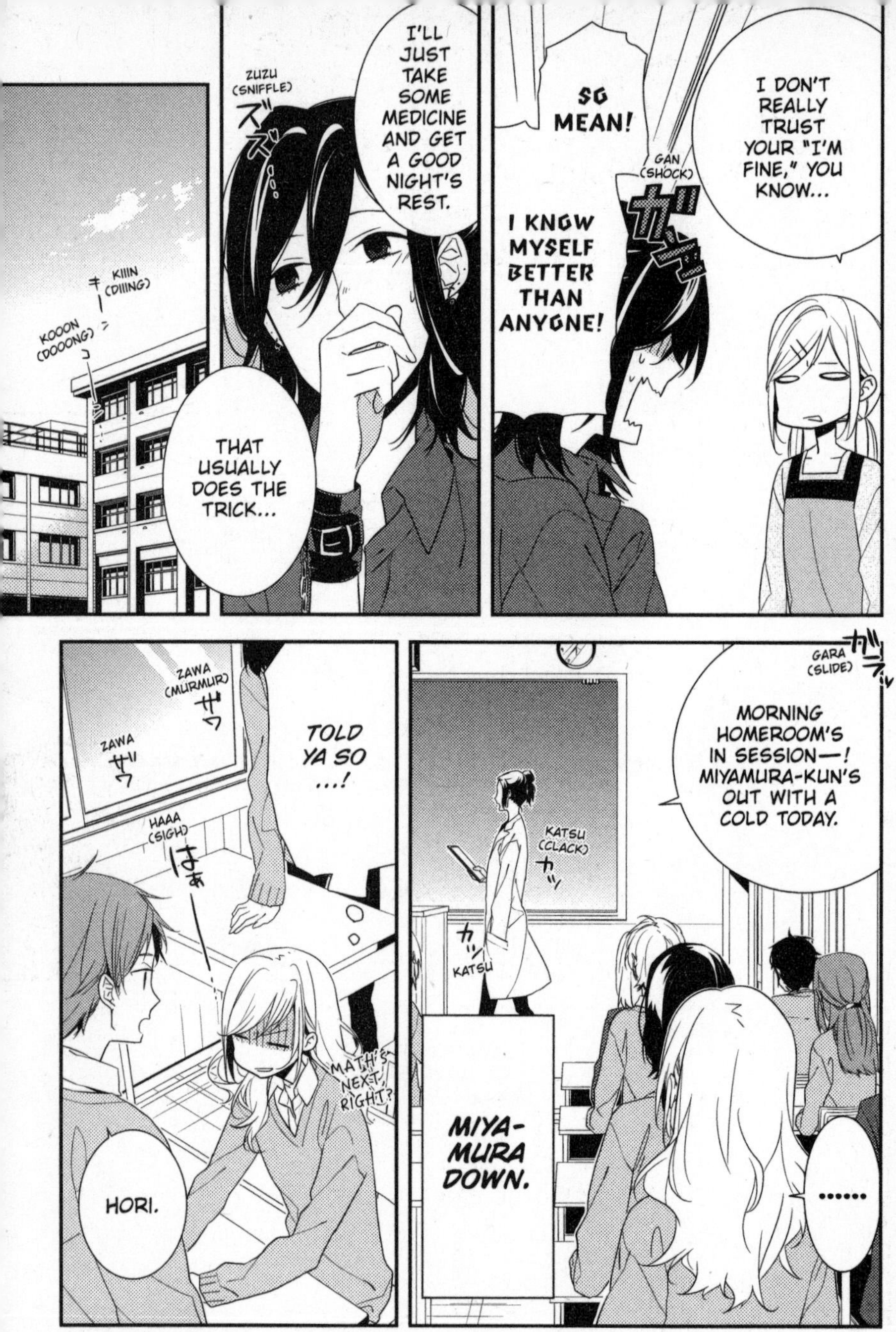
I DON'T REALLY TRUST YOUR "I'M FINE," YOU KNOW...
SO MEAN!
GAN (SHOCK)
I KNOW MYSELF BETTER THAN ANYONE!
I'LL JUST TAKE SOME MEDICINE AND GET A GOOD NIGHT'S REST.
ZUZU (SNIFFLE)
THAT USUALLY DOES THE TRICK...
KIIIN (DIIING)
KOOON (DOOONG)
GARA (SLIDE)
MORNING HOMEROOM'S IN SESSION—! MIYAMURA-KUN'S OUT WITH A COLD TODAY.
KATSU (CLACK)
KATSU
MIYA-MURA DOWN.
......
ZAWA (MURMUR)
ZAWA
TOLD YA SO ...!
HAAA (SIGH)
MATH'S NEXT, RIGHT?
HORI.

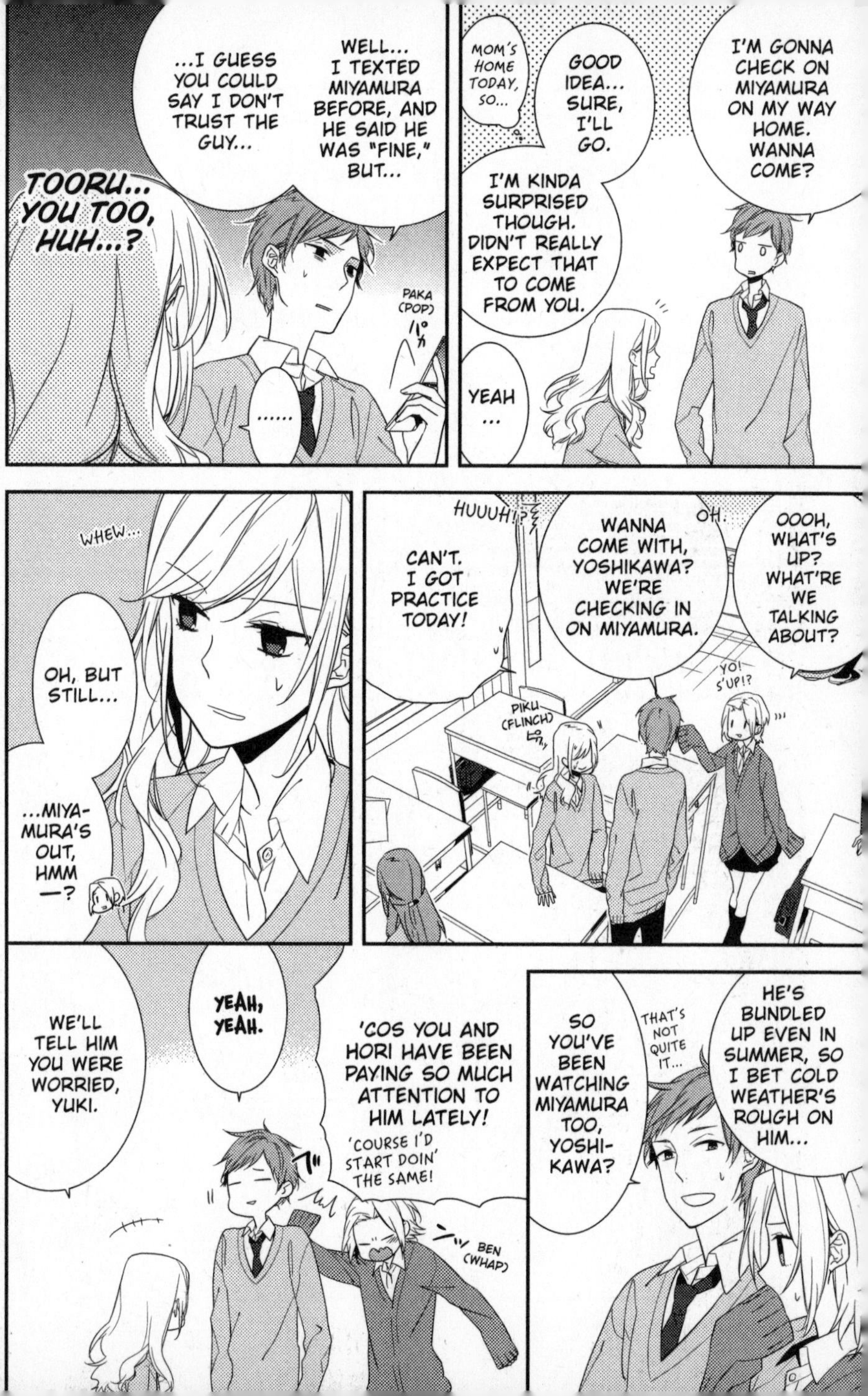
I'M GONNA CHECK ON MIYAMURA ON MY WAY HOME. WANNA COME?
GOOD IDEA... SURE, I'LL GO.
MOM'S HOME TODAY, SO...
I'M KINDA SURPRISED THOUGH. DIDN'T REALLY EXPECT THAT TO COME FROM YOU.
YEAH ...
WELL... I TEXTED MIYAMURA BEFORE, AND HE SAID HE WAS "FINE," BUT...
...I GUESS YOU COULD SAY I DON'T TRUST THE GUY...
TOORU... YOU TOO, HUH...?
PAKA (POP)
......
OOOH, WHAT'S UP? WHAT'RE WE TALKING ABOUT?
OH.
YO! S'UP!?
WANNA COME WITH, YOSHIKAWA? WE'RE CHECKING IN ON MIYAMURA.
HUUUH!?
CAN'T. I GOT PRACTICE TODAY!
PIKU (FLINCH)
WHEW...
OH, BUT STILL...
...MIYA-MURA'S OUT, HMM —?
HE'S BUNDLED UP EVEN IN SUMMER, SO I BET COLD WEATHER'S ROUGH ON HIM...
THAT'S NOT QUITE IT...
SO YOU'VE BEEN WATCHING MIYAMURA TOO, YOSHI-KAWA?
'COS YOU AND HORI HAVE BEEN PAYING SO MUCH ATTENTION TO HIM LATELY!
'COURSE I'D START DOIN' THE SAME!
BEN (WHAP)
YEAH, YEAH.
WE'LL TELL HIM YOU WERE WORRIED, YUKI.

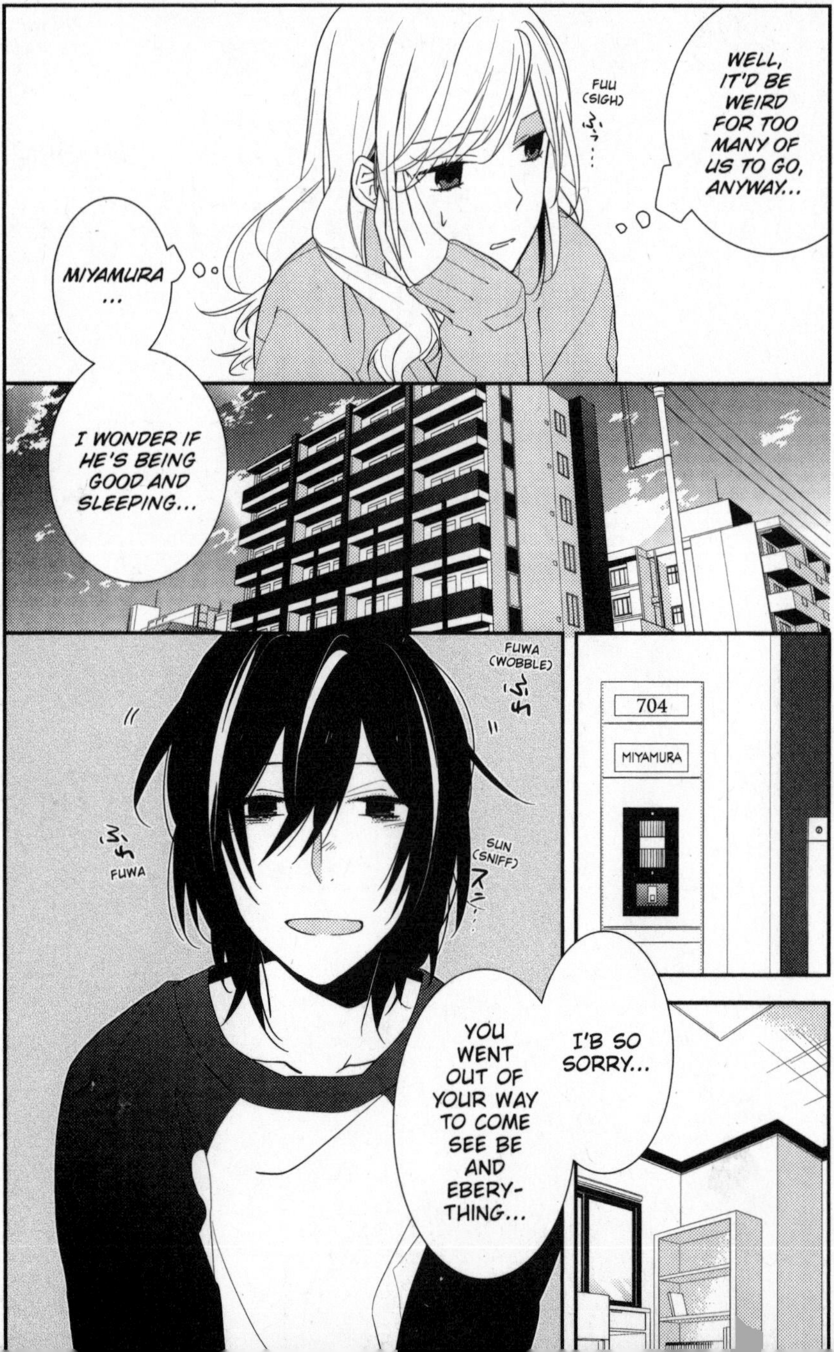
WELL, IT'D BE WEIRD FOR TOO MANY OF US TO GO, ANYWAY...
FUU (SIGH)
MIYAMURA ...
I WONDER IF HE'S BEING GOOD AND SLEEPING...
704
MIYAMURA
FUWA (WOBBLE)
SUN (SNIFF)
FUWA
I'B SO SORRY...
YOU WENT OUT OF YOUR WAY TO COME SEE BE AND EBERY-THING...

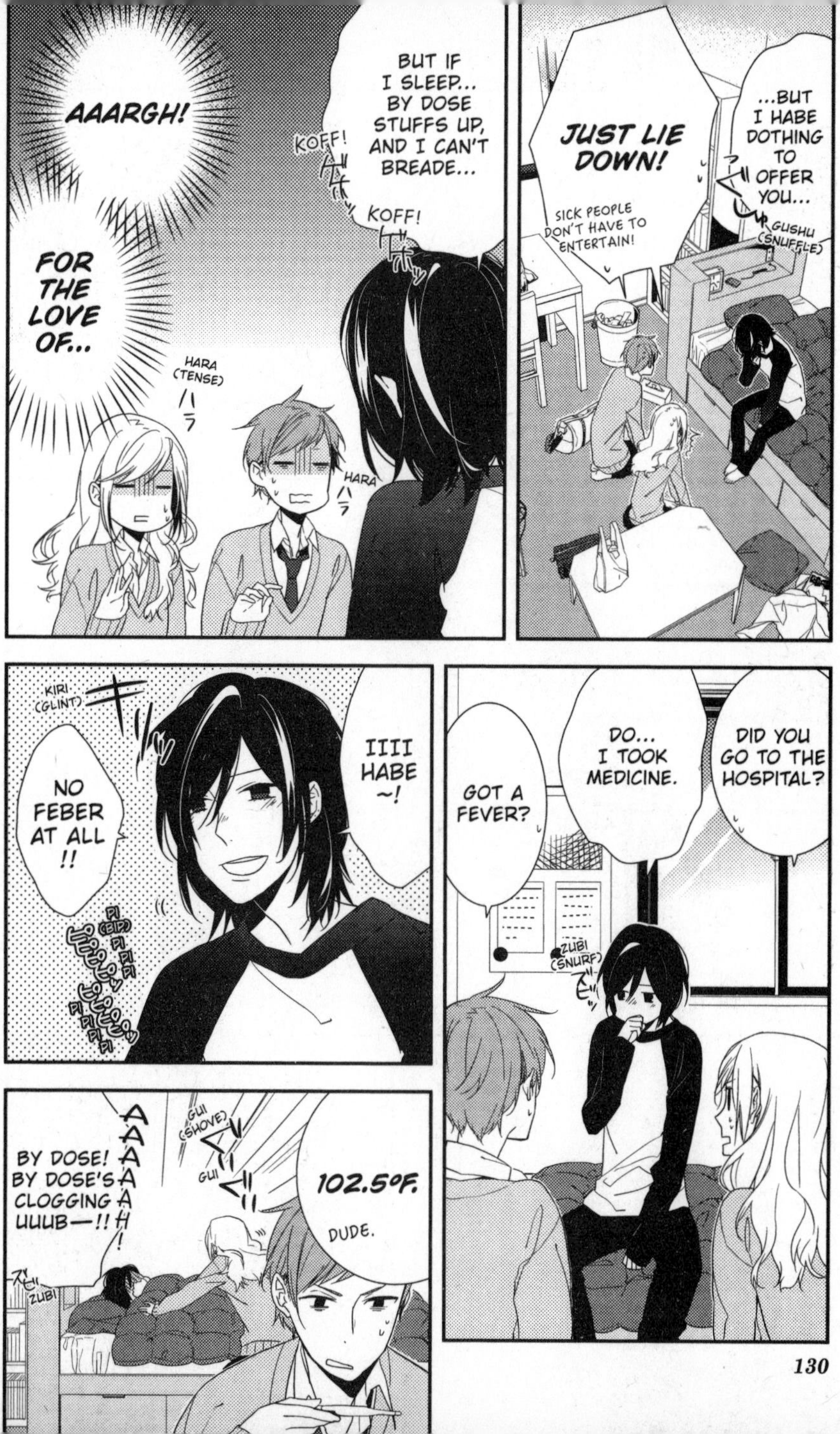
...BUT I HABE DOTHING TO OFFER YOU...
GUSHU (SNUFFLE)
JUST LIE DOWN!
SICK PEOPLE DON'T HAVE TO ENTERTAIN!
BUT IF I SLEEP... BY DOSE STUFFS UP, AND I CAN'T BREADE...
KOFF!
KOFF!
AAARGH!
FOR THE LOVE OF...
HARA (TENSE)
HARA
DID YOU GO TO THE HOSPITAL?
DO... I TOOK MEDICINE.
GOT A FEVER?
ZUBI (SNURF)
IIII HABE ~!
NO FEBER AT ALL !!
KIRI (GLINT)
PI (BIP) PI PI PI
PI PI PI PI
102.5°F.
DUDE.
GUI (SHOVE)
GUI
AAAAAAH!
BY DOSE! BY DOSE'S CLOGGING UUUB—!!
ZUBI

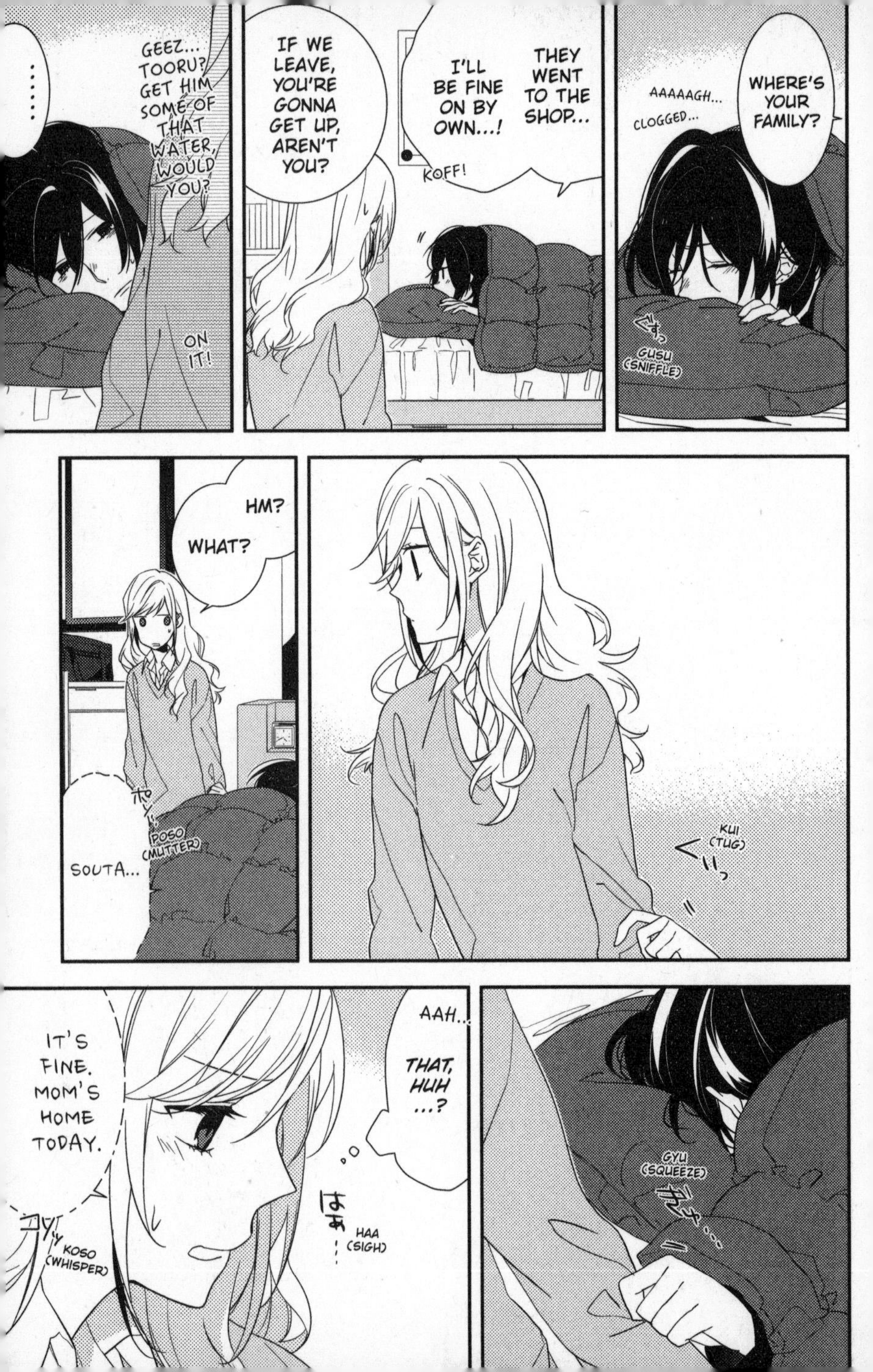
WHERE'S YOUR FAMILY?
AAAAAGH... CLOGGED...
GUSU (SNIFFLE)
THEY WENT TO THE SHOP...
I'LL BE FINE ON BY OWN...!
KOFF!
IF WE LEAVE, YOU'RE GONNA GET UP, AREN'T YOU?
GEEZ... TOORU? GET HIM SOME OF THAT WATER, WOULD YOU?
ON IT!
......
KUI (TUG)
HM?
WHAT?
POSO (MUTTER)
SOUTA...
GYU (SQUEEZE)
AAH...
THAT, HUH ...?
HAA (SIGH)
IT'S FINE. MOM'S HOME TODAY.
KOSO (WHISPER)

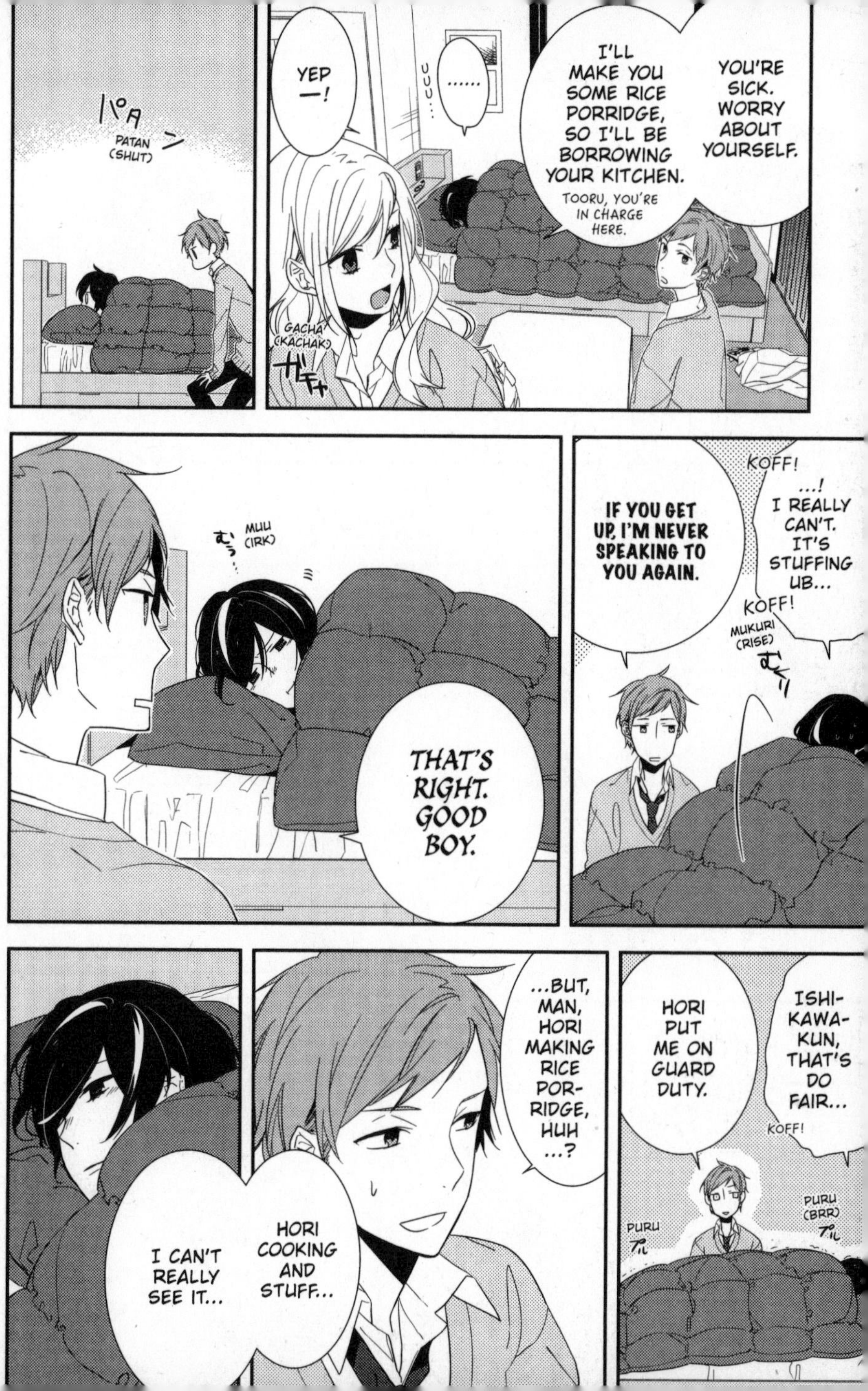
YOU'RE SICK. WORRY ABOUT YOURSELF.
I'LL MAKE YOU SOME RICE PORRIDGE, SO I'LL BE BORROWING YOUR KITCHEN.
TOORU, YOU'RE IN CHARGE HERE.
......
UUU...
YEP—!
GACHA (KACHAK)
PATAN (SHUT)
KOFF!
...! I REALLY CAN'T. IT'S STUFFING UB...
KOFF!
IF YOU GET UP, I'M NEVER SPEAKING TO YOU AGAIN.
MUKURI (RISE)
MUU (IRK)
THAT'S RIGHT. GOOD BOY.
ISHI-KAWA-KUN, THAT'S DO FAIR...
KOFF!
HORI PUT ME ON GUARD DUTY.
PURU (BRR)
PURU
...BUT, MAN, HORI MAKING RICE POR-RIDGE, HUH...?
HORI COOKING AND STUFF...
I CAN'T REALLY SEE IT...

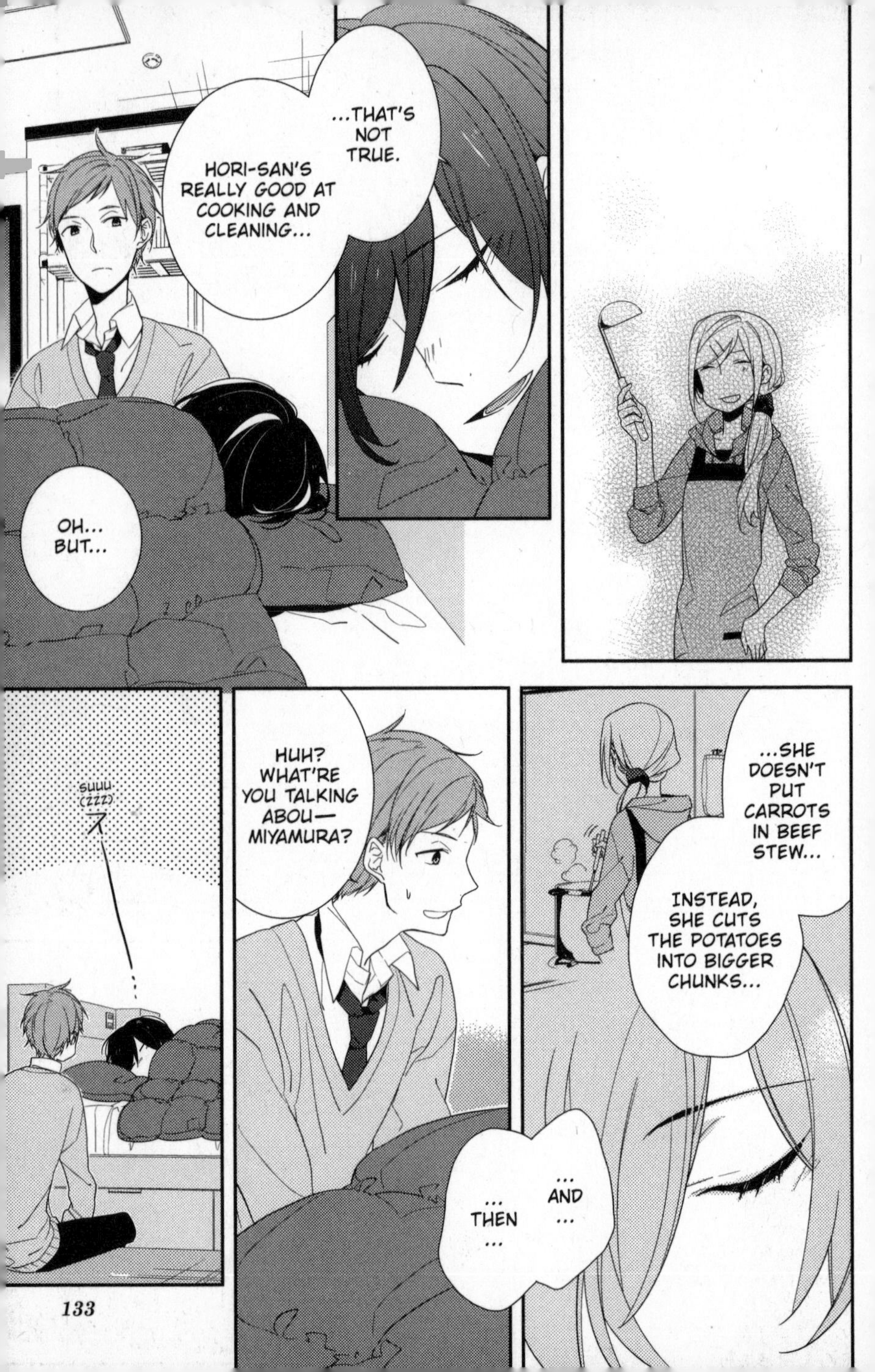
...THAT'S NOT TRUE.
HORI-SAN'S REALLY GOOD AT COOKING AND CLEANING...
OH... BUT...
...SHE DOESN'T PUT CARROTS IN BEEF STEW...
INSTEAD, SHE CUTS THE POTATOES INTO BIGGER CHUNKS...
... AND ...
... THEN ...
HUH? WHAT'RE YOU TALKING ABOU— MIYAMURA?
SUUU (ZZZ)
ス

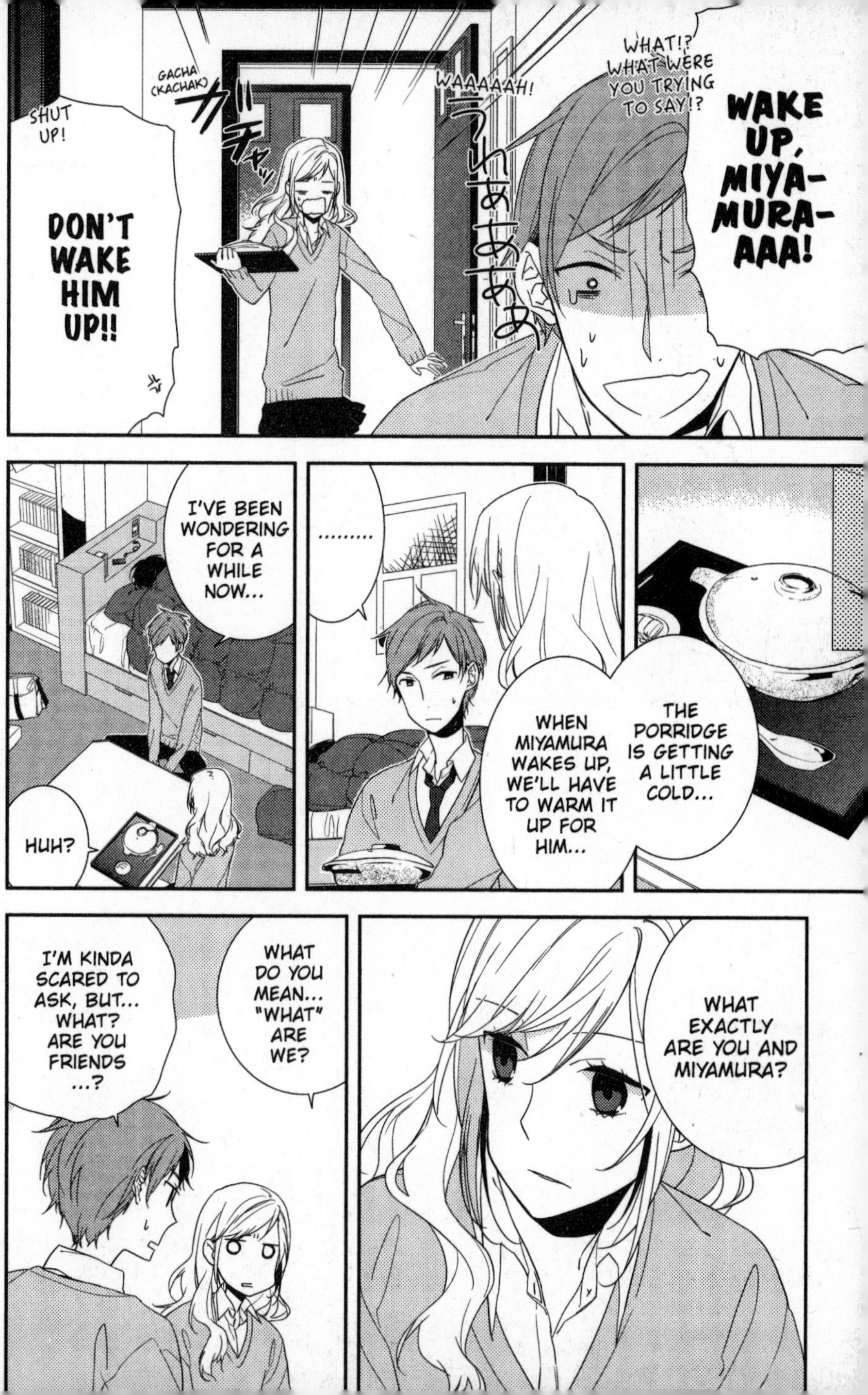
WHAT!? WHAT WERE YOU TRYING TO SAY!?
WAKE UP, MIYA-MURA-AAA!
WAAAAAH!
うわあああ
GACHA (KACHAK)
ガチャッ
SHUT UP!
DON'T WAKE HIM UP!!
THE PORRIDGE IS GETTING A LITTLE COLD...
WHEN MIYAMURA WAKES UP, WE'LL HAVE TO WARM IT UP FOR HIM...
....
I'VE BEEN WONDERING FOR A WHILE NOW...
HUH?
WHAT EXACTLY ARE YOU AND MIYAMURA?
WHAT DO YOU MEAN... "WHAT" ARE WE?
I'M KINDA SCARED TO ASK, BUT... WHAT? ARE YOU FRIENDS ...?

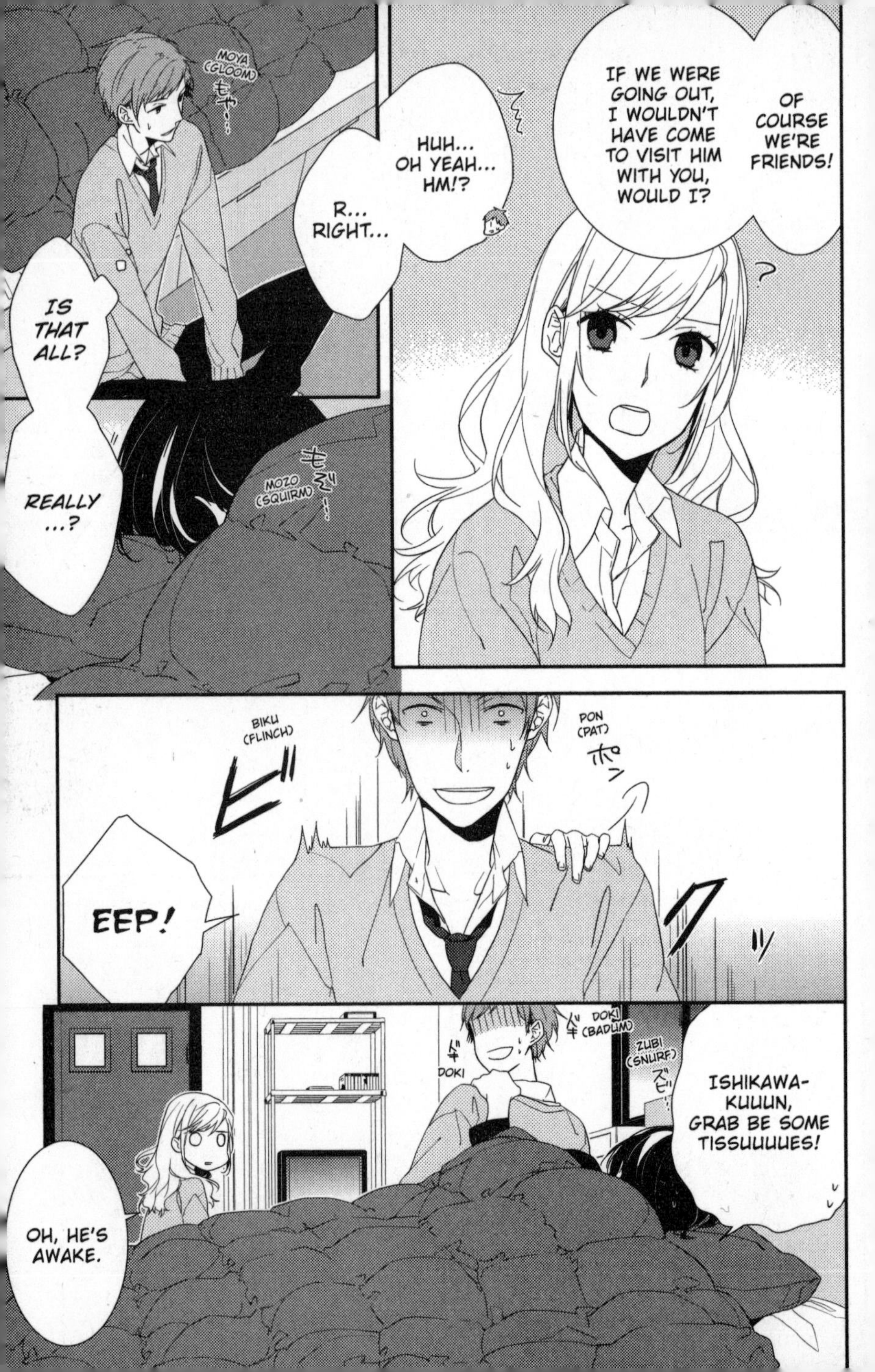
OF COURSE WE'RE FRIENDS!
IF WE WERE GOING OUT, I WOULDN'T HAVE COME TO VISIT HIM WITH YOU, WOULD I?
HUH... OH YEAH... HM!?
R... RIGHT...
MOYA (GLOOM)
IS THAT ALL?
REALLY ...?
MOZO (SQUIRM)
PON (PAT)
BIKU (FLINCH)
EEP!
ISHIKAWA-KUUUN, GRAB BE SOME TISSUUUUES!
ZUBI (SNURF)
DOKI (BADUM)
DOKI
OH, HE'S AWAKE.

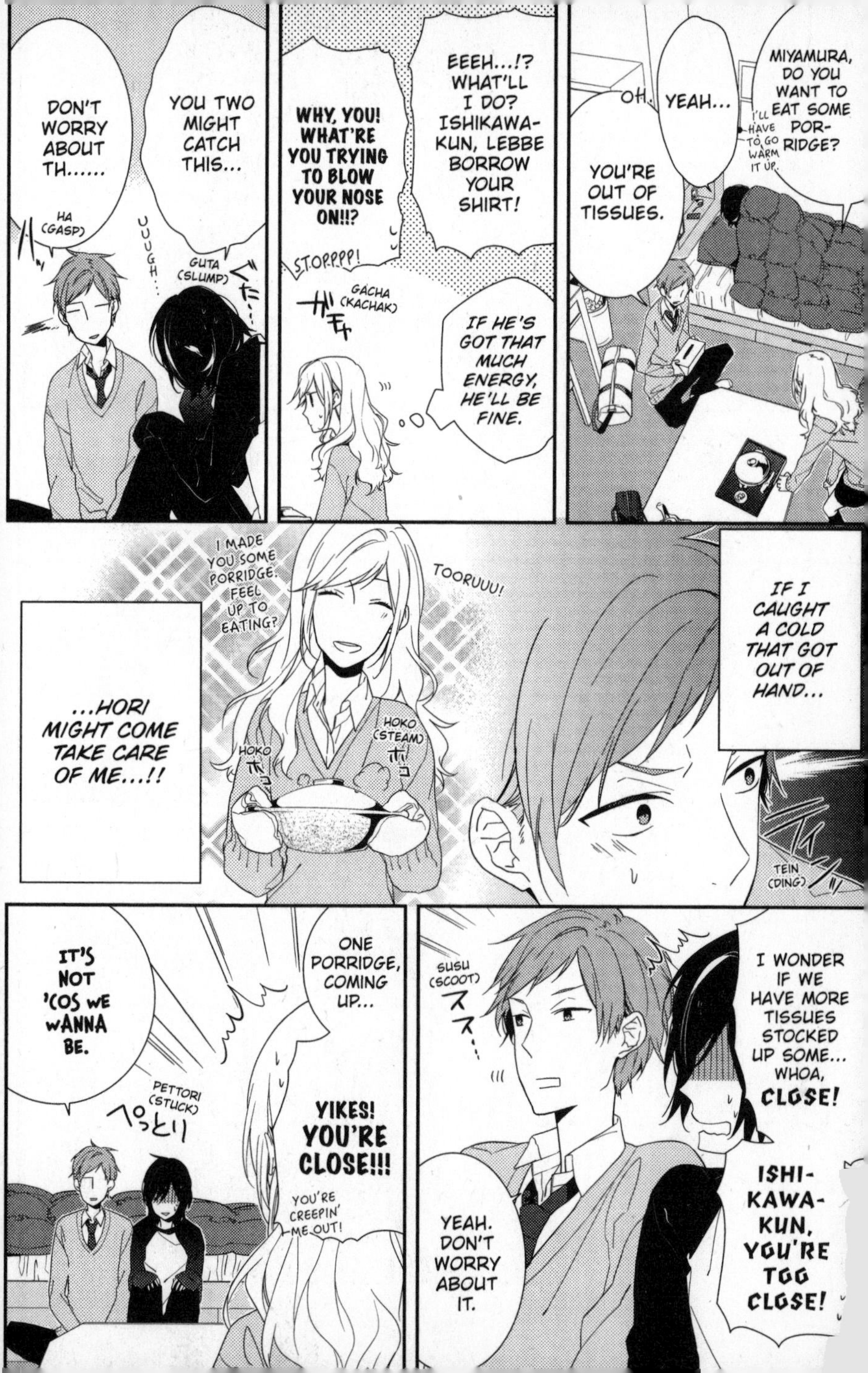
MIYAMURA, DO YOU WANT TO EAT SOME PORRIDGE?
I'LL HAVE TO GO WARM IT UP.
YEAH...
OH.
YOU'RE OUT OF TISSUES.
EEEH...!? WHAT'LL I DO? ISHIKAWA-KUN, LEBBE BORROW YOUR SHIRT!
WHY, YOU! WHAT'RE YOU TRYING TO BLOW YOUR NOSE ON!!?
STOPPPP!
GACHA (KACHAK)
IF HE'S GOT THAT MUCH ENERGY, HE'LL BE FINE.
YOU TWO MIGHT CATCH THIS...
UUUGH...
GUTA (SLUMP)
DON'T WORRY ABOUT TH......
HA (GASP)
IF I CAUGHT A COLD THAT GOT OUT OF HAND...
TEIN (DING)
TOORUUU!
I MADE YOU SOME PORRIDGE. FEEL UP TO EATING?
HOKO (STEAM)
HOKO
...HORI MIGHT COME TAKE CARE OF ME...!!
I WONDER IF WE HAVE MORE TISSUES STOCKED UP SOME... WHOA, CLOSE!
SUSU (SCOOT)
ISHIKAWA-KUN, YOU'RE TOO CLOSE!
YEAH. DON'T WORRY ABOUT IT.
ONE PORRIDGE, COMING UP...
YIKES! YOU'RE CLOSE!!!
IT'S NOT 'COS WE WANNA BE.
PETTORI (STUCK)
YOU'RE CREEPIN' ME OUT!

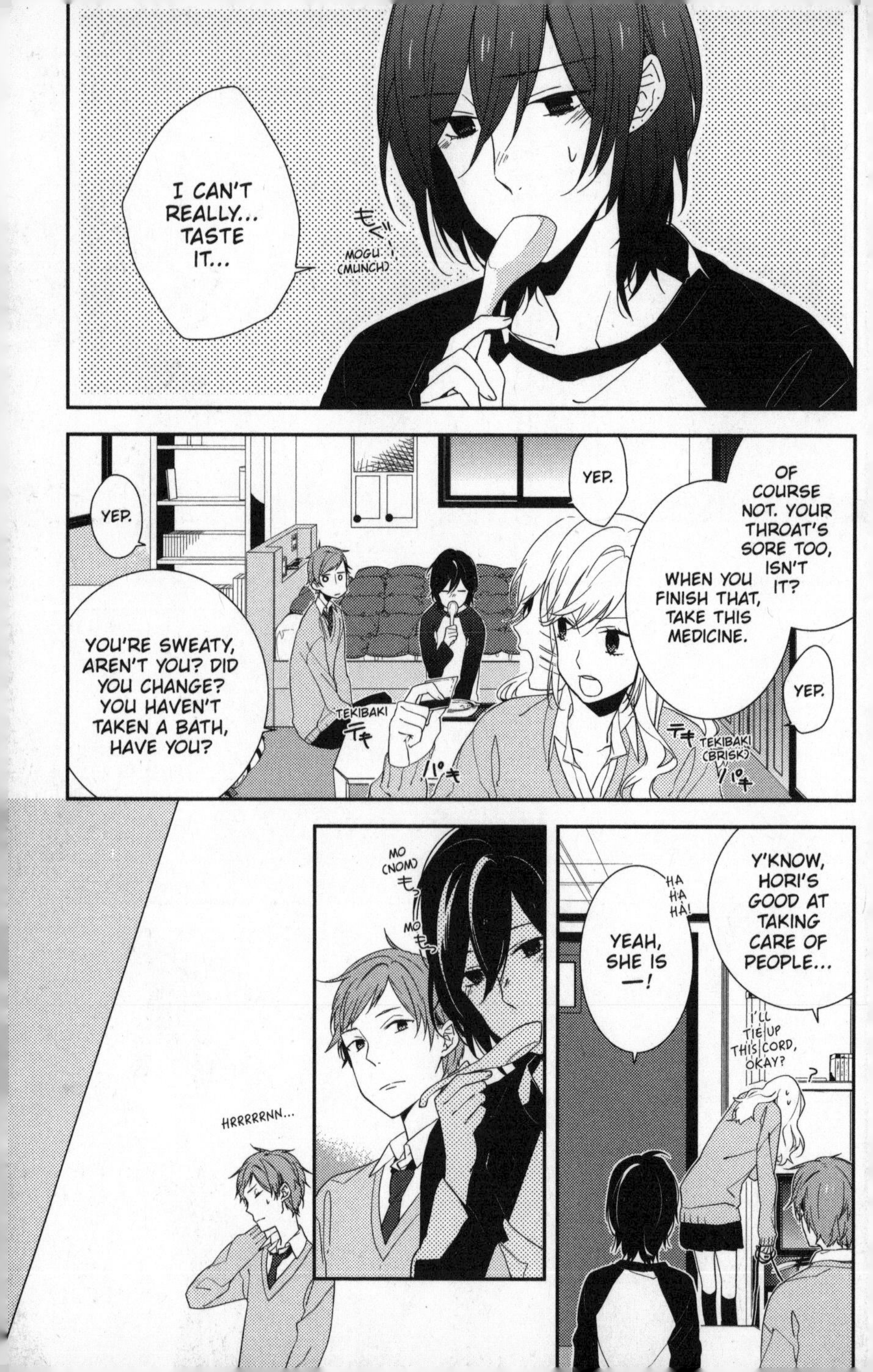
I CAN'T REALLY... TASTE IT...
もぐ
MOGU (MUNCH)
OF COURSE NOT. YOUR THROAT'S SORE TOO, ISN'T IT?
YEP.
WHEN YOU FINISH THAT, TAKE THIS MEDICINE.
YEP.
テキパキ
TEKIBAKI (BRISK)
YOU'RE SWEATY, AREN'T YOU? DID YOU CHANGE? YOU HAVEN'T TAKEN A BATH, HAVE YOU?
YEP.
テキパキ
TEKIBAKI
Y'KNOW, HORI'S GOOD AT TAKING CARE OF PEOPLE...
HA HA HA!
YEAH, SHE IS—!
I'LL TIE UP THIS CORD, OKAY?
MO (NOM)
MO
HRRRRRNN...

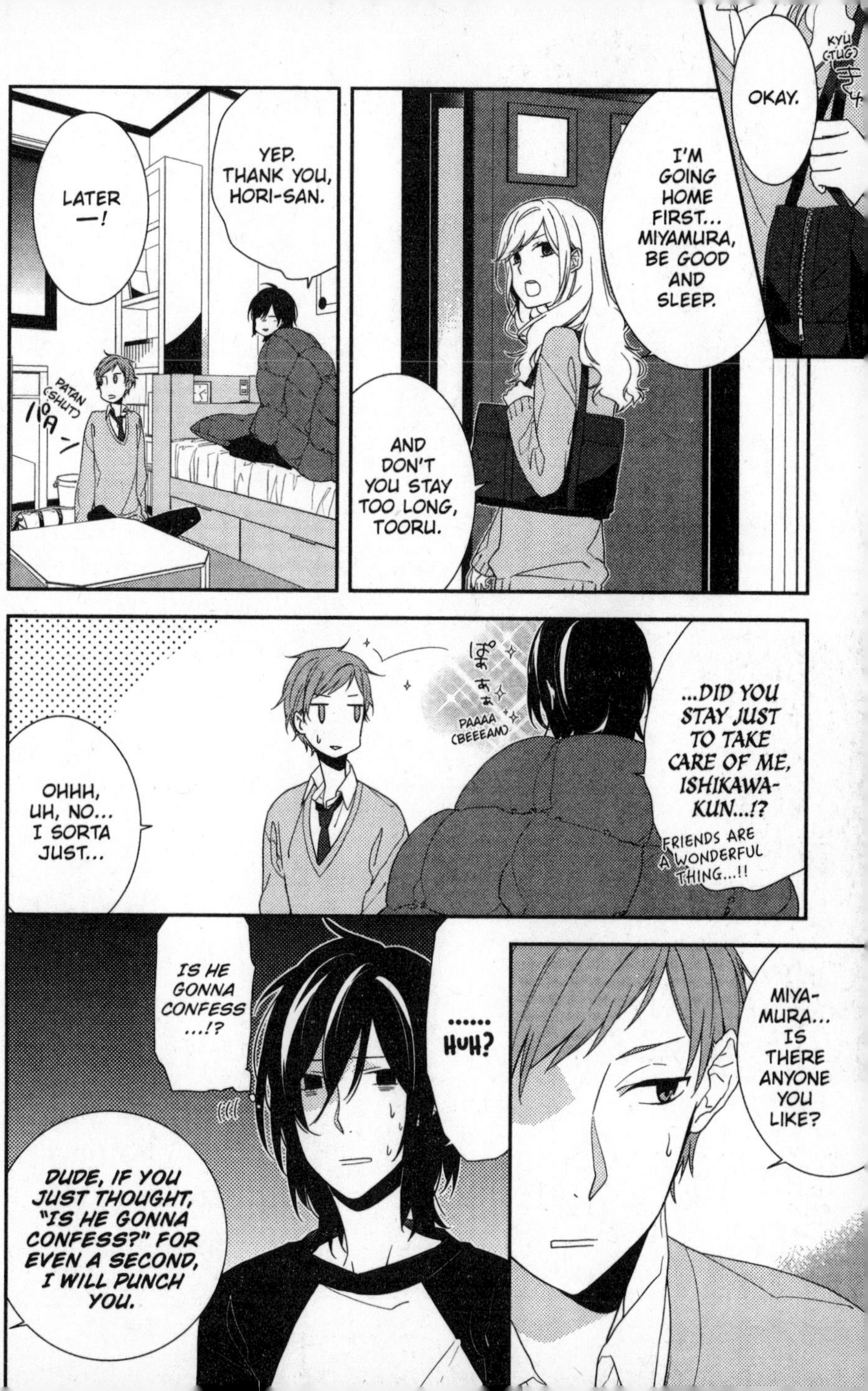
KYU (TUG)
OKAY.
I'M GOING HOME FIRST... MIYAMURA, BE GOOD AND SLEEP.
AND DON'T YOU STAY TOO LONG, TOORU.
YEP. THANK YOU, HORI-SAN.
LATER—!
PATAN (SHUT)
...DID YOU STAY JUST TO TAKE CARE OF ME, ISHIKAWA-KUN...!?
FRIENDS ARE A WONDERFUL THING...!!
PAAAA (BEEEAM)
OHHH, UH, NO... I SORTA JUST...
MIYA-MURA... IS THERE ANYONE YOU LIKE?
...... HUH?
IS HE GONNA CONFESS ...!?
DUDE, IF YOU JUST THOUGHT, "IS HE GONNA CONFESS?" FOR EVEN A SECOND, I WILL PUNCH YOU.

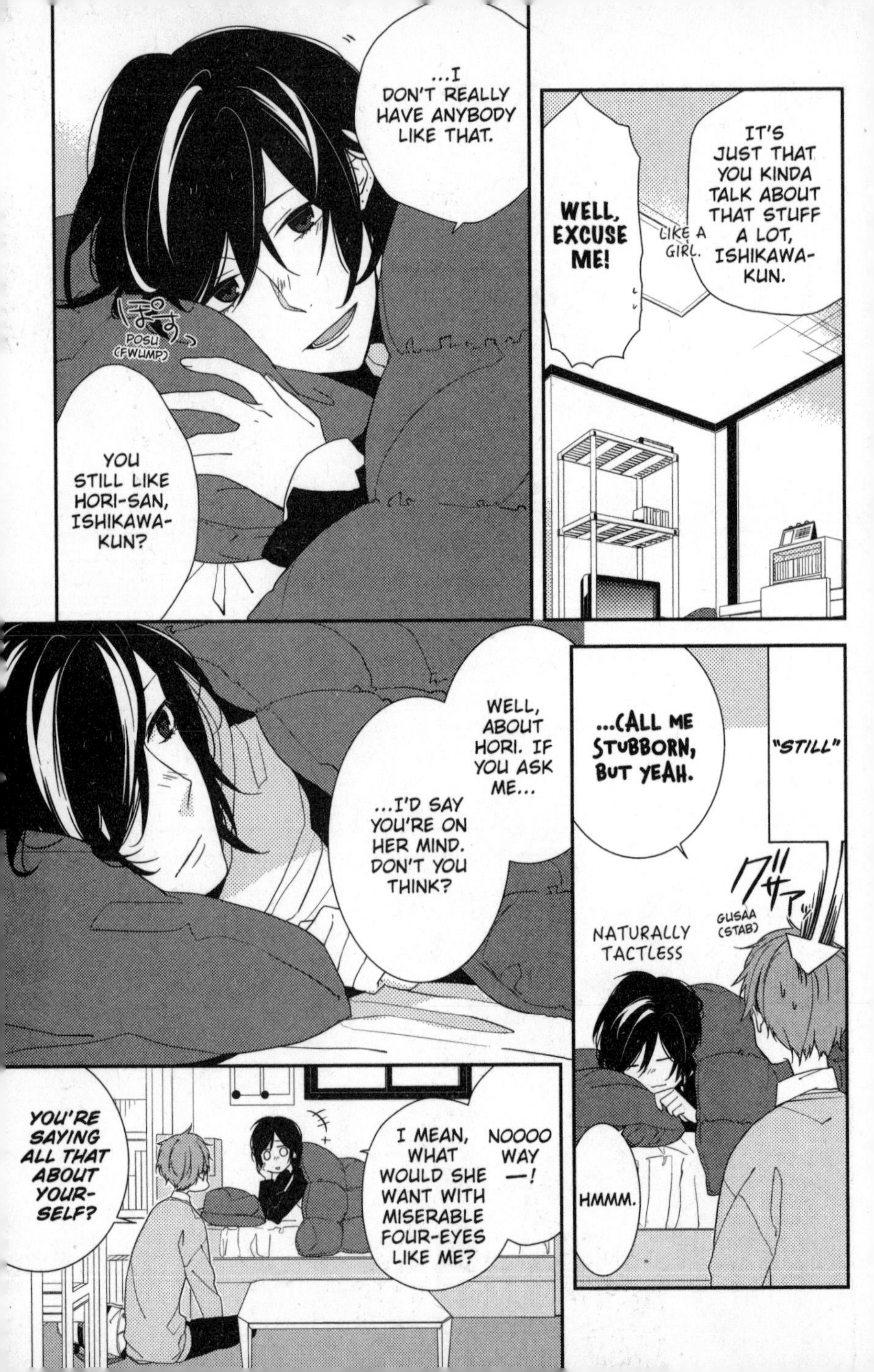
IT'S JUST THAT YOU KINDA TALK ABOUT THAT STUFF A LOT, ISHIKAWA-KUN.
LIKE A GIRL.
WELL, EXCUSE ME!
...I DON'T REALLY HAVE ANYBODY LIKE THAT.
ぽすっ
POSU (FWUMP)
YOU STILL LIKE HORI-SAN, ISHIKAWA-KUN?
"STILL"
...CALL ME STUBBORN, BUT YEAH.
グサァッ
GUSAA (STAB)
NATURALLY TACTLESS
HMMM.
WELL, ABOUT HORI. IF YOU ASK ME...
...I'D SAY YOU'RE ON HER MIND. DON'T YOU THINK?
NOOOO WAY—!
I MEAN, WHAT WOULD SHE WANT WITH MISERABLE FOUR-EYES LIKE ME?
YOU'RE SAYING ALL THAT ABOUT YOURSELF?

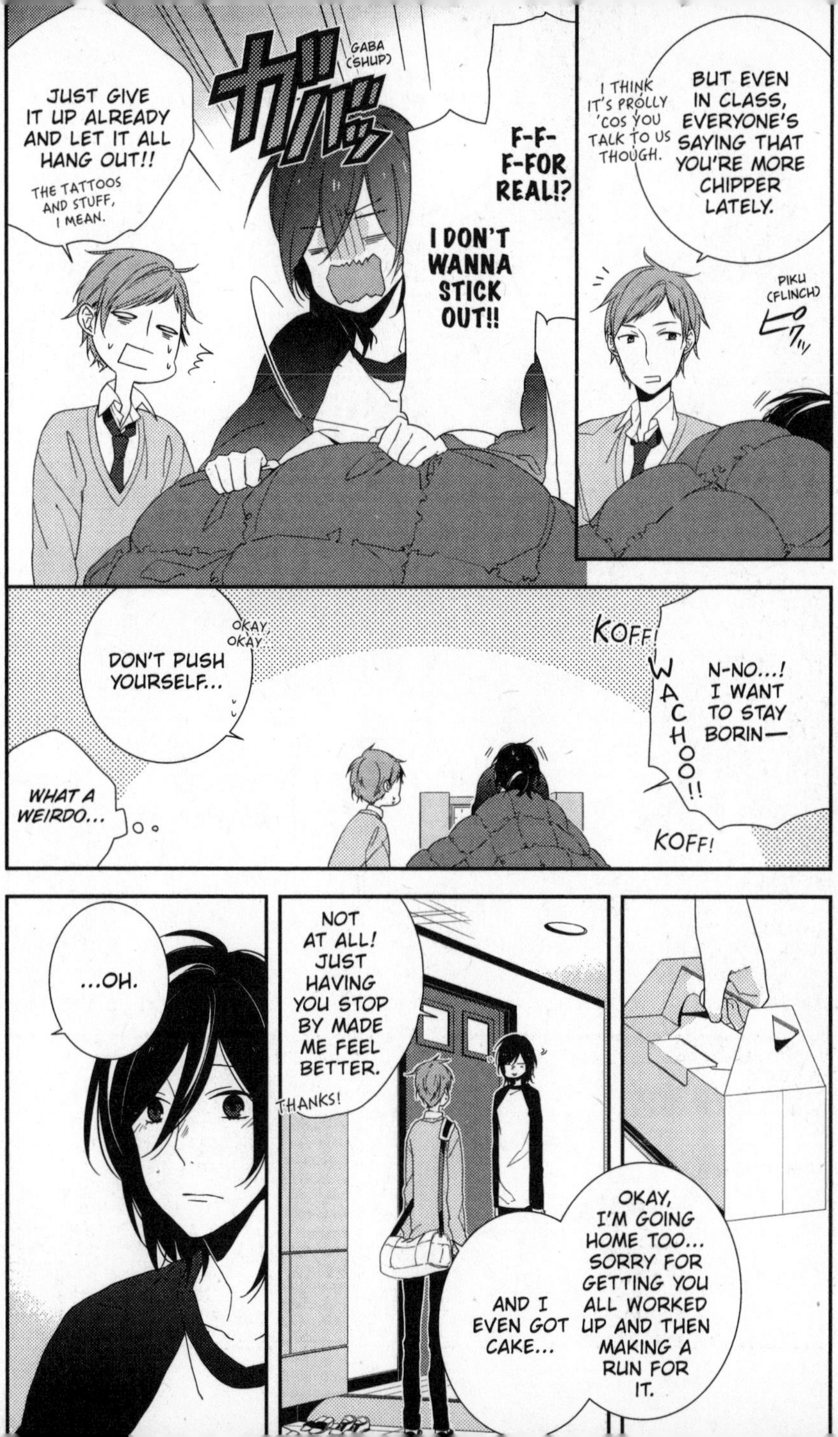
I THINK IT'S PROLLY 'COS YOU TALK TO US THOUGH.
BUT EVEN IN CLASS, EVERYONE'S SAYING THAT YOU'RE MORE CHIPPER LATELY.
PIKU (FLINCH)
GABA (SHUP)
F-F-F-FOR REAL!?
I DON'T WANNA STICK OUT!!
JUST GIVE IT UP ALREADY AND LET IT ALL HANG OUT!!
THE TATTOOS AND STUFF, I MEAN.
KOFF!
N-NO...! I WANT TO STAY BORIN—
WACHOO!!
KOFF!
OKAY, OKAY
DON'T PUSH YOURSELF...
WHAT A WEIRDO...
OKAY, I'M GOING HOME TOO... SORRY FOR GETTING YOU ALL WORKED UP AND THEN MAKING A RUN FOR IT.
AND I EVEN GOT CAKE...
NOT AT ALL! JUST HAVING YOU STOP BY MADE ME FEEL BETTER.
THANKS!
...OH.

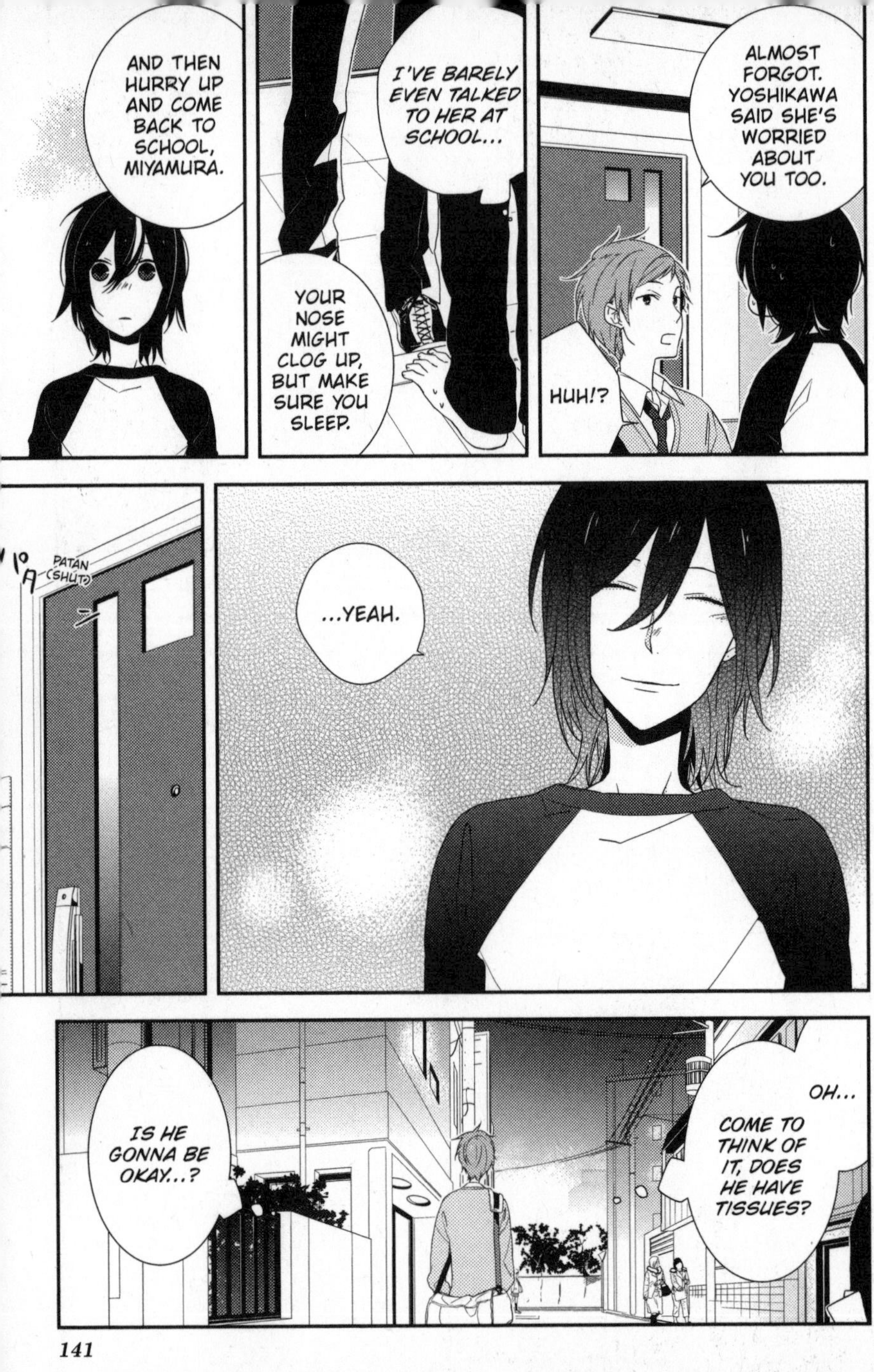
ALMOST FORGOT. YOSHIKAWA SAID SHE'S WORRIED ABOUT YOU TOO.
HUH!?
I'VE BARELY EVEN TALKED TO HER AT SCHOOL...
YOUR NOSE MIGHT CLOG UP, BUT MAKE SURE YOU SLEEP.
AND THEN HURRY UP AND COME BACK TO SCHOOL, MIYAMURA.
...YEAH.
PATAN (SHUT)
OH... COME TO THINK OF IT, DOES HE HAVE TISSUES?
IS HE GONNA BE OKAY...?

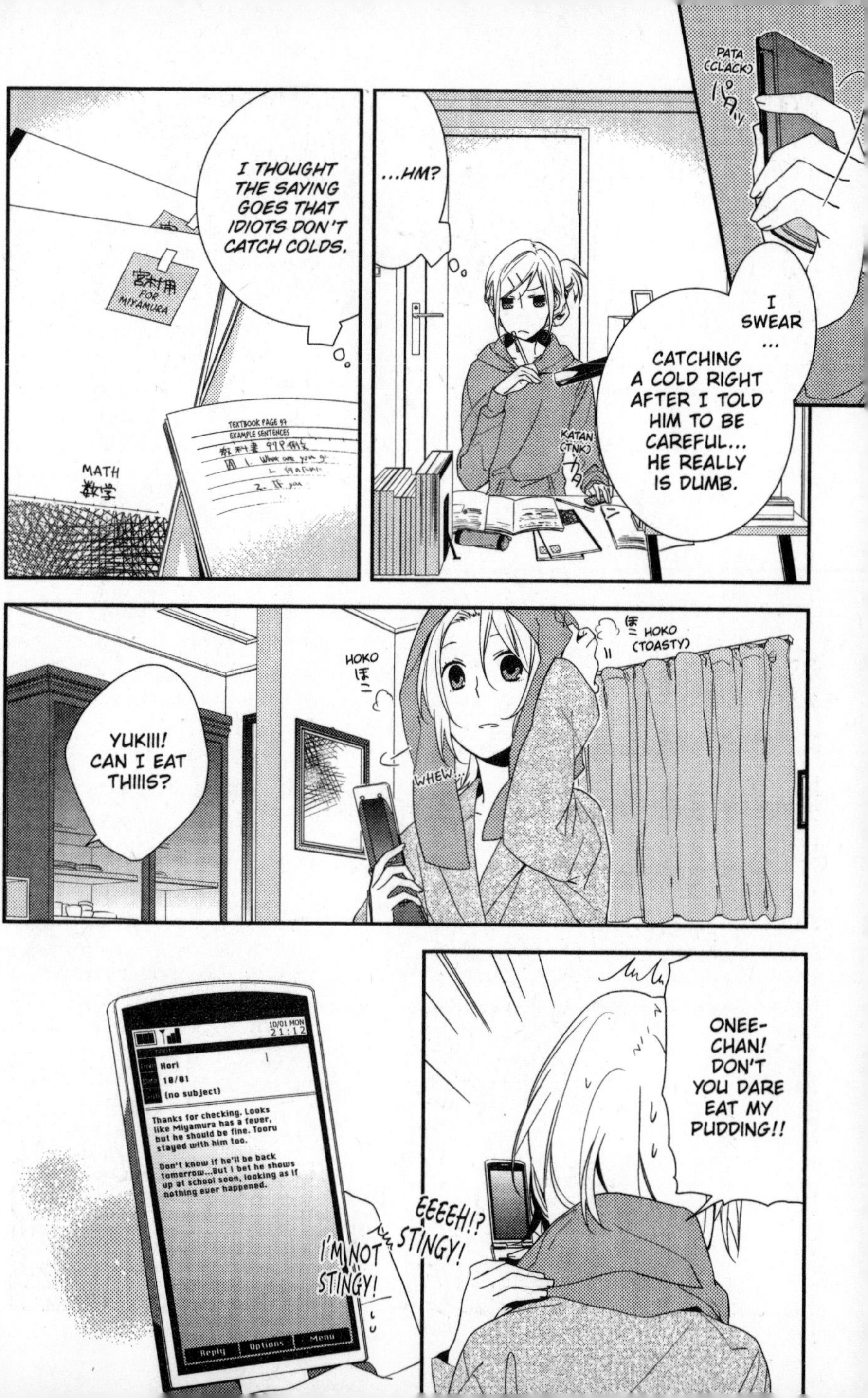
PATA (CLACK)
I SWEAR... CATCHING A COLD RIGHT AFTER I TOLD HIM TO BE CAREFUL... HE REALLY IS DUMB.
...HM?
KATAN (TNK)
I THOUGHT THE SAYING GOES THAT IDIOTS DON'T CATCH COLDS.
FOR MIYAMURA
TEXTBOOK PAGE 97 EXAMPLE SENTENCES
MATH
HOKO (TOASTY)
HOKO
WHEW...
YUKIII! CAN I EAT THIIIS?
ONEE-CHAN! DON'T YOU DARE EAT MY PUDDING!!
EEEEH!? STINGY!
I'M NOT STINGY!
10/01 MON
21:12
Hori
10/01
(no subject)
Thanks for checking. Looks like Miyamura has a fever, but he should be fine. Tooru stayed with him too.
Don't know if he'll be back tomorrow...But I bet he shows up at school soon, looking as if nothing ever happened.
Reply
Options
Menu

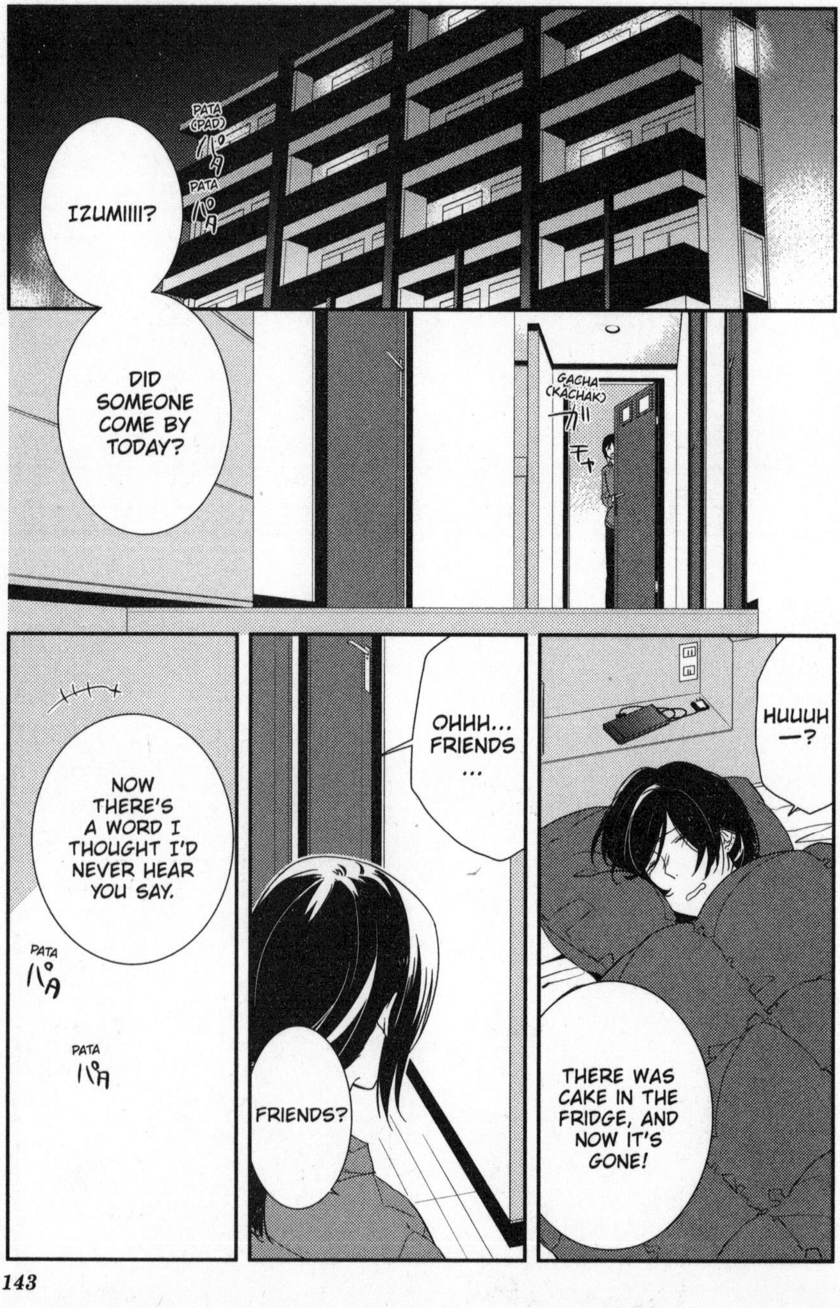
IZUMIIII?
PATA (PAD)
パタ
PATA
パタ
DID SOMEONE COME BY TODAY?
GACHA (KACHAK)
ガチャ
HUUUH—?
THERE WAS CAKE IN THE FRIDGE, AND NOW IT'S GONE!
OHHH... FRIENDS...
FRIENDS?
NOW THERE'S A WORD I THOUGHT I'D NEVER HEAR YOU SAY.
PATA
パタ
PATA
パタ

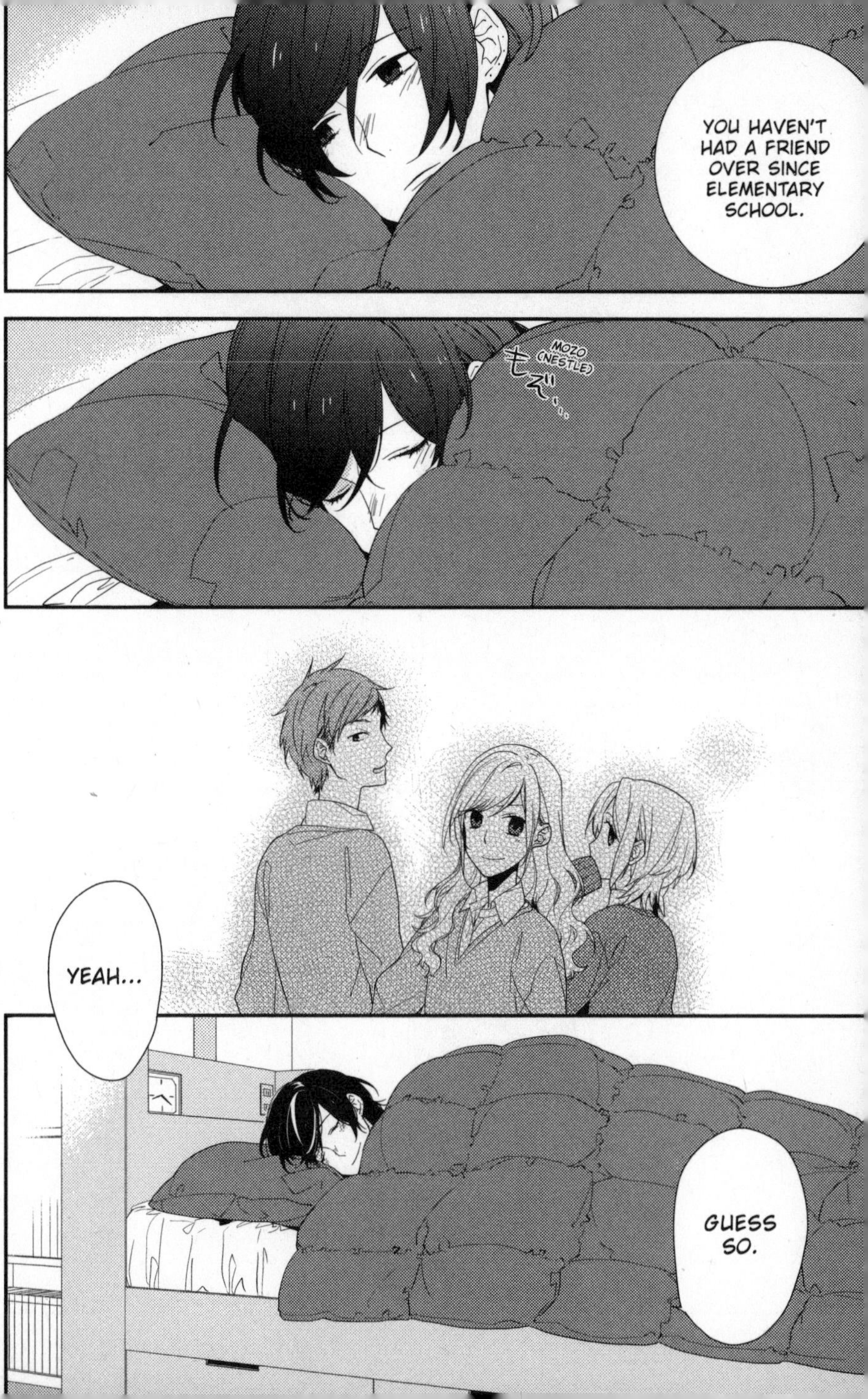
YOU HAVEN'T HAD A FRIEND OVER SINCE ELEMENTARY SCHOOL.
もぞ...
MOZO (NESTLE)
YEAH...
GUESS SO.

HORIMIYA

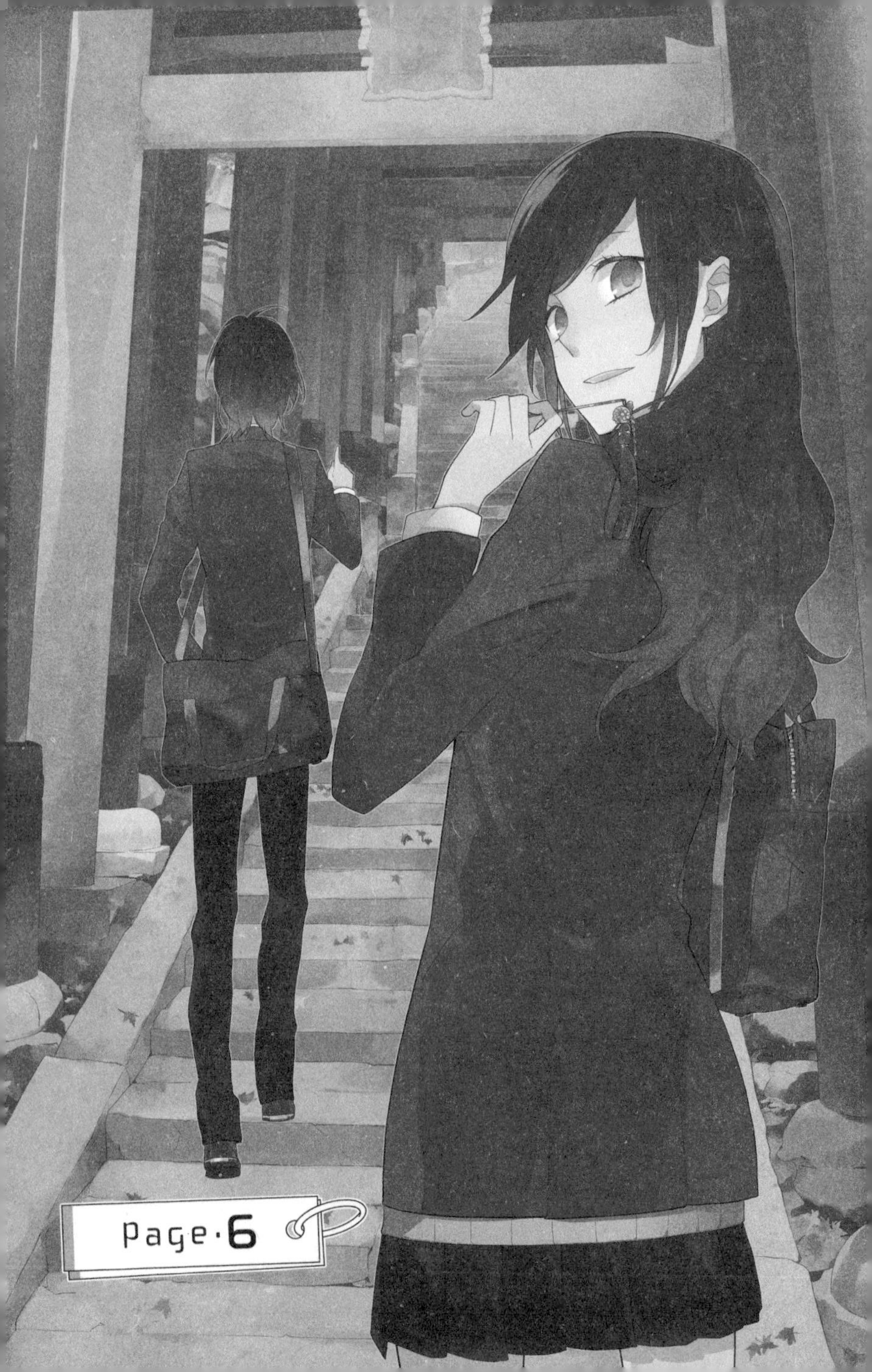
page·6

HORIMIYA

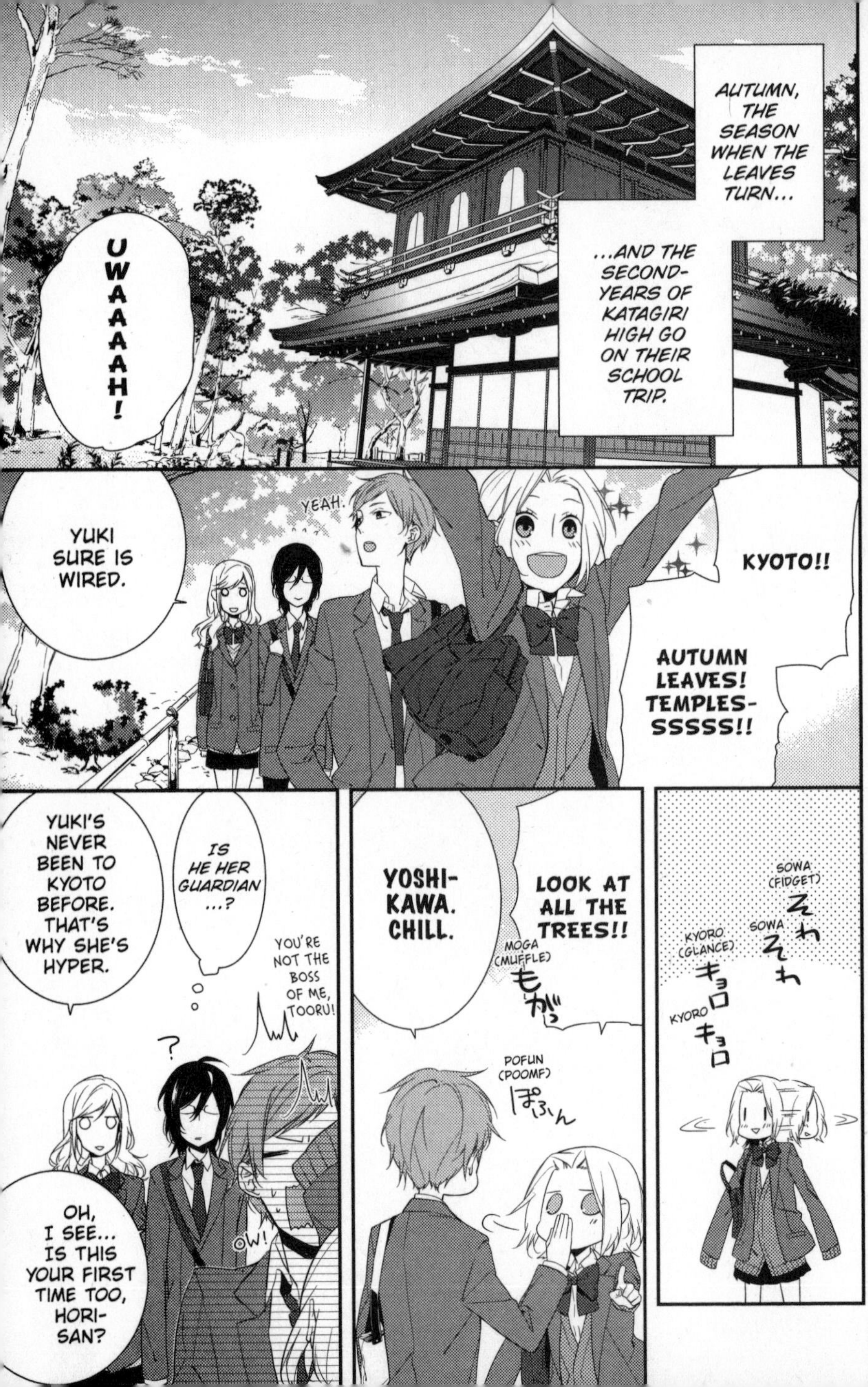
AUTUMN, THE SEASON WHEN THE LEAVES TURN...
...AND THE SECOND-YEARS OF KATAGIRI HIGH GO ON THEIR SCHOOL TRIP.
UWAAAAAH!
KYOTO!!
AUTUMN LEAVES! TEMPLES-SSSSS!!
YEAH.
YUKI SURE IS WIRED.
SOWA (FIDGET)
そわ
SOWA
そわ
KYORO (GLANCE)
キョロ
KYORO
キョロ
LOOK AT ALL THE TREES!!
YOSHI-KAWA. CHILL.
MOGA (MUFFLE)
もがっ
POFUN (POOMF)
ぽふん
IS HE HER GUARDIAN ...?
YUKI'S NEVER BEEN TO KYOTO BEFORE. THAT'S WHY SHE'S HYPER.
YOU'RE NOT THE BOSS OF ME, TOORU!
?
OW!
OH, I SEE... IS THIS YOUR FIRST TIME TOO, HORI-SAN?

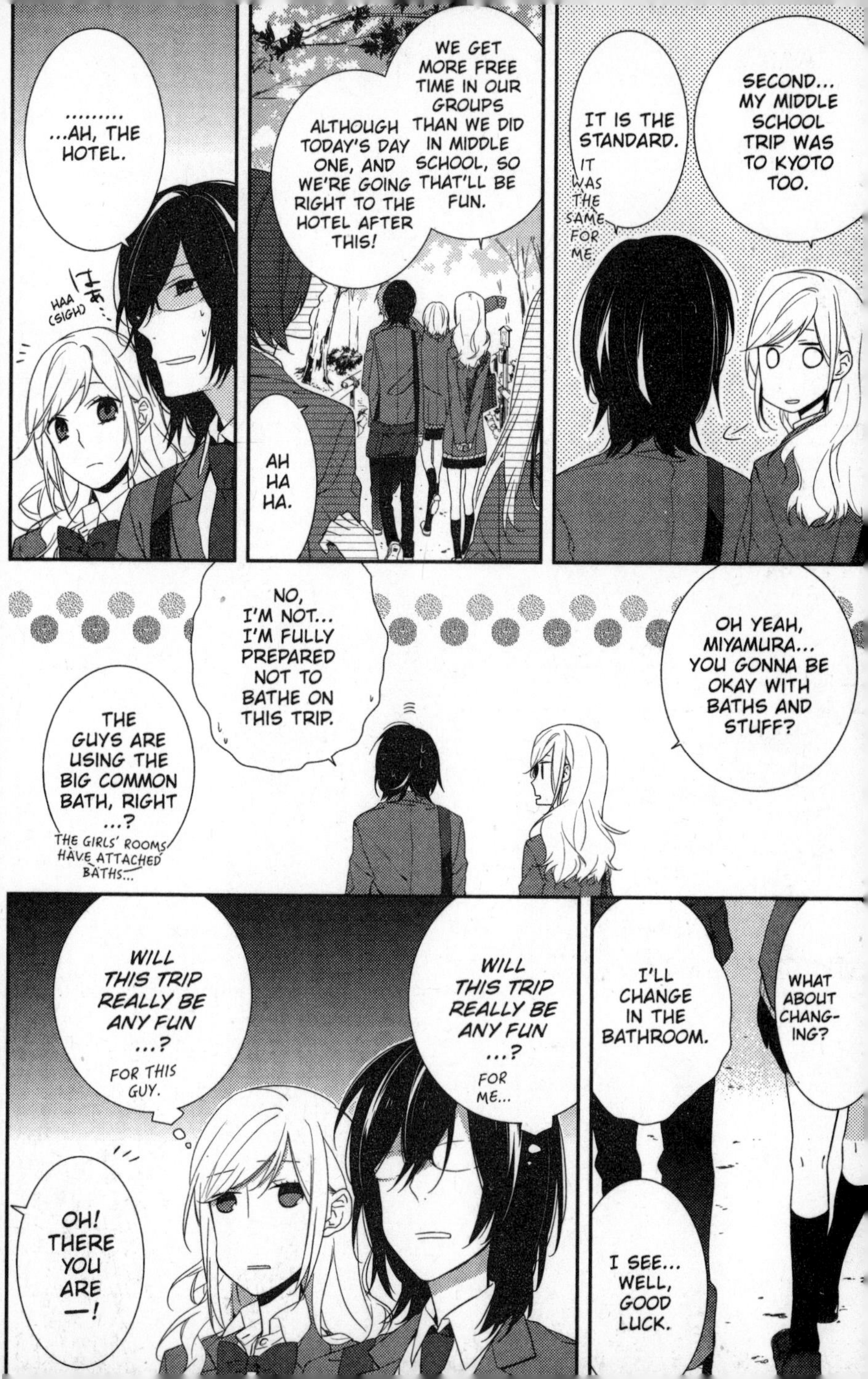
SECOND... MY MIDDLE SCHOOL TRIP WAS TO KYOTO TOO.
IT IS THE STANDARD.
IT WAS THE SAME FOR ME.
WE GET MORE FREE TIME IN OUR GROUPS THAN WE DID IN MIDDLE SCHOOL, SO THAT'LL BE FUN.
ALTHOUGH TODAY'S DAY ONE, AND WE'RE GOING RIGHT TO THE HOTEL AFTER THIS!
AH HA HA.
....AH, THE HOTEL.
はぁ
HAA (SIGH)
OH YEAH, MIYAMURA... YOU GONNA BE OKAY WITH BATHS AND STUFF?
NO, I'M NOT... I'M FULLY PREPARED NOT TO BATHE ON THIS TRIP.
THE GUYS ARE USING THE BIG COMMON BATH, RIGHT ...?
THE GIRLS' ROOMS HAVE ATTACHED BATHS...
WHAT ABOUT CHANG-ING?
I'LL CHANGE IN THE BATHROOM.
I SEE... WELL, GOOD LUCK.
WILL THIS TRIP REALLY BE ANY FUN ...?
FOR ME...
WILL THIS TRIP REALLY BE ANY FUN ...?
FOR THIS GUY.
OH! THERE YOU ARE—!

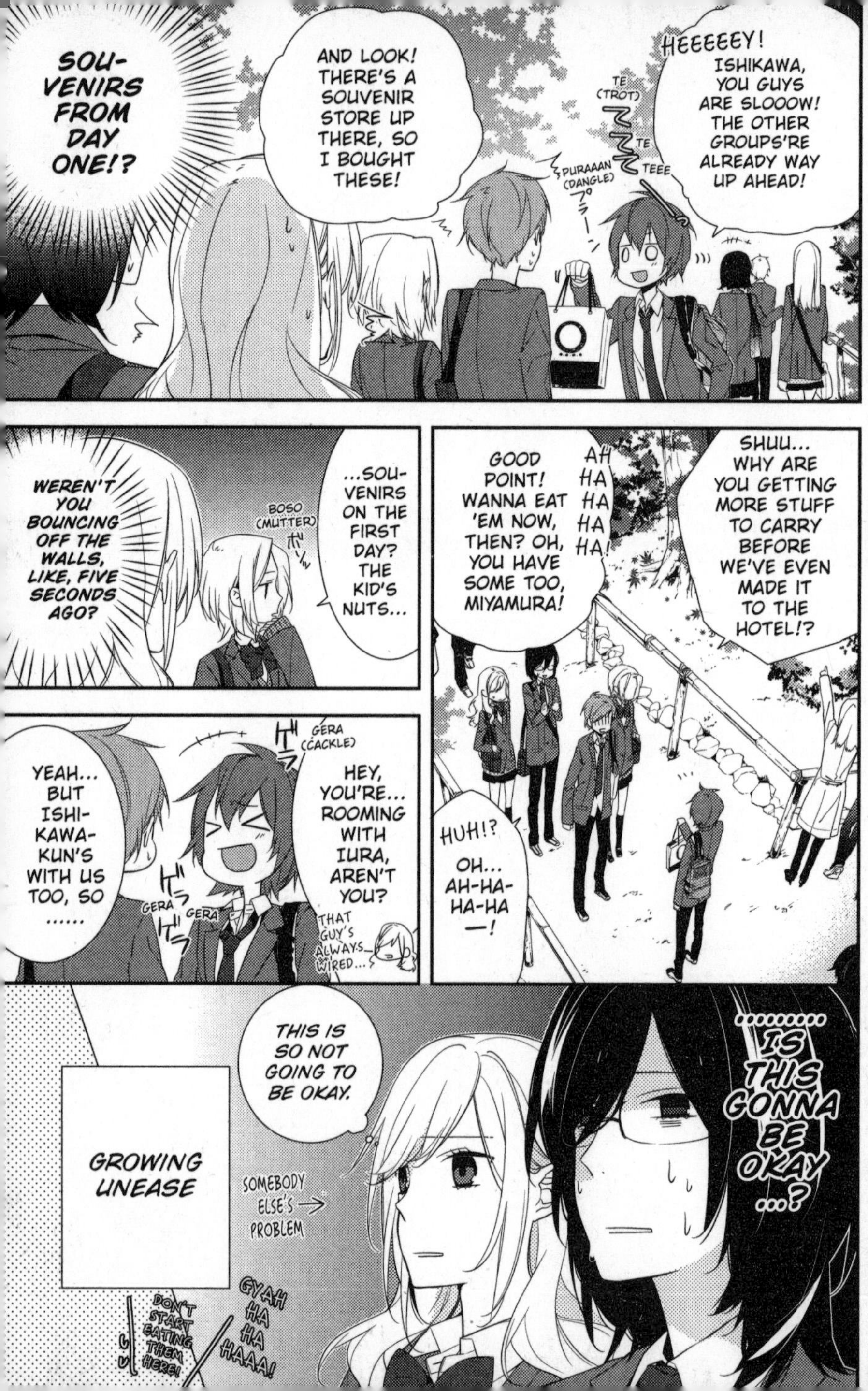
HEEEEEY! ISHIKAWA, YOU GUYS ARE SLOOOW! THE OTHER GROUPS'RE ALREADY WAY UP AHEAD!
TE (TROT) TE TEEE
PURAAAN (DANGLE)
AND LOOK! THERE'S A SOUVENIR STORE UP THERE, SO I BOUGHT THESE!
SOU-VENIRS FROM DAY ONE!?
SHUU... WHY ARE YOU GETTING MORE STUFF TO CARRY BEFORE WE'VE EVEN MADE IT TO THE HOTEL!?
GOOD POINT! WANNA EAT 'EM NOW, THEN? OH, YOU HAVE SOME TOO, MIYAMURA!
AH HA HA HA HA!
HUH!?
OH... AH-HA-HA-HA—!
...SOU-VENIRS ON THE FIRST DAY? THE KID'S NUTS...
BOSO (MUTTER)
WEREN'T YOU BOUNCING OFF THE WALLS, LIKE, FIVE SECONDS AGO?
GERA (CACKLE)
HEY, YOU'RE... ROOMING WITH IURA, AREN'T YOU?
THAT GUY'S ALWAYS WIRED...
GERA GERA
YEAH... BUT ISHI-KAWA-KUN'S WITH US TOO, SO ......
..........IS THIS GONNA BE OKAY...?
THIS IS SO NOT GOING TO BE OKAY.
SOMEBODY ELSE'S PROBLEM
GROWING UNEASE
GYAH HA HA HAAA!
DON'T START EATING THEM HERE!

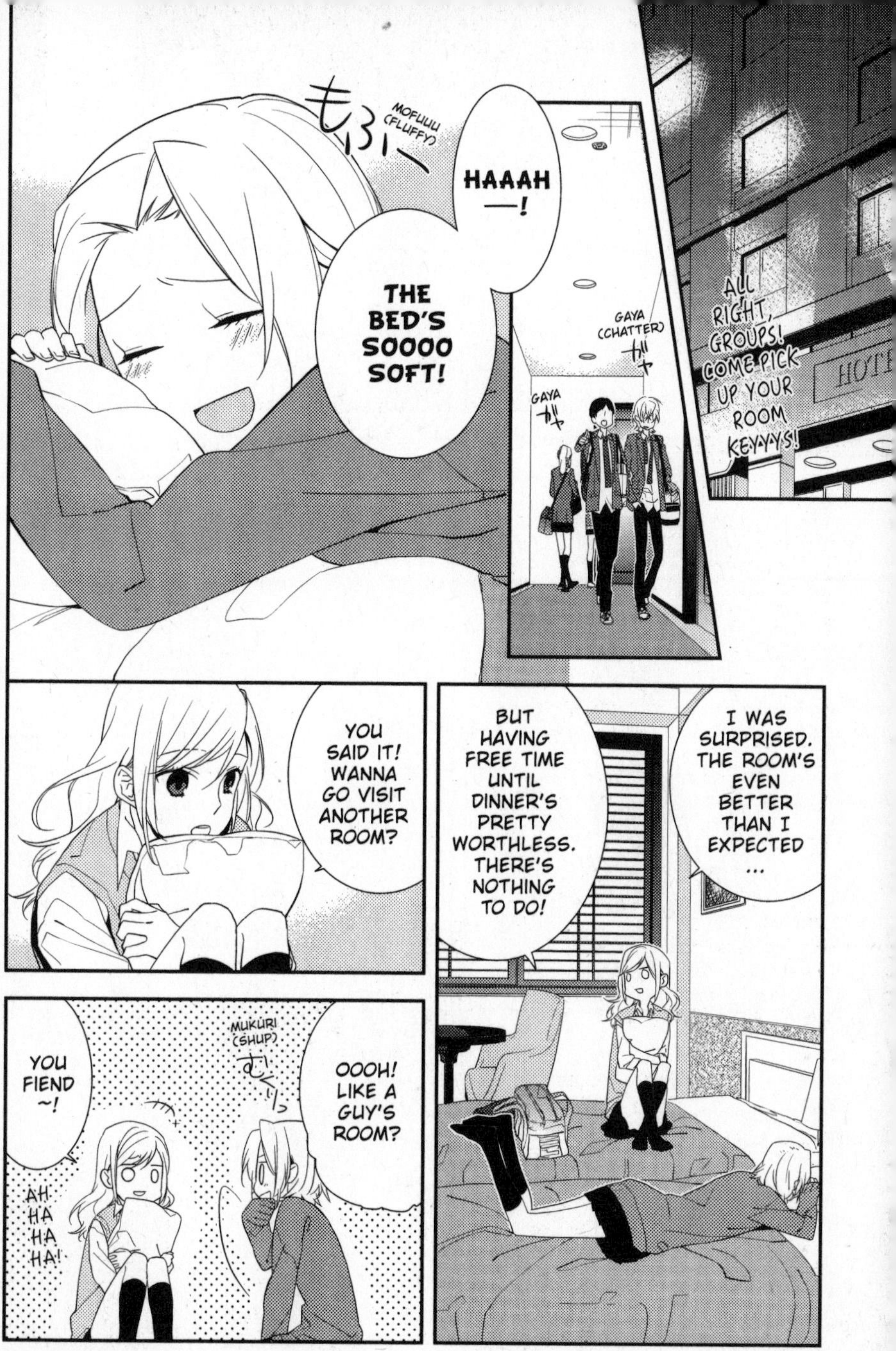
ALL RIGHT, GROUPS! COME PICK UP YOUR ROOM KEYYYS!
GAYA (CHATTER)
GAYA
MOFUUU (FLUFFY)
HAAAH—!
THE BED'S SOOOO SOFT!
I WAS SURPRISED. THE ROOM'S EVEN BETTER THAN I EXPECTED ...
BUT HAVING FREE TIME UNTIL DINNER'S PRETTY WORTHLESS. THERE'S NOTHING TO DO!
YOU SAID IT! WANNA GO VISIT ANOTHER ROOM?
OOOH! LIKE A GUY'S ROOM?
MUKURI (SHUP)
YOU FIEND~!
AH HA HA HA!

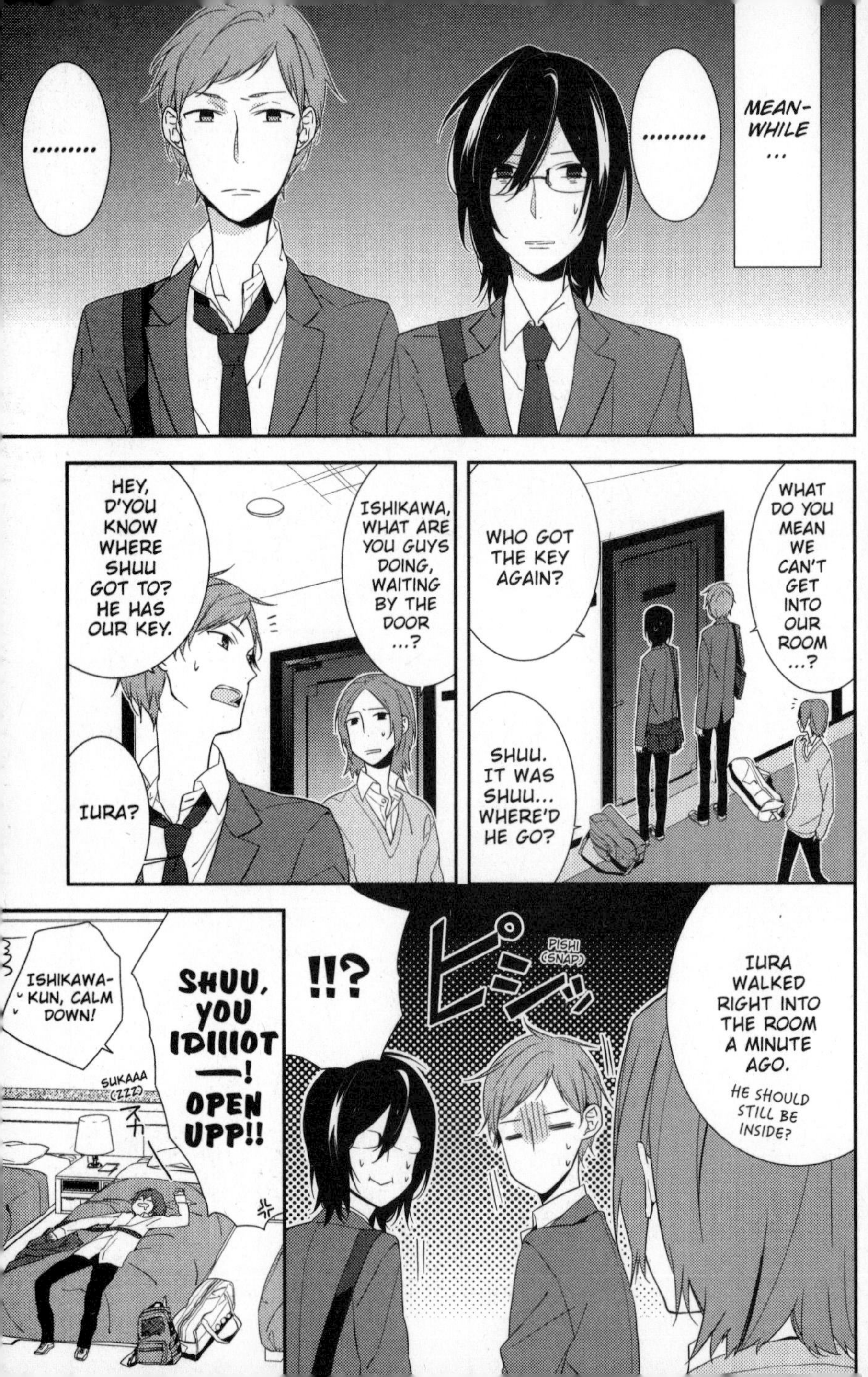
MEAN-WHILE ...
....
....
WHAT DO YOU MEAN WE CAN'T GET INTO OUR ROOM ...?
WHO GOT THE KEY AGAIN?
SHUU. IT WAS SHUU... WHERE'D HE GO?
ISHIKAWA, WHAT ARE YOU GUYS DOING, WAITING BY THE DOOR ...?
HEY, D'YOU KNOW WHERE SHUU GOT TO? HE HAS OUR KEY.
IURA?
IURA WALKED RIGHT INTO THE ROOM A MINUTE AGO.
HE SHOULD STILL BE INSIDE?
PISHI (SNAP)
!!?
SHUU, YOU IDIIIOT—! OPEN UPP!!
ISHIKAWA-KUN, CALM DOWN!
SUKAAA (ZZZ)

OKAY, OKAYYY! GEEEEZ!

I SAID I WAS SORRYYY!

FUAA (YAWN)

PORI (SKRITCH) PORI

OH.

HANG ON.

...HM, NOT A BAD IDEA. WE STILL GOT TIME TILL THEN?

WE GOT TO PUT OUR STUFF DOWN ANYWAY.

LET'S JUST TAKE IT EASY UNTIL DINNER!

THERE, THERE. EASY.

KUWA (ROAR)

AT LEAST LET US IN BEFORE YOU FALL ASLEEP, YOU MORON!

UURGHH...

Day 1

18:00~

Common bath *Boys only
·18:00~ Class 1, Groups 1~
·18:30~ Class 1, Group 5~
Bathe in order, 30 min. pe
However, groups from C
will go in after dinner, s

Those who did not bath
should take their baths
tailed tim

CLASS 1, GROUP 1

NNN...

ARE YOU AWAKE NOW?

PARA (FLIP)

LET ME CHECK REAL QUICK...

Schedule

Day 1	
18:00~	Common bath *Boys only ·18:30~ Class 1, Groups ·18:30~ Class 1, Group 5 Bathe in order, 30 min. C However, groups from C will go in after dinner, s

Those who did not bath
should take their baths a
For more detailed tim

Dinner

| 19:00~ | To be eaten in the rooms designated for
Be sure to be on time.
·Classes 1–3 – Sakura Room, Hotel
·Classes 4–6 – Plum Room, Hotel
Each group leader must confirm
group members are present.

*After dinner, all group lead
Sakura Room to report their |

Free time.
·Boys bathe in the co
~ Boys bathe in the co

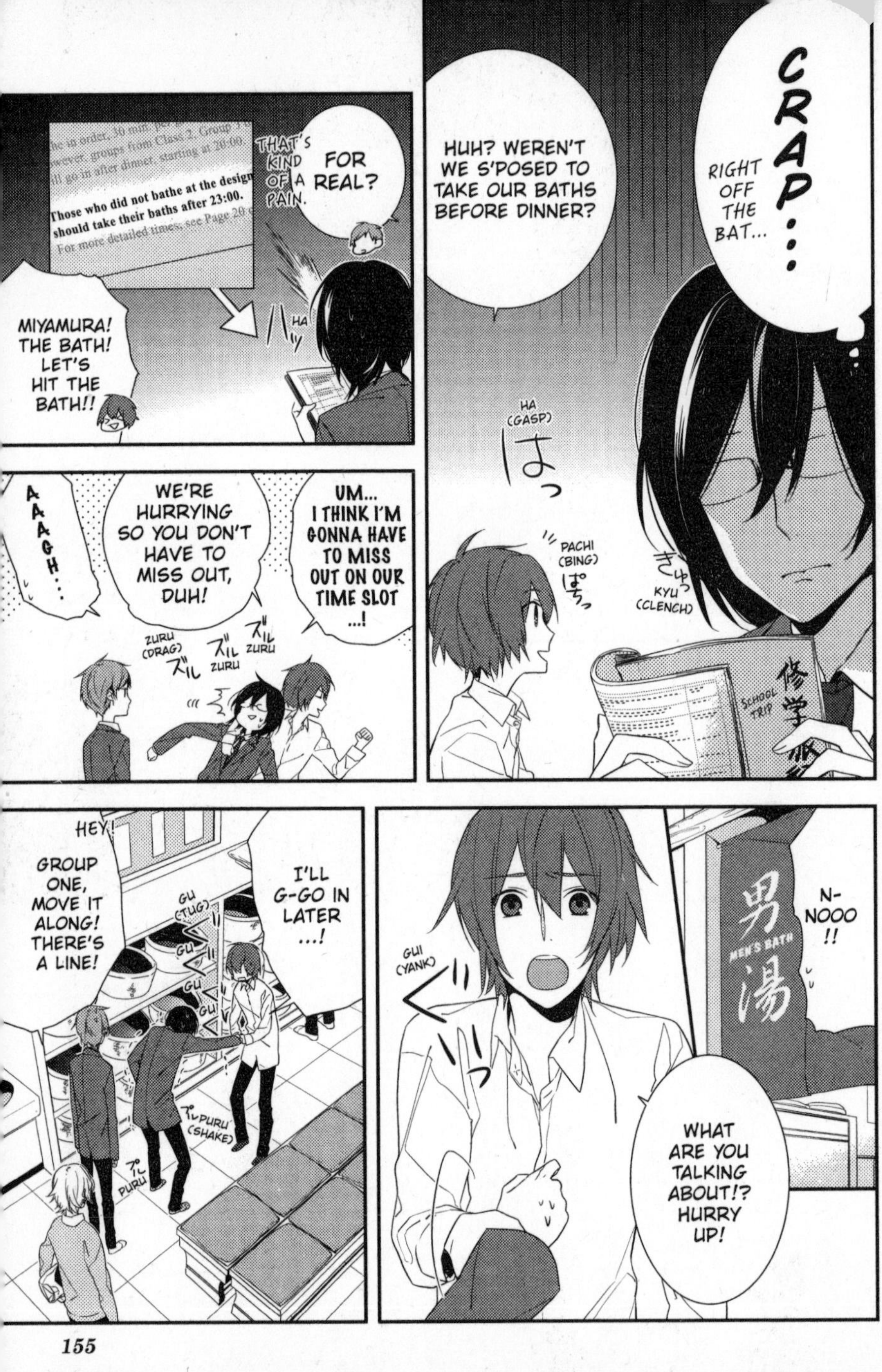
CRAP...
RIGHT OFF THE BAT...
HUH? WEREN'T WE S'POSED TO TAKE OUR BATHS BEFORE DINNER?
HA (GASP) はっ
PACHI (BING) ぱちっ
KYU (CLENCH) きゅっ
SCHOOL TRIP
FOR REAL?
THAT'S KIND OF A PAIN.
he in order, 30 min. per g
owever, groups from Class 2, Group
ill go in after dinner, starting at 20:00.
Those who did not bathe at the design
should take their baths after 23:00.
For more detailed times, see Page 20
HA ハッ
MIYAMURA! THE BATH! LET'S HIT THE BATH!!
UM... I THINK I'M GONNA HAVE TO MISS OUT ON OUR TIME SLOT ...!
WE'RE HURRYING SO YOU DON'T HAVE TO MISS OUT, DUH!
AAAGH...
ズル ZURU
ズル ZURU
ZURU (DRAG) ズル
N-NOOO!!
男湯 MEN'S BATH
GUI (YANK)
WHAT ARE YOU TALKING ABOUT!? HURRY UP!
I'LL G-GO IN LATER ...!
HEY! GROUP ONE, MOVE IT ALONG! THERE'S A LINE!
GU (TUG)
GU
GU
GU
プル PURU (SHAKE)
プル PURU

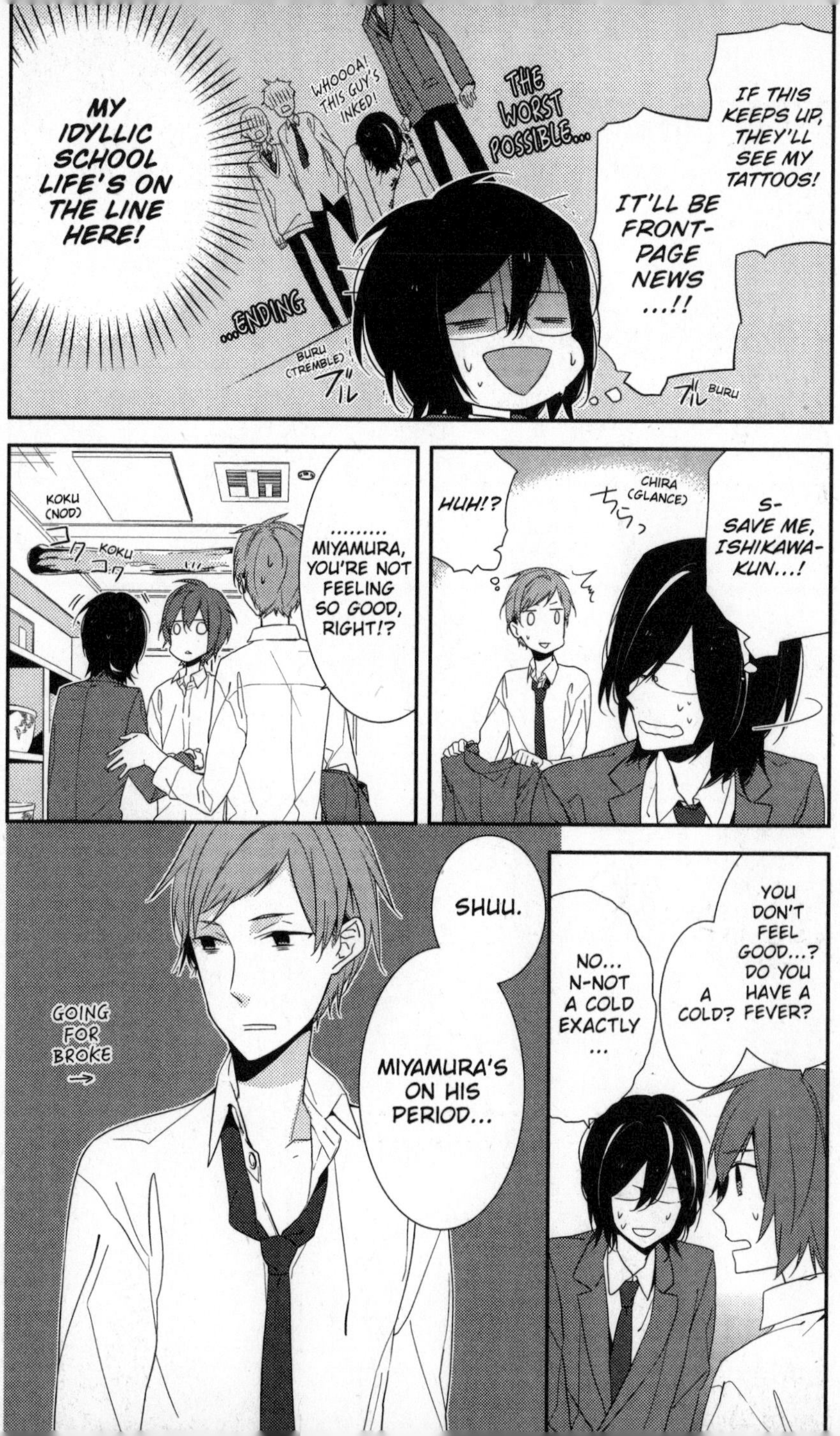
IF THIS KEEPS UP, THEY'LL SEE MY TATTOOS!
IT'LL BE FRONT-PAGE NEWS ...!!
THE WORST POSSIBLE...
WHOOOA! THIS GUY'S INKED!
MY IDYLLIC SCHOOL LIFE'S ON THE LINE HERE!
...ENDING
BURU (TREMBLE)
BURU
S-SAVE ME, ISHIKAWA-KUN...!
CHIRA (GLANCE)
HUH!?
.... MIYAMURA, YOU'RE NOT FEELING SO GOOD, RIGHT!?
KOKU (NOD)
KOKU
YOU DON'T FEEL GOOD...? DO YOU HAVE A FEVER?
A COLD?
NO... N-NOT A COLD EXACTLY ...
SHUU.
MIYAMURA'S ON HIS PERIOD...
GOING FOR BROKE →

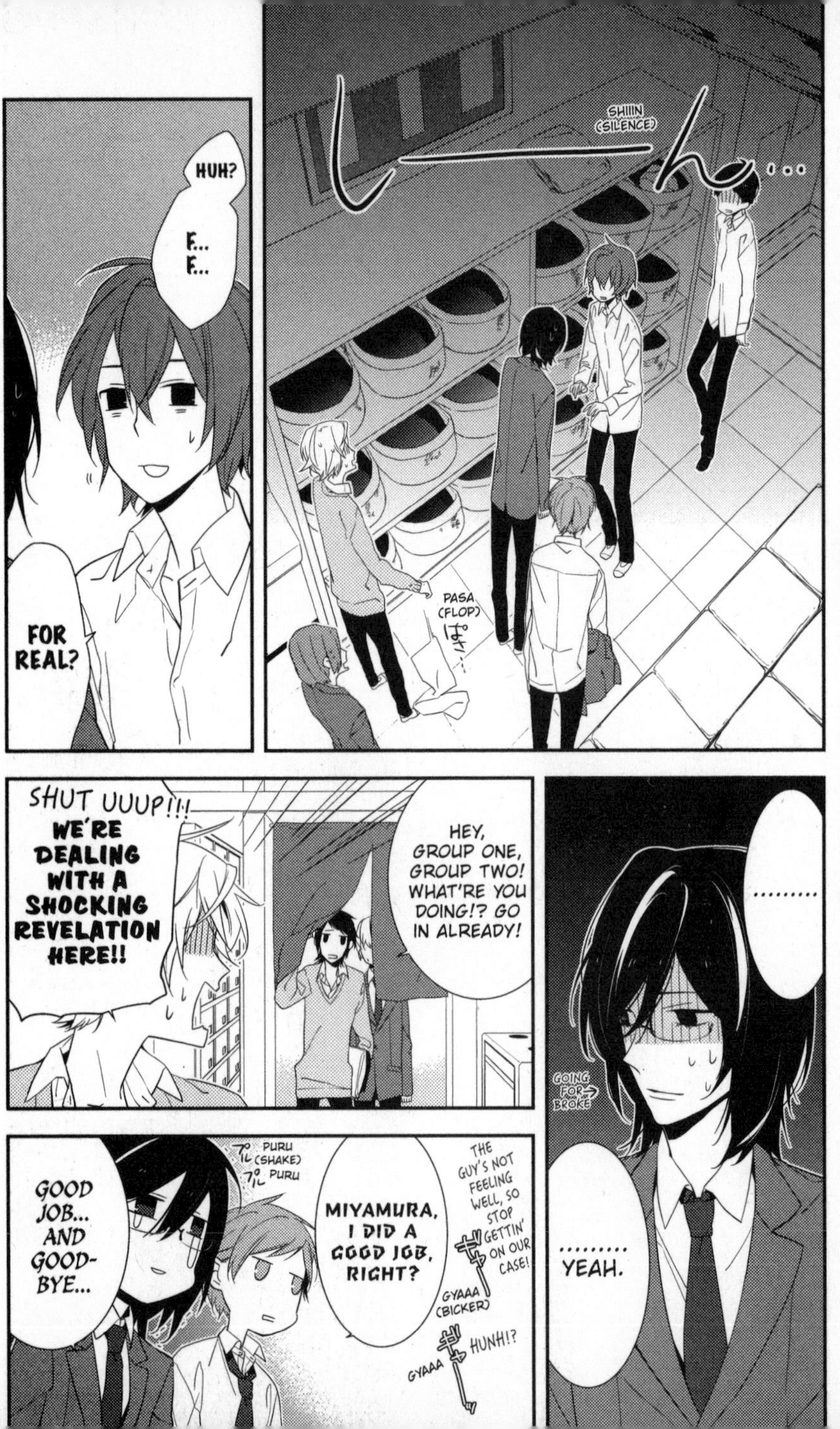

SHIIIN (SILENCE)
しーん…
PASA (FLOP)
ぱさ…
HUH?
F... F...
FOR REAL?
....
GOING FOR BROKE
.... YEAH.
HEY, GROUP ONE, GROUP TWO! WHAT'RE YOU DOING!? GO IN ALREADY!
SHUT UUUP!!!
WE'RE DEALING WITH A SHOCKING REVELATION HERE!!
THE GUY'S NOT FEELING WELL, SO STOP GETTIN' ON OUR CASE!
GYAAA (BICKER)
HUNH!?
GYAAA
MIYAMURA, I DID A GOOD JOB, RIGHT?
PURU (SHAKE) PURU
GOOD JOB... AND GOOD-BYE...

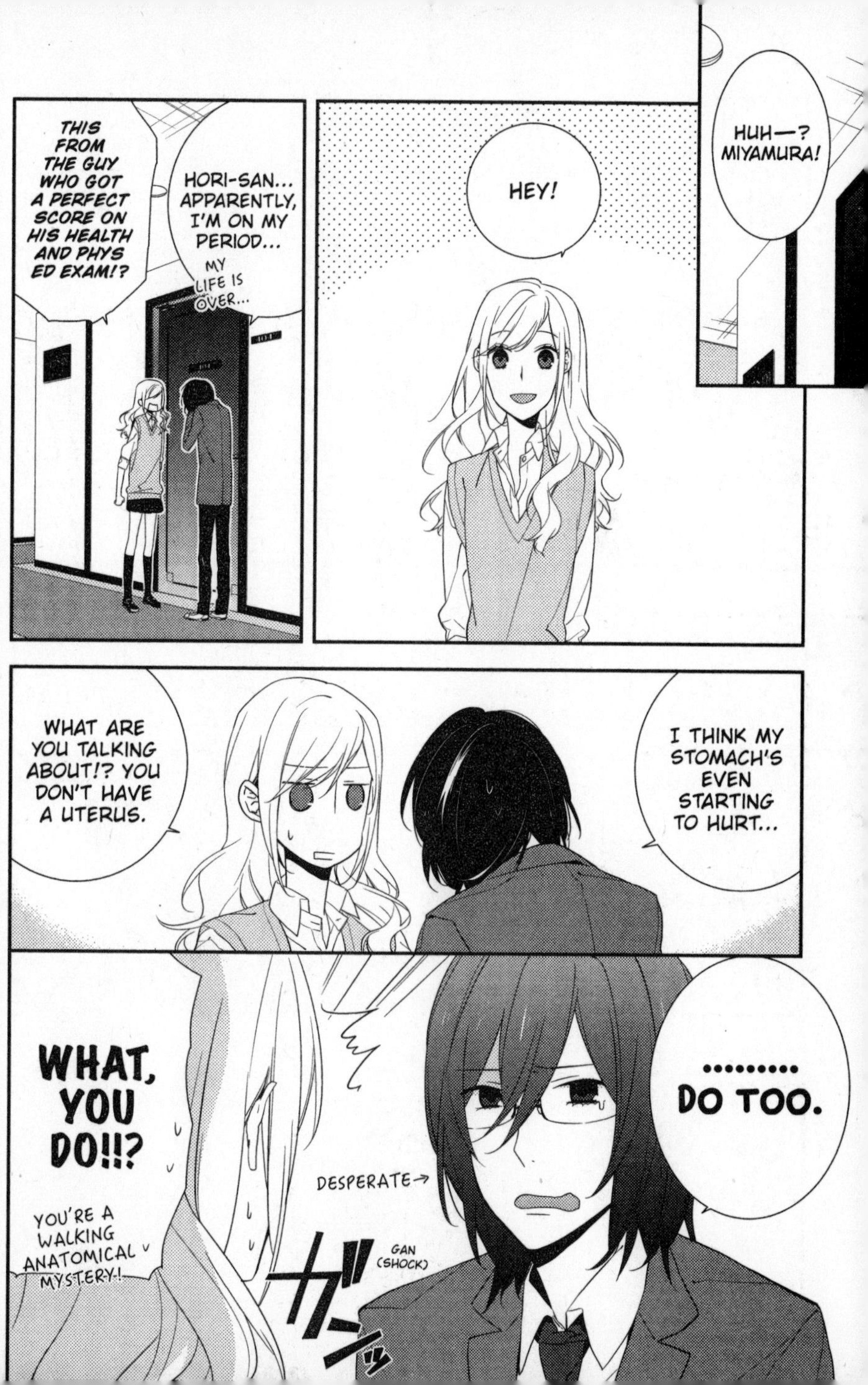
HUH—? MIYAMURA!
HEY!
HORI-SAN... APPARENTLY, I'M ON MY PERIOD...
MY LIFE IS OVER...
THIS FROM THE GUY WHO GOT A PERFECT SCORE ON HIS HEALTH AND PHYS ED EXAM!?
I THINK MY STOMACH'S EVEN STARTING TO HURT...
WHAT ARE YOU TALKING ABOUT!? YOU DON'T HAVE A UTERUS.
.... DO TOO.
DESPERATE→
GAN (SHOCK)
WHAT, YOU DO!!?
YOU'RE A WALKING ANATOMICAL MYSTERY!

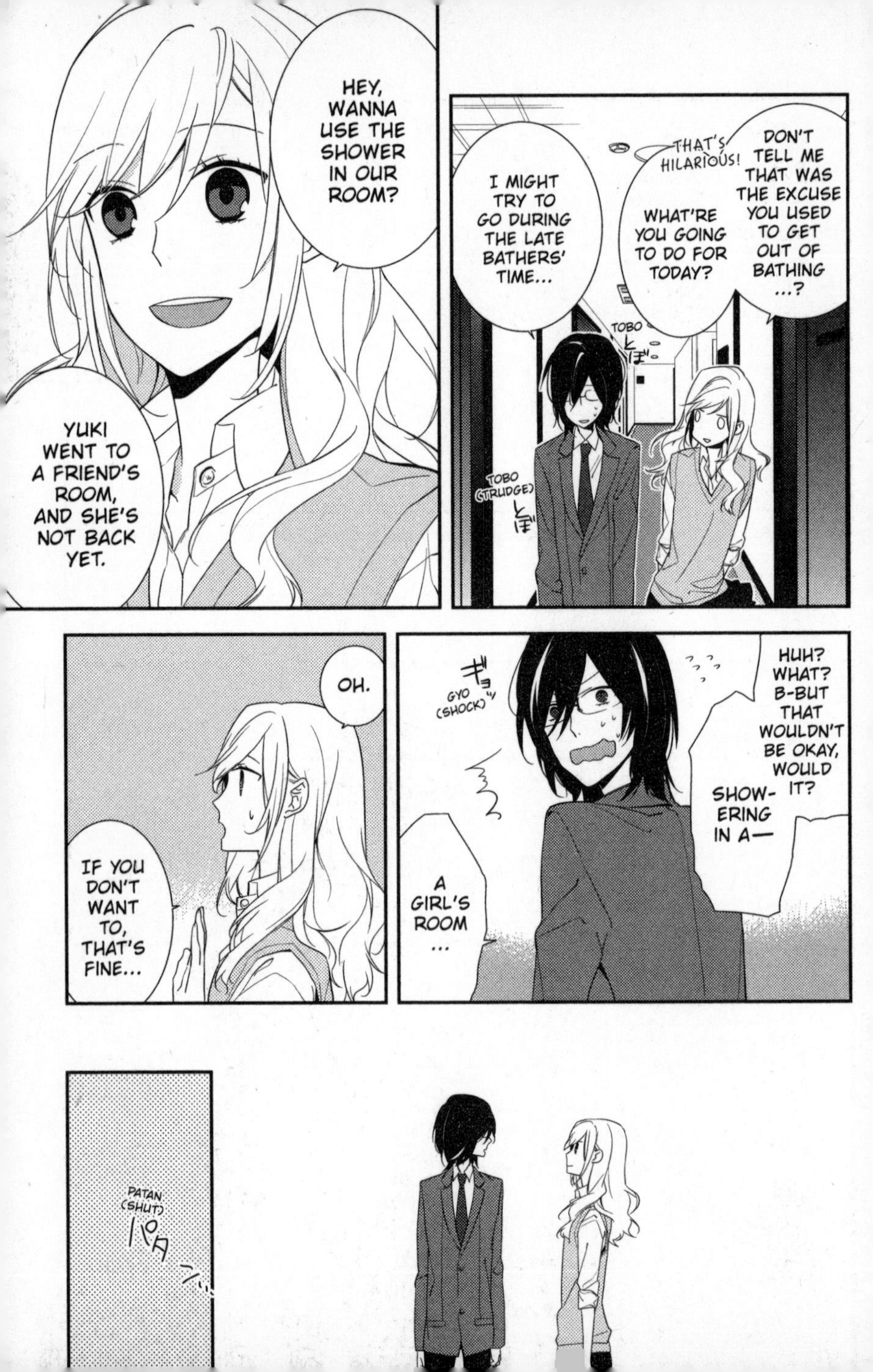

DON'T TELL ME THAT WAS THE EXCUSE YOU USED TO GET OUT OF BATHING...?
THAT'S HILARIOUS!
WHAT'RE YOU GOING TO DO FOR TODAY?
I MIGHT TRY TO GO DURING THE LATE BATHERS' TIME...
TOBO
TOBO (TRUDGE)
HEY, WANNA USE THE SHOWER IN OUR ROOM?
YUKI WENT TO A FRIEND'S ROOM, AND SHE'S NOT BACK YET.
HUH? WHAT? B-BUT THAT WOULDN'T BE OKAY, WOULD IT?
SHOW-ERING IN A—
GYO (SHOCK)
A GIRL'S ROOM ...
OH.
IF YOU DON'T WANT TO, THAT'S FINE...
PATAN (SHUT)

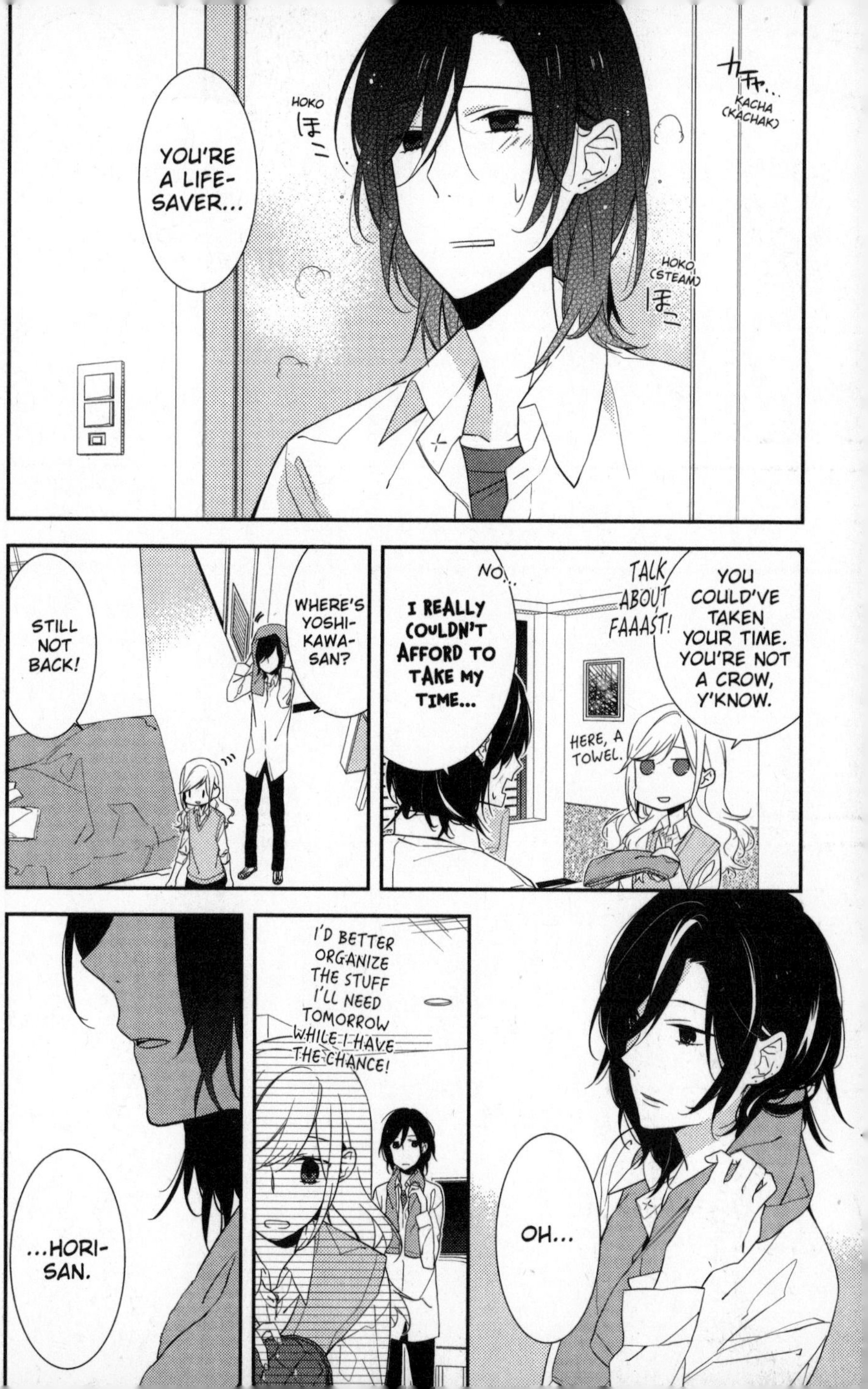
カチャ...
KACHA (KACHAK)
HOKO (STEAM) ほこ
HOKO ほこ
YOU'RE A LIFE-SAVER...
YOU COULD'VE TAKEN YOUR TIME. YOU'RE NOT A CROW, Y'KNOW.
TALK ABOUT FAAAST!
NO...
I REALLY COULDN'T AFFORD TO TAKE MY TIME...
HERE, A TOWEL.
WHERE'S YOSHIKAWA-SAN?
STILL NOT BACK!
OH...
I'D BETTER ORGANIZE THE STUFF I'LL NEED TOMORROW WHILE I HAVE THE CHANCE!
...HORI-SAN.

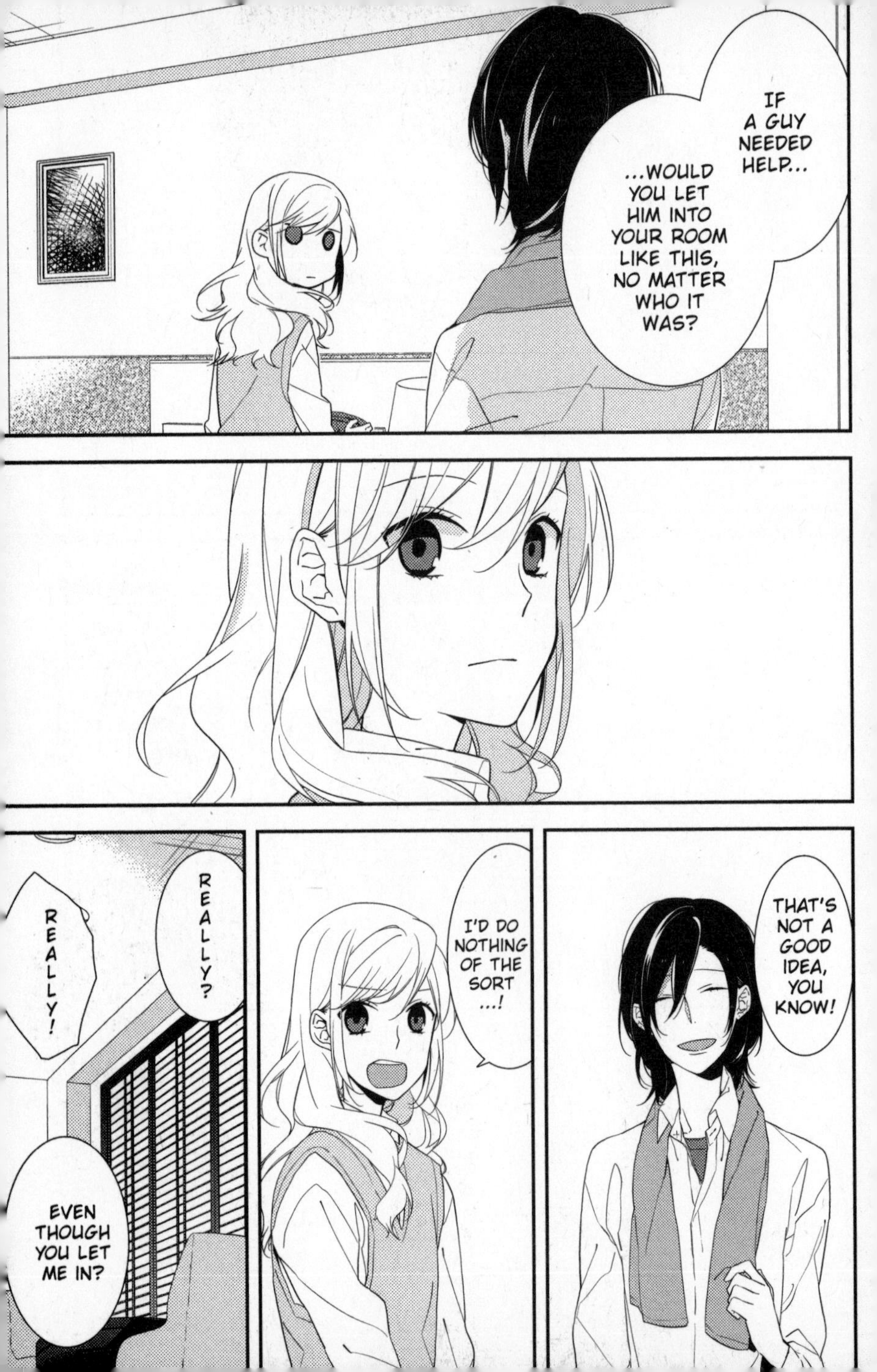
IF A GUY NEEDED HELP...
...WOULD YOU LET HIM INTO YOUR ROOM LIKE THIS, NO MATTER WHO IT WAS?
THAT'S NOT A GOOD IDEA, YOU KNOW!
I'D DO NOTHING OF THE SORT ...!
REALLY?
REALLY!
EVEN THOUGH YOU LET ME IN?

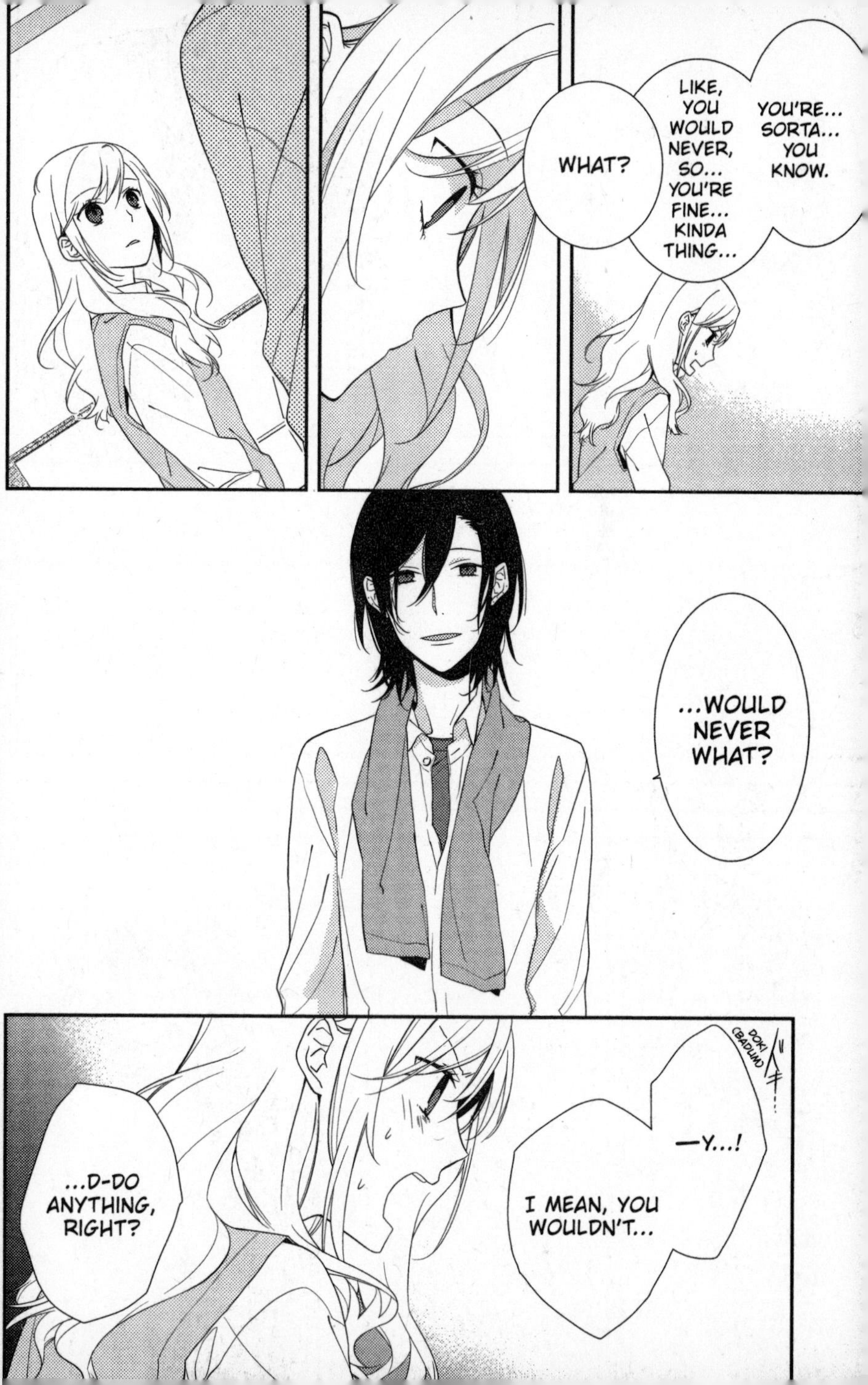
YOU'RE... SORTA... YOU KNOW.
LIKE, YOU WOULD NEVER, SO... YOU'RE FINE... KINDA THING...
WHAT?
...WOULD NEVER WHAT?
DOKI (BADUMP)
—Y...!
I MEAN, YOU WOULDN'T...
...D-DO ANYTHING, RIGHT?

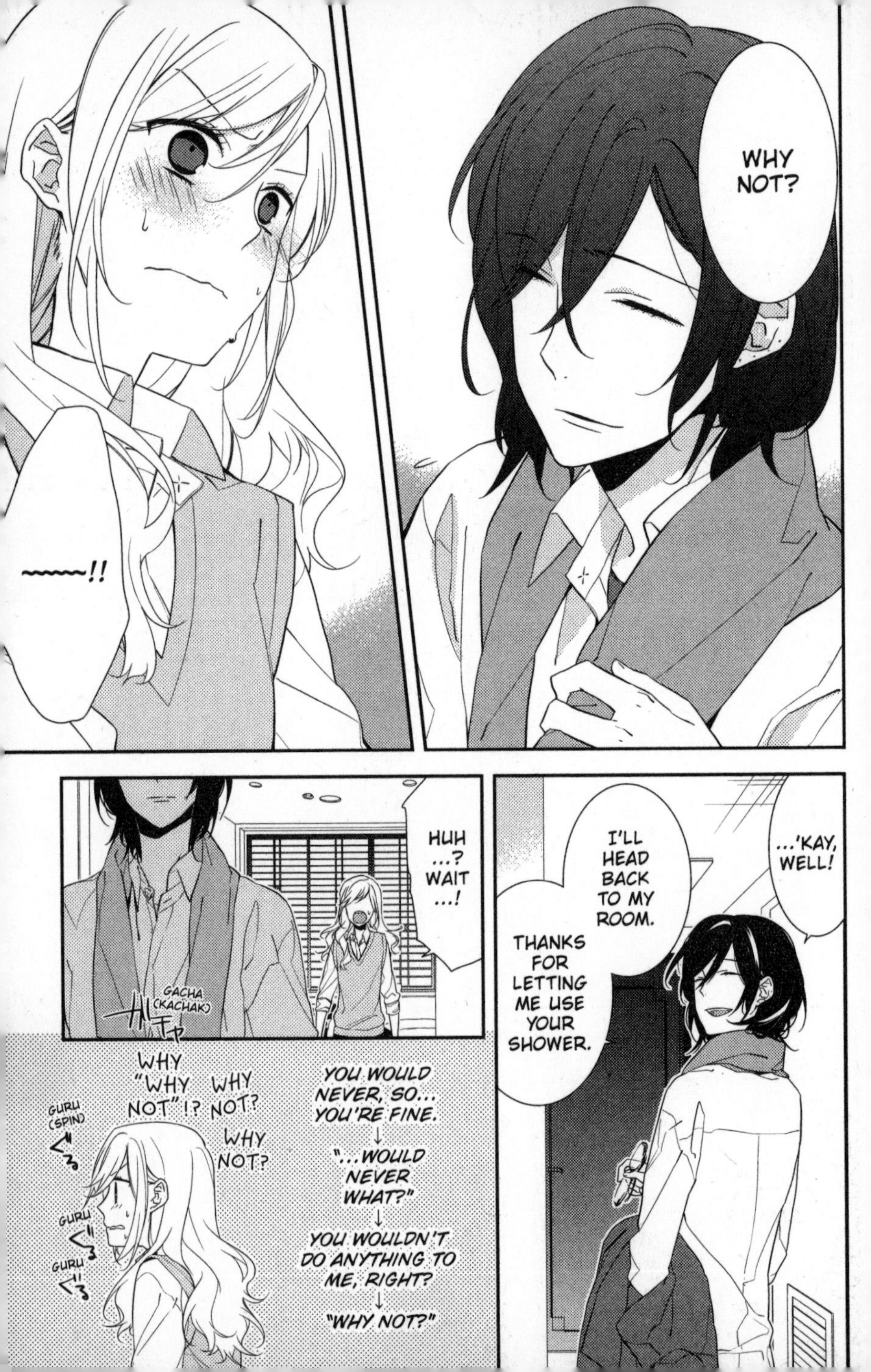
WHY NOT?
~~~~!!
...'KAY, WELL!
I'LL HEAD BACK TO MY ROOM.
THANKS FOR LETTING ME USE YOUR SHOWER.
HUH ...? WAIT ...!
GACHA (KACHAK)
YOU WOULD NEVER, SO... YOU'RE FINE.
↓
"...WOULD NEVER WHAT?"
↓
YOU WOULDN'T DO ANYTHING TO ME, RIGHT?
↓
"WHY NOT?"
WHY "WHY NOT"!?
WHY NOT?
WHY NOT?
GURU (SPIN)
GURU
GURU
~~~~

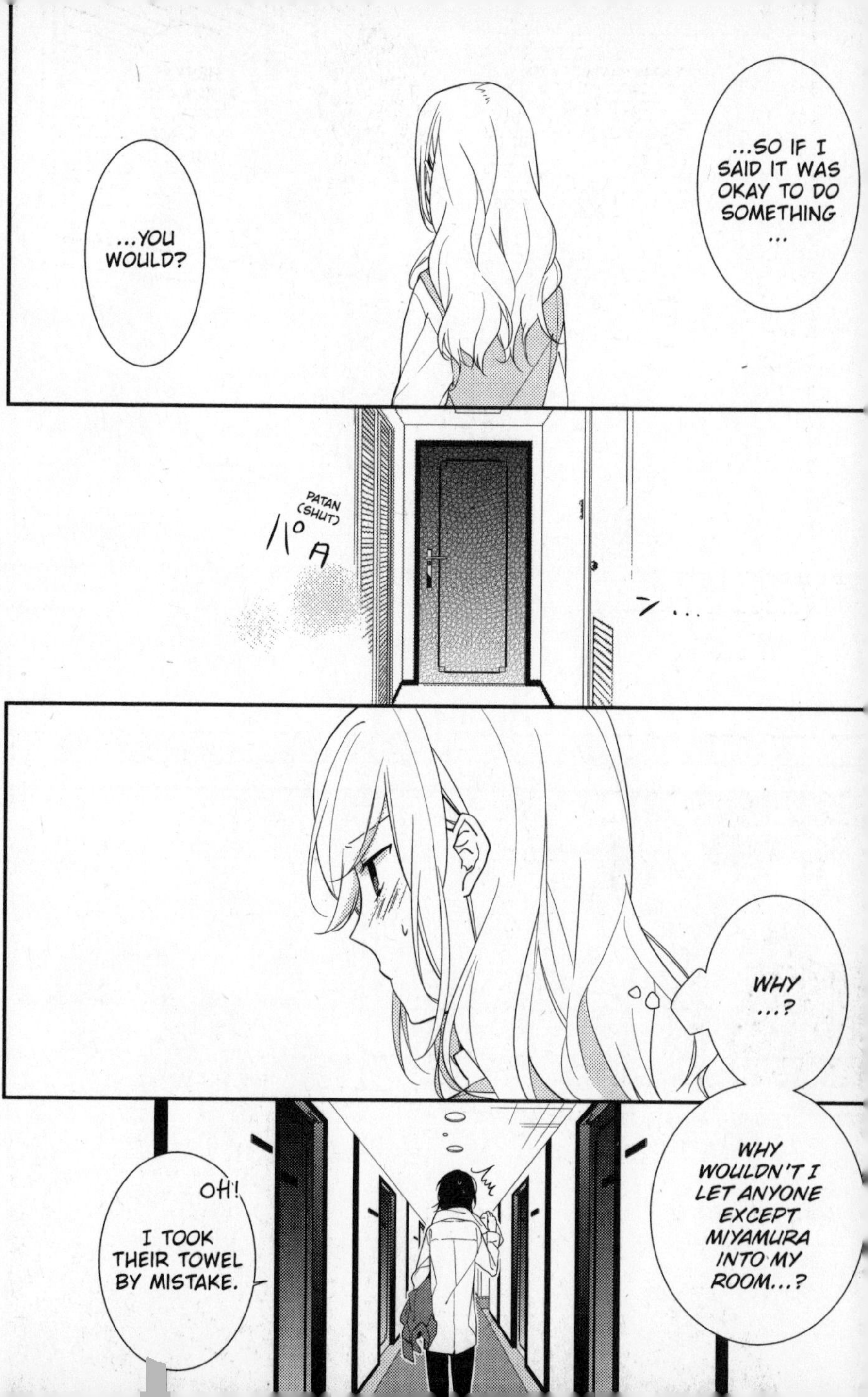
...SO IF I SAID IT WAS OKAY TO DO SOMETHING ...
...YOU WOULD?
PATAN (SHUT)
WHY ...?
WHY WOULDN'T I LET ANYONE EXCEPT MIYAMURA INTO MY ROOM...?
OH!
I TOOK THEIR TOWEL BY MISTAKE.

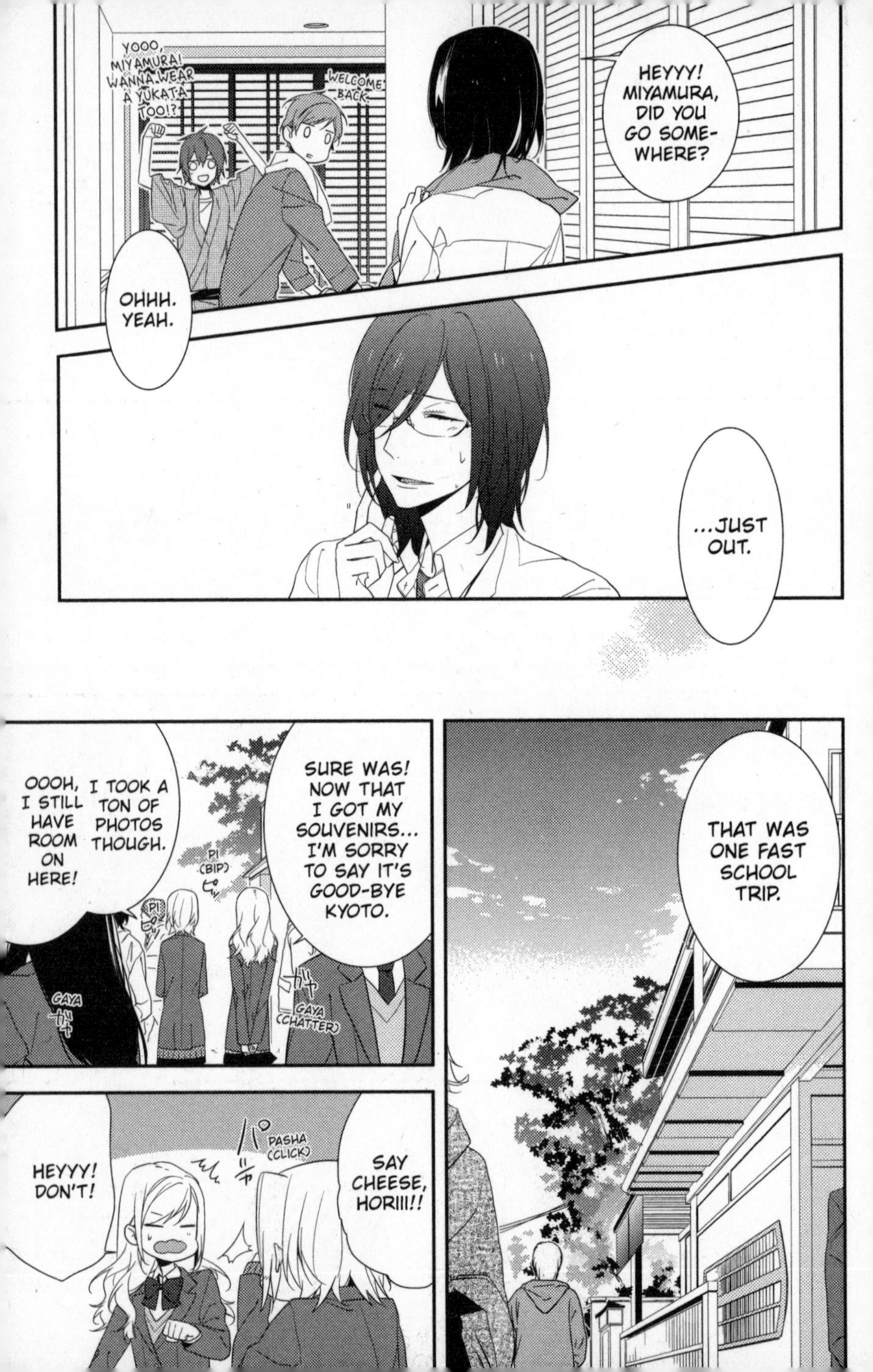
HEYYY! MIYAMURA, DID YOU GO SOME-WHERE?
WELCOME BACK.
YOOO, MIYAMURA! WANNA WEAR A YUKATA TOO!?
OHHH. YEAH.
...JUST OUT.
THAT WAS ONE FAST SCHOOL TRIP.
SURE WAS! NOW THAT I GOT MY SOUVENIRS... I'M SORRY TO SAY IT'S GOOD-BYE KYOTO.
GAYA (CHATTER)
PI (BIP)
PI
I TOOK A TON OF PHOTOS THOUGH.
OOOH, I STILL HAVE ROOM ON HERE!
GAYA
SAY CHEESE, HORIII!!
PASHA (CLICK)
HEYYY! DON'T!

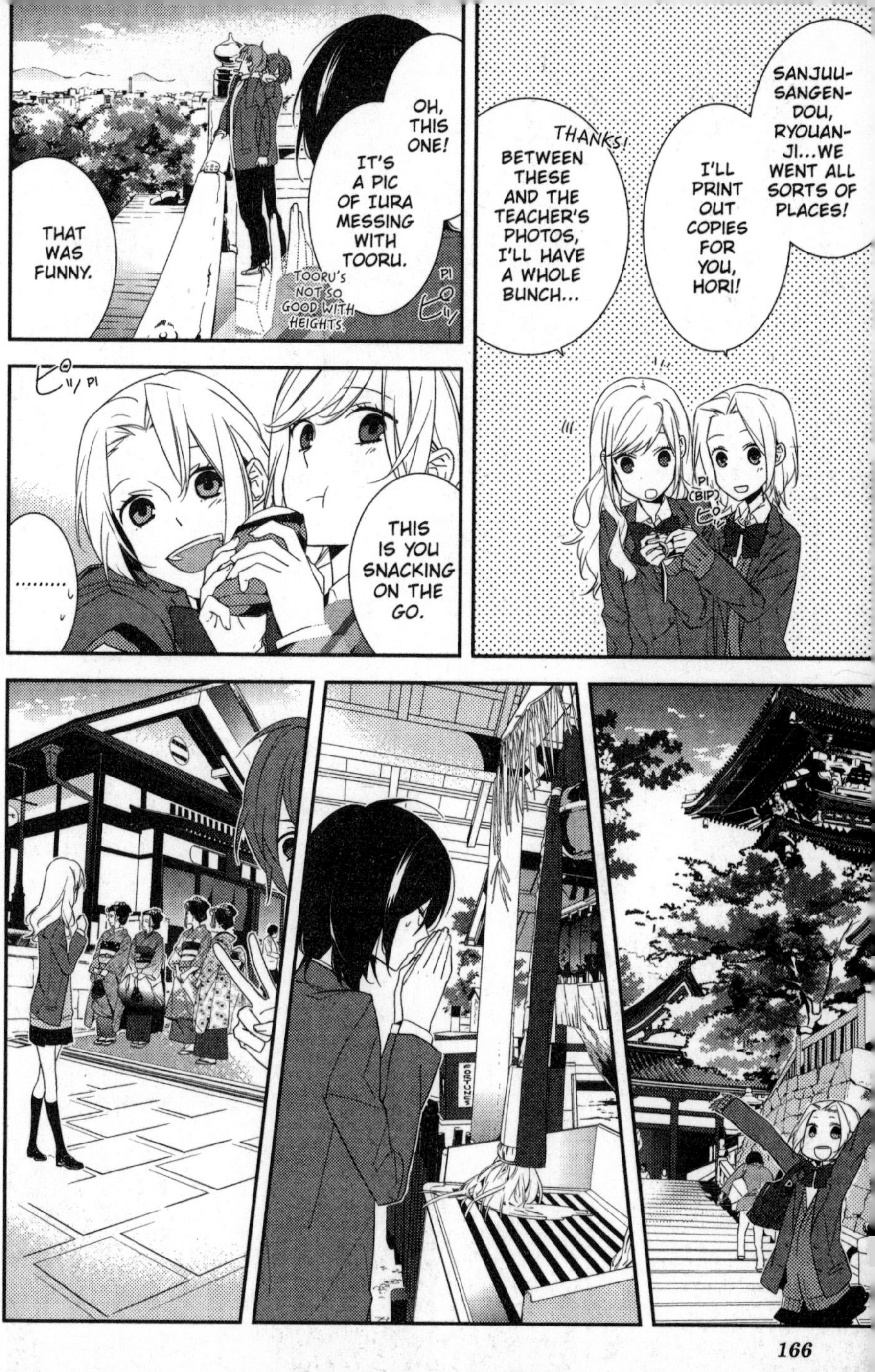
SANJUU-SANGEN-DOU, RYOUAN-JI...WE WENT ALL SORTS OF PLACES!
I'LL PRINT OUT COPIES FOR YOU, HORI!
THANKS!
BETWEEN THESE AND THE TEACHER'S PHOTOS, I'LL HAVE A WHOLE BUNCH...
PI (BIP)
OH, THIS ONE!
IT'S A PIC OF IURA MESSING WITH TOORU.
PI
TOORU'S NOT SO GOOD WITH HEIGHTS.
THAT WAS FUNNY.
THIS IS YOU SNACKING ON THE GO.
PI
....
FORTUNES

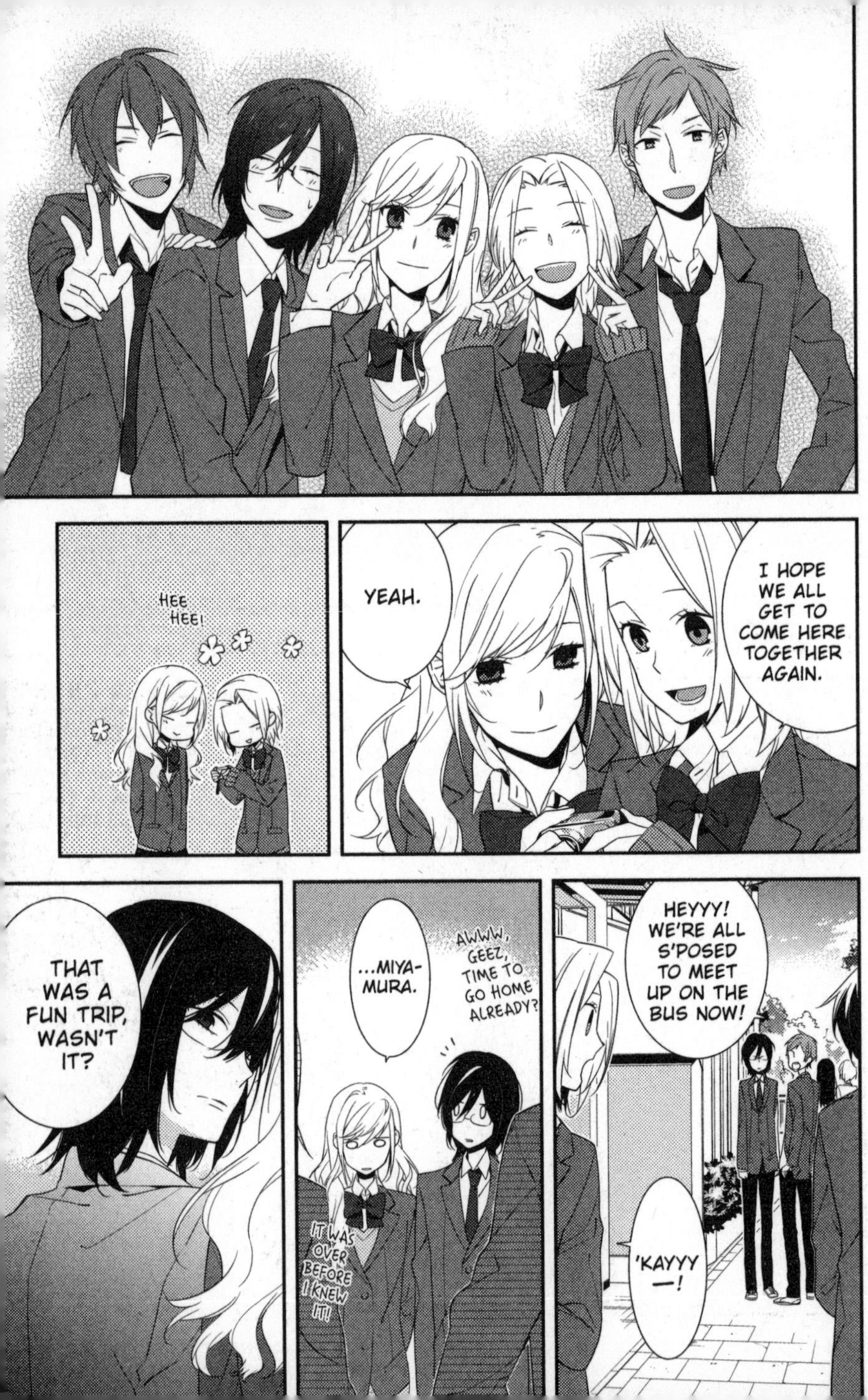
I HOPE WE ALL GET TO COME HERE TOGETHER AGAIN.
YEAH.
HEE HEE!
HEYYY! WE'RE ALL S'POSED TO MEET UP ON THE BUS NOW!
'KAYYY—!
AWWW, GEEZ, TIME TO GO HOME ALREADY?
...MIYA-MURA.
IT WAS OVER BEFORE I KNEW IT!
THAT WAS A FUN TRIP, WASN'T IT?

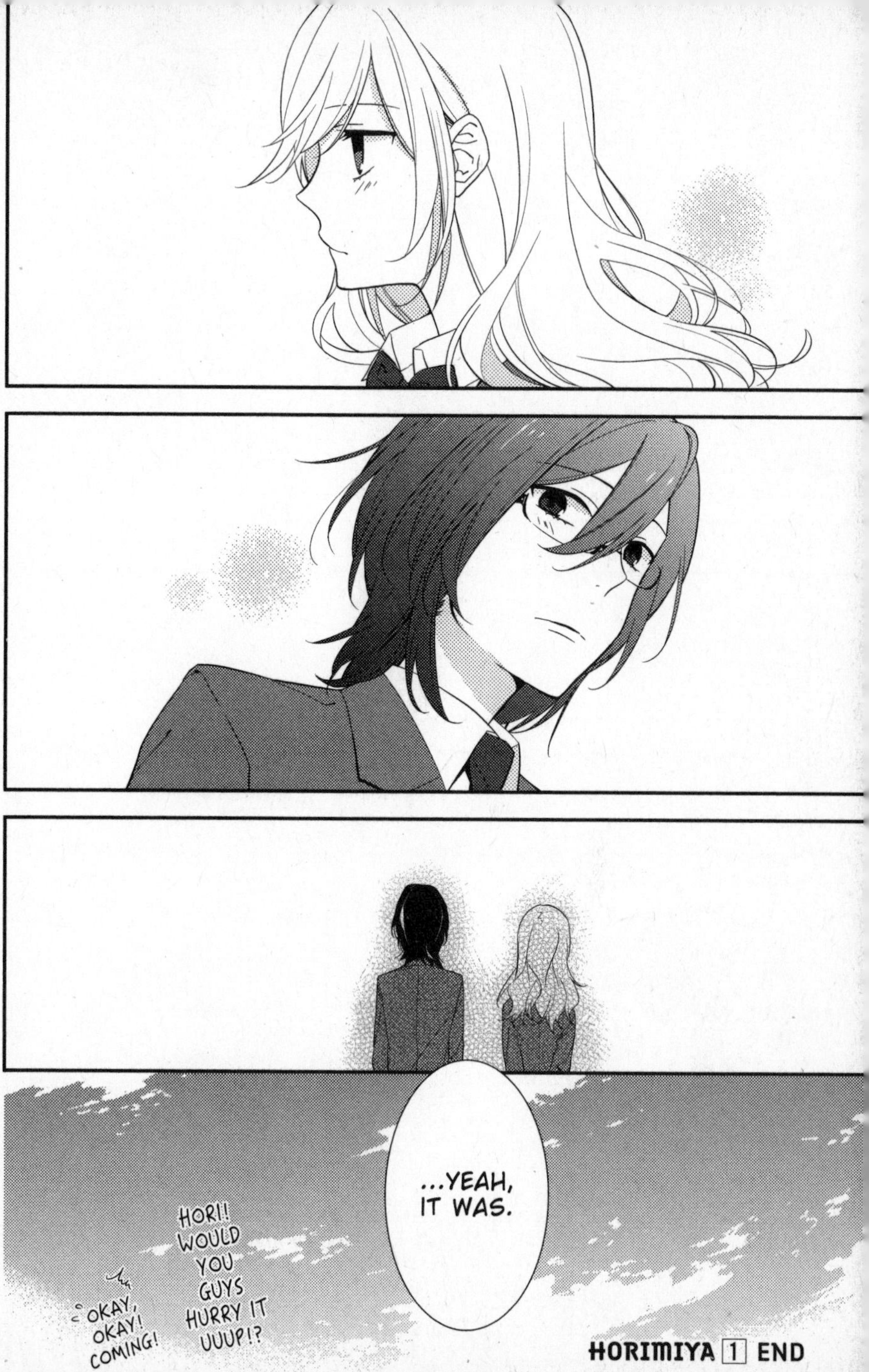
...YEAH, IT WAS.
HORI! WOULD YOU GUYS HURRY IT UUUP!?
OKAY, OKAY! COMING!
HORIMIYA 1 END

To Be Continued...

Translation Notes

Page 7 – *Moe*
Moe is a geeky, fetish-like obsession with something cute, usually a certain category of girl (maids, little sisters) or piece of clothing (glasses, school uniforms). Also used as an interjection when something triggers the obsession.

Page 99 – Attendance roster
In Japanese schools, instead of students going to different classrooms for different subjects, the teacher generally comes to the students.

Page 166 – Sanjuusangen-dou and Ryouan-ji
Two famous temples in Kyoto. Sanjuusangen-dou is famous for having one thousand life-sized statues of the thousand-armed Kannon, and Ryouan-ji is known for its Zen garden.

BONUS MANGA • MYAMURA

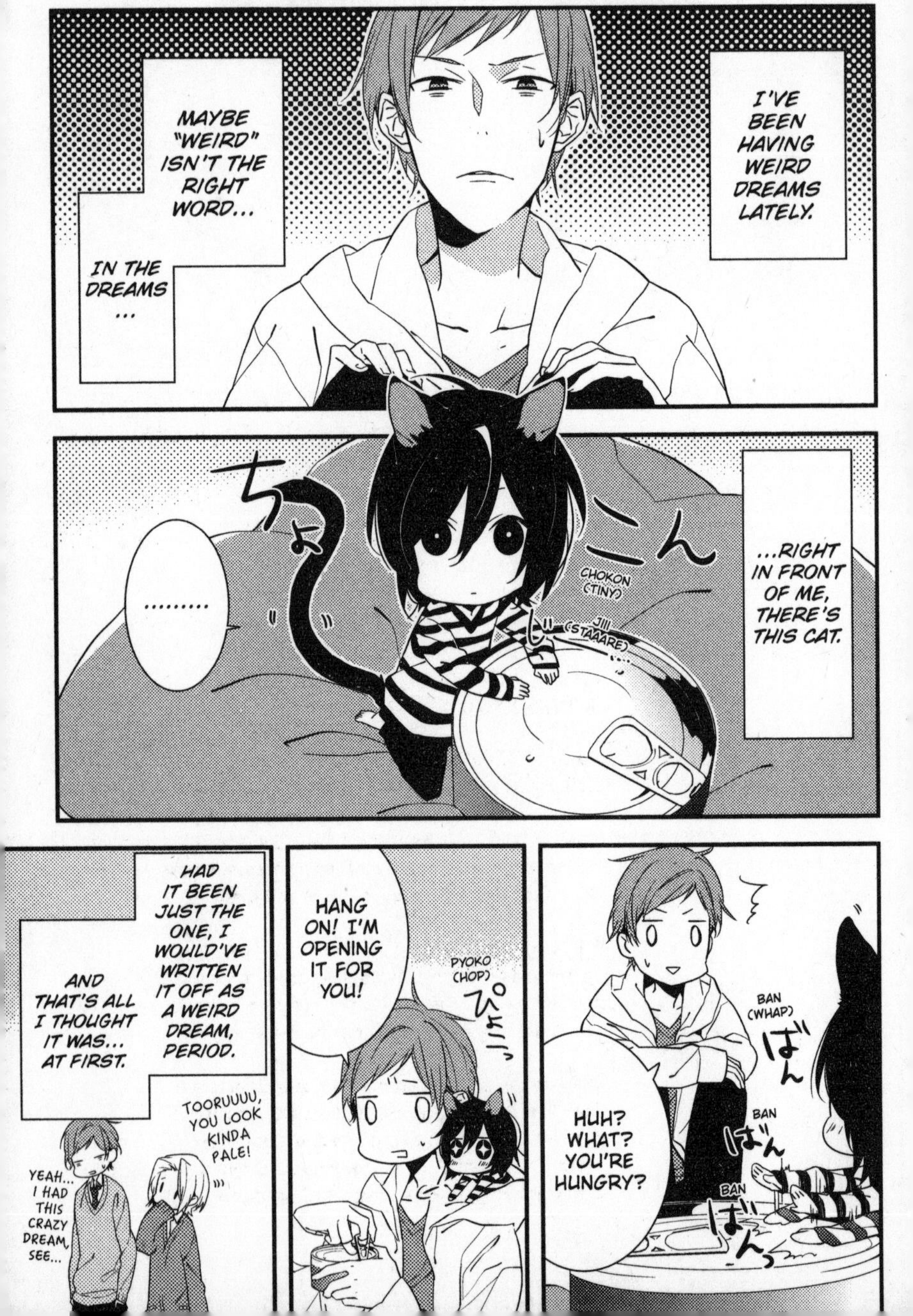

I'VE BEEN HAVING WEIRD DREAMS LATELY.
MAYBE "WEIRD" ISN'T THE RIGHT WORD...
IN THE DREAMS...
...RIGHT IN FRONT OF ME, THERE'S THIS CAT.
ちょこん
CHOKON (TINY)
じぃ
JIII (STAAARE)
....
BAN (WHAP)
ばん
HUH? WHAT? YOU'RE HUNGRY?
BAN
ばん
BAN
ばん
HANG ON! I'M OPENING IT FOR YOU!
PYOKO (HOP)
ぴょこ
HAD IT BEEN JUST THE ONE, I WOULD'VE WRITTEN IT OFF AS A WEIRD DREAM, PERIOD.
AND THAT'S ALL I THOUGHT IT WAS... AT FIRST.
TOORUUUU, YOU LOOK KINDA PALE!
YEAH... I HAD THIS CRAZY DREAM, SEE...

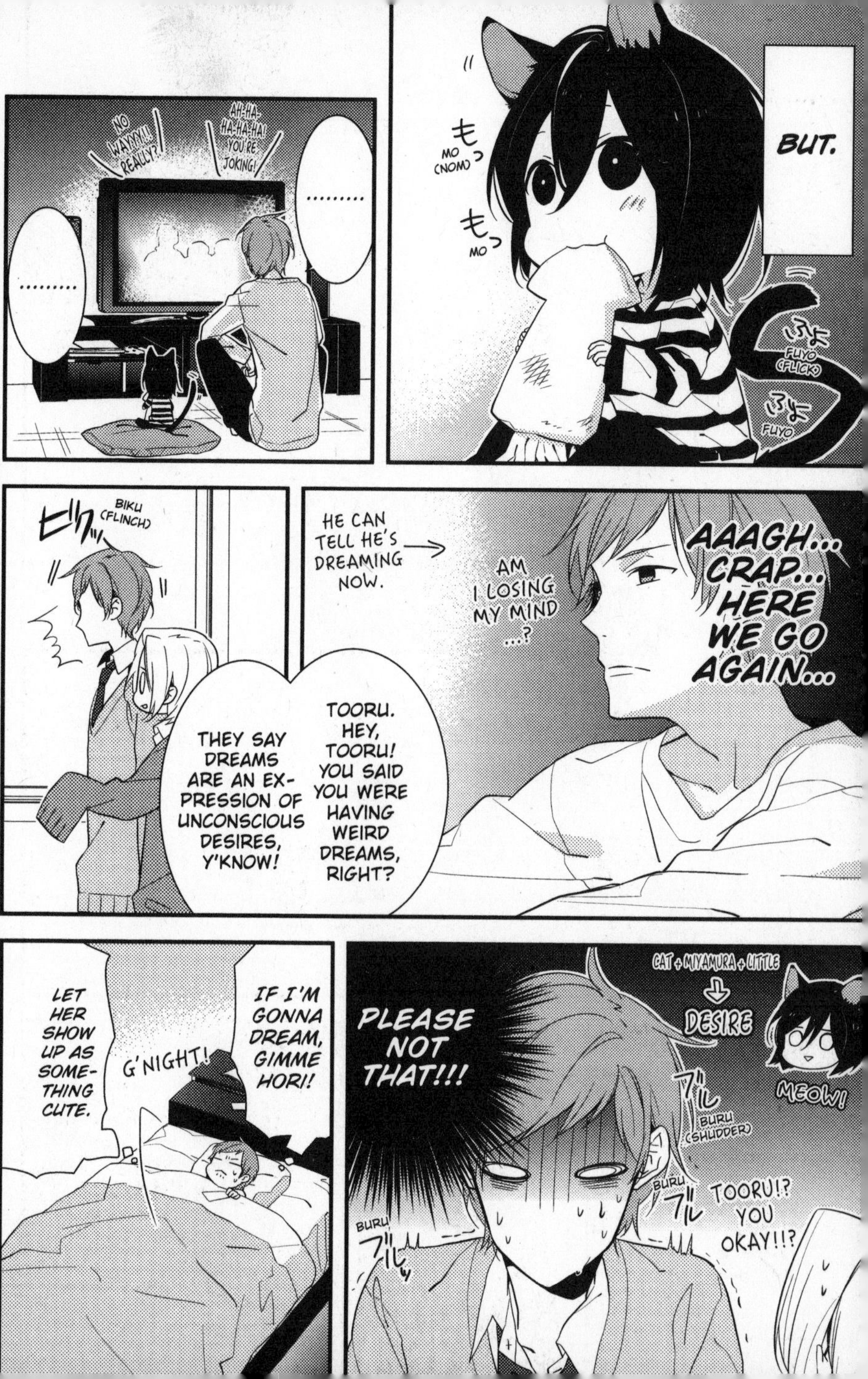
BUT.
も MO (NOM)
も MO
ふよ FUYO (FLICK)
ふよ FUYO
NO WAYYY!! REALLY?
AH-HA-HA-HA-HA! YOU'RE JOKING!
....
....
AAAGH... CRAP... HERE WE GO AGAIN...
AM I LOSING MY MIND ...?
HE CAN TELL HE'S DREAMING NOW.
TOORU. HEY, TOORU! YOU SAID YOU WERE HAVING WEIRD DREAMS, RIGHT?
THEY SAY DREAMS ARE AN EXPRESSION OF UNCONSCIOUS DESIRES, Y'KNOW!
ビクッ BIKU (FLINCH)
CAT + MIYAMURA + LITTLE
DESIRE
MEOW!
PLEASE NOT THAT!!!
ブル BURU (SHUDDER)
BURU ブル
TOORU!? YOU OKAY!!?
BURU ブル
IF I'M GONNA DREAM, GIMME HORI!
LET HER SHOW UP AS SOMETHING CUTE.
G'NIGHT!

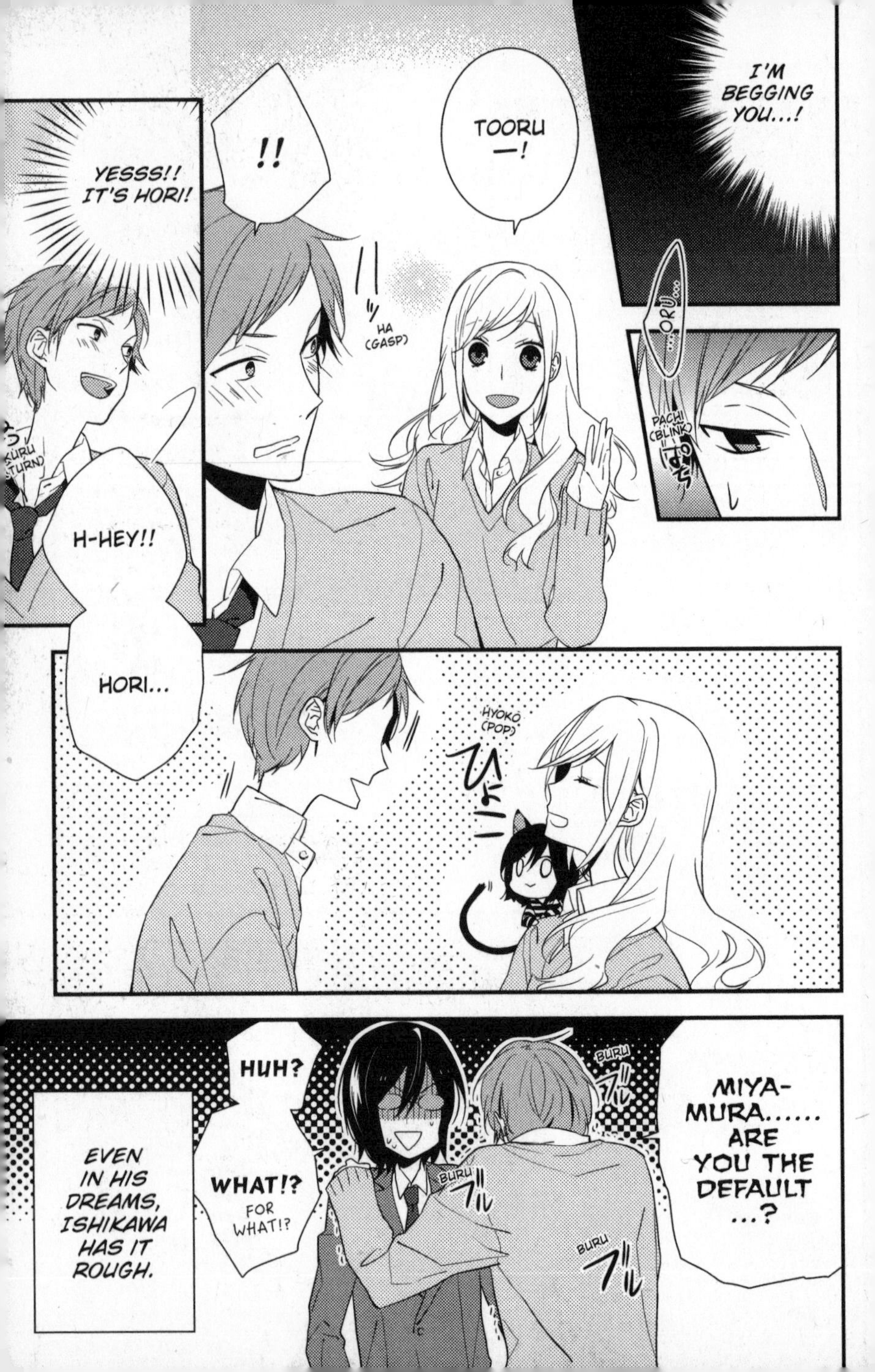

I'M BEGGING YOU...!
...ORU...
PACHI (BLINK)
TOORU —!
!!
HA (GASP)
YESSS!! IT'S HORI!
KURU
H-HEY!!
HORI...
HYOKO (POP)
MIYA-MURA...... ARE YOU THE DEFAULT ...?
BURU
BURU
BURU
HUH?
WHAT!?
FOR WHAT!?
EVEN IN HIS DREAMS, ISHIKAWA HAS IT ROUGH.

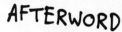

AFTERWORD

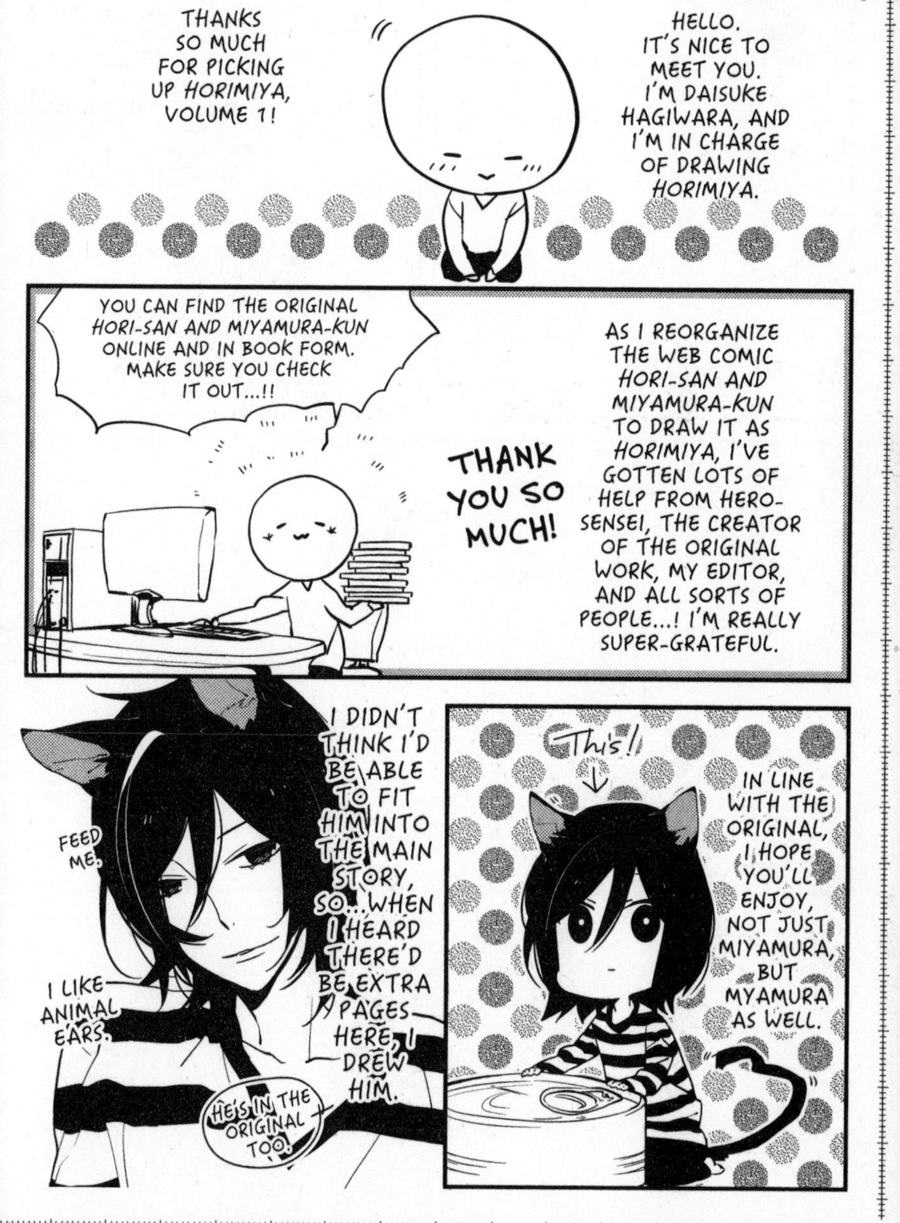
HELLO. IT'S NICE TO MEET YOU. I'M DAISUKE HAGIWARA, AND I'M IN CHARGE OF DRAWING *HORIMIYA*.
THANKS SO MUCH FOR PICKING UP *HORIMIYA*, VOLUME 1!
AS I REORGANIZE THE WEB COMIC *HORI-SAN AND MIYAMURA-KUN* TO DRAW IT AS *HORIMIYA*, I'VE GOTTEN LOTS OF HELP FROM HERO-SENSEI, THE CREATOR OF THE ORIGINAL WORK, MY EDITOR, AND ALL SORTS OF PEOPLE...! I'M REALLY SUPER-GRATEFUL.
THANK YOU SO MUCH!
YOU CAN FIND THE ORIGINAL *HORI-SAN AND MIYAMURA-KUN* ONLINE AND IN BOOK FORM. MAKE SURE YOU CHECK IT OUT...!!
This!
IN LINE WITH THE ORIGINAL, I HOPE YOU'LL ENJOY, NOT JUST MIYAMURA, BUT MYAMURA AS WELL.
I DIDN'T THINK I'D BE ABLE TO FIT HIM INTO THE MAIN STORY, SO... WHEN I HEARD THERE'D BE EXTRA PAGES HERE, I DREW HIM.
FEED ME.
I LIKE ANIMAL EARS.
HE'S IN THE ORIGINAL TOO.

ALL SORTS OF OTHER CHARACTERS WILL BE SHOWING UP DOWN THE ROAD...
...AND I'D BE THRILLED IF YOU WATCH OVER THEIR STUDENT DAYS.
BUT WE'RE THE MAIN CHARAC-TERS!

ALL RIGHT! HERE'S HOPING WE'LL MEET AGAIN ...!
PLEASE KEEP CHEERING ME ON ...!!

Staff

ORIGINAL WORK:
HERO-SAMA
"HORI-SAN AND MIYAMURA-KUN"

ASSISTANT: YOSSAN

EDITOR: ISHIKAWA-SAMA

Special thanks

SCARLET BERIKO-SAMA

MONIKICHI-SAMA

MY FRIENDS AND FAMILY, WHO ENCOURAGED ME

AND EVERYONE WHO PICKED UP THIS BOOK!

THANK YOU!

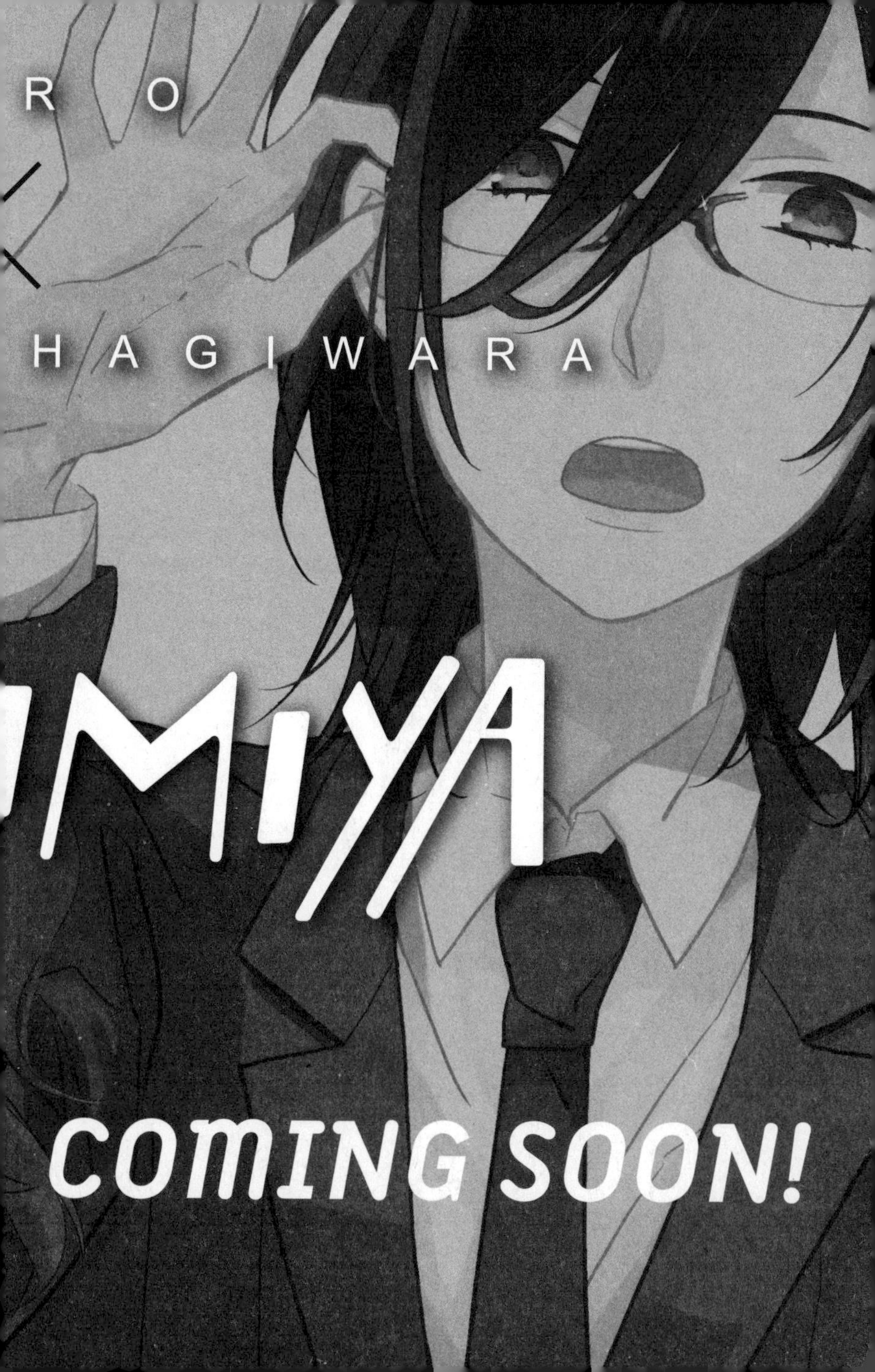

R O
H A G I W A R A
MIYA
COMING SOON!

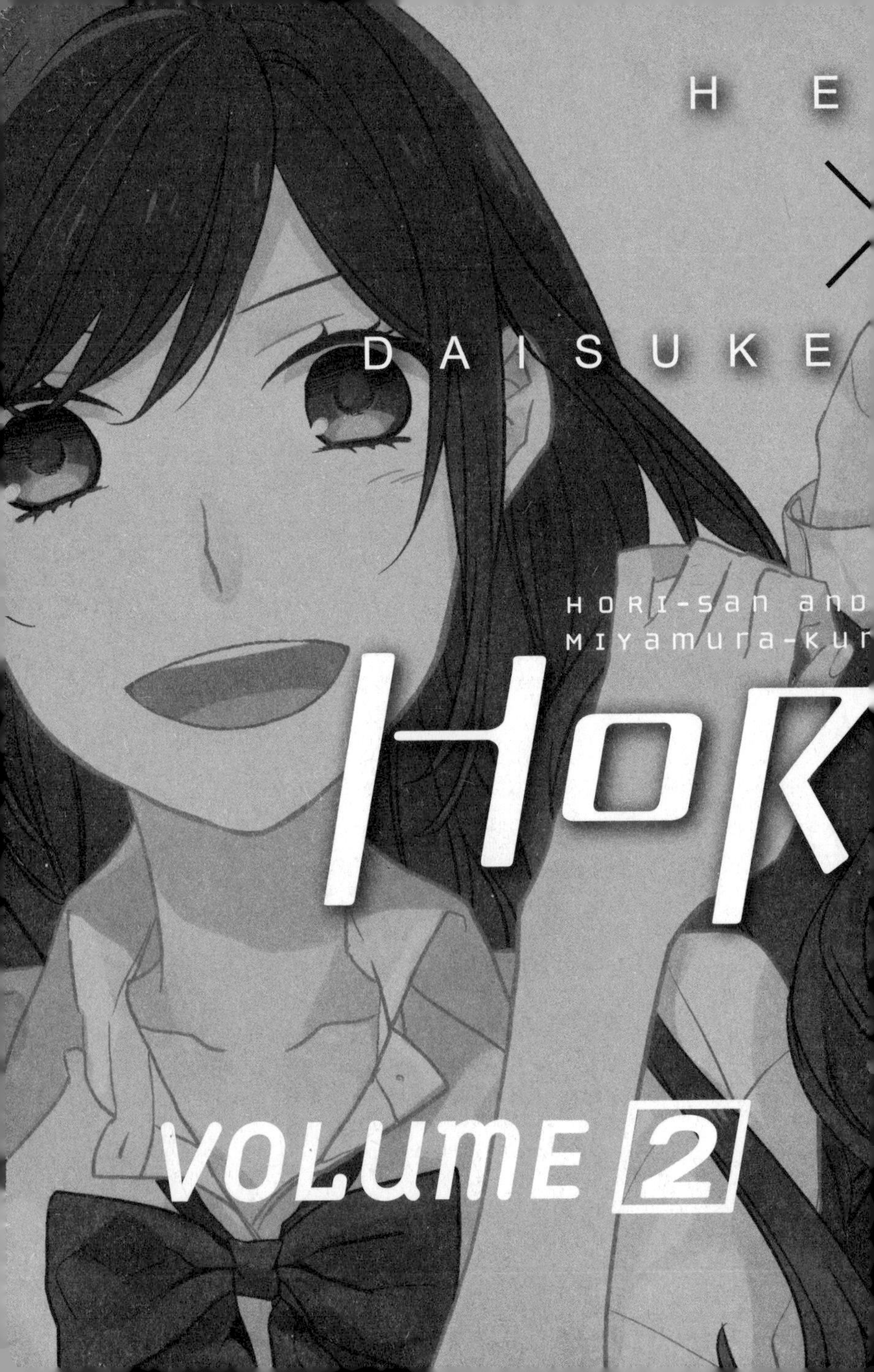

HE
DAISUKE
HORI-san and
MIYamura-ku
HOR
VOLUME 2

HERO × DAISUKE HAGIWARA

Translation: Taylor Engel
Lettering: Alexis Eckerman

This book is a work of fiction. Names, characters, places, and incidents are the product of the author's imagination or are used fictitiously. Any resemblance to actual events, locales, or persons, living or dead, is coincidental.

HORIMIYA vol. 1
© HERO · OOZ
© 2012 Daisuke Hagiwara / SQUARE ENIX CO., LTD. First published in Japan in 2012 by SQUARE ENIX CO., LTD. English translation rights arranged with SQUARE ENIX CO., LTD. and Yen Press, LLC through Tuttle-Mori Agency, Inc.

English translation © 2015 by SQUARE ENIX CO., LTD.

Yen Press
1290 Avenue of the Americas
New York, NY 10104

Visit us at yenpress.com
facebook.com/yenpress
twitter.com/yenpress
yenpress.tumblr.com

First Yen Press Edition: October 2015

Yen Press is an imprint of Yen Press, LLC. The Yen Press name and logo are trademarks of Yen Press, LLC.

The publisher is not responsible for websites (or their content) that are not owned by the publisher.

ISBNs: 978-0-316-34203-2 (paperback)
        978-0-316-35657-2 (ebook)
        978-0-316-35659-6 (app)

10 9 8

WOR

Printed in the United States of America

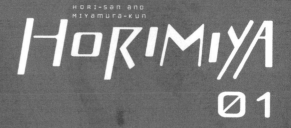

HORI-san and
MIYamura-kun

HORIMIYA

01

C ONTENTS ✶

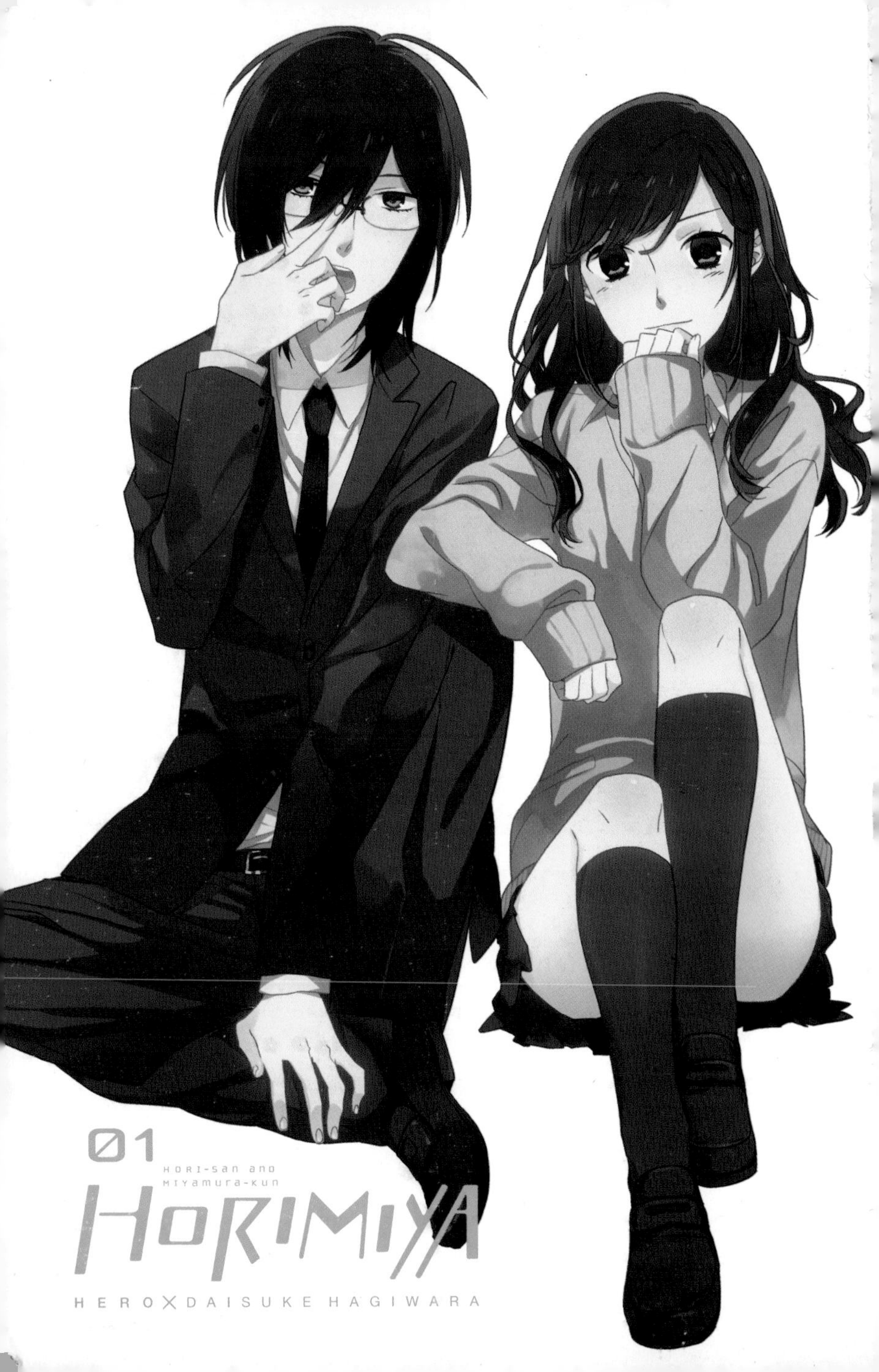
01
HORI-san and
MIYAMURA-KUN
HORIMIYA
HERO×DAISUKE HAGIWARA

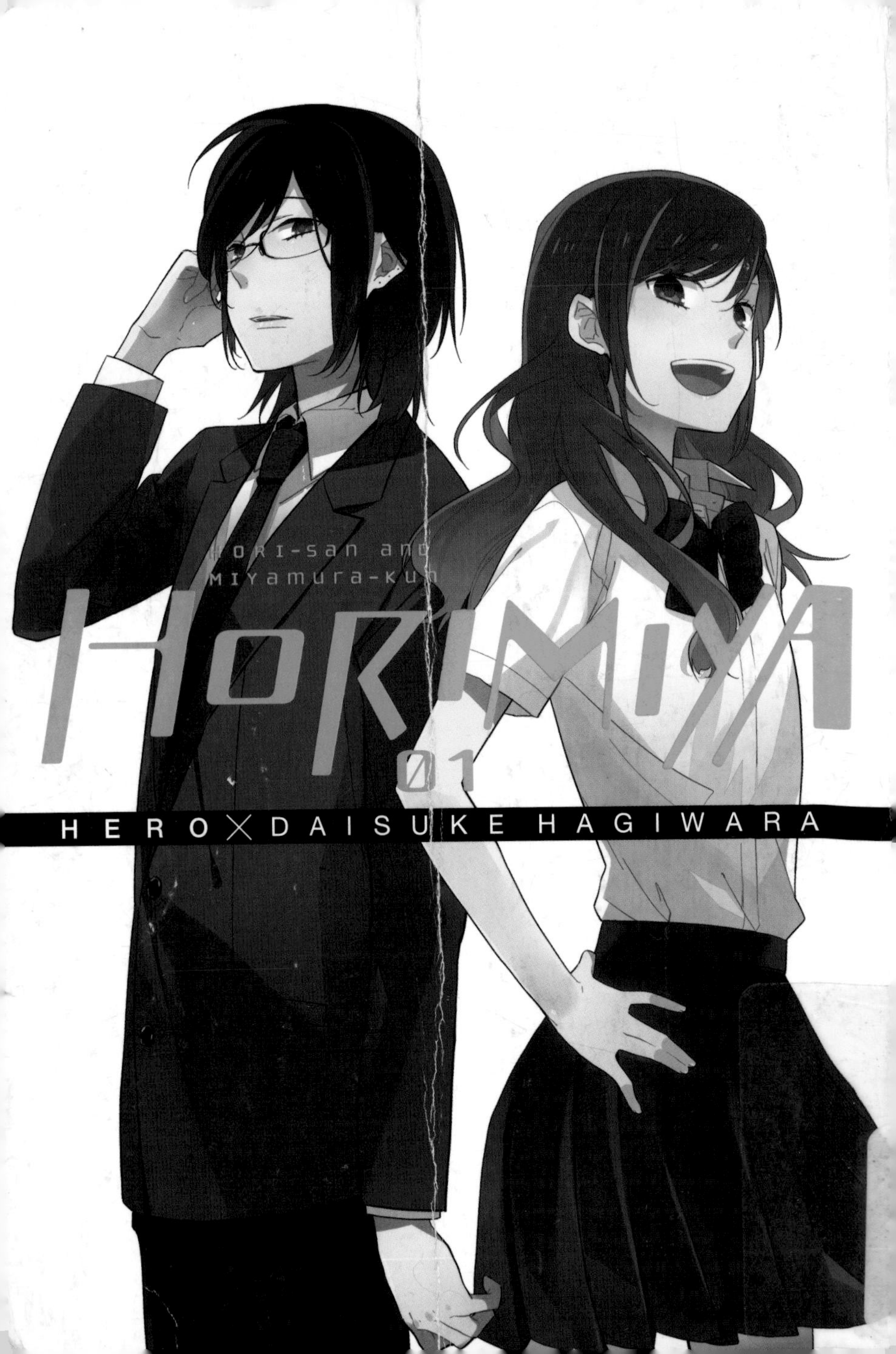
HORI-san and
MIyamura-kun
HORIMIYA
01
HERO × DAISUKE HAGIWARA